RICHARD J. GOY

FLORENCE

a walking guide to its architecture

YALE UNIVERSITY PRESS • NEW HAVEN AND LONDON

Designed by Emily Lees
Printed in China

Library of Congress Cataloging-in-Publication Data

Goy, Richard J. (Richard John), 1947–
Florence : a walking guide to its architecture / Richard J. Goy.
pages cm
Includes bibliographical references and index.
ISBN 978-0-300-20987-7 (paperback)
1. Architecture – Italy – Florence – Tours. 2. Walking – Italy – Florence – Tours.
3. Florence (Italy) – Buildings, structures, etc. – Tours. 4. Florence (Italy) – Tours.
I. Title.
NA1121.F7G68 2015
720.945'511 – dc23
2014043044

A catalogue record for this book is available from the British Library

Frontispiece: The city centre from San Miniato, with the Palazzo Vecchio (left),
Cappelle Medicee (centre) and the cathedral group (right centre)

Contents

The Centro Storico and the *Quartiere* of the City

Preface

The basic purpose of this book is fairly simple: to provide a succinct, portable and comprehensive guide to the architecture of Florence. While there are numerous popular guidebooks to the city, only the excellent and authoritative *Guida rossa*, published by the Touring Club Italiano (TCI), provides a reliable and comprehensive guide to the city's architecture; unfortunately, it is available only in Italian, and thus of little use to many English-speaking visitors. There are a couple of other helpful pocket guides, *Guida di Firenze architettura* by Carlo Cresti and others (first edn, 1992), and also Guido Zucconi's *Firenze: guida all'architettura* (1995); both are extremely useful, albeit selective, and again both published in Italy.

There thus appeared to me to be a gap, a *raison d'être* for such a guide. The intention is to be as comprehensive as space allows, and I have taken the history of Florence's architecture from the Romanesque period up to the recent past, including, for example, the ground-breaking new children's hospital at Careggi, completed in 2008.

In almost no other city, however, with the possible exception of Rome, is architecture so closely intertwined with the other arts as it is in Florence; from the Medicean sculptures in the Loggia dei Lanzi to Fra Angelico's frescoes at San Marco, these three arts are indivisibly interrelated; I have therefore made at least a brief reference to most of the many remarkable treasures of art and sculpture with which the city is extraordinarily richly endowed.

Florence is so immediately and universally recognised as the birth-place of the Renaissance, and thus of many central elements of modern western civilisation, that many people are unaware of the fact that the city had a 'pre-Renaissance' of great cultural importance more than a century earlier than the buildings of Brunelleschi, the paintings of Botticelli and the texts of Alberti and Ficino. One could, for example, cite the 1290s, the decade in which the great new cathedral of Santa Maria del Fiore and the Palazzo Vecchio were both begun; when Giotto painted and when Dante was writing the *Vita nuova*; or the 1340s and 1350s, when Boccaccio and Petrarch wrote, and when the elegant campanile of the cathedral was rising. High medieval Florence was a wealthy, refined city full of extraordinary creative gifts a century before the broader rediscovery of the classical world and the patronage of Cosimo de' Medici, *pater patriae*.

If this small guide has two primary functions, one is therefore to broaden the visitor's appreciation of the whole millennial span of the city's architectural history both before and after the Renaissance; the other is to try and persuade the visitor to explore, to stray beyond the traditional highlights of the Uffizi, the Accademia, the cathedral and the Palazzo Pitti, essential though they are; also to appreciate the medieval fabric of Borgo Santi Apostoli and the homonymous church; the massive power of the city's medieval gates; the splendid Baroque façade of San Gaetano; the neo-Byzantine orientalism of the synagogue; the Art Nouveau Galleria Vichi; and the remarkable Modern Movement railway station of Santa Maria Novella. There is not a single major architectural style from the last millennium that does not have some representation in the city and its surroundings, and they can all be sought and admired.

Following the principles of my earlier guide to Venice, I have again omitted the type of tourist information usually found in popular guides. There are two reasons: first, that of space, since its omission permits the maximum amount of architectural information within a reasonably compact format. Secondly, because such information almost always has some built-in obsolescence, and any references to hotels and restaurants or the opening hours of museums are all subject to change.

Courtyard of a house on Borgo Santa Croce

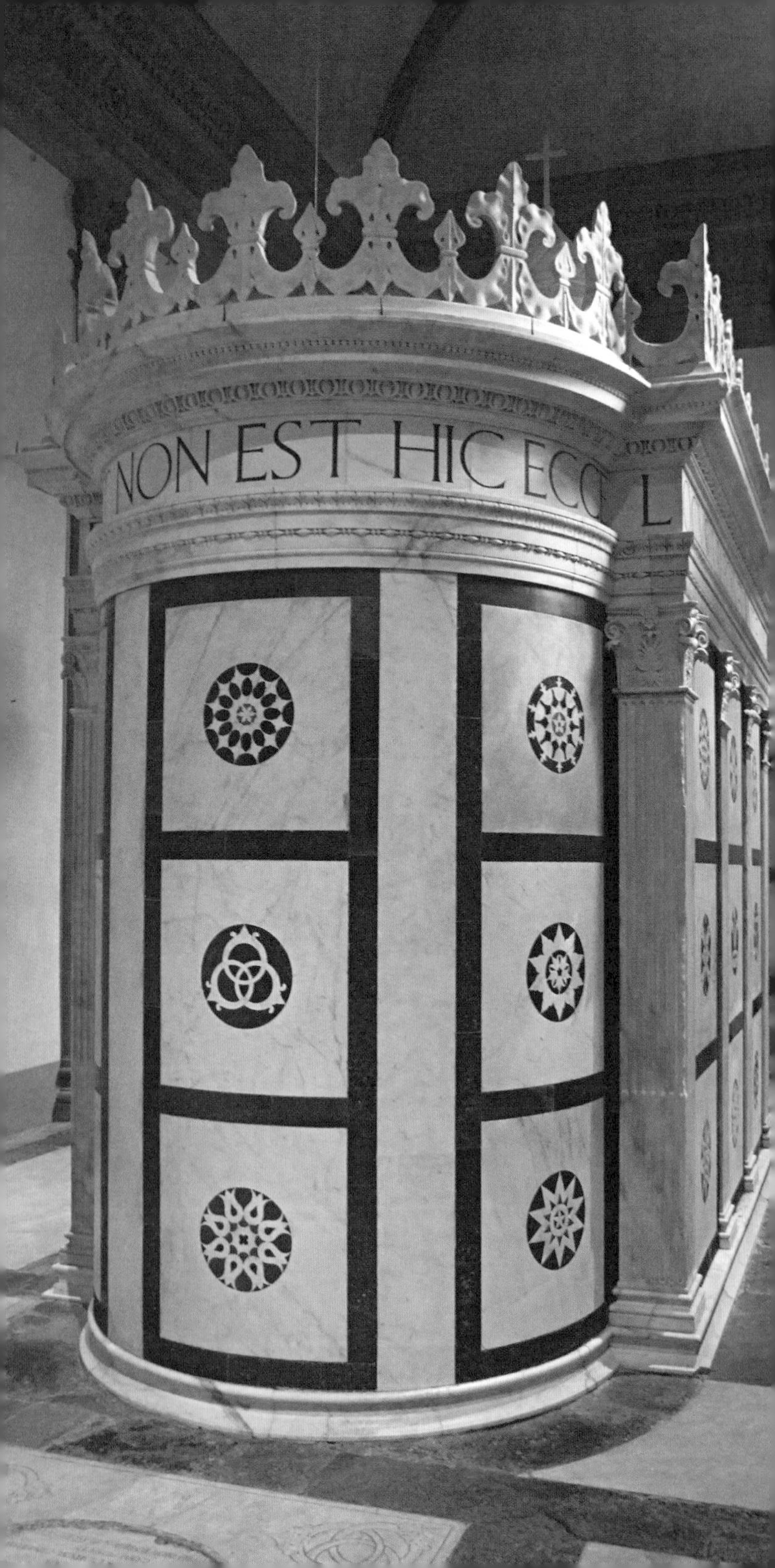
NON EST HIC ECC
L

Acknowledgements

I have accumulated a number of debts while compiling this guide, which I am delighted to acknowledge. At a practical level, I must thank all at the Hotel Universo, for their excellent accommodation and friendly, helpful assistance; to the restaurant Da Guido for providing splendidly robust local cuisine; and to Wilma and her colleagues at the bar Le Cappelle Medicee for their warm hospitality.

Special thanks are due to Professore Architetto Romano del Nord and, in particular, to his colleague Architetto Cristina Donati, both at CSPE, for taking time to give me a guided tour of their wonderful new children's hospital at Careggi; the illustration of their new hospital entrance block at Careggi is reproduced with their kind permission: copyright CSPE; IPOSTUDIO; Elio di Franco and photographer Alessandro Ciampi. All the other photographs are by me.

Once again, warmest thanks are due to Gillian Malpass, Emily Lees and Hannah Jenner at Yale, for supporting and encouraging my efforts, and for bringing them – once again – to such elegant fruition.

Finally, thanks once more to Barbara and Catherine, and to Angela, all of whose enthusiastic appreciation of the many delights of Florence now matches my own. No visit is now complete without a family picnic up at Fiesole. This book is therefore dedicated to them.

The Rucellai Monument at San Pancrazio by Leon Battista Alberti, *circa* 1465–7

Introduction

A POLITICAL OUTLINE

The Roman city of Florentia was established by the emperor Augustus (27 BC–AD 15) and this settlement is discussed briefly under the urban history section below. The Roman town flourished, such that by the reign of Diocletian (AD 245–313) Florentia was the capital of the Roman region of Tuscia et Umbria, with borders very similar to those re-established by the Medici many centuries later. Like much of northern and central Italy, the city was badly damaged by the series of 'barbarian' invasions following the decline of the Roman Empire, notably that of the Goths in AD 405. They were defeated, however, by the Florentine leader Stilicone, who re-established Christianity here, after the earlier attempt by (St) Miniato, who had been martyred in AD 250.

The reign of the Ostrogoth Theodoric (493–526), whose capital was at Ravenna, was one of peace and prosperity; it was followed by the rule of the Byzantine Narses (553–70), when the Lombards invaded the peninsula. A degree of urban renewal began in the Carolingian period (768–814) and continued intermittently over the following two centuries.

Florence flourished again during the tenth and eleventh centuries. During this period the great baptistery was constructed, as well as a number of other examples of this highly characteristic local Romanesque style, notably San Miniato al Monte. At the beginning of the twelfth century Florence began the expansion and conquest of adjacent towns and cities that were to form the nucleus of the future state. The principal and recurring conflict was with Siena, with one of many open battles in 1174, although the city's relationship with Pisa was often equally difficult and frequently bellicose.

In 1207 Florence secured a notable victory over Siena at Montalto. The notorious division of the former city into two factions, Guelphs and Ghibellines, began shortly afterwards, in 1216, as the result of the murder of Buondelmonte dei Buondelmonti by a group led by the Uberti and Lamberti; he was killed for failing to honour his pledge to

Santa Maria Novella: the Chiostro Verde

marry a member of the Amidei, and instead married a Donati. The Guelph faction was to ally itself to the papacy, while the Ghibellines were generally allied with the Holy Roman emperor. The city waged a further war against Siena in the years 1229–35. In 1248, following the arrival in Florence of the son of Federico II, the Holy Roman emperor, the Guelphs were exiled. In December of the same year, civic reform brought about the appointment of a *capitano del popolo*, who governed with twelve men, the Anziani. In 1251 the Guelphs were readmitted. A few months later, in turn, a number of Ghibellines were driven from the city. In 1257 a further expulsion of Ghibellines led to the destruction of the houses of the Uberti, which stood on the site to be occupied a few decades later by the Palazzo Vecchio.

On 4 September 1260 the decisive battle of Montaperti took place between Florence and its Guelph allies (including Lucca), and Siena and its own Ghibelline allies. Florence was soundly defeated, and the first popular government fell; this time many Guelphs fled or were exiled from the city for the next six years. Dozens of Guelph properties in the city were destroyed, and the Ghibellines began their vital ascendancy in the capital. In 1280 a truce was established between Guelphs and Ghibellines. Two years later, the *arti* (guilds) were established and their statutes registered; there were initially three, then six, and then twelve *arti*; the numbers were finally later increased to seven *arti maggiori* and fourteen *arti minori*. In 1293 the so-called Secondo Popolo was inaugurated; this popular government was notable for the publication of the Ordinamenti di Giustizia (Ordinances of Justice). The Ordinamenti affected profoundly the political structure of the city. Their publication represented the triumph of the 'new' merchant *borghesia* over the old 'magnates' (banking clans) and it left 147 of these formerly powerful clans, both Guelph and Ghibelline, politically 'out in the cold'. They included such illustrious families as the Frescobaldi, the Bardi and the Mozzi.

In 1300 the Florentine Guelphs subdivided into the Whites (*bianchi*) and the Blacks (*neri*); the latter (mostly consisting of older noble clans) continued to support the papacy, whereas the *bianchi* opposed its influence and generally allied themselves with the guilds. In the same year, Dante Alighieri was elected as one of the priors of the ruling council. Two years later, the *bianchi*, including Dante, were exiled from the city.

In an attempt to establish a more stable government that could rise above this factionalism, a series of foreign rulers was selected to govern the city, and to provide more objective, non-partisan rule; in 1313

Robert of Anjou (Roberto d'Angiò) was chosen to govern for five years, and later, in 1342, Gualtieri di Brienne, duke of Athens, this time *in perpetuo*. Within a year, however, the city had risen against his despotic rule, and he was forced out. In 1346 the two great banking houses of the Peruzzi and Bardi both failed; in the same period, the disaster of the Black Death killed a significant proportion of the population, including the city's chronicler, Giovanni Villani. As elsewhere, the city took some time to recover the numbers and economic activity following this disaster. In 1378 the Ciompi, the powerful and numerous wool workers' guild, rioted against their conditions and wages; after three months they were brutally suppressed, but the economic damage was very serious.

The early fifteenth century was marked by the rise of the Medici, originally from the Mugello, a district along the Sieve river, 20 km NE of the city; the first important member of the dynasty that was to shape the city's history for 300 years was Giovanni di Bicci (b. 1360), elected *gonfaloniere* (chief justice) in 1421, and who established the family's banking fortune. Giovanni was modest and cautious, but when he died in 1429 he was said to be the second richest man in the city. His son Cosimo, posthumously given the title of *pater patriae*, father of the nation, was born in 1389. He succeeded his father as head of the bank in 1429. Cosimo il Vecchio was an extremely astute banker, extending Giovanni's notable achievement and developing the international banking network over much of western Europe; on his death, he was perhaps the wealthiest man in Europe. Also an able politician, he weathered the treacherous waters of Italian inter-state rivalries better than most; his unofficial party and networks of influence made him the de facto ruler of the city, although in theory it remained a republic. Cosimo was also an important patron of the arts and the new humanist movement that was taking root in Florence. He was a noted bibliophile and patronised the writers Poggio Bracciolini, Marsilio Ficino and Leonardo Bruni; he patronised Donatello (generously), Brunelleschi and Lorenzo Ghiberti; he also appointed Michelozzo to be the family's 'house architect' for much of his life.

At one time or another the Medici bank had branches in Rome, Naples, Pisa, Milan, Venice, Ancona, Avignon, Bruges, Lyon, London and Geneva. The Rome branch was by far the most important, since the Medici were bankers to a succession of popes.

In 1433 Cosimo was exiled, following a conspiracy to overrule his power by the Albizzi and Guadagni. He returned barely a year later, and continued to rule for thirty years until his death in 1464, during which time he commissioned a succession of artistic and architectural masterpieces.

Piero, Cosimo's son, known as 'il Gottoso' (the gouty), had been born in 1416; he succeeded his father in 1464, but had poor health and died only five years later. In 1449 Lorenzo, Piero's first son, was born, later to be called 'il Magnifico' (the Magnificent); twenty years later he married Clarice Orsini, from a powerful, wealthy Roman family. Following Piero's early death, Lorenzo succeeded him in turn, in a seamless transfer of power.

The notorious Pazzi conspiracy took place in 1478; Lorenzo's younger brother Giuliano was murdered in the cathedral by an alliance of opponents led by the Pazzi; Lorenzo himself was wounded but escaped. With popular support, there followed a bloody reckoning in which the perpetrators of the conspiracy were tracked down and put to death. Lorenzo's rule is generally seen today as a period of outstanding cultural achievement, and, like Cosimo, he was a remarkable patron of the arts and literature as well as a highly accomplished poet. The fortunes of the Medici bank declined significantly in this period, however, since Lorenzo showed little interest in its expansion or its efficient management.

The latter part of Lorenzo's rule was overshadowed by the rise of the Dominican friar Girolamo Savonarola, who was in Florence from 1481; his powerful sermons against excess and his notorious 'bonfire of the vanities' (destruction of books, jewellery and other supposedly decadent luxury goods) gained widespread popular support; but he was later tried for heresy, and was executed in the Piazza della Signoria on 23 May 1498.

Lorenzo had died in 1492; two years later the Medici were driven into exile. A republican form of government followed for the next eighteen years, loosely modelled on the Venetian system; then, in 1512, the Medici were allowed to return. In 1519 Cardinal Giulio de' Medici, archbishop of the city, ruled, and following a failed assassination attempt in 1522, was elected pope, as Clement VII, in 1523. In the same year, Alessandro de' Medici, natural son of Lorenzo, duke of Urbino, was sent by the pope to govern the city. This rule was confirmed by the Holy Roman emperor Charles V in 1531. In the following year the constitution was revoked, and Alessandro was given the title of the first duke of Florence. Six years later, in 1537, he was murdered by Lorenzino di Pierfrancesco de' Medici; Cosimo, Pierfrancesco's uncle (from the other branch of the clan) and the son of Giovanni delle Bande Nere, was chosen as his successor; he was proclaimed grand duke in 1569, but died five years later. The titles of duchy and grand duchy, however, established the automatic right of succession, and his son Francesco I succeeded him, ruling until 1587. Francesco was an eclectic ruler, and the principal patron of the polymath and equally eclectic Bernardo Buontalenti. The period saw the rise of Mannerism as an art movement. Francesco was succeeded in turn by his brother Ferdinando, who ruled from 1587 to 1609.

Ferdinando was followed by his son Cosimo II (r. 1609–21), and then his son in turn, Ferdinando II, who had a remarkably long reign from 1621 to 1670. Although the political power of the Tuscan state declined significantly in the period from the rule of Ferdinando I, that of Ferdinando II was generally enlightened, with great emphasis on public works. Cosimo III, his son again, ruled from 1670 to 1723, by which time Tuscan political power and influence had waned still more. Finally, the last – and most ineffectual – Medici 'ruler' was Gian Gastone (1723–37).

Following the extinction of the Medici, and the Treaty of Vienna (1734), after 1737 the Florentine state was ruled by the dukes of Lorraine (Lorena), again governing as grand dukes. In 1790 Pietro Leopoldo renounced the title in favour of his second son, who ruled as Ferdinando III. This succession lasted until Napoleon's invasion of 1799; two years later Tuscany became part of his 'Kingdom of Etruria'.

In 1814 the Bonapartists were removed and Grand Duke Ferdinando III was welcomed back. Ten years later, he was succeeded by his son Leopoldo II. In 1848 Leopoldo fled the city for some months, and a democratic government was installed; in 1859 he fled once more, this time permanently. In the following year Tuscany became part of the united kingdom of Sardinia, which became the kingdom of Italy in 1861. From 1865 to 1870 Florence was briefly the capital of the newly united state, and many radical works took place on the city's fabric; many more were continued after the permanent transfer of the capital to Rome. Since that date Florence has remained the capital of the region of Tuscany, which (like most of the other twenty Italian regions) corresponds in its extent very closely to the historic boundaries of the city states, in this case those of the duchy and grand duchy.

During the rise of Fascism, Mussolini made the city one of the centres of his increasing power, making important speeches here, notably in 1930 in the Piazza della Signoria, attended by more than 100,000 people. The city was extensively damaged by the retreating Germans in 1944 during the Second World War.

URBAN HISTORY

Knowledge of the earliest settlements on the city's site has increased notably over the last few decades, following major archaeological investigations, particularly in the 1980s, which have reached back to evince settlement in the Copper Age (*circa* 3000 BC); previously, the earliest known remains dated from the Villanova period, around 800 BC. For some time prior to the definitive town established by the Romans, the site had already become an important crossing point of the Arno, and a meeting place of several routes, notably those up the river valley and the passes northwards across the Apennines.

The formal establishment of the Roman city of Florentia took place in the era of Augustus. It was a classically planned settlement, with two principal axes: the north–south axis on the line of the present Via Roma and Calimala, and the east–west axis of Via degli Strozzi and the Corso. At the NW side of the central intersection, on the site of the present Piazza della Repubblica, was the forum. The Roman city measured eight urban blocks from east to west and six from north to south, the perimeter walls being aligned with the present Via dei Tornabuoni (west), Via dei Cerretani and Piazza del Duomo (north), and Via del Proconsolo (east). Its southern alignment was probably originally parallel to the northern one.

During the period of Hadrian (AD 117–38) there was an important regeneration of the town, which included the extension and realignment of the southern section of the city walls, so that they stood roughly parallel to the river. They also now enclosed the new theatre, which today lies below Via dei Gondi and part of the Palazzo Vecchio, and other new buildings, including a large textile factory, the remains of which were discovered in the Piazza della Signoria in the 1980s excavations. Further east, still beyond the walls, was the amphitheatre, also built in Hadrian's period, and which lies below Via Torta, Via dei Bentaccordi and the houses of the Peruzzi. At this stage the town contained several thousand inhabitants, and had a port district on the river, a little further downstream, near the present Piazza Carlo Goldoni.

In 393 the church of San Lorenzo was established as the cathedral, just outside the walls to the north. Across the river, Santa Felicità was founded in the same era, while perhaps a little later, in the fifth century, two further Christian basilicas were established: Santa Reparata, near the north gate, and Santa Cecilia near the south one, on the present Piazza della Signoria.

The prosperous reign of the Ostrogoth Theodoric (493–526), whose capital was at Ravenna, was followed by a further degree of urban renewal in the Carolingian period (768–814), which continued to the end of the millennium; by *circa* 1000–50 the town's population had increased from an estimated 5,000 to perhaps 20,000. Pressure on space within the Roman walls resulted in their expansion and reconstruction, first around 1000 and again in 1078; the latter were the so-called Matildine walls, since they were built under the rule of the Countess Matilda. They became known in time as the 'first circle', although, including the Roman walls, they were actually the third; Dante refers to them as the 'ancient circle'. The Matildine walls followed closely the alignment of the old Roman walls on the north, west and east sides, but on the south they took in a further strip of land towards the Arno.

The eleventh century was also a period of growth and prosperity for the town, as can be seen today in a number of surviving buildings and fragments. It was the era of Florentine Romanesque architecture, most spectacularly seen in the baptistery of San Giovanni and at San Miniato; but also at the cathedral of Fiesole, the façade of the Badia Fiesolana, and on a modest scale at Santo Stefano al Ponte and San Salvatore al Vescovo. The Ponte Vecchio was probably first built *circa* 1000, on a site very close to the Roman crossing; it was rebuilt after flood damage in 1117, and more definitively in 1345, the reconstruction that largely survives today.

During this period much of the basic urban structure of the Roman settlement survived. In this period, too, the first craft and trade guilds began to emerge, based on the increasingly important activities of international trade and banking; above all, of wool and the textile industry. They evolved together with the fortified houses and towers that were to become such a distinctive feature of the mature medieval city. As the city grew in size and numbers, settlement also began just outside the walls, along the main roads that led towards Pisa, Arezzo, Rome and Prato. And so a new circle of walls was built, very rapidly, in the years 1173–5, to enclose these new inner suburbs. Their route can be traced today: clockwise, they ran along the banks of the Arno to the present Ponte alla Carraia, then followed Via del Moro, Via del Giglio, Via del Canto dei Nelli, Via dei Pucci, Via Maurizio Bufalini and Via Sant'Egidio, Via Verdi and Via dei Benci to reach the river again at the Ponte alle Grazie. The Mugnone stream was diverted further west so that it ran beyond the new walls. There was also a protective palisade for the first time in the Oltrarno, extending between the two future bridgeheads, and running along Via dei Serragli, Via Sant'Agostino, Via Guicciardini, and then parallel to the river, before reaching Piazza dei Mozzi. The area thus enclosed nearly doubled the area of the city within the new defences.

Inside the walls there appeared increasing numbers of defensive towers. They were attached to houses, and were occupied only during periods of civil strife, when the families 'retreated' into them, depending on the stocks of food that the towers contained. At first, the towers were built by individual families for their exclusive use, but during the course of the twelfth century *società delle torri* ('tower consortia') were formed by groups of families of similar political affiliation, with their houses clustered around the base of the tower.

Outside these still fairly constricting walls was a broad circle of extensive monastic houses and friaries, and other religious establishments such as hospitals and hospices, with their orchards, vineyards and market gardens. They included the notable Dominican friary of Santa Maria Novella (founded in 1221), the equally important Franciscan house of Santa Croce (1226), the Carmelite house of the Carmini (1250), and that of the Servites at the Santissima Annunziata (1250). In front of each was a substantial open square, sometimes based on a pre-existing suburban market, but also used by the mendicant orders for preaching to large crowds.

Pressure on land within the walls continued, with particularly high densities along the bank of the Arno, the waters of which were essential for the all-important textile industry. To improve communication across the river, the Ponte alla Carraia was first built in 1220, and the Ponte Rubaconte (alle Grazie) a little later, in 1237. With one upstream of the centre and the other downstream, they took pressure off the previously solitary span, the Ponte Vecchio, and in turn generated further development in their vicinity. In 1252 a fourth bridge was built, the Ponte Santa Trinità, thus completing the four historic links across the river, which have survived today, roughly equally spaced through the city centre.

After 1215, as noted, the city became polarised into two parties or factions, the Guelphs and Ghibellines. In 1248 the Guelphs were exiled

Ponte Vecchio, 1345, from the Lungarno Archibusieri

from the city, but returned three years later, when several prominent Ghibelline families were in turn driven from Florence. In 1255 construction of the Palazzo del Podestà (the Bargello) was begun as the residence and power base for the city's new elected governor. Three years later again, the Ghibellines were driven from Florence and the houses of the Uberti, one of their leading clans, were destroyed. The Palazzo dei Priori (begun 1299, later known as the Palazzo Vecchio) was later to be built on the site. The Guelph–Ghibelline struggles polarised the city until, in 1260, the Ghibellines won a decisive victory at Montaperti and many Guelphs fled; their houses and towers were now destroyed. This was the era of the Primo Popolo (1250–60); following a peace between Guelphs and Ghibellines (1280), peace and prosperity returned, and, with the inauguration of the Secondo Popolo (1293) a number of major public works were undertaken. They included the Palazzo dei Priori and, after 1284, an extensive new ring of city walls, the *ultima cerchia* or last circle. This enormous engineering project took half a century to complete (to 1333), and the new walls enclosed a vastly increased area of land, including all the surrounding religious houses and hospitals. On the north bank, the Mugnone stream was diverted yet again, so that it still lay beyond the new circle of walls.

Several tracts of this wall have survived today, although much was lost in the nineteenth-century urban 'improvements'. On the north bank, its course is marked by Giuseppe Poggi's avenues: Viale della Giovine Italia, Viale Antonio Gramsci, Viale Giacomo Matteotti, Viale Spartaco Lavagnini, Viale Fratelli Rosselli. In the Oltrarno, the new walls took in the whole built-up area, and ran along Viale Lodovico Ariosto, Viale Francesco Petrarca, around the south edge of the present Giardino di Boboli, and NE to Porta San Niccolò. The overall effort was prodigious: the walls were 8.5 km (5.2 miles) long, 11.6 m (38 ft) high, had seventy-three towers, and were broken by fifteen monumental gates, a number of which also survive. The extent of these walls was to define the city for the next five centuries, and it was only in the later nineteenth century that significant development began to take place beyond them.

The new walls formed part of a campaign of urban works that included the paving of streets (begun as early as 1237) and the layout of new roads, notably in the northern part of the historic centre. They included Via dei Martelli and the present Via Ricasoli, Via San Zanobi, Via Santa Reparata and Via Gino Capponi. These streets, together with the pre-existing axes of Borgo Pinti and Via San Gallo, gave the whole northern quarter a distinctively 'planned' quality, with long, straight, parallel routes linked by a small number of cross axes.

The figure of Arnolfo di Cambio is of pivotal importance in this period. Not only was he associated with the landmark Palazzo dei Priori, but he also began the great new cathedral of Santa Maria del Fiore in 1296. Thereafter, these two monuments became symbols of the two poles of power in the city: the Church and the people, separated from each other by a modest but highly significant distance of a few hundred metres. Towards the end of the thirteenth century and into the fourteenth, too, a new genre of *palazzo*, rather than *casa-torre*, began to be built by a number of the wealthiest families: the Spini, Peruzzi and Mozzi, most of them notable bankers.

During the fourteenth century the city's population continued to grow. In 1200 Florence probably contained approximately 50,000 people; by the century's end the figure had roughly doubled, making Florence one of the largest cities in Italy, after Milan, Venice and Naples. A series of laws and ordinances attempted to impose order and dignity on the urban realm; they included regulations regarding the cladding of façades with stone (*pietra forte*) up to a certain height: around 10 m (32.8 ft) on façades to a major public square. One of the last and best of the private palaces in this period is Palazzo Davanzati, built in the 1330s by the Davizzi, and with an all-stone façade. This period of general growth and prosperity concluded in the 1330s; Giotto had begun the campanile of the cathedral (1334), and the building of Orsanmichele added a further civic monument to the city centre. A disastrous flood of the Arno in 1333, however, was followed by the devastating plague of 1348, abruptly terminating work on all major capital projects for a generation, since the economy contracted to reflect the population crisis. Although a slow recovery was made, and in 1376 the construction of the Loggia dei Lanzi was to add a further major civic structure to the city's administrative heart, the violent unrest of the Ciompi revolts two years later dealt a further blow to stability. A period of oligarchical government was followed immediately by the rise to power of Giovanni di Bicci de' Medici, and then his son, Cosimo il Vecchio. Florence became an archbishopric in 1419.

In the early fifteenth century the works of Brunelleschi and the writings and influence of Leon Battista Alberti were to transform not solely the city but also the entire peninsula, as the principles and philosophies of the Renaissance spread to Milan and Venice, to Rome and Naples. Brunelleschi's cupola for the cathedral became a new icon for the city, a masterpiece of technical skill and religious and cultural symbolism. Brunelleschi worked in a medieval city, the principal elements of which had been defined (or redefined) by Arnolfo in the early fourteenth century. But Brunelleschi's churches of San Lorenzo and Santo Spirito were major new urban landmarks, with a completely different architectural vocabulary, even though their liturgical and social-urban functions were not fundamentally new. However, his proposal to form a grand new piazza onto the river at Santo Spirito (never executed), and the beginnings of the formation of the Piazza della Santissima Annunziata announced a new urban formality, and an attempt to 'externalise' the humanist principles of harmony, symmetry and proportion that is seen inside the early Renaissance building: outside, now, into the public realm.

Under the Medici, the city became more of an expression of the will and power of the dynasty. After a relatively short period in the new family palace on the Via Larga (by Michelozzo, begun 1444), their move, first to the Palazzo Vecchio and then to Palazzo Pitti, had profound consequences for the form of the city. The construction of the Uffizi, and its physical link to Palazzo Pitti via the Corridoio Vasariano, created an entire complex of connected structures, collectively forming the hub of political power. At the same time, Medici patronage elsewhere, notably at San Lorenzo and San Marco, rendered their influence over the city's form all-pervasive. The construction, first, of the Fortezza da Basso (1534) and then the Fortezza del Belvedere (1590) enhanced the Medici's physical domination of the city. In this period, too, the later sixteenth and early seventeenth centuries, further development began along the new routes in the northern quarter, within the city walls, but thus far little developed. Here there remained ample space for gardens and houses that were part-*palazzo* and part-villa.

The seventeenth century, the era of the Baroque, was essentially one of slow decline in the city, both economically and in terms of its political power and influence. The phased aggrandisement of Palazzo Pitti by successive grand dukes masked a contradictory geo-political reality, although a small number of rich, notable churches were constructed in the new style: Ognissanti and San Gaetano, as well as the grandiose Cappella dei Principi.

The end of the house of Medici marked the transfer of the city to the Lorraine (Lorena), who, despite a greatly reduced economy, concentrated their attention on public works, including schools, hospitals and libraries. This emphasis was continued throughout the nineteenth century both up to and beyond Unification in 1860. The Napoleonic era brought the closure of the monastic and religious houses here, as elsewhere, and the appropriation of many of their works of art.

A number of works of modernisation took place within the city walls in the early and mid-nineteenth century. They included the first railway station (1846) and the new district of Barbano, centred on the large Piazza Maria Antonia (today Piazza dell'Indipendenza).

But the most radical alterations to the city's fabric in several centuries came with the decision to demolish most of the old city walls, which took place in the years 1865–9. In the former year Florence had been established as the capital of the newly united Italy (although it was to be only a temporary status), and these works were intended to transform the city into a worthy modern capital, whose population also grew rapidly and dramatically within a few years. The intention was to remove the perceived restricting effects of the fortified ring, and link the city with the new suburbs beyond. Giuseppe Poggi was responsible for the master planning, and specifically for the boulevards that were set out in place of the city walls, and the formal squares in the locations of the principal city gates, notably Piazza Beccaria and Piazza della Libertà. Closely associated with these major interventions was the setting out of new inner suburbs, on land as yet under-developed, just inside the line of the walls: Mattonaia (east), Maglio (north-east) and Le Cascine (west). The last had been begun in 1855 before the walls were taken down. In the same period Poggi built the Viale dei Colli and Piazzale Michelangelo, on the hills to the south-east. Towards the end of the century, in 1881, the destruction of the central district of the Mercato Vecchio and the Ghetto was begun, with the loss of many historic buildings; in its place the grandiose Piazza della Repubblica was set out.

In the twentieth century further radical works of modernisation were carried out. In 1915 a new Piano Regolatore (general develop-ment plan) was published; although it did not become operational until 1924, it provided a structure for major new expansions in several peripheral locations. The new industrial zone of Rifredi (begun in 1918) was one of these, the location for a large FIAT works. In 1933 the new, much larger railway station of Santa Maria Novella was begun, necessitating further demolitions, and in the following year the general development plan was reviewed. In 1933–5 demolitions took place to the north and west of San Lorenzo to 'improve' its urban setting, while in 1936 still further destruction took place in the crowded zone just north of Santa Croce, although the planned new rational development was never executed. In 1933 the new autostrada Firenze-Mare was inaugurated, and in 1934 the new hospitals at Careggi were begun.

The city was badly damaged during the Second World War, culminating in 1944, when the retreating Nazis destroyed all the Arno bridges except the Ponte Vecchio. Although the bridge itself survived, many substantial buildings at both bridgeheads were blown up; they were rebuilt in the 1950s, as were the other lost bridges. Other significant post-war developments included three new bridges: Ponte Vespucci (1954–7), Ponte da Verrazzano (1967–9) and Ponte all'Indiano (1969–76). A number of new residential districts were also built beyond the old walls including Sorgane (south-east), the Isolotto (south-west) and Rovezzano (east), as well as the completion of the extensive sports complex at Campo di Marte, begun in the 1930s, but with a much later post-war phase completed in 1986.

THE ARCHITECTURE OF THE CITY: TYPOLOGIES

Fortified Towers (Torri)

The recorded history of domestic architecture in Florence begins in the thirteenth century, with the construction of fortified towers. At the end of the eleventh century it was said that there were only five in the city; by 1180 there are documentary records of thirty-five, although there existed perhaps as many as a hundred. The ultimate locations of around twice that number have been traced today, and some fifty survive in whole or in part. Torri were built immediately adjacent to the owners' house, and were linked to it; they were inhabited only in times of urban unrest. The towers were built of stone, were generally square on plan, and relatively tall and narrow, usually with four or five floors. The earliest statute governing the società delle torri (tower consortia) is from 1137. A tower was thus sometimes collectively owned by several families of similar political allegiance. Sometimes, too, these residential clusters were extensive, occupying a whole city block; in fact, the ultimate aim of many prominent families or groups of families was to acquire such an entire block for obvious reasons of security. Such were the aims achieved, for example, by the Amidei, Uberti, Donati and Peruzzi.

Palaces (Palazzi)

Towards the end of the thirteenth century individual families began to build sizeable new palaces for themselves. These families were those who had acquired power, both financial, through banking and trade, and political. The construction of the Palazzo del Popolo (Bargello) acted as an important catalyst in this process. Although to modern eyes it appears highly fortified, and more of a castle than a *palazzo*, it established a new vocabulary for translation into the private sphere. One of the first of this generation was Palazzo Mozzi, 1260–73, built by an extremely wealthy banking family, who were later disenfranchised by the Ordinamenti di Giustizia of 1293, which consolidated power in the hands of the *borghesia* and the merchants. Palazzo Mozzi stands at the south bridgehead of the Ponte alle Grazie, and thus had considerable strategic importance. Even more strategic were the twin palaces of the Frescobaldi and the Spini, which functioned almost as private city gates, one at each end of the Santa Trinità bridge. These marked a transition between the fortified Bargello and the more mature palaces of the early Renaissance. Although they were crowned by a prominent crenellation, they also had rows of large windows, which contradicted their quasimilitary appearance; and they no longer had towers attached to them. These *palazzi* generally contained commercial activities on the ground floor, with residential accommodation above; servants' quarters were usually in the attic.

The few palaces of the early fourteenth century that have survived are refinements of the appearance of the earlier ones; at Palazzo Davanzati and Palazzo dei Giudici the crowning crenellation has now gone, often replaced later by a spacious covered loggia or *liagò*, a common element on the Florentine palace well into the Renaissance. Windows are large, arched and regularly spaced. The cladding of the façades, too, is now more refined: Palazzo Davanzati is faced with smooth ashlar, with only the lowermost order slightly more boldly rusticated. The next decisive stage in the evolution of the Florentine *palazzo* was Michelozzo's massive new structure for the Medici on the Via Larga (Cavour), begun in 1444. The most imposing palace yet seen in the city, it set a new standard with its three orders of graduated rustication and large, regular *bifore* (two-light windows); the whole exterior is capped by a massive cornice. The building was a hollowed cube, with an elegant square courtyard (*cortile*) in the centre, completely different from the palace's powerful external impression; together, though, they expressed the two different worlds of the Medici: rich, powerful, even ruthless on the outside, refined patrons of the humanist Renaissance inside. Palazzo Medici set a precedent that was to be followed by several others: by Luca Pitti, by the Gondi, above all by Filippo Strozzi. A highly intellectual variant can be seen in Alberti's Palazzo Rucellai, where the use of the classical orders and flat, refined rustication resulted in a much more scholarly version of the typology.

Other, later Renaissance palaces retained some of the elements of these earlier works: strong rustication to the ground floor and regular, rhythmically spaced, arched windows. But they were less powerfully monumental, and the upper floors were often faced with render, rather than stone: an early example is Palazzo Pazzi (begun 1458), then Palazzo Horne, Palazzo Rosselli del Turco and others, well into the sixteenth century. The return of the republic (1494–1512) brought a brief period of relative austerity in façade design (Palazzo Guadagni, Palazzo Ginori), but in the 1520s Raphael's Palazzo Pandolfini and Baccio d'Agnolo's Palazzo Bartolini brought a new 'Romanising' approach, with aediculed, pedimented windows, an approach developed further at Palazzo Uguccioni (1549). Still later in the sixteenth century and into the seventeenth, the increasingly Mannerist work of Ammannati and Buontalenti can be seen at Palazzo Pucci and the Palazzo Nonfinito, by the two architects respectively. Further into the century, this rather eclectic approach was continued by Gherardo Silvani, exemplified by his Palazzo Strozzi del Poeta and Bernardino Radi's Palazzo delle Missioni, with their broken pediments and Mannerist fenestration. The most notable palace of the later seventeenth century was Palazzo Corsini al Parione, on which most of the leading architects of the era worked over several decades: Alfonso Parigi the younger, Pietro Tacca, Pier Francesco Silvani and Antonio Maria Ferri. In its composition the extremely large palace recalls Roman examples such as Palazzo Barberini.

Few new palaces were built in the last decades of the grand duchy; by the time of the Lorraine governments, most of the very limited funds in the city were spent on public works.

Churches, Monasteries and Friaries

In Florence, the cathedral of Santa Maria del Fiore and the adjacent baptistery form a unique complex. The baptistery, although of a form common to a number of Italian cities, is one of the oldest structures in Florence, and is essentially Romanesque. The cathedral, rebuilt on a massively increased scale by Arnolfo di Cambio and his successors in an undecorated Gothic style in the early fourteenth century, was finally complete only when Brunelleschi's extraordinary cupola and lantern were added a century later.

As for the rest of the city's churches, as in most Italian cities there is a clear distinction between parish foundations and religious houses. Until the end of the first millennium, Florence was effectively a single parish, that of Santa Reparata, together with the adjacent baptistery. After *circa* 1100, though, smaller local parishes began to be established, and according to tradition, eventually numbered thirty-six. In addition, there were a dozen more important priory foundations; they were the most ancient, and comprised Santi Apostoli, Santa Cecilia, Santa Felicità, San Frediano, San Lorenzo, Santa Maria degli Alberighi, San Pancrazio, San Pier Maggiore, San Pier Scheraggio, San Procolo, San Remigio and Santo Stefano al Ponte. Some of these are now lost. The churches of both groups, however, were generally very small. The earliest that survive today typically have a basilica plan, with a central nave and two narrower, lower side aisles, and usually terminating in a semicircular apse at the east end. A few evince their Romanesque origins with decorated marble façades (Santo Stefano al Ponte): several also made use of recycled Roman capitals and columns in their interiors.

The story of the Florentine parish church is typically one of frequent alteration over the centuries, sometimes enlargement, often for a mixture of reasons: stylistic modernisation; structural necessity; liturgical changes; the benefaction of a wealthy parishioner, who might bequeath a chapel or an altar. Very few remain unaltered today. Most of the early medieval survivors remained through the Gothic period, and were then joined by a few newcomers: the rebuilt Santa Trinità, for example. With the Renaissance came more radical change: a new stylistic language and wealthy patronage, above all of the Medici, who transformed the entire complex of San Lorenzo into their own architectural legacy. Other wealthy families also patronised their own local churches: the Rucellai at San Pancrazio and the Barbadori at Santa Felicità.

Many Florentine churches lack their main façades, which were sometimes designed, but often never built. In the late sixteenth century and the seventeenth, though, a number of notable façades appeared: Santa Trinità, San Gaetano and Ognissanti, all rich variants of early Baroque. They were followed later in the seventeenth century by San Giovan-

nino and San Firenze, although there was virtually no church-building activity after that, other than some modernisation of interiors.

Many monastic and religious houses were of a different order of magnitude from the numerous small parish foundations. By definition, they were more extensive, since they had to accommodate all the residential and administrative quarters, kitchens and refectories for the monks or friars. By 1400 there were no fewer than eighty-five within the city walls, many combining the functions of conventual house and hospital or hospice. By far the most conspicuous were the great houses of the mendicant orders of friars, of which there were five: Santa Maria Novella (Dominican, 1221), Santa Croce (Franciscan, 1226), Santissima Annunziata (Servite, 1250), Santo Spirito (Augustinian, 1250) and Santa Maria del Carmine (Carmelites, 1268). In the same period, too, the Cistercians settled at San Frediano, the Umiliati at Ognissanti and the Vallombrosians at Santa Trinità and Santa Maria Maggiore. Despite the Napoleonic suppression, many of these churches and monasteries survive today.

Their stylistic development mirrors that of the parish churches, albeit sometimes on a far greater scale: the great naves of Santa Croce and Santa Maria Novella had a capacity of 2–3,000 to hear the mendicant preachers. And again on a much more lavish scale, the religious houses were patronised by the wealthy bankers and merchants of the city, perhaps most notably of all at Santa Croce, where the Bardi and Peruzzi commissioned dazzling fresco cycles by Giotto.

Wealthy, and particularly Medici, patronage of the friaries and hospitals became even more prominent in the Renaissance; San Marco was richly endowed – and largely rebuilt – by the Medici; the Pazzi paid for the chapter house and family chapel at Santa Croce; while the wealthy *arti* also continued their sponsorship: the Arte della Seta (Por Santa Maria), for example, at the Ospedale degli Innocenti. Many religious and hospital complexes still evince the elegant refinement of the early Renaissance, notably the cloisters and library of San Marco (by Michelozzo), the colonnades of San Paolo, the Innocenti (by Brunelleschi) and the Badia Fiorentina (by Bernardo Rossellino).

Public Loggias (Logge)

There are several of these in the city, most associated with market activities: the Loggia del Mercato Nuovo (1547–51, by Giovanni Battista del Tasso, funded by the Medici), the Loggia del Pesce or Fishmarket

Santa Croce: the Pazzi chapel: right side of the façade

(1567, by Vasari; formerly in the Mercato Vecchio, today relocated), the Loggia del Grano (1619, by Giulio Parigi). A few others have trade or guild associations, for example those of the Tessitori and the Bigallo. The Loggia della Signoria, however, remains unique.

Tabernacles

These are a widespread feature in the more historic parts of the city, and are said to have first appeared in the thirteenth century. They usually take the form of an altarpiece set into an aedicule, and are frequently located at the corners of a street or piazza; they usually contain (or contained) a sacred and locally venerated image, frequently of the *Virgin and Child*. The images are in a variety of media from fresco (often now in extremely poor condition) to statues of marble. Those of particular significance are noted in the text.

Villas and Gardens

The earliest villas in the territories immediately surrounding the city were almost all based on a nucleus of an earlier, medieval fortified farmhouse or castle. Michelozzo's early modernisation of Careggi for the Medici (after 1457) rendered it still half-castle and half-villa, and even the much later modernisation of La Petraia by Buontalenti (after 1576) retained the imposing castle tower in the centre, with the villa wrapped around it. The first true villa, built wholly anew, was that at Poggio a Caiano, built by Giuliano da Sangallo, again for the Medici, in the years 1485–94, but embellished later. It was extremely influential, both for its rational, refined planning and for its elegant external appearance. It was also influential for its gardens and its relationship with the surrounding landscape, factors that became increasingly important with the later villas of La Ferdinanda, the extensions to Palazzo Pitti and the laying out of the Giardino di Boboli. Although the most prominent, the Medici were by no means alone in establishing these bases for semi-rural escape; many Florentine clans did the same, from the earlier banking dynasties of the Bardi to the later generations of the Strozzi, Capponi and many others. In the seventeenth and eighteenth centuries villas were modernised again or created anew; Villa Corsini at Castello is a good example of the radical modernisation of a fifteenth-century house, again with notable gardens. A few houses in the outer fringes of the city also had something of the character of a villa, several with extensive gardens. The last of the line can be said to be Poggio Imperiale, begun in 1767 and completed forty years later; an imposing pile in a highly restrained neo-Classical style, it bridges the era from the last of the Lorraine dynasty to the new world order imposed on Italy by Napoleon.

Fortifications

Most of the great circle of the city walls was destroyed in the mid-nineteenth century, but a few significant sections remain in the Oltrarno. A number of the massive city gates also survive, several now stranded in the centre of traffic roundabouts. Porta San Gallo, Porta alla Croce and Porta al Prato are the oldest (all built in 1284), while Porta San Frediano (1332) is the largest survivor; others include the Porta Romana (1326) and Porta San Niccolò (1324). The two principal fortresses are the Fortezza da Basso (1534) and the Forte di Belvedere (1590–95). Their significantly different designs reflect their topography, although they were intended by the Medici to face potential threats from both within and outside the city, and thus present powerful defences on both faces. The Belvedere, in particular, guarded the important and vulnerable approach to the city from Rome.

HOW THE CITY IS BUILT

Bricks and Tiles

Most of Florence is built of brick, but it is almost always concealed, either by a substantial cladding of stonework or by a smooth layer of external rendering. There was no tradition in Florence of using brick as a facing material in its own right, or of the development of decorative detailing in brick, as there was, for example beyond the Apennines, in Bologna, Ferrara and Venice. Only one major historic palace in Florence is of facing brickwork: Palazzo Grifoni Budini Gattai (1563–74), probably by Ammannati. Since the city had ample stone supplies very close at hand, and a very strong tradition of stonemasonry, this is not surprising. Tiles are the almost universal roofing material, and only very rarely is lead or some other material used. The baptistery, uniquely, is roofed with white marble.

Florentine kilns are recorded since at least the early fourteenth century, although they were located outside the walls because of the fire risk; many were just outside the city, in the Oltrarno. They were also closer to the clay fields for the basic materials. The kilns generally produced lime as well as firing clay, and they also manufactured roof tiles.

Stone and Marble

Stone is undoubtedly the dominant visible building material in the city. The most notable quarries in Tuscany, and among the most famous in the world, are the marble quarries of Carrara, some 100 km north-west of Florence. They were quarried by the Romans in huge quantities, and after the fall of the Roman Empire much of this marble was recycled for use elsewhere; many columns, capitals and bases, in particular, were dragged from the ruins of antiquity for reuse. Several churches in Florence have reused classical capitals in their colonnades. This reuse was partly because transporting long distances from the quarries to the destination city was extremely slow and expensive. The Carrara quarries were revived partly as a result of the demand in Florence for the construction of the cathedral and its campanile in the early fourteenth century. The market continued to expand into the fifteenth century and the Renaissance. Marble, though, remained relatively rare and costly, and even that from the much closer quarries of Prato, which produced a highly regarded dark green marble, was generally used sparingly. In the city as a whole, marble was used in only very limited quantities, and it was usually sourced via the department of works, the *opera* of the cathedral.

The use of other types of stone, however, was far more widespread. Florence was exceptionally fortunate in having good-quality stone quarries not far beyond the city walls; there was even one – in the Boboli hillside – within them. This stone is called *pietra forte*, an arenaceous limestone with a warm, sandy, yellow-brown coloration. Until the later thirteenth century stone was generally used as what is known as random rubble, uncoursed and unfaced. Fully finished, dressed stone was used only for elements such as quoins, door and window surrounds, and on important buildings such as churches.

From the late thirteenth century and throughout the fourteenth demand in the city increased dramatically, partly for the construction of the Bargello and then the Palazzo Vecchio. In both of these buildings, coursed blocks are used, but with a rusticated finish, an appearance that became as popular for private palaces as it was for major public buildings.

Although *pietra forte* effectively became *the* stone of Florence (much like *pietra d'Istria* did for Venice), in the fifteenth century a new taste developed, this time for *pietra serena*, a type of calcareous sandstone or *macigno*. It was first used by Brunelleschi for the interiors of his churches and chapels, and thereafter it became extremely popular, although its use was controlled by the Medici and was confined to the most prestigious structures, almost exclusively churches or other public buildings. It is generally bluish-grey in colour, with a fine, even texture that makes it ideal for carving capitals and other architectural elements. The principal quarries were south of Monte Ceceri, near Settignano, Maiano and Vincigliata, just north-east of the city. Both of these stone types were thus very easily accessible.

Timber and Other Materials

The other most important building materials were timber and sand; in both cases the costs and issues associated with transportation were the principal factors in the management of the industry. Sand and gravel were obtained very locally indeed: from the Arno itself, where it was freely and easily dredged, and where its removal assisted in maintaining the river's navigability. Timber was required in huge quantities, although fortunately much of Tuscany was heavily forested. Even in the early nineteenth century it was estimated that one third of the entire region was still under timber. Much was relatively accessible via the Vallombrone and the upper valley of the Arno. Huge tracts of upland forest estates were owned by the cathedral, and timber supplies were thus obtained through the *opera*, as marble was. Timber was generally worked on site, rather than in remote workshops. The construction industry also required limited amounts of ironwork, for locks, hinges, gates and railings. Mining and smelting took place some distance from the city; the iron mines on the island of Elba were among the most important on the Mediterranean, and had been mined since before Roman times. The ore was then distributed in Tuscany, to small smelting works in the Mugello and elsewhere, where in some cases the iron was worked into finished goods. In others, the basic metal was brought to Pistoia and Florence for further manufacture.

Vernacular Features

Florentine architecture developed a number of characteristic features, some of them unique to the city, or rarely found elsewhere. In domestic buildings, as in many medieval cities where space was highly restricted, the cantilevering of upper floors to provide more space was fairly widespread; these jetties are locally known as *sporti*, and are of stone or timber.

The uppermost floor of a palace was often occupied by a full-width covered loggia, sometimes known (as in Venice) as a *liagò*. The roof above was supported on a stone or timber colonnade. The *liagò* was used for the practical function of drying washing, and by the owner to take the air on summer evenings, when the city is often stiflingly hot.

Façades themselves were often terminated with dramatically extended, overhanging roof eaves. This allowed the safe dispersal of water from the occasional torrential rainstorms; it also protected the surface of the façade below, which was usually finished with render, and was sometimes decorated with *sgraffito* or fresco paintings. Both techniques were used, notably in the sixteenth and seventeenth centuries, although time has caused the loss of many examples. Fresco decoration seems to have become popular from the early sixteenth century. The rich, complex *sgraffito* decoration of the Palazzo di Bianca Cappello by Bernardino Poccetti (1579–80) led to a widespread interest in the technique throughout the city.

Rustication of stonework was widespread in the larger houses and palaces, its origins dating back to the early medieval towers, and to the Palazzo del Popolo and the Palazzo Vecchio. In the thirteenth and fourteenth centuries its use was partly symbolic and partly practical; even well into the Renaissance, the latter consideration remained important, and the massive rustications and barred high-level windows of Palazzo Medici were a real reflection of the potential for civil unrest. By the mid-sixteenth century, although most palaces retained relatively easily defensible ground storeys (barred high-level windows), the upper floors were now filled with large arched windows, usually with rusticated surrounds. Most such palaces displayed the owner's *stemma* (coat of arms), either in the centre of the façade or on a prominent outer corner.

As noted above, free-standing loggias were also common features, sometimes for public use such as markets, sometimes private, for example, Alberti's notable loggia for the Rucellai. These private loggias were used to celebrate important family events such as a marriage and a baptism; they were also used to display the wares that the family produced, such as wine and fabrics.

CRAFTS AND GUILDS

The building crafts were organised into guilds in Florence, much as they were in every major Italian city in the early and high Middle Ages; by around 1300 there may have been as many as seventy specialist guilds or *arti* in the city. The Ordinamenti di Giustizia of 1293 radically reorganised not only the guild system but also the government of the city itself, thenceforth to be based on the major guilds. Smaller *arti* were amalgamated, such that there were now only twenty-one, seven major and fourteen minor. One of these latter was the Arte dei Maestri di Pietra e Legname, masters working in both stone and timber, which itself later absorbed several other smaller, more specialist building crafts. This was very unusual in Italy, and in most other cities guilds remained much more numerous and fragmented; in Florence, this consolidated arrangement lasted until beyond the end of the republic in 1512, and the reinstatement of the Medici. By the end of the fourteenth century the building *maestri* may already have been the most numerous of all the Florentine *arti*, perhaps 20 per cent of the entire total, and by now included almost all of the construction crafts.

In 1532 Alessandro de' Medici consolidated the guilds even further, and the fourteen minor guilds were now reduced to just four. The new Arte dei Fabbricanti ('makers') included not only all the building crafts but also the workers in metals and furniture makers; in fact, almost every man in the city who made or built anything. The new statutes were approved in 1544; the new 'super-guild' now covered the whole Tuscan state, not solely the capital. Slowly, the guilds became less organisations of master craftsmen and more and more an agency of government, subject to the direct authority of the Medici grand dukes. The physical transfer of the administrative base of the Fabbricanti into the Uffizi at the end of the sixteenth century, where all centralised departments of government also had their offices, merely reflected their emasculated role as simply one bureaucratic department among thirteen. Still further consolidation followed in 1583 when the Fabbricanti were united with the food guilds; a single *arte* now replaced what had once been fourteen individual minor trades and crafts. The guild survived in this form until 1770, when, under Pietro Leopoldo, the guilds lost their remaining power and individuality as corporate entities.

FLORENCE TODAY AND TOMORROW

The city took a considerable time to recover from the floods of 1966, the damage from which, in every sphere of life, was enormous. The principal immediate cause was a torrential storm, but the effects were exacerbated to a devastating extent by factors such as deforestation and lack of regular excavation of the river Arno and its tributaries. The entire city was flooded to a depth of up to several metres; several dozen died; 14,000 families were made homeless; and countless works of art, documents and archives were damaged or destroyed. The world rallied to the city's aid, and although some irreparable damage was done (to Cimabue's painted Crucifix in Santa Croce, for example), the city's historic fabric today is in fairly good condition. The only remaining visible signs of this catastrophic event are the gauge marks carved onto many of the city's buildings, a dramatic reminder of the depths to which Florence was inundated.

A wealthy regional capital, and one of the world's most famous 'cities of art', this extraordinary patrimony brings with it many problems and challenges. One is the continuous and apparently endless round of restorations; during the time of compiling this guide, for example, the following major monuments were at least partly under scaffolding: Santa Croce, the Ponte Vecchio, the Carmini, the cathedral, the Uffizi and the Arcispedale di Santa Maria Nuova.

There are other familiar problems relating to the *centro storico*, common to so many historic cities: the extremely high cost of buying property and of maintaining it; the resultant depopulation of the centre, with the consequential loss of the usual everyday shops and amenities; the increase in the cost of living, seriously worsened by the inflationary effects of mass tourism – Florence is one of the most expensive cities in Italy. Although much of the centre is largely pedestrianised, the city still has acute problems of air pollution, partly the result of its location in the centre of a shallow bowl of surrounding hills; this can be such that the view from Fiesole is frequently obscured by a greyish-yellow haze, causing serious damage not only to the health of the Florentines but also visible corrosion and erosion of its monuments. As can be clearly seen, the misleadingly named *pietra forte* puts up little resistance to this modern *inquinamento* (pollution), and many famous external sculptures have been replaced by replicas, the originals now in the relative safety of the museums.

The demands of mass tourism are relatively well managed, although the extraordinary global popular appeal of Michelangelo's *David* and the Uffizi means that it is no longer realistic to visit either without booking in advance; at the same time, ironically, most of the 'lesser' museums (Museo Horne, Palazzo Davanzati, even the splendid Museo dell'Opera del Duomo) are often enticingly empty. And unlike Venice, Florence does not have to deal with the additional logistical challenge of 3,000 day trippers simultaneously pouring out of a giant cruise liner.

Issues of infrastructure and modernisation have given rise to extensive and highly controversial debates in recent years. The notorious international competition and master plan for the redevelopment of the former FIAT plant at Novoli, for example, were promptly abandoned with a change of city government in the late 1980s. Instead, the district has been partially developed in a piecemeal manner, with the most prominent new building the equally controversial Palazzo di Giustizia by Leonardo Ricci. Also highly divisive has been the new tramline connecting Santa Maria Novella with Scandicci, along the Viale delle Cascine, and with a new bridge across the Arno. Another, considerably more massive infrastructure project, involving the construction of a new TAV (Treni di Alta Velocità) high-speed rail station at Rifredi, and a long tunnel (the *tubone*) below the northern part of the city, has been equally mired in controversy, even as work continues on site. Santa Maria Novella is a terminus station, and this important but extremely expensive project is intended to provide the city with a new 'through' station (by Norman Foster) on the TAV line from Bologna to Rome; most of the rest of the line (Bologna–Rifredi and Florence–Rome–Naples–Salerno) is already complete and in use. These examples all represent a major historic city trying to adapt to transformational issues of modern infrastructure.

For all of its difficulties, however, Florence remains an enormously attractive and human-scale city, easy to explore, surrounded by the legendary Tuscan landscape, and with a great variety of treasures in addition to its world-famous monuments and works of art. It gave the Renaissance to the world, but the city has far more depth and range to its history than simply that unique period of genius and creativity. And its achievements are, of course, by no means confined to the visual arts. Its linguistic and literary heritage is the richest and most important in all Italy, with the triumvirate of Dante, Boccaccio and Petrarch still pivotal figures in European literary history. The city's Maggio Musicale music festival is noted throughout Europe; its textile and leather industries – seriously challenged from abroad though they now are – remain of extremely high quality; its culinary and viticultural standards are justly and universally renowned, and the Mercato San Lorenzo and the nearby *trattorie* are temples to fine food and wine. Florence truly has an extraordinary amount to teach us, in just about every sphere of human creativity and achievement.

A NOTE ON TOPOGRAPHY AND THE WALKS

Most of the routes in the early sections of this book are best undertaken on foot, since the city's historic centre is relatively small. Little electric buses (four routes) run by the city's transport agency, ATAF, also traverse the *centro storico*. To cover the zones a little further out, a combination of walking together with the city's bus service is probably the best answer. Most of the outermost districts are best reached by car, although again, many (like Fiesole, Galluzzo and Settignano) can be reached easily by bus, which is usually reliable and cheap.

The guide is generally organised on the basis of starting in the *centro storico* (historic centre), then discussing the inner ring of districts (the historic *quartieri*), and finally the further settlements such as Fiesole and Poggio a Caiano.

Although Florence is a relatively easy city to explore on foot, and much of the *centro storico* is largely pedestrianised, there are one or two topographical quirks of which it is useful to be aware. One relates to the naming of streets; many were renamed in the nineteenth century, particularly after Unification, and Florence's designation as capital in 1865. The best known is the Via Cavour, on which Palazzo Medici is located, known for centuries beforehand as the Via Larga. In many cases, the old name is indicated *in situ* below the present one. Another feature is the designation of *canto* (corner) at many important intersections, the *canto* generally being identified with a major adjacent palace. A further minor Florentine quirk is the appellation of 'Piazza', which is applied to almost any public space, regardless of size, even the tiniest, which elsewhere might be a *cortile* or, at the most, a *piazzetta*.

A trickier matter is that of street numbering; some decades ago, the city council decided to adopt two different numbering systems, one for commercial premises (red) and the other for private residences (blue or black); the result is a system that apparently benefits the postal services but almost nobody else, and means that a single building can sometimes have a selection of different numbers, some in *rosso*, others in *nero*. Where necessary, these numbers are denoted in the text by an 'n' or an 'r'.

Centro Storico

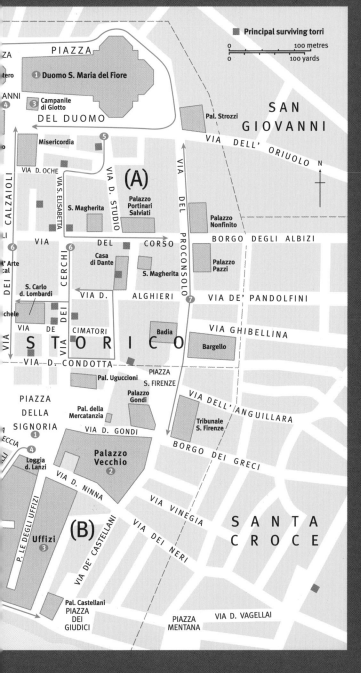

Principal surviving torri

0 ——— 100 metres
0 ——— 100 yards

PIAZZA

① Duomo S. Maria del Fiore

③ Campanile di Giotto

DEL DUOMO

Pal. Strozzi

SAN GIOVANNI

VIA DELL' ORIUOLO

N

Misericordia

VIA D. OCHE

(A)

VIA D. STUDIO

VIA S. ELISABETTA

S. Magherita

Palazzo Portinari Salviati

Palazzo Nonfinito

VIA DEL PROCONSOLO

VIA

CALZAIOLI

DEI

VIA

DEL

CORSO

BORGO DEGLI ALBIZI

Palazzo Pazzi

l' Arte cal

CERCHI

Casa di Dante

S. Magherita

⑦

VIA DE' PANDOLFINI

S. Carlo d. Lombardi

VIA D.

ALGHIERI

chele

DEI

VIA GHIBELLINA

VIA

DE

CIMATORI

Badia

Bargello

S T O R I C O

VIA D. CONDOTTA

Pal. Uguccioni

PIAZZA S. FIRENZE

PIAZZA DELLA SIGNORIA

Pal. della Mercatanzia

Palazzo Gondi

VIA DELL' ANGUILLARA

ECCIA

④

①

VIA D. GONDI

Tribunale S. Firenze

Loggia d. Lanzi

VIA D. NINNA

Palazzo Vecchio

②

BORGO DEI GRECI

P. LE DEGLI UFFIZI

(B)

Uffizi

③

VIA DEI NERI

VIA DEI CASTELLANI

VIA D. NINNA

VIA VINEGIA

SANTA CROCE

Pal. Castellani

PIAZZA DEI GIUDICI

PIAZZA MENTANA

VIA D. VAGELLAI

A: The Cathedral and its Environs

B: Piazza della Signoria, Palazzo Vecchio and the Uffizi

C: Piazza della Repubblica and Surroundings

The Cathedral and its Environs

This first itinerary covers the historic religious heart of the city, centred on the cathedral, as distinct from the political heart, centred on the Palazzo Vecchio and the Piazza della Signoria. It discusses the world-famous group of monuments on the Piazza del Duomo, the square that surrounds the cathedral, as well as part of the historic centre as far S as the Corso.

1 CATHEDRAL OF SANTA MARIA DEL FIORE (THE DUOMO)

The principal religious monument of the city; one of the greatest and most imposing churches in the world, said to be the fourth largest in volume. Its majestic cupola, the masterpiece of Filippo Brunelleschi, remains the iconic image of the city, visible from many locations in the surrounding hills. Although the cathedral was constructed over a very long period (the present façade was completed only in 1887), its facing materials of pink, green and white marble create a richly unified composition with the adjacent baptistery and campanile.

2, 3

Santa Maria del Fiore stands on the site of the earlier, much smaller church of Santa Reparata, first built in the late fourth or early fifth century; it was rebuilt in the eleventh century in the form of a Roman-esque basilica. In the twelfth century Santa Reparata became the city's cathedral, replacing San Lorenzo. This church had an aisled nave of six bays and three semicircular eastern apses, the central apse larger than the flanking ones. Its façade stood some distance forward of the present cathedral's west front and it extended eastwards for half the length of the present nave.

By the late thirteenth century the city had increased dramatically in both size and wealth, such that Santa Reparata was now considered too small; after tentative attempts to enlarge the church, in 1294 Arnolfo di Cambio was appointed by the Signoria (the city's govern-ment) to build anew. The first stone was laid on 8 September 1296, and the dedication was to Santa Maria del Fiore, the *fiore* being the lily, emblem of the city and symbol of the Virgin Mary. The basic plan

1   The cathedral: oblique detail of the façade by Emilio de Fabris, 1876–87

of the church was to be a Latin cross. Before his death in 1302, Arnolfo had begun the façade, considerably wider than Santa Reparata, and had taken up the nave flank walls to a certain height. After his death, work slowed considerably. In 1331 a new board, the Magistrati dell'Opera, was established to manage the works, progress on which now gathered momentum with funding by the wealthy Arte della Lana (wool workers' guild). In 1334 Giotto was appointed chief master, but he concentrated on beginning construction of the campanile, and died only three years later. Giotto's successor, Andrea Pisano, also worked almost solely on the campanile. Around 1350 Francesco Talenti was appointed in turn, and although he completed the campanile, in 1359, by 1356 his attention had also turned back to the church itself.

At this stage the eastern part of Santa Reparata still stood, as did the *canonica* (canons' residence) to the S, and the monastic buildings; further E stood the little church of San Michele Visdomini. Talenti produced a new model of the proposed cathedral. The plan was still basically a Latin cross, but the number of nave bays was reduced to four, although each was increased in size, and the proposed height of the nave vault was increased. Talenti also proposed a large cupola at the crossing. By 1364 the first three nave bays were complete, but Talenti was then dismissed. Three years later a commission of architects and sculptors (including Neri di Fioravante and Benci di Cione) was called on to approve the revised proposal of Lapo Ghini, Talenti's colleague and successor. This proposal included a modified plan for the eastern apses. The cupola proposed by Talenti was to be increased in diameter from approximately 36 m to 41 m (approx. 119 to 135 ft); it was to stand on an octagonal drum with circular windows, as it is today. Ghini completed almost all the structure of the nave, but Talenti then returned as master, until *circa* 1370, by which date the form of the cupola and eastern apses had been defined. In 1378 the nave vault was complete; two years later the aisle vaults were also completed. Work continued until 1421 on the three arms of the transepts and chancel, and the drum to carry the cupola.

In 1418 a competition was launched for the design of the cupola; it was won by Lorenzo Ghiberti and Brunelleschi. The role of the former was to be very limited, however, and soon Brunelleschi alone took control of the work. It was completed up to the base of the lantern in 1436.

The construction of such a massive structure had long been considered a major challenge, but Brunelleschi's scheme was daring and innovative. He proposed to build the cupola without timber centering or formwork, an approach that had probably never been tried before, certainly not since the classical era; in fact, sourcing the massive timbers that would have been necessary for the temporary supports was itself a possibly insurmountable challenge. To achieve this, he designed and constructed two 'shells' of brickwork, an inner, heavier one (approx. 2 m, or 6 ft 6 in., thick) and a lighter outer one, with a matrix of brick ribs between the two to stiffen them into an integrated whole. The main function of the outer shell was to support the external tile cladding, and a staircase was built between the two shells to reach the lantern at the top. The cupola was built upwards and inwards from the drum in a 'spiral' manner, such that it was self-supporting at every stage in the process; the bricks themselves were laid in a herringbone pattern to provide further integrity. Iron chains were also inserted to reduce the tendency to spread. The top of the cupola (excluding the lantern) is 91 m (approx. 300 ft) from the ground.

A final competition was then held for the design of the crowning lantern, which was again won by Brunelleschi. Construction began in 1443, but he died three years later. It was continued under Michelozzo di Bartolomeo, and then Bernardo Rossellino, but was finally completed only in 1468 under Andrea del Verrocchio's supervision. The long construction period was partly the result of the extreme logistical difficulties in hauling the marble up to such a height and placing it in position. The lantern takes the form of an octagonal classical *tempietto*, and is the size of a small chapel; in the same period Brunelleschi also designed the four exedrae, which rise just below the circular windows of the drum and between the cupolas of the three tribunes or eastern apses. Their appearance is related to that of the lantern, with deep niches separated by paired pilasters, in a refined early Renaissance style.

The Exterior

The S flank is the oldest part of the cathedral. Like the rest of the exterior, it is clad with white Carrara marble, with decorative rectangular panelling in green Prato marble. On the wall adjacent to the campanile is a relief of the *Annunciation*, dated 1310. Nearby is the Porta del Campanile, with a *Virgin and Child* in the lunette, once attributed to Andrea Pisano, now generally given to Simone Talenti. Next, further E, is the rich Porta dei Canonici, 1378, by Piero di Giovanni Tedesco 4 and others. In the lunette: another *Virgin and Child*, by Niccolò di Pietro Lamberti, 1395.

The E end of the cathedral is characterized by the vast massing of the three equal arms of the transepts and chancel, all rising towards Brunelleschi's great cupola. The exteriors of these three arms each have five facets, with tall Gothic two-light windows on each face. Above the lower order, raking buttresses support the considerably smaller upper order, crowned by a small but incomplete cupola, abutting the base of the octagonal drum. The drum has a large oculus (*occhio*) on each face; just above, before the springing of the cupola itself, it was intended to construct eight marble-clad galleries. Only one facet was completed, in 1506–15, by Baccio d'Agnolo. Its design was not considered a success – Michelangelo notoriously described it as looking like 'a cage for crickets' – and the remaining seven were never built, the rough masonry surviving to this day. Several proposals for the galleries' completion, in the form of models, survive in the Museo dell'Opera di Santa Maria del Fuore.

Brunelleschi's cupola has eight facets, clad with large terracotta tiled panels and divided by stone ribs. His crowning *tempietto* is a further 20 m (approx. 66 ft) tall, and again has eight facets, supported by raking stone buttresses and capped by a tall pyramidal roof, with a gilded orb and cross. Its form is loosely based on the Tower of the Winds in Athens.

The N face of the exterior: the Porta della Mandorla (1391–7) was made by several masters, including Giovanni d'Ambrogio, Piero di Giovanni Tedesco and Niccolò Lamberti. The rich relief in the spandrel above the lower arch is by Nanni di Banco, and in the lower lunette was an *Annunciation* attributed to Jacopo della Quercia, today in the Museo dell'Opera. In the gable, within a *mandorla* (almond), is the *Assumption of the Virgin, with St Thomas*, by Nanni di Banco.

West façade

The original W façade was designed by Arnolfo di Cambio, but was completed only up to the top of the central portal. It was a rich, complex work in late Gothic style, but was dismantled in 1587. It contained sculpted works by Nanni di Banco, Donatello and Niccolò Lamberti, all now in the Museo dell'Opera (see below). The demolition was decreed by Grand Duke Francesco I, and was undertaken by Bernardo Buontalenti. The condition of the façade just prior to its dismantling was recorded in a notable drawing by Bernardino Poccetti, also in the Museo.

2 The cathedral from Piazzale Michelangelo, with (left to right) the campanile of the Badia, the cupola of the Cappella dei Principi, the cathedral campanile, the Bargello tower and the cupola of the cathedral

3 The cupola of the cathedral from Via dei Servi

4 The cathedral: the Porta dei Canonici

5 The cathedral: one of the smaller cupolas over the south transept

6 The cathedral: detail of one of Brunelleschi's exedrae and an oculus

7 The cathedral cupola from the south-west

8 The cathedral: the façade, by Emilio de Fabris, and Brunelleschi's cupola, 1418–36, and lantern, 1443–68

9 The cathedral: nave interior, begun by Arnoldo di Cambio, 1296

The façade then remained unadorned until 1843, when Nicola Matas proposed a new west front. In 1859 a public competition was launched, but was then postponed for two years as a result of political upheavals and Italian Unification in 1860. A series of disputes and two highly controversial competitions then followed, before a final decision on the design was reached in 1867.

The present rich neo-Gothic façade was built in 1871–87 to a design by Emilio de Fabris. It was completed after his death in 1883 by Luigi del Moro. The theme of the decoration is the greatness of Christianity and the importance of the Virgin Mary. Among the principal figures in the niches of the buttresses are *St Antonino, Archbishop of Florence* (+1459), and *Pope Eugenius IV*. The three bronze doors are by Augusto Passaglia (left and centre) and Giuseppe Cassioli (right); their reliefs depict scenes from the *Life of the Virgin*. On the upper gallery: the *Virgin and Child*, flanked by the *Twelve Apostles*, also by Passaglia.

The Interior

The cathedral interior has a vast, noble simplicity, approaching severity. Other than the stained-glass windows, there is almost no integral decoration. It is 153 m (approx. 505 ft) long, 38 m (approx. 125 ft) wide across the nave and aisles, and 90 m (approx. 297 ft) across the transepts. The plan is a modified Latin cross, with a nave of only four extremely large square bays, relatively narrow aisles (each one half the width of the nave) and an octagonal crossing. The three equal arms of the cross extend N, E and S from this huge central space. Articulation of the nave is by massive compound piers and pilasters, which support the very simple pointed arches of the main arcade and then rise to a prominent cornice, which is, in fact, a continuous walkway on corbels. Above this cornice: simple quadripartite vaults with stone ribs and plain plaster to the webs. In the centre of each bay of the clerestory is a large oculus. The aisles are similarly detailed, but on a considerably reduced scale. The cathedral contains one of the finest collections of stained glass in Italy, with a total of forty-four windows.

The floor is of polychrome marble, with rich geometrical patterns; it was begun in 1526 to a design by Baccio d'Agnolo, but took more than a century to complete.

Below the W part of the nave is a crypt, actually the remains of the earlier church of Santa Reparata, excavated in 1965–74. The excavations revealed a complex series of successive buildings and alterations, some

Roman, others early Christian. Near the foot of the stairs in the SE corner: tomb slab of Brunelleschi, the only artist of Florentine birth buried in the church.

Back in the church itself: monuments etc. in the nave:

Inside the W wall: mosaic of the *Coronation of the Virgin, circa* 1290, originally in the baptistery. Adjacent: a large clock, decorated by Paolo Uccello, 1443. On the W wall: three circular stained-glass windows, designed by Ghiberti: *St Lawrence with Angels*; *Assumption*; *St Stephen with Angels*.

Right aisle: first bay: near the corner: bust of *Filippo Brunelleschi*, probably from his death mask, made by his adopted son, Andrea Cavalcanti, 1446. Adjacent, within a wooden aedicule: statue of *Isaiah*, attributed to Donatello. Further along in the same bay: bust of *Giotto*, by Benedetto da Maiano, 1490. Fourth bay, just before the Porta della Canonica: bust of *Marsilio Ficino*, the neo-Platonist philosopher, by Andrea Ferrucci, 1521. The adjacent stained-glass window is by Agnolo Gaddi, 1394–5.

The crossing and cupola: the inner surface of the cupola was intended by Brunelleschi to be clad with mosaics rather like those in the adjacent baptistery. Instead, it is decorated with a vast fresco of the *Last Judgement* by Giorgio Vasari (until his death in 1574) and Federico Zuccari, 1572–9. In the oculi of the drum: seven fine stained-glass windows, 1443–5 (one, by Uccello, is lost), with scenes from the *Life of Christ*, designed by Uccello (2), Andrea del Castagno (1), Donatello (1) and Ghiberti (3).

The cupola can be climbed; access is adjacent to the Porta della Canonica (S) or the Porta della Mandorla (N). From the lantern there is a remarkable panoramic view of the city and its surrounding hills.

In each of the three arms of the tribunes are five square chapels, all lit with Gothic two-light windows containing fine stained-glass images of saints set into aedicules. The programme was proposed by Brunelleschi and Ghiberti in 1435; they were made by Ghiberti.

To the SE of the central octagon is the 'old sacristy', or that of the canons. Above the entrance: *Ascension* in enamelled terracotta by Luca della Robbia, 1451. Donatello's splendid *cantoria* (choir loft) of 1439 was formerly located above the doorway, but was removed in 1688, and is now in the Museo dell'Opera. Chancel: E chapel: two kneeling angels in white glazed terracotta by Luca della Robbia; and a bronze reliquary urn by Ghiberti.

North sacristy (of the Masses or of the Servites): above the doorway: relief of the *Resurrection* by Luca della Robbia, 1442. Bronze doors also by Luca, with Michelozzo and Maso di Bartolomeo. Above the doorway was Luca della Robbia's equally magnificent *cantoria*, also now in the Museo. The sacristy interior is almost entirely clad with rich intarsia panels of timber, in *trompe l'oeil* perspective, 1436–65, by various artists including Giuliano and Benedetto da Maiano. N transept: set into the floor is a gnomon (1475), once used for solar observations through a window in the cupola lantern.

Left aisle: first bay: figure of *Joshua*, probably by Donatello. Second bay: portrait bust of *Antonio Squarcialupi* by Benedetto da Maiano, 1490. Adjacent, to the right, are notable memorials to two *condottieri* (mercenary captains), both *trompe l'oeil* frescoes; the first is to *Sir John Hawkwood* (Giovanni Acuto) by Uccello, 1436; the other is to *Niccolò da Tolentino* by Andrea del Castagno, 1456. Fourth bay, near the Porta della Mandorla: famous portrait of *Dante and his Worlds*, in which the poet holds a copy of the *Divine Comedy*, by Domenico di Michelino, 1465. The setting is contemporary Florence; to the rear, on the right, the city is now dominated by Brunelleschi's newly completed cupola.

2 BAPTISTERY OF SAN GIOVANNI BATTISTA

One of the city's most notable monuments, and the most remarkable survivor from Florence's first era of greatness. Its dedication is to the patron saint of the city, and for centuries it has played a pivotal role in the religious and social life of Florence. Together with countless other Florentines, Dante was baptised here, and refers to 'il bel San Giovanni' in the *Divine Comedy* (*Inferno*, XIX, 17). Its origins and early history remain obscure, despite centuries of speculation and numerous theories. According to one long-held tradition, it was originally a Roman temple, dedicated to Mars. The first written record of a church on this site dates from 897, although the present basic structure is believed to date from the fifth or sixth century, built in association with Santa Reparata; San Giovanni may well have been constructed on earlier Roman foundations, and its form suggests oriental influence, perhaps from Turkey, Armenia or Syria. It was reconsecrated on 6 November 1059 by Pope Nicholas II, also formerly bishop of Florence, following major works of alteration. These included the addition of the third order of the enclosing fabric; the pyramidal roof was built *circa* 1150; its lantern was added in 1174. A little later (*circa* 1202) the original semicircular apse was replaced by the present rectangular sanctuary, containing the high altar. Between 1059 and 1128 San Giovanni served as the city's cathedral. While Santa Maria del Fiore was patronised by the Arte della Lana, the baptistery was patronised by the equally important guild of Calimala (merchants).

The plan is a regular octagon, with the principal faces towards the cardinal points of the compass, and thus with the E face directly opposite the façade of the cathedral. There are many other examples of this centralised form in Italy, including the baptisteries at Pisa (begun 1152), Cremona (1167) and Parma (begun 1196). In the medieval period, baptisms took place only three times a year, at Easter, Pentecost and Epiphany, so a generous centralised space was necessary for the large numbers who assembled. The octagon also has religious symbolism. In the biblical account, creation was completed on the seventh day. The eighth day marks Christ's Resurrection and the beginning of a new, redeemed creation, into which Man is incorporated through baptism.

The Exterior

10   The baptistery is clad with two colours of marble: white from Luni (Carrara) and green from Prato. Each facet has three orders and three bays; the lower two orders read together and have three semicircular arches at the top of the second order, on polygonal columns whose bases align with the square pilasters of the lower order. The lowermost order is filled with rectangular marble panels, while the second has stylised semicircular arches below an aediculed window set into the centre of each bay. At the angles are 'zebra'-striped quoins. The slightly later uppermost order is much simpler, with rectangular panels set in three groups of three, and surmounted by a rich cornice. The sanctuary (*scarsella*) projects to the W, and is detailed in a very similar manner to the body of the church.

11   The other notable features of the exterior are the doorways on each of the three other faces, N, E and S. The doors on the S portal were originally on the E face. They were completed by Andrea Pisano in 1330 (signed and dated at the top) and put into position in 1336. They remained on the E face until 1452, when they were transferred to accommodate Ghiberti's Porta del Paradiso. Pisano's doors are made of gilded bronze, and contain twenty-eight relief panels, all set in Gothic quatrefoil frames. The upper twenty contain scenes from the *Life of St John the Baptist*, while the lowermost eight contain the *Virtues*.

10 The baptistery from the south-west

11 The baptistery: detail of Andrea Pisano's south portal, 1330–36

12 The baptistery: detail of Ghiberti's Porta del Paradiso, begun 1425 (*Joseph Sold to the Merchants*)

13 The baptistery: interior of the cupola, with mosaics, begun 1270, completed early fourteenth century

The N door is known as the Porta alla Croce. It is the first of the two made by Lorenzo Ghiberti, 1403–24, but with many assistants, including Masolino, Donatello, Michelozzo and Uccello. Ghiberti won a famous competition in 1401, with rival proposals from Brunelleschi and Jacopo della Quercia. His winning *formella* (maquette), together with Brunelleschi's proposal, is now in the Bargello. The composition generally follows Pisano's earlier precedent, again with twenty-eight panels, but here the upper twenty depict *New Testament* scenes, in five rows of four, beginning at the bottom. The lowermost two rows depict the *Evangelists* and the *Fathers of the Latin Church*. Above the portal is the *Sermon of the Baptist* by Giovan Francesco Rustici, bronze, 1506–11 (now a copy; original in the Museo dell'Opera).

The E portal now contains Ghiberti's celebrated Porta del Paradiso (Gates of Paradise), the name first given to it by Michelangelo. In fact, the area between a baptistery and a cathedral was traditionally known as the *paradiso*, a reference both to the Garden of Eden and original sin and to baptism and heavenly redemption. Ghiberti was commissioned in 1425; the initial design, established by the Arte di Calimala, was to have twenty-four panels, depicting an iconographic programme devised by the humanist scholar Leonardo Bruni. Instead, Ghiberti proposed a radically different programme of only ten, much larger, rectangular panels of *Old Testament* stories, rather than the Gothic framing used on the other two doors. The panels are of gilded bronze and took twenty-two years to complete. Stylistically, they are quite different from the two earlier doors, with rich, expressive reliefs, and with the foreground figures almost fully cast in the round. Again, Ghiberti was assisted by others, including his sons Tommaso and Vittorio, Michelozzo, Bernardo Cennini and Benozzo Gozzoli. During the disastrous floods of 1966, several panels became detached; they were all removed and restored, and are now in the Museo dell'Opera. The panels now on the doors are therefore copies. The ten panels read from left to right and from the top to the bottom, beginning with *Adam and Eve* and ending with *Solomon and the Queen of Sheba*, some panels containing two biblical episodes. The intermediate panels depict: *Cain and Abel*; *Noah*; *Abraham*; *Jacob and Esau*; *Joseph*; *Moses*; *Joshua*; *Saul and David*. Around the frame are twenty-four small niches containing figures of *Prophets* and *Sibyls*, alternating with little roundels containing portraits of Ghiberti's contemporaries, and a self-portrait (right side of the left leaf, fourth from the top). Above the portal is a sculpted group of the *Baptism of Christ*, begun by Andrea Sansovino in 1502–5 and completed by Vincenzo Danti in 1569; again, the original is now in the Museo. Flanking the portal: two porphyry columns, originally classical, given by the Pisans to Florence in 1115. All of the exterior is currently (2015) under restoration.

The Interior

An octagonal plan, 25.6 m (approx. 84 ft) in diameter, its appearance broadly derived from the Pantheon in Rome. Two orders, the lower formed of fourteen monolithic columns of Middle Eastern granite, probably of classical origin, with gilded Corinthian capitals; square fluted white marble pilasters at the angles. The sanctuary is also framed by square fluted pilasters, above which is a large double chancel arch.

The main walls of the octagon behind the lower order are clad with geometrical patterns of marble. Above the architrave: paired arched openings to the *matroneo* (women's gallery), with three pairs to each face; above again is an attic with square panels in which mosaic figures are set. The cladding is of white and green marble, like the exterior, with geometric decoration. Above rise the eight internal facets of the cupola.

The floor is covered with marble mosaic (begun 1209), in various geometrical forms, and with figures of the *Signs of the Zodiac*. It resembles the contemporaneous mosaic floor at San Miniato al Monte, completed in 1207. In the centre, a large plain octagon marks where the baptismal font was originally located; it was demolished in 1576, together with the choir.

The inner surface of the cupola is clad entirely with mosaics, as is the barrel-vaulted sanctuary, the only such complete cycle in the city. The mosaics in the sanctuary are the oldest, begun in 1225 by Jacopo da Torrita. Those around the double arch at the front depict *Christ*, the *Virgin Mary*, *Prophets* and *Apostles*. On the intrados of the vault itself: four telamons kneeling on Corinthian capitals and supporting a wheel, on which are more *Prophets* and *Patriarchs*, with the *Mystic Lamb* in the centre.

Within the main cupola, the decoration was begun in 1270 and completed in the early fourteenth century. At the top, around the lantern: symbolic plants and animals. In the next row: *Christ among the Seraphim* and the *Orders of Angels*. In the next row, in the three panels towards the *scarsella*: *Last Judgement*, with Christ as Judge enthroned in the centre; He is flanked by the blessed (left) and the damned (right). On the other five faces are (from top to bottom) stories from *Genesis*; scenes of the lives of *Joseph, Mary and Christ*;

stories of *St John the Baptist*. The mosaic decoration in the gallery is later, *circa* 1300 to 1330. All the mosaics show a strong Venetian-Byzantine influence, and were probably mostly made by Venetians from the workshops of San Marco.

Among the other artefacts in the baptistery: the font was made by a follower of Andrea Pisano (1371), with six reliefs of baptisms. To the right of the high altar: sepulchre of Baldassare Cossa, the antipope John XXIII, 1421–7. The gilded bronze figure is by Donatello, the base, with three *Virtues* set in niches, is by Michelozzo. To the left of the high altar: two Roman sarcophagi, adapted to become Christian tombs, one (1230) for Giovanni da Velletri, bishop of Florence.

3   THE CAMPANILE 'OF GIOTTO'

The free-standing bell-tower stands just S of the cathedral, towards its W end. Its rich, elegant appearance has rendered it another of the iconic images of the city, and it is often claimed to be the most beautiful campanile in Italy. The tower is 84.7 m (approx. 279 ft) tall, with a square plan of 14.45 m (approx. 48 ft). The design was intended to harmonise with that of the cathedral, although it was not begun until July 1334, by which time the cathedral had been under construction – intermittently – for around forty years. Like the cathedral itself (but not the baptistery), the campanile has three colours of marble cladding: pink (from the Maremma), white from Carrara and green from Prato. The tower is reinforced by octagonal buttresses at the corners, and terminates with a boldly projecting balustrade, supported on a series of corbels with trilobate arches. The campanile was originally reached by a bridge from the flank of the cathedral into its N face, at the level of the first cornice, but this access was already lost by the early 1400s. All the surviving original sculptures are today in the Museo dell'Opera, and have been replaced by copies.

The initial design was by Giotto, who completed only the lowermost order before his death in 1337. He was succeeded by Andrea Pisano, who continued Giotto's proposal as far as the second order, but then modified the original intention for the two successive orders, with rows of niches for statues and a similar blind order. After 1348 Pisano took no further part in the works, and after a gap of two years Francesco Talenti completed the remainder, by 1359. The three different hands are clearly legible in the resulting tower, whose overall design has an

14   Campanile: the upper orders, completed 1359

15   Campanile: detail of the lower order with relief panels and statues in niches

16   Campanile of Giotto, begun 1334: detail of the bell chamber

ascending hierarchy of orders of progressively greater height, broadly following Giotto's original intention.

15   Giotto's lowermost order has a series of hexagonal *formelle* (relief panels) set into rectangular panels. They were probably designed by him, although executed by Pisano, and represent the *Creation of Man* and *Crafts and Industries*. The five on the face towards the cathedral are by Luca della Robbia and were put in place in 1437–9, after the bridge had been removed. On the upper register, the panels, again by Pisano, are lozenges, and represent the *Virtues*, the *Planets*, the *Liberal Arts* and the *Sacraments*. The last are attributed to Alberto Arnoldi.

The next order contains sculpted figures set into niches, four to each face; the figures (*Patriarchs*, *Kings*, *Prophets* and *Sibyls*) were all originally by Pisano, but some were replaced in 1466 by works by Donatello and Nanni di Bartolo.

Above this order is a similar one, but with blind panels. The next two orders (by Talenti) have a different character. On each face is a pair of large *bifore* (two-light windows), the two lights divided by very slender colonnettes, and with a pointed arch above. The *bifore* have richly carved outer frames. The upper of these two orders is very similar to the lower, but the paired *bifora* windows are slightly taller.

16   Finally, the uppermost order is considerably taller again; each face contains a single, very large, open traceried window to the bell chamber. The window has three lights, again subdivided by extremely slender colonnettes, and with a large pointed arch above. The tower terminates with a substantial machicolated cornice.

4 AROUND THE PIAZZA SAN GIOVANNI AND THE PIAZZA DEL DUOMO

Begin on the S side, at the Loggia del Bigallo, and proceed clockwise around the perimeter of Piazza San Giovanni and the Piazza del Duomo.

Loggia del Bigallo: S side, corner of Via dei Calzaiuoli. Generally attributed to Alberto Arnoldi, chief master of the cathedral, and built in 1352–8. It originally housed the Compagnia della Misericordia, which in 1425 joined with the Compagnia del Bigallo. The latter had been founded by St Peter Martyr in 1244, principally to care for orphan children. The name Bigallo derives from a village of that name beyond Bagno a Ripoli, where the Compagnia had a hospital. In 1489 the two *compagnie* split, and the Loggia was used solely by the Bigallo; abandoned children could be placed there and taken into care.

The modest structure measures three bays by one, with two open round-headed arches at the external corner, forming the loggia itself; the whole is capped by a boldly oversailing roof. The corner element is said to be the work of Ambrogio di Renzo, and is richly decorated with reliefs (*Prophets, Angels, Virtues, Ecce Homo, Christ Blessing* and the *Annunciation*). In the second bay on the N face: a small Gothic arched doorway leading to stairs to the upper-floor hall. Above the N arch of the open bay: three small tabernacles, added after 1425. They contain figures of *St Peter Martyr* (left), the *Virgin and Child* (centre) and *St Lucy*, by a follower of Nino Pisano.

On the upper floor: elegant Gothic *bifore* with trilobate heads, one paired window to each bay. On the façade below the *bifore* (centre and right): remains of frescoes contemporary with the tabernacles.

Inside the lower loggia: set in a rich tabernacle by Noferi d'Antonio (1515): *Virgin and Child between Two Angels*, by Arnoldi, 1359–64. On the walls: fragments of contemporary frescoes.

Inside: the upper Sala dei Capitani contains a fresco of the *Madonna della Misericordia* (Virgin of Mercy), probably from the workshop of Bernardo Daddi, with the earliest-known depiction of the city (*circa* 1342), illustrated as a forest of fortified palaces and towers, with the baptistery in the centre. Another fresco, *circa* 1384, relocated here from the exterior, shows *Children Reunited with their Mothers*. Still another depicts scenes from the *Life of Tobias*, patron of the Compagnia, *circa* 1380. Also in the little museum: a triptych, again by Daddi, *circa* 1333.

Palazzo Arcivescovile: Piazza San Giovanni no. 3, W side. First built in 1287–95 for Bishop Andrea de' Mozzi; partially rebuilt for Archbishop Andrea Buondelmonti after a fire in 1533. The reconstruction was by Giovanni Antonio Dosio, 1573–84. The façade was rebuilt again in 1893–5 by Felice Francolini, part of a general reordering of the piazza: restrained and neo-Classical, four orders, with mezzanines alternating with the principal floors. Eleven bays, with three large pedimented portals in *pietra serena*. The ground floor is given over to commercial activity; the *piano nobile* has windows with alternating triangular and segmental pediments. A bold coat of arms (*stemma*) of Archbishop Agostino Bausa on the outer corners.

Inside: a central courtyard (*cortile*) with Doric colonnades on three sides; the upper loggia is Ionic. The staircase of honour and courtyard itself are by Bernardino Ciurini, early eighteenth century. The courtyard gives access to the little church of **San Salvatore al Vescovo**, today subsumed within the Palazzo. Eleventh-century Romanesque in origin, but largely rebuilt by Ciurini (1727); the only surviving early element is part of the façade onto Piazza dell'Olio to the W (*circa* 1220). This fragment is a small-scale member of the same family as the baptistery and San Miniato: three arched bays in white Carrara and green Prato marble; three semicircular arches on semi-columns, the central one containing the portal, the outer two blind, and filled with decorative panelling in green and white marble; six rectangular panels in each bay. The rest of the façade is plain, with an oculus to the upper order. Inside the remodelled church: extensive eighteenth-century frescoes, including *Adoration of the Shepherds* by Giovanni Domenico Ferretti (1735).

Continuing to the N side of the piazza:

On the corner of Borgo San Lorenzo: remains of the **Torre dei Marignolli**, much altered and absorbed within adjacent later structures. Clad partly with fine ashlar to the lower sections, random rubble towards the top. Family arms above the side portal. Continuing E:

Casa dell'Opera di San Giovanni: Piazza San Giovanni no. 7. Based on a tower; two bays wide, two original storeys and a low mezzanine. Most of the *casa* itself is fifteenth century, with a typical courtyard (accessible). The piazza portal is a good early Renaissance work, with a semicircular pediment. In the lunette: statuette of the young *St John the Baptist*, flanked by a pair of eagles (symbol of the Arte di Calimala), copy of a work by Michelozzo, now in the Bargello.

Continuing E along the N side of Piazza del Duomo: between Via Ricasoli and Via dei Servi, wrapped around the N transept of the cathedral: several medieval and Renaissance houses, many altered later, including no. 5 (fifteenth century), with rusticated arches and an elegant three-bay *liagò*. On the corner of Via dei Servi (nos. 25 and 28r) is **Palazzo Strozzi Niccolini**; also known as Palazzo Naldini or del Riccio; sixteenth-century Renaissance, on the site of the houses of the Tedaldi, and in which Donatello's studio was once housed (plaque). A substantial but simple façade to Via dei Servi (nos. 2–4), ten bays, the lower part incorporating earlier stonework. The building was modernised by Gherardo Silvani in the later seventeenth century, including the staircase and the Via dei Servi façade.

No. 9 is the **Museo dell'Opera del Duomo**. Begun by Brunelleschi in 1432 for the Magistratura dell'Opera, the body that oversaw con-

17   Loggia del Bigallo: detail of the east end

18   Loggia del Bigallo: detail of Gothic niches, added after 1425

19   San Salvatore al Vescovo: detail of the west portal, with thirteenth-century marble cladding

20   Piazza del Battistero: the early Renaissance portal of the Opera di San Giovanni

struction of the cathedral. Much altered over the centuries; little original fabric remains. After 1331 the Magistratura was sponsored by the Arte della Lana.

The present museum was founded in 1891. It contains an important collection of sculptures and artefacts made in association with the building of the cathedral, baptistery and campanile. It was radically modernised and reordered in 1990. Above the portal: marble bust of *Cosimo I de' Medici* by Giovanni Bandini, 1572.

Principal Works of Art and Artefacts

The Museo is currently (2014–15) undergoing extensive alteration and enlargement, so the notes below may not reflect the new arrangement once it reopens.

In the courtyard (now with a glass roof): two large groups of figures, originally located above the N and E doors of the baptistery, respectively: *Sermon of the Baptist* by Giovan Francesco Rustici; and *Christ and the Baptist*, begun by Andrea Sansovino, completed by Vincenzo Danti, 1569. Some of the original gilded bronze panels from the Porta del Paradiso are also usually on display here.

In the adjacent vestibule, through the *pietra serena* doorway: glazed and enamelled terracotta works by Andrea della Robbia and his workshop. On the wall: marble bust of *Brunelleschi*, sometimes attributed to Andrea Bandini, sixteenth century.

Sala dell'Antica Facciata del Duomo: the principal ground-floor hall contains sculptures removed from the incomplete medieval cathedral façade when it was dismantled in 1587. Among the works by Arnolfo di Cambio: *Pope Boniface VIII*, *Virgin and Child*, *St Reparata*, *Virgin of the Nativity*; also four figures of the Evangelists: *Mark* and *Luke* by Nanni di Banco, *John* by Donatello and *Matthew* by Bernardo Ciuffagni. In a small room at the side: scale model of a re-creation of the medieval façade, with further small sculpted figures. At the right end of the hall is the Sala dei Corali, containing relief panels from the cathedral choir (Baccio Bandinelli and Giovanni Bandini, 1547–72) and panel paintings; at the end is a small facetted chapel containing rich reliquaries. Adjacent, in the hallway known as the Lapidarium: collection of family arms and other stone fragments.

Halfway up the stairs, off the half-landing, is Michelangelo's superb *Pietà*; late 1540s or early 1550s, but never completed. The figure of Nicodemus at the back is a self-portrait.

Upstairs: the principal hall is the Sala delle Cantorie, in which are figures of *Kings*, *Sibyls* and *Prophets* from the campanile, by Andrea Pisano. The highlights are the two magnificent white marble choir galleries (in fact, organ lofts), both formerly on the walls of the crossing of the cathedral. The first is by Luca della Robbia, *circa* 1431–8; the other is by Donatello, 1433–40. They remained in the cathedral until 1688. Both are mounted at their original height; the della Robbia has the original relief panels hung below the *cantoria* at low level, so they can be seen more easily, with copies set into the *cantoria* above. Both are richly expressive, Luca's with singers and musicians, Donatello's with dancers.

Adjacent is the Sala delle Formelle, containing the original *formelle* (relief panels) from the campanile, transferred here in 1965–7. Many have been cleaned and restored. See notes on the campanile above. The hexagonal panels are mostly by Andrea Pisano; five are by the della Robbia. The lozenge-shaped ones are by Pisano and Maso di Banco.

Leading off the corner of the Sala is a narrow corridor containing historic building equipment and tools, leading in turn to the display of the original wooden model of Brunelleschi's cupola, his death mask and further contemporary models for the lantern and drum. These are followed by a series of large wooden models for the completion of the cathedral façade (*circa* 1590), and finally, by an exhibit of the nineteenth-century façade proposals by Matas and others.

Leading off the Sala delle Cantorie in the other direction is a small lobby leading to the Sala dell'Altare d'Argento: artefacts from the baptistery, including a fine silver Crucifix. At the far end of the hall: splendid silver dossal of *St John the Baptist*, a masterpiece of the silversmith's craft (restored 2009–11). The panels are by different hands: the central figure is by Michelozzo; the outer flanking panels are by Antonio Pollaiolo, Verrocchio, Bernardo Cennini and Antonio Salvucci. In the same hall: two figures of the *Annunciation*, attributed to Jacopo della Quercia. Also usually in this room: Donatello's striking *St Mary Magdalene*, a gaunt, skeletal figure carved in wood, *circa* 1455.

Back Outside in the Piazza

On the corner of Via dell'Oriuolo (Canto dei Bischeri; no. 10) is the imposing **Palazzo Strozzi di Mantova** or **Guadagni-Riccardi**. In 1593 a pre-existing house owned by the Bischeri was bought by Alessandro and Vincenzo Guadagni, who comprehensively modernised the façade,

24 including the portal, with its balcony. The architect was perhaps Gherardo Silvani, who also added the Guadagni arms. In the eighteenth century the palace passed to Anna Riccardi Strozzi, whose son Carlo extended it S to Via dell'Oriuolo in 1640; this S façade has five bays and a strongly rusticated portal. In 1871 the building passed to the Strozzi di Mantova and it was further extended by Felice Francolini. In 1989 it was acquired by the regional government and, after a long restoration (2008), now houses the region's offices. A powerful façade to the piazza; seven bays and three storeys plus attics, with a rusticated portal, as are the windows: pedimented on the ground and first floors, square to the second. Inside is a large irregular courtyard, on the ground floor of which are stables. The *piano nobile* is reached by a grandiose stair, built after 1730; ceiling decoration by Luigi Catani.

The S side of the Piazza del Duomo was reordered in 1826–30. In order to open this hitherto congested corner, and give more visual 'room' for the massive S transept of the cathedral, the building line was straightened and moved further S. The **Palazzi dei Canonici**, three similar blocks, are by Gaetano Baccani (1826–30), in a reticent neo-Classical manner; ground-floor arcades and two upper floors plus attics, all with regularly spaced rectangular windows. In the principal, central block, the balcony is supported by four columns, with figures of *Arnolfo di Cambio* and *Brunelleschi* by Luigi Pampaloni, 1830. Between the second and third blocks is the tiny Piazza del Capitolo, in which is the **Palazzo del Capitolo dei Canonici**, on the site of San Pietro in Celoro. This was one of the thirty-six ancient parishes of the city, but was suppressed in 1448. After 1680 it housed the canons' archive, until in 1778 this was relocated to the Biblioteca Laurenziana and the Biblioteca Magliabechiana. The simple façade is probably late seventeenth century.

Adjacent, at the W end, no. 19 (corner of Via dei Calzaiuoli), is the administrative base of the

Arciconfraternità della Misericordia: Its origins lie in the Società Nuova di Santa Maria, founded in 1244 by the Dominican friar St Peter Martyr, with the role of caring for the sick and arranging burials. In 1329 the confraternity was legally recognised by the *comune*. From 1425 to 1489 it was fused with the Compagnia del Bigallo, but thereafter was independent again (see the Bigallo, above). It was permanently established on the present site in 1576. A pre-existing building was restored by Alfonso Parigi (1576–8), and further renovated in 1781 by

21   Museo dell'Opera: the *cantoria* of
Luca della Robbia, *circa* 1431–8

22   Museo dell'Opera: the *cantoria* of
Donatello, 1433–9

23   Museo dell'Opera: relief panel from the
campanile depicting builders, by Andrea
Pisano, *circa* 1348–50

24   Piazza del Duomo: the seventeenth-
century Palazzo Strozzi di Mantova:
entrance portal

Stefano Diletti. The Arciconfraternità continues to flourish today, with around 2,500 full members (*fratelli*) and thousands more subscribing members; for centuries members were instantly recognisable by their black hoods and capes. Among other activities, they provide ambulance services for the city.

The present building reflects several modernisations since the eighteenth century. The main ground-floor hall is the Sala di Compagnia. On the end wall: sculpted *Virgin and Child* by Benedetto da Maiano; two kneeling angels by Giovanni della Robbia. To the left is the little oratory, with seventeenth-century decoration, and a sculpture of *St Sebastian*, again by Benedetto. The glazed terracotta altarpiece by Andrea della Robbia was originally in the Sassetti chapel in the Badia Fiesolana.

5 SOUTH OF THE PIAZZA DEL DUOMO

The next section of the itinerary takes us around the rectangular block of the old city bounded by the piazza (N), Via dei Calzaiuoli (W), Via del Proconsolo (E) and the Corso (S). This last was the Roman *decumanus*, extending E from the forum (the present Piazza della Repubblica) to the E gate, next to the present junction with Via del Proconsolo. The quarter remains densely built-up, with a number of labyrinthine medieval alleys and early fortified towers. It is closely associated with Dante.

Via dello Studio runs S from the piazza just E of the Canonica, down to the Corso. Good views of the cathedral cupola. In the fourteenth century the university was located here, in the houses of the Tedaldini. On the corner of Via della Canonica is the substantial **Torre dei Pierozzi**, or di Sant'Antonino, with a terracotta bust of the canonized *Antonino Pierozzi*, and descriptive plaque (1731); Pierozzi, a Dominican bishop, who was born here, also became *cancelliere* of the Opera. The tower has four storeys and a rectangular plan. On the next block S (W side) is a single-storey workshop, still used by the Opera del Duomo for preparing stone and marble for the cathedral. At no. 1: coats of arms frescoed onto the wall, originally four, mostly now lost, one depicting a dove (the Holy Spirit).

Just E of Via dello Studio, Via dei Bonizzi leads into Piazza San Benedetto. **San Benedetto** was first recorded in 1032, and was one of the thirty-six early medieval parishes. Its entrance was originally on Via dello Studio. The present structure is mostly from 1702, with a simple façade; arched window over the portal. Deconsecrated in 1771.

Via delle Oche runs E–W between Via dei Calzaiuoli and Via dello Studio. At no. 3: **Palazzo degli Scolari**, later Altoviti and Benivieni, the latter modernising it in the sixteenth century. At nos. 5–7: a bank stands on the site of the former synagogue (Italian rite), lost at the end of the Second World War. A little further, no. 20r is **Palazzo dei Visdomini**, with a tall tower, nearly surrounded by the *palazzi* of the Canonica. On the façade: a quotation from Dante below the family coat of arms.

Via Sant'Elizabetta runs N–S between Via delle Oche and the Corso. A little way down on the W side (no. 15): remains of an unidentified tower, much altered. Further S, on the little Piazza Sant'Elizabetta, stood **San Michele alle Trombe**, destroyed in the eighteenth century. In the NW corner of the piazza is the notable **Torre della Pagliazza** (no. 3), unique in the city because it has an elliptical plan. One of the oldest surviving towers; excavations (1983–4) indicated a Roman origin, perhaps originally a *piscina* (fish pond). In the sixth century it probably formed part of the city's defensive walls, built *circa* AD 541 by the Byzantines to defend Florence from the Goths. In the twelfth and thirteenth centuries it was used as the campanile for the adjacent church. It was also used for a time as a women's prison. The irregular fenestration represents many different uses over the centuries. In 1988 it was restored and incorporated into the Hotel Brunelleschi by Italo Gamberini. The brick paving is well preserved, as is the lower part of the tower itself. On the SE corner of the piazza is the six-storey **Torre dei Ricci**; a large arched ground-floor opening and a symmetrical main elevation. Via Sant'Elizabetta now reaches the Corso. On the two corners (N side) are two more *torri*: on the NW corner is **Palazzo Donati Ricci** with its tower; two large arched portals. On the other corner (NE) is the Torre dei Ghiberti (see below).

Via del Corso, north side: Turn E along the Corso, towards Via del Proconsolo. At nos. 5 and 7 is the extensive **Palazzo Portinari Salviati**. Originally built by the Portinari, the banking family, on the site of their earlier medieval houses; Folco Portinari was the father of Dante's Beatrice and founder of the Spedale (later Arcispedale) di Santa Maria Nuova. It is claimed that Dante first met Beatrice here in May 1274. It was later owned by the Da Cepparello and now by the Banca Toscana. The present twelve-bay palace was built in two phases. The first seven bays to the right (no. 7), with a central portal, formed the first stage (1470–80), originally built around two courtyards, the first later converted into a *salone*. Perhaps by Michelozzo, who had close ties with the family. Refined colonnades with acanthus capitals. In 1538 ownership passed to the Spedale; in 1546 Jacopo Salviati, closely related by marriage to the Medici, acquired the house and enlarged it. These works were perhaps by Ammannati, *circa* 1565–70. At the end of the seventeenth century the westernmost five bays were added (no. 5), extending to Via dello Studio.

The street façade is late seventeenth century (but in a sixteenth-century manner); three orders; rectangular single lights to the ground floor, with rusticated surrounds to the original arched portal. The *piano nobile* and second floor have regular, large, arched windows with rusticated surrounds to the first storey, square lights set into larger arched surrounds to the second.

Inside: the first courtyard is now the banking hall. Tuscan order, with robust stone colonnades, acanthus-leaf capitals and a flat continuous entablature; all in *pietra serena*. Above: a series of roundels with reliefs set into them. Fifteenth-century frescoes to the end wall. The Cortile degli Imperatori has porticoes on two sides, and vaults frescoed with sixteen scenes from the *Story of Ulysses*, by Alessandro Allori, 1580. Off the courtyard is the Sala dell'Udienza, a small but richly decorated hall, formerly with a loggia to the garden. Adjacent is a chapel dedicated to St Mary Magdalene; frescoed, and an altarpiece by Allori, *circa* 1580. The first-floor rooms contain fifteenth-century decorated timber ceilings and late eighteenth-century ceiling frescoes of mythological scenes by Tommaso Gherardini. The palace also has a fine collection of modern art, acquired or commissioned by the Banca Toscana.

La Madonna de' Ricci: N side of the Corso, a little further w. The
26 full dedication is to Santa Margherita in Santa Maria de' Ricci. Built in 1508, although the façade was added by Gherardo Silvani, 1604–10. The lower order consists of a spacious three-bay loggia, with semicircular arches. Above the central arch: arms of the Landini, who funded the work. Second order: a single central pedimented Baroque window with a balcony.

The interior was modernised in 1769 by Zanobi del Rosso. A single nave, restrained Baroque, all in *pietra serena*; a heavy, semicircular chancel arch, flanked by pilasters. The square chancel has a cupola on pendentives, frescoed by Agostino Rosi. Shallow barrel-vaulted chapels down

25 Torre della Pagliazza, sixth to twelfth centuries, restored 1970

26 Santa Margherita in Santa Maria de' Ricci: detail of upper window and balcony, 1610, by Gherardo Silvani

27 Torre dei Giuochi, attached to the Casa di Dante, fourteenth century, but heavily restored in 1875

each side. On the nave vault: fresco of the *Assumption* by Lorenzo del Moro (early eighteenth century?). On the walls of the lateral chapels: eight paintings by Giovanni Camillo Sagrestani showing scenes of the *Life of the Virgin*. On the high altar: *Virgin and Child* by Jacopo da Milano, commissioned in 1350 by Rosso de' Ricci, set in a marble pedimented aedicule. Continuing W:

Casa-Torre dei Ghiberti (delle Vedove): Via del Corso no. 48r, corner of Via Sant'Elizabetta, thirteenth century; originally part of the extensive properties of the Erborati and Adimari. The complex formed an *insula* to defend the local population. In the early fifteenth century it was owned by Jacopo and Lorenzo Ghiberti, the artists. Its unusual plan is a parallelepiped. The Corso façade has a large arched doorway and six upper levels; that to Via Sant'Elizabetta was much altered in the nineteenth century. Irregular fenestration, with some Gothic arched lights filled in. On the other corner is the **Torre Donati**, and immediately abutting it, right, the **Torre dei Ricci** (see above).

Via del Corso, south side: Halfway along, at no. 33r, is the thirteenth-century **Torre dei Donati**, with a plaque bearing an inscription from Dante, recording the murder of Corso Donati by the Cerchi. Originally owned by the Corbizzi, then the Donati, who became extinct in 1616. At the SW corner of Via Santa Margherita, a little further W, is the **Torre dei Giuochi** (no. 2); reconstructed in 1875 after it had become ruinous. At no. 13 (left side, just before Via dei Calzaiuoli) is the **Casa Lapi**, sometimes attributed to Brunelleschi.

6 FROM THE CORSO TO THE PIAZZA DELLA SIGNORIA

This itinerary continues the previous one, and is directly to the S, covering the block bounded by the Corso (N), Via dei Calzaiuoli (W), Via del Proconsolo and Piazza San Firenze (E), and the Piazza della Signoria (S). Like that above, the zone is intimately associated with Dante.

Via dei Cerchi: Runs N–S from the Corso down to the Piazza della Signoria. At the SW corner of the junction with Via dei Tavolini: remains of the twelfth-century **Torre dei Galigai**, with a Dante inscription; two large arched openings on the ground floor; three floors above. Almost opposite, on Via dei Tavolini (N side) is the **Torre della Bella** (no. 4r), with later rectangular windows. On the next block of Via dei Cerchi, continuing S: another **Torre dei Galigai** (W side) and the **Torre dei Cerchi** directly opposite on the E side (no. 20). Via dei Cerchi now crosses Via dei Cimatori, with yet another Galigai tower on the NW corner and another **Torre dei Cerchi** on the SE corner, the Canto alla Quarcona, again twelfth century.

A short way E along Via dei Cimatori is the tiny Piazza dei Cerchi, on which stands the fourteenth-century **Palazzo Rinuccini**. Stone facing and large arches to the ground floor and mezzanine, while the piazza façade has two upper floors on *sporti* and with arched windows. Returning to Via dei Cerchi, and continuing S, its last section becomes Via della Farina. At the S end is **Palazzo Giugni** (see Piazza della Signoria, below).

Via della Condotta: Runs E–W from Via dei Calzaiuoli to Piazza San Firenze. Named after the four Ufficiali della Condotta, who held office for a year, and were responsible for paying troops for the *condotta della guerra* ('conduct of war'). The street was also once known as the Via del Garbo; at the E end was the Porta del Garbo. 28

It contains a number of medieval houses: near Via dei Calzaiuoli, at no. 52r (N side, corner of Vicolo dei Cerchi) is the eleventh-century **Torre degli Alepri**, much restored. A relatively wide façade: three bays and five storeys. Also near the W end (corner of Via delle Farine) is the **Palazzo delle Farine**, formerly of the Antellesi. Built for Giuliano dell'Antella in the late fourteenth century, it marks the transition from *casa-torre* to the earliest 'proper' *palazzo*. After the Antellesi moved into Piazza Santa Croce, it was sold to Cosimo I, who installed his flour officials here, hence the name. A stone-faced ground floor with large arches for shops and workshops; the upper floors plastered, the remains of stone arched windows still visible. An Antellesi coat of arms on the outer corner, below which is a fifteenth-century *Virgin and Child*, attributed to Jacopo della Quercia.

Also on the S side (next block) between Vicolo dei Cerchi, Via dei Cimatori and Via Condotta is **Palazzo dei Cerchi** or Riccardi; a well-preserved medieval palace, late fourteenth century, faced with stone and absorbing earlier *torri* of the same family, and of the Alepri. Three large arched bays to the first order; arched windows to the three upper orders.

Further E along Via della Condotta, at the junction with Via dei Cerchi (NE corner) is **Palazzo Giugni**. Another notable late fourteenth-century house, with dramatic *sporti* to the W façade. The ground floor has three large rusticated stone arches, but the upper orders have four bays, arched to the first floor, square to the second and third.

Via dei Magazzini: Runs N–S from Via Dante Alighieri to the Piazza della Signoria. On the E side (nos. 18–20) is the **Torre dei Sacchetti**, with a broad façade: two large arched openings at street level; three upper floors, three bays wide. At the junction with Via Dante is **San Martino del Vescovo**. Near the location of an earlier San Martino, founded *circa* 1000, and possibly the church in which Dante Alighieri married Gemma Donati, since it was their local parish (but see below). The present church is a little oratory, built *circa* 1400; in 1441 it was assigned by Antonino Pierozzi, then archbishop, to the Compagnia dei Dodici Buonomini, 'twelve good men', whose role was to assist citizens who had fallen into poverty. The Dodici still dispense charity today. On the exterior: seventeenth-century tabernacle by Cosimo Ulivelli with a sculpture showing *St Martin Dispensing Alms*. Inside: a simple vaulted hall, with ten lunettes filled with frescoes (school of Domenico Ghirlandaio), depicting the life of the patron saint and scenes of contemporary Florentine life; all *circa* 1480–90.

On the E side of the piazza is the Pretura, within the courtyard of which can be seen the ancient façade of the Badia Fiorentina (see below).

In the SE corner of the little piazza is the **Torre della Castagna**, one of the best-preserved towers, and one of few that retain their original height. Probably early eleventh century, because in 1038 it was ceded by the emperor Corrado to the nuns of the adjacent Badia, to be used for their defence. The nuns, in turn, ceded it back to the city in 1282; thereafter, it was used for meetings of the priors of the guilds, before the construction of the Palazzo Vecchio. It was restored in 1921. The tower has a square plan and three very tall principal levels. The lowest two floors are of squared ashlar, while the upper levels are random and unsquared; arched lights with square lintels. Today it contains a small collection of Garibaldi memorabilia.

Via Dante Alighieri: Runs E–W from Via del Proconsolo to Via dei Cerchi. Halfway along the N side, corner of Via Santa Margherita, is the so-called **Casa di Dante**. Originally medieval, but largely reconstructed in a picturesque manner by Giuseppe Castellucci (1910), incorporating the truncated thirteenth-century tower-house of the Giuochi.

On the upper floors (access from Via Santa Margherita no. 1) is a small museum dedicated to the poet, reordered in 2008, and containing various editions of his works and much detail of contemporary Florentine life.

Via Santa Margherita runs N up the side of the Casa di Dante. On the right is **Santa Margherita dei Cerchi**, first recorded in 1032. In 1353 it was patronised by the Cerchi, Donati and Adimari (arms above the portal). It was also the burial place of the Portinari, Beatrice's family; Dante may have married Gemma Donati here. A very simple façade, with arched portal and three oculi with striped marble surrounds; perhaps later insertions. Inside: a rectangular nave without aisles, very simple (and very dark). Altarpiece of the *Virgin and Child Enthroned with Four Female Saints* by Neri di Bicci. Left side: monument to Monna Tessa (+1327), who inspired Folco Portinari to found the Spedale di Santa Maria Nuova. On the right altar: *predella* (small panel painting) by Domenico di Michelino.

Via dei Calzaiuoli, east side: One of the principal streets of the *centro storico*, it runs S from Piazza San Giovanni into the Piazza della Signoria. In 1841–4 the street was widened, with new façades, most in a neo-Classical manner, but the southernmost block had been set out to this width in 1383, and thus remained unaltered. On the NE corner, adjacent to the Misericordia, are the remains of **San Cristoforo degli Adimari**, today the confraternity's ambulance station.

At the S end, corner of Via dei Cimatori, is

San Carlo dei Lombardi: Begun in 1284 by Arnolfo di Lapo, continued by Benci di Cione and Neri di Fioravante in 1349, and completed by Simone Talenti in 1404. Originally dedicated to St Michael and St Anne, it was occupied by the Capitani (governors) of Orsanmichele until the latter was converted into their church. In 1616 the dedication was altered to San Carlo Borromeo, following its concession to a company of Lombards living in the city. The fairly simple façade, all in *pietra forte*, with corner pilasters, is crowned by a pitched roof supported on arched corbels; a large late Gothic portal, with an oculus above. 30

Inside: a rectangular nave with an open timber trussed roof, terminating in a tripartite chancel, divided by octagonal columns, supporting pointed arches and vaults. Late fourteenth-century fresco decoration around the chancel arch. In the chancel: *Lamentation over the Dead Christ* by Niccolò di Pietro Gerini, 1385–90. On the two side walls: four early eighteenth-century frescoes in lunettes, badly deteriorated, depicting scenes from the *Life of St Charles Borromeo*.

Nearby, at nos. 2–12r, corner of Via dei Cimatori, is the fourteenth-century **Palazzo dei Buonaguisi**. The four-bay façade to Via dei Calzaiuoli has large rusticated stone arches to the ground floor and simple square lights (altered) to the mezzanine. The upper levels are rendered, with rectangular windows.

31   **Via dei Calzaiuoli, west side**: On the northernmost block, between Piazza di San Giovanni and Via dei Tosinghi: two much-altered **Torri Adimari** (nos. 11 and 13), the gap between them filled in with a later hotel.

The principal monument on this side is the unique structure known as **Orsanmichele**.

On the block bounded by Via dei Lamberti (S) and Via Orsanmichele (N). Its origins lie in an eighth-century oratory, dedicated to San Michele in Orto ('in the orchard'), from which the present corruption derives. In 1290 Arnolfo di Cambio built a loggia here for the storage and distribution of grain. It was destroyed by fire in 1304, and rebuilt after 1337 by Francesco Talenti, Benci di Cione and Neri di Fioravante. They rebuilt the loggia to form a covered market hall, in a larger, more impressive form, but the arches were filled in by Simone Talenti, 1367–80, and two further storeys were built on top. The work was completed in 1404, the function of the upper storeys being to store grain. During the fourteenth and fifteenth centuries the building became a place of pilgrimage, as a result of the presence of a miracle-working image of the Virgin. Towards the end of the fifteenth century the market functions were transferred elsewhere, and the ground-floor hall was converted into a church, to be used as a base for the trade guilds.

The Exterior

All four façades are finished with fine *pietra forte* ashlar. The main features of the lowermost orders are the large arches with Gothic three-light windows with complex, refined stone tracery. In between the infilled arches is a series of tabernacles, one for each of the principal guilds, and each containing a statue of the guild's patron saint. The present statues are copies, the originals now being on display in the first-floor hall. The names of the guilds and statues are as follows:

28 Via della Condotta: general view towards the east

29 The eleventh-century Torre della Castagna

30 San Carlo dei Lombardi, 1349–1404; detail of the portal and façade, by Neri di Fioravante and Benci di Cione

31 Via dei Calzaiuoli: the west side with Orsanmichele (centre)

32   Orsanmichele: the west façade and main portal

33   Orsanmichele: niche of the guild of smiths or farriers (Fabbri / Maniscalchi) copy of *St Eligio* by Nanni di Banco, 1415

34   Orsanmichele: relief panel of the guild of stonemasons, by Nanni di Banco, 1408

35   Orsanmichele: terracotta roundel of the *Madonna della Rosa* (guild of physicians and pharmacists) by Luca della Robbia

East face (Via dei Calzaiuoli), from the left side: first tabernacle: Arte di Calimala (cloth merchants), *St John the Baptist*, by Albizo di Piero and Lorenzo Ghiberti, 1412–16; second tabernacle: Arte di Mercatanzia (merchants), originally contained *St Louis of Toulouse* by Donatello, today in the Museo dell'Opera at Santa Croce, and replaced by the *Incredulity of St Thomas* by Verrocchio, 1467–93; third tabernacle: Arte dei Giudici e Notai (judges and notaries), bronze figure of *St Luke* by Giambologna, replacing that by Niccolò di Pietro Lamberti, today in the Bargello.

South face (Via dei Lamberti), from the left side: first tabernacle: Arte dei Linaiuoli, Rigattieri e Sarti (workers in linen, dealers and tailors), *St Mark*, copy of an early work by Donatello, 1411–13; second tabernacle: Arte dei Pelliciai (leather-workers), *St James* and a relief of his *Decapitation*, attributed to Lamberti; third tabernacle: Arte dei Medici e Speziali (physicians and pharmacists), marble *Madonna della Rosa*, attributed to Piero di Giovanni Tedesco, *circa* 1400; fourth tabernacle: Arte dei Setaiuoli e degli Orafi (silk and gold workers), bronze *St John the Evangelist* by Baccio da Montelupo, 1515, replacing one by Orcagna, today at the Ospedale degli Innocenti.

West face (Via dell'Arte della Lana): first tabernacle: Arte del Cambio (bankers and money-changers), bronze *St Matthew* by Ghiberti, 1419–22; second tabernacle: Arte dei Lanaiuoli (wool workers), bronze *St Stephen* by Ghiberti, 1428; third tabernacle: Arte dei Maniscalchi or Fabbri (farriers or blacksmiths), marble *St Eligio* by Nanni di Banco, 1415. Also on this face: main portal by Lamberti, 1410. [32] [33]

North face (Via Orsanmichele): first tabernacle: Arte dei Beccai (butchers), marble *St Peter*, today attributed to Brunelleschi, 1408–13; second tabernacle: Arte dei Conciapelli (tanners), marble *St Philip* by Nanni di Banco, *circa* 1415; third tabernacle: Arte dei Maestri di Pietra e Legname (stonemasons and carpenters), marble statues of the *Quattro Santi Coronati* (Four Crowned Martyrs) by Nanni di Banco; fourth tabernacle: Arte degli Armaiuoli (armourers), bronze *St George*, copy of the marble figure by Donatello. Directly above four of the tabernacles are glazed terracotta roundels of the arms of the relevant *arti*, by the della Robbia workshop: they represent the Mercatanzia, Beccai, Seta and Maestri di Pietra. The remaining roundels were originally frescoed. [34] [35]

The two upper orders are both detailed in a very similar manner: Gothic *bifore* with trilobate heads, one to each bay, set inside a larger stone relieving arch. String courses at sill level, and the whole façade capped by a cornice supported on small stone trilobate Gothic arches.

The Interior

The ground-floor church has six bays, two rows of three, with simple rib vaults supported by square stone piers with typical fourteenth-century capitals. The vaults and pilasters were all frescoed in the late fourteenth century and the early fifteenth. On the vaults are Old Testament *Prophets* and *Patriarchs*, while on the pilasters are figures of *Saints*. In the stained-glass windows: stories from the *Life of the Virgin*, 1395–1405, by Niccolò di Pietro Gerini. In the NW corner a stair built into the pilaster is the original access to the upper floors. Adjacent, in the ceiling, is the hole through which sacks of grain were raised to the upper floors; built into the wall nearby are the chutes that brought it back down to the ground floor.

In the SE bay is the celebrated tabernacle by Andrea Orcagna, 1355–9, a richly decorated work, with intarsia decoration of many types of marble. The aedicule has cusped round-headed arches on all four faces, supported by elaborate piers, the whole surmounted by tall triangular pediments, and with pinnacles on each corner. Around the base: octagonal reliefs of the *Life of the Virgin*. On the back face: an extremely rich, complex relief of the *Assumption*, 1359. The altarpiece is the *Madonna delle Grazie*, 1347, by Bernardo Daddi, which substituted the original miracle-working fresco, destroyed in the fire of 1304. At the outer corners and on the upper pediment: statuettes of *Angels*, *Prophets* and *Apostles*. At the summit: *Christ the Redeemer*. The adjacent altar (left) is that of St Anne, with a marble group of *St Anne with the Virgin and Child* by Francesco Giamberti, 1526.

The upper halls are reached by a bridge (1569) from the adjacent Palazzo dell'Arte della Lana (q.v.). They have fine brick vaulting on heavy stone piers and columns. The original tabernacle statues are usually on display in the lower hall. A modern 'spiral' stair leads from the first floor to the second; a splendid open wooden roof, formerly spanning the hall with no internal columns (the central columns were added in 1844).

On Via dei Calzaiuoli S of Orsanmichele (W side) is **Palazzo dei Cavalcanti**, originally fourteenth century; side façade to Via Porta Rossa. Its rusticated stone ground-floor arcade is contiguous with that of the adjacent **Casa della Compagnia di Orsanmichele**, the two together having nine bays in all, and occupying the whole block. The ground floor is surmounted by a tall mezzanine with simple square lights; above are three further storeys, the first *piano nobile* also with stone arched lights (most altered). Further again, on the piazza (no. 4a), corner of Via Calimaruzza, is the **Palazzo dell'Arte dei Mercatanti**, whose symbol, an eagle and a bolt of cloth, is set in a series of roundels on the lower façade. The ground- and first-floor façades, clad in stone, are original: stone arches to the ground floor, rectangular lights to the first.

7 VIA DEL PROCONSOLO AND PIAZZA SAN FIRENZE

The west side: An important artery running S from the SE corner of the Piazza del Duomo into Piazza San Firenze. It follows the line of the city's Roman east wall, and also that of the first medieval walls, *circa* 1085. It is flanked by several notable buildings. In the road in front of the Badia is marked the location of one of the Roman bastions.

La Badia (Abbazia) Fiorentina: West side, opposite the Bargello. 36 Founded in 978 by Willa, mother of the marquis of Tuscany, Ugo, for Benedictine nuns. The formal dedication is to Santa Maria Assunta. The present complex is the result of a series of interventions, of which that of Arnolfo di Cambio (after 1285) is the most important. Arnolfo reduced the earlier nave to a single volume, with pointed arches, although maintaining the original orientation of the Romanesque church, with the chancel to the E. The plan was almost a Greek cross, with broad transepts to N and S, and a tiny chapel in the SW corner, opposite the campanile. At the E end the chancel was flanked by two smaller chapels, all three with cross vaults. The façade of this E end onto Via del Proconsolo has four tall single-light windows, the two larger central ones representing the original chancel inside.

In 1330 the upper part of the campanile was rebuilt to a hexagonal plan, with two orders of tall two-light windows, and surmounted by a slender spire. At the end of the fifteenth century the Chiostro degli Aranci was added by Bernardo Rossellino, and in the early sixteenth century the Pandolfini chapel was built, formed out of the little chapel of Santo Stefano.

In 1627–31 the interior was again radically reorganised by Matteo Segaloni, and turned through 90 degrees, so that the main axis is now N–S, with a new deep chancel, with a semicircular apse, at the S end. A new entrance was formed at the N end, onto Via Dante Alighieri.

Entering from the N portal: Corinthian atrium, *circa* 1494, by Benedetto da Rovezzano, with two orders of columns down the sides.

Immediately to the left: the tiny Bonsi chapel, sixteenth century. Next, also left: the large cubic form of the Pandolfini chapel, with a hemi-spherical cupola. In 1373 Boccaccio gave readings from Dante's *Divine Comedy* here; they continued into modern times. Just beyond the chapel is the entrance from Via del Proconsolo, with a portal also by Rovezzano. On the right side of the atrium a portal (perhaps by Giuliano da Sangallo) gives access to the large courtyard.

The church interior: an approximate Greek-cross plan, with deco-rated timber ceiling (*circa* 1630), above which are the earlier painted timber trusses of Arnolfo. On the entrance wall: fragments of late fourteenth-century frescoes. Below them: sepulchre of Giannozzo Pan-dolfini (+1456), by the Rossellino workshop. On the right side, adjacent to the base of the campanile: *Virgin and Child between St Leonard and St Lawrence* by Mino da Fiesole, 1464–70. Around the corner to the right: tomb of Bernardo Giugno, again by Mino, of similar date. In the right transept: entrance to the chapel of San Mauro, by G.B. Balatri, 1660–64, frescoes by Vincenzo Meucci, 1717. To the right of the chancel steps is the little square Cappella dello Spirito Santo.

A doorway on the right wall nearby leads to the Chiostro degli Aranci; adjacent stairs lead to the upper loggia. An attractive early Renaissance work by Bernardo Rossellino, 1432–8. Rectangular, five bays by three, with two superimposed Ionic colonnades, the columns supporting segmental arches. On the walls of the upper level: twelve fresco lunettes depicting the *Story of St Benedict*, 1436–9, probably by Giovanni di Consalvo.

Back in the church: the deep chancel has a semicircular apse. The vault and apse are frescoed by Giovanni Domenico Ferretti (1733–4); wooden choir stalls by Francesco del Tasso, 1502.

Left transept (the original chancel): the carved *cantoria* encloses the remains of the high altarpiece, an *Assumption* by Vasari, 1568. Below the *cantoria* is the marble and porphyry tomb of Ugo, marquis of Tuscany, who died in 1001, son of the foundress of the Badia; again by Mino da Fiesole, 1469–81. To the left of the transept is the chapel of San Bernardo, with detached frescoes by Nardo di Cione. Returning towards the N entrance, on the flank wall to the right is the *Apparition of the Virgin to St Bernard*, a masterpiece by Filippino Lippi, *circa* 1485.

Piazza San Firenze: west side
Palazzo Gondi: Piazza San Firenze no. 1. By Giuliano da Sangallo for Leonardo Gondi, and built 1490–1501; modelled on the earlier palaces

of the Medici and Pitti. It was originally built with only six bays and two portals. In 1874 the façade was extended to the left by Giuseppe Poggi, who added the seventh bay and the third portal; he also added the façade to Via dei Gondi. Today, therefore, the main E façade is symmetrical. The ground floor has a large central portal; both upper floors have relatively small arched windows. All the major openings are surrounded by radiating rustication. The façade, capped by a bold cornice, incorporates graduated rustication: the ground floor has prominent cushion rustication; that to the first floor is less pronounced, while the second floor has smooth ashlar. In the late seventeenth century Antonio Maria Ferri and Matteo Bonechi finally completed the interiors. Inside: an elegant central courtyard, with the original impressive staircase. Today, the main entrance is at no. 1 Via dei Gondi, and a new stair, added by Poggi, leads to the *piano nobile*. The building is still owned by the Gondi.

Via del Proconsolo and Piazza San Firenze: east side: From N to S: just S of the junction with Via dell'Oriuolo is

Santa Maria in Campo: Of very ancient but uncertain origin; one of the thirty-six medieval parish churches of the city. In 1228 it was assigned to the see of Fiesole, as it remains today. The simple Renaissance façade was altered in the sixteenth century (reconsecrated 1585); inside is a simple, rather narrow nave, with little ornament. Four Baroque side chapels plus the chancel, enriched with stucco decoration.

Palazzo Nonfinito: Via del Proconsolo no. 12. Begun in 1593 for Alessandro Strozzi by Bernardo Buontalenti, who completed only the heavy, richly Mannerist first order of the façade. Strozzi had acquired a number of smaller houses from the Pazzi for his new palace. The upper orders were completed after Buontalenti's dismissal in 1600; they are attributed to Giovanni Battista Caccini or Matteo Nigetti, probably under Vincenzo Scamozzi's direction, and continuing after the latter's death in 1616; Nigetti was a close friend of Roberto Strozzi. Buontalenti's first order is powerfully modelled, clad with flat rusticated stonework, and with prominent cushion rustication at the external corners. The façade has seven bays, with the massive central portal (by Caccini) flanked by two groups of three large aediculed windows, with heavy Baroque pediments and bold sills on console brackets. The bizarre pediments derive from bats' wings. The N and S façades are shorter, five bays, but treated in the same manner. The upper order is much simpler: single windows between pilasters, the windows with alternating triangular and segmental pediments. Above the first floor: a modest attic with simple square windows, where the second *piano nobile* was intended to be.

Inside: the unusual Palladian courtyard is probably by Lodovico Cigoli, 1602–4, with a lower order of Serlianas supported on paired Tuscan columns. The *piano nobile* has pedimented lights with balconies, alternating with smaller, simpler, rectangular windows; a very simple attic. The grandiose stair is by Santi di Tito. The building remained in Strozzi ownership until the end of the eighteenth century; in 1814 it was acquired by the Tuscan government, and now contains the Museo Nazionale di Antropologia ed Etnologia, established in 1869, and one of the most important in Italy.

Palazzo Pazzi Quaratesi: Via del Proconsolo no. 10; corner of Borgo degli Albizi. Sometimes known as the Palazzo della Congiura, in recognition of Francesco de' Pazzi's plot against the Medici that originated here in 1478. After the plot, the palace was confiscated by the Medici, and after various owners in 1593 it was bought by the Strozzi, who sold it to the Quaratesi in 1796. In 1931 it was acquired by the Istituto Nazionale della Previdenza Sociale, which restored it after 1945. The architect was probably Giuliano da Maiano, 1458–69, possibly after an initial concept by Brunelleschi, whose patron was Jacopo de' Pazzi. The simple but imposing façade has three orders and nine bays; the ground floor has two principal bays with rectangular lights on each side of the central round-arched portal; the façade is clad with rusticated stonework up to the first-floor sills, while the upper two orders have plain render, which might have been decorated with *sgraffito* or painted rustication. All the upper windows are *bifore* set within an arched outer frame; a small attic with little oculi, one per bay. The façade terminates with boldly projecting eaves. In the elegant, square courtyard: a three-bay colonnade on three sides, all in *pietra serena*. The capitals incorporate dolphins (the family arms) and a representation of the vase containing the sacred flame that Pazzino de' Pazzi brought back from the Holy Land in 1088 after the First Crusade. Above the colonnade are *bifore* like those on the façade. Around the top is a colonnaded *liagò*, now glazed in. Also in the courtyard: original family coat of arms by Donatello; that on the façade is a copy. The present stair to the *piano nobile* rises in the front *androne*, but was originally in the courtyard.

36 Piazza San Firenze, with the campanile of the Badia (left) and the Bargello (right)

37 Palazzo Gondi, 1490–1501, by Giuliano da Sangallo: detail of the rusticated façade

38 Palazzo Nonfinito, by Bernardo Buontalenti, begun 1593: detail of ground-floor window

39   Palazzo del Bargello from
the north-west, with the Torre
Volognana at the front corner;
first stage, 1255–61, by Neri di
Fioravante

40   Palazzo del Bargello:
north-west corner of the
courtyard

41   Palazzo del Bargello:
Donatello's bronze *David*
(foreground), *circa* 1440, and
St George (behind), *circa* 1416

No. 16r is the former guildhall of the **Arte dei Giudici e Notai** (judges and lawyers); plaque. Early fourteenth century, abutting an eleventh-century tower. The interior contains important frescoes, some badly damaged; they include the earliest known images of Dante and Boccaccio. Some are by Jacopo di Cione, 1366; others by Ambrogio di Baldese, *circa* 1406. These may include the ceiling vault fresco, with the symbol of the city.

Palazzo del Bargello: East side, between Via Ghibellina and Via della Vigna Vecchia. One of the most important medieval buildings in the city. Begun in 1255 as the Palazzo del Capitano del Popolo, who was elected to serve for one year as the city's supreme governor. From the late thirteenth century to 1502 it was the residence of the *podestà*, the chief magistrate, traditionally a non-Florentine. In 1574 it began to be used as the base for the Capitano di Giustizia or Bargello, and for the city's security police; prisons were also formed here in this period. In the nineteenth century the prisons were closed, and the building was restored in 1858–65 by Francesco Mazzei, with neo-medieval internal decoration by Gaetano Bianchi. The Museo Nazionale del Bargello was established here in 1865, and contains a remarkable collection of sculptures (notably by Donatello, Michelangelo and Giambologna), and other works of art and artefacts.

The new palace incorporated the exceptionally tall Torre Volognana, 39 on the corner of Via Ghibellina. It was built in stages; the first (1255–61) consisted of the front wing onto Via del Proconsolo. It was damaged by fire in 1323, and in the reconstruction, by Neri di Fioravante (1340–45), this wing was increased in height to incorporate the new Salone del Consiglio Generale. The central courtyard and the E block (to Via dell'Acqua) were built *circa* 1280–1300, and were also raised in height in 1316–20. The courtyard stairs were added by Neri in 1346–67.

The exterior is massively impressive, faced with stone and with bold crenellation around the top, supported on corbels. Its overall impression is severe, with small *bifore* to the first floor, and a single large *bifora* on the S façade lighting the council hall. In the NW corner the **Torre Volognana** rises 57 m (approx. 187 ft), with single-light openings at the top; it is also capped by corbelled crenellation.

Entrance is usually via the doorway in the Torre Volognana, and thence into the courtyard, which has a three-bay colonnaded portico on three 40 sides: stout octagonal piers supporting large stone arches. The interior of the colonnade is cross-vaulted. On the upper floors: windows in the form of trilobate *monofore* and *bifore*, set below shallow arched heads. On the fourth side of the cortile is the E side wall of the council hall.

On the walls around the courtyard and within the colonnade is a rich collection of reliefs and sculptures from the fifteenth century onwards, including works by Benedetto da Maiano, Francesco Laurana, Giambologna and Ammannati. Off the E side of the courtyard is a hall dedicated to medieval sculpture, with work by Arnolfo di Cambio and others. The doorway below the staircase leads to the Sala del Michelangelo, a large hall with four works by Buonarroti: *Drunken Bacchus* (1497), the *Pitti Tondo* (1503–5), a bust of *Brutus* (*circa* 1540s) and the small *Apollo*, unfinished. There are also fine works by Benvenuto Cellini, Giambologna (notably *Mercury*), Baccio Bandinelli, Ammannati and others.

The external stair rises to a first–floor loggia, from which the principal rooms are reached. Halfway up the stair is a portal added by Giuliano da Sangallo in 1502. In the upper loggia: small bronzes by Giambologna.

The impressive Salone del Consiglio Generale occupies most of the W wing. It has just two very large vaulted square bays, and contains notable sculptures by Donatello, including the *Marzocco* (symbol of the city), 1418–20; the young marble *David* (1408–9); the famous bronze David (*circa* 1440); *St George and the Dragon* in low relief and the fine *St George* (*circa* 1416), both formerly at Orsanmichele. Other early fifteenth-century works include: *St Giovannino* and busts by Desiderio da Settignano; and two figures of *St John the Baptist*, one perhaps by Michelozzo, the other also perhaps by Desiderio. On the wall: two trial panels made by Ghiberti and Brunelleschi for the competition for the second doors of the baptistery.

There are six further rooms on the first floor. The Islamic room (Sala della Torre); the Carrand Room (furniture and artefacts); the chapel of St Maria Maddelena, with frescoes from the school of Giotto (*circa* 1340); the Ivories room; the Bruzzichelli room (furniture); and the Maiolica room, with maiolica from the Medici collections.

On the second floor are: the Giovanni della Robbia room; the Andrea della Robbia room (SE and E); the Verrocchio room (S); Baroque sculpture and medals room; small bronzes room; and the armoury (N wing).

On Via della Vigna Vecchia, immediately S of the Bargello, is the **Chiesa Evangelica dei Fratelli**, 1879, neo-Gothic, by Teodorico Rossetti, and funded by Conte Piero Guicciardini.

San Firenze: Piazza San Firenze, E side. A substantial complex of buildings occupying the block between Via dell'Anguillara and Borgo dei Greci. Its origins are in the ancient church of San Firenze (Fiorenzo), founded in 1174 and donated to the Congregation of the Oratory by Pope Urban VIII in 1640. The old church was then replaced by a new Baroque church by Pietro da Cortona (begun 1645), with funding by Giuliano de' Serragli. The dedication is to San Filippo Neri. This new church stood just N of the old. Construction proceeded very slowly, however, and after 1668, when work restarted under Pier Francesco Silvani, its scale was reduced significantly. After Silvani's death (1675), it was completed in 1715, with a façade by Ferdinando Ruggieri. The final stage (1772–5) consisted of the demolition of the ancient church and the construction of the oratory on the S side of the site, by Zanobi del Rosso. The oratory was given a façade to match that of the church, with a linking block in the centre, containing the entrance to the conventual buildings.

The principal façade: the two outer wings are treated almost identically. Each has a very broad single bay, defined by a giant order of paired fluted Corinthian pilasters at the outer corners, and with a central pedimented portal surmounted by a single rectangular light. The 42 façade is capped by a segmental pediment, above which rises a square attic. At the upper outer corners: reversed half-pediments.

The church façades are enlivened by sculpted groups above the 43 portals, above the second-order windows and on the skyline; their white marble contrasts strongly with the *pietra forte*. The sculptures to the church are by Gioacchino Fortini (1715), those to the oratory by Pompilio Ticciati and Giovanni Nobili.

The central block is much more restrained: five bays and three orders, all with rectangular windows, surmounted by triangular pediments (first order), segmental pediments (second order) and square heads (third order). An arched portal in the middle, below a balcony.

The Interiors

San Filippo Neri: completed by Gioacchino Fortini after the death of Silvani. A long nave without aisles with a semicircular apse to the chancel. The detailing is rich and monumental but restrained. Two orders, the upper clerestory lit by rectangular windows; a flat ceiling. The articulation consists of flat, fluted Corinthian pilasters, with the two orders divided by a deep entablature. Between the pilasters are altars, with altarpieces set into stone aedicules. A carved, decorated stone chancel arch, beyond which is the apse, covered by a hemispherical vault. The high altar is flanked by Corinthian columns, and the altarpiece is set into another large stone aedicule, curved on plan. The paintings to the lateral altars are by Giuseppe Pinzani, Alessandro Gherardini and others. The high-relief panels above the lateral portals, depicting the *Life of St Philip Neri*, are by Fortini. The statues flanking the high altar (*Charity* and *Purity*) are also by Fortini. Frescoes to the apse ceiling are by Niccolò Lapi, 1715.

The oratory: again a rectangular nave without aisles, terminating in a semicircular apse, but its length is shorter than that of the nearby church. Ionic columns support the choir and organ lofts. Less brightly coloured than the church interior, but rich stucco decoration by Domenico and Giuliano Rusca. Above and below the choir galleries: frescoes by Filippo Burci and Gesualdo Ferri. Central ceiling fresco: *Assumption* by Giuliano Traballesi, 1775.

The conventual buildings: to the rear of the central entrance portal is a grandiose staircase by Zanobi del Rosso. The building is by Giovanni Filippo Ciocchi, 1745–9. It is centred on a rectangular cloister towards the rear, three bays by five. The work shows the influence of Borromini, notably in the capitals of the pilasters and the fenestration.

Much of the building is occupied today by the Corte d'Assise (assize courts) and associated administration.

On the next block S, bounded by the Borgo dei Greci and Via dei Leoni, is **Palazzo Columbia-Parlamento**. The present building is *circa* 1865, but stands on the site of a fifteenth-century structure in the location of one of the ancient Roman gates, the Porta Peruzza.

42   San Firenze: façade of the oratory

43   San Firenze: detail of the portal of San Filippo Neri; sculpture by Gioacchino Fortini, 1715

Piazza della Signoria, Palazzo Vecchio and the Uffizi

Historical Note

The Piazza della Signoria has been the city's political heart since the late thirteenth century, but its settled history is much older. Archaeological excavations (1982–9) revealed layers of settlement from the pre-Roman era onwards. From the period of Hadrian (r. AD 117–38), a baths complex was identified in the E part, and the remains of an imposing portico towards the S. Nearby (SW corner) were remains of a textile workshop of some size. From the later Roman and early Christian era the basilica of Santa Cecilia was identified, perhaps fifth century (W side, near Palazzo Lavisan), and that of San Romolo, of similar date, towards the N; from the early medieval period was found evidence of the complex of houses and towers of the Uberti and others of the defeated Ghibelline faction, from the eleventh century onwards. The Uberti tower was located near the Porta della Dogana of the Palazzo Vecchio.

The role of the piazza as the heart of temporal power was established with the foundation of the Palazzo dei Priori (Palazzo Vecchio) towards the S end of the city, some way from the ecclesiastical heart of the baptistery and the cathedral. The choice of location was a clear reflection of the separation of civil and ecclesiastical power in the republic, as well as recognition of the defeat of the Ghibellines.

The piazza developed organically, with no original 'master plan' to guide succeeding generations. The original nucleus of the Palazzo dei Priori itself was a compact rectangular structure, with its entrance at the N end, aligned with the axis of Via dei Cerchi. The piazza, however, was enlarged significantly towards the W in conjunction with the construction of the Loggia dei Lanzi (1376–82), and this also shifted its centre of gravity. Thereafter, Via dei Calzaiuoli became a more important N–S axis than Via dei Cerchi, since it provided the most direct route to the ecclesiastical heart, terminating at its N end between the cathedral and the baptistery.

44   The Uffizi from the Lungarno Torrigiani; completed by Buontalenti and Alfonso Parigi, 1580

Sculptures

Other than those in the Loggia dei Lanzi (see below), the following sculptures are located within the piazza itself. In the N centre: equestrian monument to *Cosimo I de' Medici*, a late bronze by Giambologna, 1594–8. It is aligned with Via dei Cerchi to the N. A little further S, abutting the NW corner of the Palazzo Vecchio, is the *Fontana del Nettuno*, by Bartolomeo Ammannati and assistants, including Giambologna, 1563–75. The work is another celebration of the Medici, and in particular Cosimo I. The giant central figure is carved from a single block of Carrara marble. The work was popularly known as il Biancone, the 'big white one', and frequently maligned; Michelangelo apparently dismissed it as a waste of good marble. Around Neptune's legs: three small figures of Tritons. The four bronze figures around the base are probably by Giambologna.

Immediately adjacent is the *Marzocco*, the heraldic lion, republican symbol of the city. The present work is a copy of Donatello's original, in *pietra serena*, transferred to the Bargello in 1885. Next, towards the S, is a modern copy (1980) of the bronze *Judith and Holofernes* by Donatello; the original is inside the Palazzo Vecchio. To the left of the present main entrance is a copy of Michelangelo's *David*. The original was set up here in 1504, but was moved to the Accademia in 1873. To the right of the entrance is the marble *Hercules and Cacus* by Baccio Bandinelli, 1534.

West Side

Dominated by the imposing pile of **Palazzo Lavisan**, by Giuseppe Landi, 1871, in a *quattrocento* revival style, modelled on Palazzo Medici and Palazzo Pitti. Built as the offices of Assicurazioni Generali, an insurance company. Nine bays; an arched ground floor, mezzanine and three upper floors, all lit by arched *bifore*. Its construction entailed the demolition of the church of Santa Cecilia and the Loggia Pisani. Restored 2010–11.

North Side

Palazzo Bombicci: no. 5, in the NW corner, with façades to Via dei Calzaiuoli (nos. 2–12r) and Via della Condotta. Fourteenth century in origin; stonework survives on the façades to the piazza and Via dei

Calzaiuoli. The latter has five large arches to the street, and a smaller portal. The upper floors are considerably later and finished with stucco. In 1786 it was enlarged by demolition of the church of San Romolo, and the piazza façade was modernised by Bernardo Fallani. On the corner of Via delle Farine is the sixteenth-century **Palazzo Guiducci**; a regular, restrained, four-bay façade, the ground floor and mezzanine clad with stone, the upper floors rendered but with rusticated quoins. Three principal upper floors, all with arched windows with rusticated surrounds, and two mezzanines.

Immediately adjacent is **Palazzo Uguccioni**, no. 7. Despite attributions to Ammannati and others, the architect is unknown, although the design was obtained in Rome by Giovanni Uguccioni, and is strongly influenced by Michelangelo and Raphael. A model was made by Mariotto di Zanobi Folfi (1549), who may also have supervised its construction. Late Roman Renaissance in style, with three bays and three orders, strongly modelled and all faced with *pietra forte*. The *alla romana* 48 façade was unique in the city at the time. The lower order is heavily rusticated, with a central arched portal and similar flanking bays. Above the portal: bust of *Francesco I de' Medici* by Giovanni dell'Opera. The two upper orders have paired columns defining the bays, Ionic below, Corinthian above, on prominent pedestals. Large rectangular windows to both floors, treated as aedicules, with segmental pediments below, triangular above. The interior has little relation to the façade, and is largely a pre-existing structure, the façade rising higher than the building behind it. **Palazzo della Condotta**, no. 9, in the NE corner, is so named because it once housed the quarters of the city's *condottieri* (mercenary captains); sixteenth century.

East Side

Palazzo del Tribunale di Mercatanzia: No. 10, extending to the corner of Via dei Gondi; fourteenth century. On part of the site of the Roman theatre, whose foundations lie below Via dei Gondi and account for the marked difference in levels. The building housed the tribunal that adjudicated on legal disputes between merchants. Four storeys, with a severe, almost undecorated appearance. Several ground-floor doorways, some altered; the first and second floors are almost identical, with five plus four bays, single-light windows with shallow arched heads. On the façade: the twenty-two arms of the guilds of the city.

45   Piazza della Signoria: equestrian statue of *Cosimo I de' Medici* by Giambologna, 1594–8

46   Piazza della Signoria: copy of Donatello's *Marzocco*

47   Piazza della Signoria: *Hercules and Cacus* by Baccio Bandinelli, 1534

48   Piazza della Signoria: Palazzo Uguccioni, detail of the façade

49   Loggia dei Lanzi: upper part of
the east façade; begun 1376

50   Loggia dei Lanzi: detail of corner
column

51   Loggia dei Lanzi: Cellini's *Perseus
with the Head of the Medusa*, 1545

South Side

Loggia dei Lanzi (della Signoria): Adjacent to the W façade of the Palazzo Vecchio. It takes its name from the *lanzi* (or *lanzichenecchi*, in full, from the German *Landsknecht*), the bodyguards of Cosimo I de' Medici, who were stationed here. The decision to build it was taken in 1350, its original function being for public festivals and ceremonies. Sometimes attributed to Orcagna, it was not begun until 1376, eight years after his death. Work was directed by Benci di Cione and Simone Talenti, and completed in 1382.

The loggia is raised on several steps above the level of the piazza, and consists of three very large bays, the semicircular arches supported by massive polygonal piers. The shape of the arches gives the loggia a rather 'proto-Renaissance' appearance. At high level in the spandrels of the arches: barbed trefoils containing reliefs of the *Cardinal and Theological Virtues*, by Agnolo Gaddi, 1384–9. The façade terminates with a decorative balustrade on cantilevered trilobate Gothic *archetti*. Above is a large roof terrace, accessible from the Uffizi galleries. Within the *archetti*: arms of the *comune* and the trade guilds. Inside the loggia: three simple rib vaults, supported on the back wall by massive corbels.

The loggia served several functions, including public proclamations and trials, until Cosimo I began to exhibit sculptures here. Today it contains a number of important works, some now in replica. Facing the loggia from the N, they are: flanking the steps: two lions, one (right) classical Roman, the other a sixteenth-century copy. The principal sculptures are: Benvenuto Cellini's bronze *Perseus with the Head of the Medusa*, 1545 (left, front), commissioned by Cosimo I, and considered Cellini's masterpiece; Giambologna's marble *Rape of the Sabines*, 1583 (right, front), commissioned by Francesco I; Giambologna's marble *Hercules and the Centaur*, 1599, right side, halfway back. In the centre towards the rear is *Menelaus* (classical Roman); near the left end (towards the Uffizi) is Pio Fedi's *Rape of Polyxena*, 1866. Along the back wall are six Roman statues, once at the Medici villa in Rome, and brought here, like the lion, in 1780.

History

The Palazzo Vecchio was built to house the Priori delle Arti, the city's governing magistrates, who lived here during their two-month period of office. During the fifteenth century and the period of republican governments (1494–1512), it became known as the Palazzo della Signoria; in 1537 Cosimo de' Medici was made duke of Tuscany, and three years later the building became the residence of the Medici, who moved here from their family palace on the Via Larga (the present Via Cavour); it then became known as the Palazzo Ducale. In 1565, however, Cosimo I transferred his court to Palazzo Pitti, which had been acquired by his wife, Eleonora di Toledo; thereafter, the present building became known as the Palazzo Vecchio. It housed the provisional national governments of 1848 and 1859; and between 1865 and 1870, during Florence's short period as the capital of the recently united Italy, the national parliament sat here. Since 1872 the palace has been the city hall, containing the mayor's apartments, the city council and numerous other offices. Many historic rooms are open to the public.

The building stands on the site of the houses and towers of the defeated Ghibelline Foraboschi. It was built in four principal stages. The original nucleus is the W section, and has a compact rectangular plan, with its longer façade towards the W and two shorter return façades to the N and S. The second, longer (E) façade was lost in later extensions. This first nucleus was begun in 1299 by Arnolfo di Cambio, although completed *circa* 1315, after his death, by others. The internal courtyard, towards the S, was modernised in 1453 by Michelozzo. The next stage of enlargement took place directly to the E, and was begun in 1343. In 1494 the Sala dei Cinquecento (Hall of the Five Hundred) was formed in this section, and in 1558–71 it was comprehensively modernised by Vasari. The next expansion consisted of a relatively small rectangular wing at the SE corner, extending to Via della Ninna and Via dei Leoni. This wing included the two superimposed suites of rooms known as the Quartiere degli Elementi and the Quartiere di Leo X. The fourth and final stage was a substantial addition at the NE corner, undertaken by Bernardo Buontalenti for Ferdinando I in 1588–96, and filling in the remaining land between Via dei Leoni and Via dei Gondi.

52 The Palazzo Vecchio is an extremely imposing castle-palace. The original W block is faced with rusticated *pietra forte*, and largely retains its
early fourteenth-century appearance. The façades are divided into three
orders by string courses, directly above which are rows of regularly
spaced *bifore* set within arched openings. They were remade in the late
eighteenth century, as was the present main entrance on the W façade.

54 Above the principal floors is an uppermost storey projecting well
forward from the plane of the façade, and supported by tall *archetti*.
Within these *archetti* are the arms of the city. The present ones are
post-1945 copies, and represent: the Capitano del Popolo; the Guelph
city; Florence and Fiesole; the papal arms; the Signoria; the Guelph
faction; the Ghibelline city; Charles and Robert of Anjou; and Louis
of Anjou, king of Hungary. At the outer corners were four gilded
marzocchi (heraldic lions), added in 1353. This uppermost storey contains
a covered walkway, which originally ran all around the perimeter; it
has a row of regularly spaced openings, and is crowned by crenellations.
Off centre to the right rises the dramatic form of the tower, 95 m
(approx. 312 ft) high overall, completed *circa* 1310 and rising sheer from
the cantilevered face of the uppermost storey. It is said to have been
built over the pre-existing fortified tower of the Foraboschi. The top
of the tower is crenellated in a similar manner to the palace itself, but
with swallow-tail battlements, a form associated with the Guelph
faction. As a means of 'advertising' the allegiance of the local lord,
Ghibelline fortifications generally adopted square-headed crenellation,
whereas the Guelphs adopted the swallow-tail form. The alignment of
the lower part of the tower can be traced in the different fenestration

53 from the main lower façade. At its pinnacle rises the tall bell-chamber,
itself crowned by semicircular arches and another swallow-tail crenellation. Near the base of the tower: a large clock, with a mechanism
dated 1667, and still functioning. Above the principal W portal (1345)
is a monogram of *Christ the King*, 1528. Flanking the portal: two marble
figures, sixteenth century, formerly used to hold a chain to bar entry
into the building.

The N façade to the piazza shows the successive stages of construction. The first five bays (right), with their crowning crenellation, are
symmetrical, and represent the extent of the original structure, with its
central portal, the Porta di Tramontana, closed in 1380 but reopened
in 1910. Further E are the sixteenth-century alterations to create the

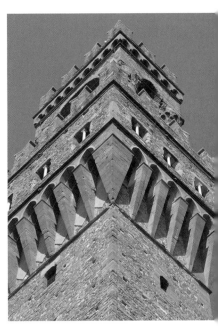

52 Palazzo Vecchio, begun 1299: the tower from the north-west

53 Palazzo Vecchio: the tower from the roof of the Loggia dei Lanzi

54 Palazzo Vecchio: south-west corner of the upper order from the roof of the Loggia dei Lanzi

Sala dei Cinquecento, while the sections further E again are the work of Buontalenti in the 1590s.

The Interior

The original nucleus consisted of two principal elements. At ground-floor level, to the N is the Camera dell'Arme, the oldest surviving element of the Palazzo, measuring three bays by two: plain square stone piers with chamfered corners, supporting robust arches and brick groin vaults. Immediately to the S is the second, larger element containing the courtyard, reached directly from the W portal. The courtyard has a slightly irregular rectangular plan, with two bays on three sides and three on the fourth (E) side. It was modernised in 1453 by Michelozzo, who added the upper-floor windows, with their arched *bifore* and high-level oculi. He also added the *sgraffito* decoration above the arch spandrels. In 1565, for the marriage of Francesco de' Medici to Giovanna d'Austria, Vasari frescoed the *loggiato* with scenes of eighteen cities of the Habsburg empire: Prague, Passau, Stein, Klosterneuberg, Graz, Freiburg, Linz, Bratislava, Vienna, Innsbruck, Eberndorf, Constanz, Neustadt and Hall. The courtyard columns were also clad with elaborate stucco decoration.

At the far side of the courtyard, opposite the W entrance, rises Vasari's double-branch staircase to the *piano nobile* (1561–71). Beyond it, to the E, is the Cortile della Dogana, originally open, but in which are the columns supporting the floor of the Sala dei Cinquecento above. Further E again is the larger Cortile Nuovo, an irregular rectangle, built by Buontalenti and Ammannati as part of the E extension, 1588–96.

The publicly accessible staterooms on the *piano nobile* are reached by Vasari's staircase. The stair gives directly into the **Sala dei Cinquecento**, a massively impressive hall (53 m long, 22 m wide, 18 m high / approx. 174 × 72 × 59 ft), extending the full depth of the Palazzo from the piazza (N) to Via della Ninna (S). It was built following the expulsion of the Medici in 1494 and the consequent establishment of a republican form of government, with a 'great council' loosely modelled on that of Venice. The hall was built by Antonio da Sangallo the elder, Il Cronaca and Francesco di Domenico, and was completed, remarkably rapidly, in just over a year. In 1502 two giant frescoes were commissioned, one from Leonardo da Vinci (*Battle of Anghiari*, 1440) and one from Michelangelo (*Battle of Cascina*, 1364). The first was begun, but then abandoned; current research is attempting to 'rediscover' the work behind Vasari's later paintings. Michelangelo's fresco was not even begun, since he was immediately summoned to Rome by the pope, only the cartoon having been drafted; a few preliminary sketches survive.

In 1563–5 the hall was modernised by Vasari for Cosimo I, and the ceiling was raised; the present decorations were also installed. The hall now became a ducal audience chamber rather than a place of government assembly, with decoration dedicated to the Medici. At the N end, the raised section is the Udienza, where the ducal throne was located; this was the first part of the hall to be modernised (1542–3, by Giuliano di Baccio d'Agnolo), and the N wall is an interpretation of the classical Roman triumphal arch.

The ceiling is richly coffered and gilded. In the centre is the *Apotheosis of the Duke* by Vasari; surrounding it are allegories of the Tuscan cities subject to Florence; victories over Pisa and Siena; and the growth and early history of Florence; all by Vasari and his workshop, including Jacopo Zucchi and Giovanni Stradano. On the walls: huge frescoes by the same workshop, depicting the wars with Pisa and Siena. Several free-standing statues are on display here. On the E wall, opposite the stairs: Michelangelo's *Victory*, 1533–4, intended for the tomb of Pope Julius II; and three *Labours of Hercules* by Vincenzo de' Rossi, 1562–84. On the W wall: Giambologna's plaster model for *Florence Victorious over Pisa*; and three more *Labours of Hercules*, again by de' Rossi's shop.

Off the W side of the hall is the little **Studiolo di Francesco I de' Medici**. Created by Vasari, with Vincenzo Borghini, in 1570–75, it has a stuccoed barrel-vaulted ceiling and is richly decorated in the Mannerist style, with bronze statuettes (by Ammannati, Giambologna and others) and pictures, representing Francesco's interests in natural science, alchemy and the arts. Adjacent is a little stair giving access to the Scrittoio (study) and the Tesoretto (small treasury), 1559–61, neither generally accessible.

Off the SE corner of the Sala dei Cinquecento is a series of rooms, the **Quartiere di Leone X**, that is, Giovanni de' Medici (son of Lorenzo il Magnifico), elected pope in 1513. The unifying decorative theme (1556–62) is the celebration of great figures from the Medici dynasty, all programmed (and partly executed) by Vasari, assisted by Giovanni Stradano and Marco da Faenza. The only room usually publicly accessible is the Sala di Leone X itself. Ceiling decoration: scenes from the life of the pontiff, with the *Capture of Milan* in the centre. On the walls: further scenes from the life of Leo X.

The other rooms in the suite are: the Sala di Cosimo il Vecchio; Sala di Lorenzo il Magnifico; Sala di Cosimo I; Sala di Giovanni dalle Bande Nere; Scrittoio; Cappella di Leone X; Sala di Clemente VII. Most of the decoration of these rooms follows the pattern above, with scenes from the lives of members of the Medici family.

A staircase adjacent to the Sala di Leone X rises to the second *piano nobile*. Directly above the apartments of Leo X is a second suite of rooms, of almost identical plans, and known as the **Quartiere degli Elementi**. They were again designed by Vasari (1555–8), assisted by Cristofano Gherardi and Marco da Faenza. The themes are allegories of the elements and classical gods and goddesses. The first room is the **Sala degli Elementi**, with *Allegories of Fire, Water, Earth and Air*. The marble fireplace is by Ammannati. Next, to the N, is the **Sala di Opi**, with the *Triumph of the Goddess Ops* on the ceiling. The floor tiling bears the date 1556. Next (NW corner) is the **Sala di Cerere**, with ceiling painting of *Ceres Seeking Proserpine*. Then (left) is the little **Scrittoio di Calliope**, with ceiling painting by Vasari. This was the room in which Cosimo I kept his personal treasures, such as jewellery, coins and statuettes.

Return to the Sala degli Elementi, and take the NE doorway into the **Sala di Giove**, and the adjacent **Terrazzo di Giunone**, originally an open terrace, but brought into the fabric by Ammannati. Verrocchio's *Putto with a Dolphin* is usually on display here. Next (SE side) is the **Sala di Ercole**, the walls decorated with the *Labours of Hercules*. Then another small study, the **Scrittoio di Minerva**. In the far SE corner of the suite is an open loggia, the **Terrazzo di Saturno**, with paintings of the god on the walls. Fine views across the city to the S, including San Miniato and the Giardino di Boboli.

Return to the Sala degli Elementi, and cross the balcony across the S end of the Sala dei Cinquecento, with a good view of the hall. We enter the suite known as the **Quartiere di Eleonora di Toledo**, wife of Cosimo I.

The first room on the right is the **Cappella di Eleonora**, entered by a marble doorway (*circa* 1543), perhaps by Ammannati. The chapel was formed out of the E bay of the Camera Verde in 1540–45 by G.B. del Tasso, and decorated by Bronzino, again in 1540–45, one of his most important works. On the walls: episodes from the *Life of Moses*. On the ceiling: *St Francis, St Jerome, St John the Evangelist* and the *Archangel Michael*. The altarpiece, also by Bronzino, is the *Lamentation*.

Adjacent to the S is the tiny **scrittoio**, with ceiling frescoes by Francesco Salviati. Straight ahead is the **Camera Verde**, with landscape

55   Palazzo Vecchio: the courtyard, modernised by Michelozzo in 1453, further elaborated in 1565 by Vasari

56   Palazzo Vecchio: ceiling of the Sala dei Cinquecento, by Giorgio Vasari, 1563–5

57   Palazzo Vecchio: tiled floor in the Sala di Opi, 1556

scenes on the walls; ceiling frescoes by Ridolfo del Ghirlandaio, 1540–42. A doorway on the S side (now closed) gave access to the bridge across Via della Ninna, and thence into the Uffizi.

The following sequence of rooms was used by the Priori and Gonfalonieri in the republican period, but later modernised by Vasari and Giovanni Stradano (1561–2). The themes of the suite are the achievements and attributes of notable women (in homage to Eleonora). The first is the **Sala delle Sabine**, with ceiling painting of the *Sabine Women Making Peace*. The next is the **Sala di Ester**, with episodes from the *Life of Queen Esther*; the frieze of *putti* (cherubs) is dedicated to Eleonora. Next is the **Sala di Penelope**, with a ceiling painting of *Penelope* and a frieze of the *Story of Ulysses*. The last is the **Sala di Gualrada**, dedicated to the young Florentine woman who (it is said) refused to kiss Otto IV, Holy Roman emperor, declaring her fidelity to her husband; the episode is recounted in the ceiling painting.

A short corridor behind the massive masonry of the tower leads to the **Cappella dei Priori**, formed in 1511–14 by Baccio d'Agnolo, and richly decorated by Ridolfo del Ghirlandaio. In the centre of the ceiling is a representation of the *Holy Trinity*, with the *Four Evangelists* in the cruciform compartments. A fine marble doorway leads into the **Sala dell'Udienza**, formed when the larger great hall here was divided into two by Benedetto da Maiano. Gilded coffered ceiling decorated with the coat of arms of the Florentine Popolo, by Giuliano da Maiano and others. The wall frescoes, illustrating mythical and allegorical figures, are by Francesco Salviati. Between this hall and the adjacent **Sala dei Gigli** is another fine marble portal, with *Justice* in the lunette, again by Giuliano and Benedetto da Maiano. The Sala dei Gigli has a ceiling decorated with gold lilies on a blue field, which, together with the frieze of *marzocchi*, is by Giuliano and assistants, 1472–6. The frescoes on the E wall are by Domenico Ghirlandaio. In this hall is usually exhibited Donatello's splendid bronze *Judith and Holofernes*, *circa* 1453–7, made for Cosimo il Vecchio.

The N doorway on the E wall leads into the **Cancelleria**, a long, narrow room, formerly the Chancellery of the Republic, where Niccolò Machiavelli worked as chancellor after 1498; sixteenth-century stucco bust, and a posthumous portrait by Santi di Tito.

Return to the Sala dei Gigli. To the E is the **Sala delle Carte Geografiche**, a hall built by Vasari (1563–5), and with wooden cupboards decorated with fifty-three maps by Dionigi Nigetti, and executed by Egnazio Danti and Stefano Buonsignori, 1581. They represent a comprehensive summary of Florentine geographical knowledge at the time.

Descending the adjacent staircase to the mezzanine, a suite of rooms was formed by Michelozzo for the Priori, by lowering the ceilings of some of the first-floor rooms. The suite contains seven rooms and a *scrittoio*. Four contain the Collezione Loeser, donated to the city by the American art critic Charles Loeser (+1928). They include works by Lorenzo di Credi; a portrait of *Laura Battiferri* (wife of Bartolomeo Ammannati) by Bronzino; and other works by Pontormo, Pietro Lorenzetti and Piero di Cosimo. In the adjacent rooms is a collection of historic musical instruments, some once owned by Ferdinando I de' Medici.

Descending back to the first floor, enter the **Ricetto**, with vault frescoed by Lorenzo Sabatini (1565); and thence (left) into the **Sala dei Dugento**. The impressive hall is part of the original nucleus of the *palazzo*, and stands directly above the Camera dell'Arme. It is not normally open to the public and is used for meetings of the city council. It has a rich coffered ceiling and frieze with the arms of the republic, all by Benedetto and Giuliano da Maiano, 1472. The two sixteenth-century marble portals are by Baccio d'Agnolo. Returning to the Ricetto, adjacent is the doorway into the **Sala degli Otto**, a small hall with a ceiling decorated with cherubs and angels, contemporaneous with the Sala dei Dugento.

3 THE UFFIZI

The construction of the imposing Palazzo degli Uffizi ('Offices') was a radical urban intervention undertaken by Cosimo I. Since 1540 Cosimo had ruled Florence from the Palazzo Vecchio, and in 1560, following the capitulation of Siena and its subsequent annexation (1555), he decided to locate in a single building the thirteen different magistracies (Uffizi) that administered this now much enlarged state. His architect, Vasari, was instructed to build this extremely large new 'annexe' to the Palazzo Vecchio, to which it is connected by a bridge. Each magistracy was to have its own entrance from the Piazzale down the centre, and a suite of rooms on the ground floor, mezzanine and *piano nobile*. The uppermost floor or gallery was intended for the use of Cosimo I. It has been claimed as the first purpose-designed office building in the western world.

It was first necessary to effect extensive demolitions, as well as the 'absorption' of the ancient church of San Pier Scheraggio, which stood at the corner of Via della Ninna.

The Uffizi were begun in 1560, but completed after Vasari's death (1574) by Alfonso Parigi and Bernardo Buontalenti *circa* 1580. By 1564 the E wing was already complete. In 1580 the W wing was extended northwards by means of an archway crossing Via Lambertesca, to link it to the Loggia dei Lanzi. The portal, the Porta delle Suppliche, is by Buontalenti, a bizarre Mannerist design, capped by a reversed split pediment.

The main building consists of two long parallel wings of accommodation, divided by an equally long, rather narrow open space, the Piazzale degli Uffizi, and united at the south end, near the Arno, by a transverse linking block. At the N end of the east wing: the remains of **San Pier Scheraggio**, originally consecrated in 1068. The church had been used for civic assemblies prior to the construction of the Palazzo Vecchio. Its left aisle had been demolished in 1410 when Via della Ninna was widened, but the rest survived and remained in use until 1743. It was restored in 1971, and now forms part of the Uffizi galleries. The remains of the nave arcade can be seen on Via della Ninna.

The Exterior

The two principal wings have a colonnaded ground floor, a fairly modest mezzanine, a principal *piano nobile* and a top floor containing the galleries. The order throughout is Doric (on Cosimo's instructions) and the two main materials are plaster and grey *pietra serena* from the Valle della Mensola. The ground-floor colonnades are divided into groups of three bays by a broad pier containing a niche for a statue. Each triple bay represents accommodation for one magistracy. Above the broad entablature the main bays are defined by flat pilasters; the mezzanine has rectangular windows, again in groups of three per bay. The principal *piano nobile* has single large rectangular lights, again in groups of three, and treated as aedicules, the central light with a segmental pediment, the outer two with triangular pediments. By contrast, the uppermost floor was originally an open loggia, but was filled in with glazed screens by Buontalenti after 1581 on the orders of Francesco I, so that the broad corridor behind could be used to display his sculpture collection. Shortly afterwards, in 1584 Buontalenti built the Tribuna, to display the Medici's most prized works, as it still does today.

Two years later again he built a theatre within the complex. A new doorway was also formed in the W wing so that the galleries here could be reached directly from the Piazzale, and here Francesco established workshops for artists and craftsmen. On the arch at the end: bust of *Cosimo I de' Medici* by Giambologna, 1585. Cosimo intended that the niches along the main façades should be filled with figures of illustrious Florentines, although the present twenty-eight figures (including Machiavelli and Giotto) were not finally installed until 1835. The SW corner of the Uffizi was badly damaged by a terrorist attack in 1993.

The Galleries

The Uffizi contain one of the most important collections of art in the world, and the gallery itself is the oldest museum of the modern era. The nucleus of the collection is that of the Medici themselves, initially the works acquired by Cosimo I, but enlarged by his successors, notably Francesco I and Ferdinando I. The latter increased significantly the antiquities in the collection and opened new rooms for the applied arts. The galleries have been open to the public since 1591, initially on request.

The following is a very brief itinerary of the principal rooms and galleries. Some temporary rearrangements are often in place; for example, the Tribuna was under restoration in 2010–11, and its works temporarily relocated in the W wing. The main entrance is on the E side, near the N end. The grand staircase leads directly up to the *piano nobile* and on to the principal galleries on the top floor. The stair passes the grandiose three-bay entrance screen to the theatre built by Buontalenti for Francesco I in 1586–9. Since 2009 a major project has been in hand to increase greatly the extent of the publicly accessible gallery space; in particular, large areas on the first floor (previously inaccessible) will be used for temporary exhibitions. The Grandi Uffizi project was well advanced when this guide went to press.

Third floor, E corridor: at the top of the staircase: busts of ten of the Medici, including *Cosimo I* by Giambologna. Following the top stair landing is an elliptical vestibule (by Zanobi del Rosso, *circa* 1780), with classical Roman statues set in niches, and sarcophagi. In the lobby are also some classical Greek pieces. The long vaulted E corridor runs the full length of the block, with ceiling decorations by Alessandro Allori, 1581. The corridor contains a fine collection of classical sculptures, mostly from the Medici collections. They were first arranged here in 1595–7. At high level, along all the corridors, is a long series of portraits of famous contemporaries, first located here in 1590 and augmented until the nineteenth century.

Rooms off the E corridor

Room 1: antique Roman sculptures

Room 2: medieval paintings: the room was remodelled by Michelucci, Gardella and Scarpa in 1956. Three *Maestà* (altarpieces of the *Virgin and Child in Majesty*), by Cimabue, *circa* 1285 (from Santa Trinità); Duccio di Buoninsegna, 1285 (the *Rucellai Madonna*, from Santa Maria Novella); and Giotto, 1310 (from Ognissanti).

Room 3: fourteenth-century Sienese paintings: *Annunciation* by Simone Martini, 1333; several works by Pietro and Ambrogio Lorenzetti: *Scenes from the Life of St Nicholas*; *Presentation in the Temple*, 1342; *Virgin and Child in Glory*, 1340.

Room 4: fourteenth-century Florentine paintings: works by Bernardo Daddi and by Orcagna and Jacopo di Cione, his brother. A *St Cecilia* in the manner of Giotto; and a *Deposition* by Giottino, 1350s.

Rooms 5 and 6 are in fact a single room: International Gothic works by Lorenzo Monaco: *Coronation of the Virgin*, 1413; Agnolo Gaddi: *Crucifixion*; Gentile da Fabriano: *Adoration of the Magi*, 1423; *Mary Magdalene and other Saints*, formerly parts of a polyptych, 1425.

Room 7: notable fifteenth-century early Renaissance paintings: Paolo Uccello: *Battle of San Romano*; famous diptych by Piero della Francesca of *Federico da Montefeltro and Battista Sforza*, *circa* 1465; other works by Domenico Veneziano (*Virgin and Child with Saints*), Masolino and Fra Angelico (*Coronation of the Virgin*).

Room 8: paintings by Filippo Lippi, including the *Virgin and Child with Two Angels*, *circa* 1465; *Coronation of the Virgin*; *Adoration of the Child*. Works by his son Filippino include two altarpieces of the *Adoration of the Magi* and the *Virgin and Child and Saints*.

Room 9: altarpiece and *Portrait of a Lady*, both by Antonio Pollaiolo. Also: two small panels by Pollaiolo of the *Labours of Hercules* and two by Botticelli of *Judith and Holofernes*.

Rooms 10 to 14: formerly small rooms and part of the theatre, now opened into one much larger hall for the finest works of Botticelli, including *Primavera*; the *Birth of Venus*; two roundels (*tondi*) of the *Virgin and Child*; and three altarpieces − *Virgin and Child with Saints* (from Sant'Ambrogio); *Coronation of the Virgin* (from San Marco); and an *Annunciation*. Other works by Botticelli include the *Adoration of the Magi* and *Portrait of a Man in a Red Hat*. In the same hall: the

Adoration of the Magi (Portinari triptych) by Hugo van der Goes; and three works by Domenico Ghirlandaio.

Room 15: remodelled by Giovanni Michelucci, 1991: works by Verrocchio and early works by Leonardo da Vinci. *Baptism of Christ* by Verrocchio, *circa* 1470; the incomplete *Adoration of the Magi* by Leonardo, 1481; *Crucifixion* by Luca Signorelli; and four works by Perugino.

Room 16, Sala delle Carte Geografiche: lined with maps designed by Stefano Bonsignori and frescoed by Lodovico Buti, 1589. It was originally an open loggia.

Room 18, the Tribuna, and the adjacent anterooms 17 and 19: the octagonal Tribuna was designed by Buontalenti for Francesco I (1584), to display his most valuable treasures. Restored in 1970 to re-create its original appearance, and again in 2010. A fine floor in *pietra dura*. In the centre: splendid octagonal table, also in *pietra dura*, by Bernardino Poccetti, 1633–49; and a fine ebony cabinet, *circa* 1650. The Tribuna contains fine classical statues, including the famous *Medici Venus* (probably made in Rome, first century BC); taken by Napoleon to Paris but returned here in 1815. On the walls: well-known portraits, many by Bronzino, including *Cosimo I*. Others by Pontormo (*Cosimo il Vecchio* and *Lorenzo il Magnifico*), the school of Raphael (*John the Baptist* and *Madonna del Pozzo*, or the *Virgin and Child with Infant St John the Baptist*) and Andrea del Sarto.

Room 19: four portraits by Perugino and two *tondi* by Luca Signorelli.

Room 20: works by German artists: Albrecht Dürer (*Adoration of the Magi*) and Cranach the elder.

Room 21: Venetian works by Giovanni Bellini (*Sacred Allegory* and the beautiful drawing of the *Lamentation over the Dead Christ*) and Giorgione (*Judgement of Solomon* and the *Infant Moses*; *Knight in Armour*, attrib.).

Room 22: Netherlandish and German portraits by Hans Memling and Hans Holbein the younger.

Room 23: north Italian paintings including three fine works by Andrea Mantegna: *Madonna delle Cave* (*Virgin of the Stonecutters*); *Cardinal Carlo de' Medici*; and the triptych from the Palazzo Ducale, Mantua.

Room 24: collection of miniatures, not always accessible. Its present appearance is by Zanobi del Rosso, 1782.

South corridor

Splendid views over the Arno and the Oltrarno. Several fine classical statues including a *Sleeping Cupid*; Roman statues of *Mars*, *Venus*.

West corridor

In the corridor itself: two figures of *Marsyas*; copy of the *Discobolos*; bust of the Roman emperor *Caracalla*; other statues of *Apollo*, *Venus* and, at the far end, a copy of the *Laocoön* by Baccio Bandinelli, 1523–5.

Room 25: opposite the entrance is Michelangelo's *Doni Tondo*, 1504, probably painted for the Agnolo Doni–Maddalena Strozzi marriage. In the room: works by Fra Bartolomeo (*Annunciation*) and others. Adjacent is the door to the Corrodoio Vasariano.

Room 26: Masterpieces by Raphael: *Portrait of Pope Leo X with Giulio de' Medici and Luigi de' Rossi*, 1517–18; *Portrait of Pope Julius II* (a good contemporary copy; the original is in the National Gallery, London); *Madonna del Cardellino* (Bullfinch), 1505–6; *Self-portrait*; *Portrait of a Young Man*, 1505–6. Also Andrea del Sarto: *Madonna delle Arpie* (Harpies), 1517.

Room 27: Mannerist paintings by Rosso Fiorentino and Pontormo: *Supper at Emmaus*, 1525.

Room 28: fine works by Titian: *Venus of Urbino*, 1538; *Flora*, circa 1520; *Portrait of Eleonora Gonzaga*, 1536–7; and *Portrait of Francesco Maria della Rovere*, 1537. Two good works by Sebastiano del Piombo: *Death of Adonis*, circa 1512, and *Portrait of a Lady*, 1512.

Rooms 29 and 30: works by Parmigianino (including the *Virgin of the Long Neck*, 1535) and Dosso Dossi.

Room 31: works by Veronese, including the *Annunciation*; the *Holy Family with St Catherine and St John*, 1562–5.

Room 32: Tintoretto: *Leda and the Swan*, 1570.

Room 33: Lavinia Fontana and sixteenth-century French painters: François Clouet.

Room 34: Lorenzo Lotto and other Lombard painters, including Giovanni Battista Moroni.

Room 35: works by Federico Barrocci.

Room 41: good works by Peter Paul Rubens, including self-portraits and the *Portrait of Isabella Brant*, 1625–6.

Room 42, Sala della Niobe: a large, spacious neo-Classical hall designed by Zanobi del Rosso in 1771 for classical statues. It contains the group of statues known as the *Niobidi*, discovered in Rome in 1583.

Room 43: works by Caravaggio, including the famous *Bacchus*, circa 1598; and by the Caracci, including *Venus* by Annibale, 1588.

Room 44: three fine works by Rembrandt, including two self-portraits.

Room 45: eighteenth-century paintings including the Venetian school: G.B. Piazzetta, G.B. Tiepolo, Francesco Guardi and Canaletto. Spanish works by Francisco Goya. French works by Chardin.

4 THE VICINITY OF THE UFFIZI AND THE PONTE VECCHIO

From the Piazza della Signoria, take the Chiasso dei Baroncelli (W of the Loggia) S to its junction with Via Lambertesca. Turn right and continue W towards Por Santa Maria. At no. 28 is the medieval **Torre Gherardini**. The tower forms part of the adjacent **Palazzo Bartolommei Buschetti** (no. 11), originally probably sixteenth century, but enlarged by the Bartolommei in 1640 also to incorporate the adjacent **Torre dei Girolami**, at the corner of Por Santa Maria. The work was organised by Ferdinando Tacca. Badly damaged in the German retreat of 1944 and extensively rebuilt. Off the N side of Via Lambertesca, the Chiasso del Buco leads into the tiny Piazzetta dei Salterelli, with the **Torre dei Salterelli** on the N side, much altered and extended. Continue into the busy Por Santa Maria, then immediately left into the Vicolo and Piazza Santo Stefano.

Santo Stefano al Ponte: First records date from 1116; the lower part of the façade is Romanesque, *circa* 1233. The central portal is of green and white marble: a rectangular doorway surmounted by an arch, and the whole surrounded by a rectangular marble frame. Two plain side portals, above each of which is a small *bifora*, also from the original construction. The upper part of the façade is early fourteenth-century Gothic, with three arched windows, and the whole is capped by a pitched roof on corbels.

Inside: the Gothic alterations transformed the three-aisle basilica into a single nave, with an open timber trussed roof at two different levels. The interior was altered again in the seventeenth century, when Baroque altars and decoration were added, and the chancel was re-faced (1631–55). The modernisation is by Pietro Tacca and Marchese Antonio Maria Bartolomei, a dilettante architect who paid for the works. In the centre of the nave, a stair descends to the crypt, also by Tacca.

At the E end of the nave: a tall chancel arch, capped by a large triangular pediment; the narrower, lower side bays are also arched. The chancel is approached by steps with a marble balustrade, a rather bizarre

Mannerist work by Buontalenti (1574). A high altar of polychrome marble, with a tabernacle by Giambologna, 1591, originally at the Arcispedale di Santa Maria Nuova. Above the chancel: a tall clerestory and a small cupola. Beyond the high altar: choir, with a richly decorated coffered Baroque ceiling.

Walk around the right side of the façade of Santo Stefano, and down the Vicolo Marzio into the Piazza del Pesce and the Lungarno degli Archibusieri. Turn left (E) and follow the impressive arches supporting the Corridoio Vasariano, towards the S end of the Uffizi. At no. 6 on the Lungarno is **Palazzo Girolami**. The site was one of several along the river owned by the Castellani, bought from them by the Girolami in 1495. The fortified house was then modernised in the early sixteenth century. An elegant loggia on the top floor; difficult to appreciate because the Corridoio runs in front of it. Confiscated by the Medici, it was returned to the Girolami, and later passed to the Cantucci and the Bourbon del Monte.

Continue E along the Lungarno, past the Uffizi. On the left is **Palazzo Castellani dei Giudici**.

Built in the mid-fourteenth century on the site of the castle-palace of the Altafronte, destroyed by a violent flood of the Arno in 1333. From 1574 to 1841 it was the seat of circuit judges dealing with civil cases, hence the present name; from then until 1966 it was the seat of the Accademia della Crusca. It was restored in 1839; since 1930 it has housed the Museo della Storia della Scienza, with an exceptionally fine collection. In 2010 it was remodelled and reopened as the Museo Galileo, with a splendid collection of scientific instruments.

The building is faced with stone, with four storeys; S façade is very plain: five bays; rusticated arches to the ground floor and two orders of arched windows above. The top floor has a loggia, originally open but today filled with glazed screens; the E façade is almost identical, again five bays, but with a prominent central portal and without the crowning loggia.

Ponte Vecchio: The only surviving medieval bridge across the Arno. The Ponte Vecchio is very close to the site of the ancient Roman bridge, which was probably a little further upstream. A medieval bridge is first recorded in 996, but was rebuilt several times over the early centuries. It collapsed in 1117 and again in the massive inundation of 1333. The present bridge is essentially the reconstruction after this last

58   The Uffizi, begun by Vasari in 1560:
detail of windows to the Piazzale

59   Ponte Vecchio, 1345, from the Lungarno
Archibusieri

60   Ponte Vecchio from the Lungarno degli
Acciaioli

61   Corridoio Vasariano, by Vasari, 1565

flood, and was begun in 1345, probably by Neri di Fioravante. Its three robust stone arches have survived countless later inundations, including the devastating flood of 1966. The little shops on top, originally forty in all, were built by the Arte della Lana for butchers and fruit and vegetable sellers; in the late sixteenth century Ferdinando I ordered their replacement by goldsmiths, silversmiths and jewellers.

59, 60   The rows of shops are cantilevered out over the flanks of the structure, and supported on raked timber corbels, *sporti*. The shops have projecting display windows, with characteristic timber shutters, known as *madielle*. In the centre of the roadway there is an open space. On the downstream side is a piazzetta, with a statue of *Benvenuto Cellini* by Raffaele Romanelli (1900); while on the upstream side three arches support the Corridoio Vasariano. Splendid views of the city and surrounding hills in both directions.

Corridoio Vasariano: This unique structure was built following Cosimo I's decision to transfer his court and residence across the river to Palazzo Pitti, and his requirement for a private secure route between Palazzo Pitti and the Uffizi. The Corridoio was built by Vasari in the extraordinarily brief time of six months in 1565. It is around 1 km long.

Its route is as follows: at the Uffizi end it is reached by a staircase between rooms 25 and 34 at the main level of the picture galleries. It turns W, to run along the S edge of the Lungarno, on fourteen tall, massive arches. It then turns S, and runs above the shops that occupy the upstream (E) side of the Ponte Vecchio. At the S end it had to wrap around the medieval Torre Mannelli on bold corbels, since the owners refused to demolish the tower. From the S bridgehead of the Ponte Vecchio it continues S, spanning Via dei Bardi on arches, and then turns SW past the façade of Santa Felicità (q.v.), to which it gives direct access. From Santa Felicità the Corridoio continues roughly parallel to Via dei Guicciardini until it joins the NE wing of Palazzo Pitti.

61   Architecturally, the Corridoio is very simple, and is lit by regularly spaced square windows. In the section that crosses the Ponte Vecchio, the windows towards the bridge are very small, round and barred, to defend against popular insurrection, whereas those towards the river are larger.

The Corridoio contains a famous display of artists' self-portraits, many from the Medici collections. They were begun in the seventeenth century by Leopoldo de' Medici, and continued by his successors. The practice of displaying portraits in the Corridoio began in the nineteenth century and today it houses around 700 works. It was opened to the public by Vittorio Emanuele II, but was damaged by war and flood and did not reopen until 1972. It was closed once more after the bomb attack in 1993 but today can be visited by appointment. Among the more notable of this huge collection are self-portraits by Guercino, Vasari, Pietro da Cortona, Andrea del Sarto, Bronzino, Jacopo Bassano, Titian, Correggio, Bernini and Luca Giordano. Foreign artists represented include Rembrandt, Van Dyck, Velázquez, Holbein the younger, Delacroix and Corot.

Piazza della Repubblica and Surroundings

This itinerary covers the W half of the inner historic centre, and is bounded to the N by Via dei Cerretani and Piazza San Giovanni; to the E by Via Roma, Calimala and Por Santa Maria; to the S by the Lungarno degli Acciaiuoli, and to the W by Via dei Tornabuoni.

This district lay within the ancient Roman walls; Via Roma and Via Calimala follow the Roman *cardus* (N–S axis), while Via degli Strozzi and its eastward continuation, Via del Corso, were the Roman *decumanus* (E–W axis). They intersected at the forum, part of the site of which is now occupied by the extensive Piazza della Repubblica. This area also lay within the first communal walls of 1078, and was densely developed in the medieval period. The Mercato Vecchio, also once on the site of the Roman forum, remained the heart of the district, but it was radically modernised between 1885 and 1895, with the wholesale destruction of dozens of medieval buildings.

The principal streets (Calimala, Via Roma, Via degli Strozzi) were all widened and straightened, and the ancient Jewish Ghetto was destroyed. Numerous medieval towers were lost, as well as the churches of Sant'Andrea, San Tommaso, Santa Maria in Campidoglio and San Pier Buon Consiglio, and the guildhalls of the Albergatori and Rigattieri. The Loggia del Pesce (fish market), which stood along the W side of the Mercato Vecchio, was dismantled and reassembled in Piazza dei Ciompi. The square was roughly doubled in size to become the present Piazza della Repubblica.

I VIA DEI CERRETANI

The itinerary proceeds generally from N to S, starting on Via dei Cerretani, a busy, important street, linking Piazza San Giovanni and the historic centre with Via dei Panzani and the railway station to the NW. On the S side, corner of Piazza dell'Olio, is **Palazzo del Bembo**, later Bezzoli Martelli, an impressive early fourteenth-century survivor. Perhaps by Arnolfo di Cambio, it represents an early development from the *torre* towards a true city *palazzo*. Five bays long and three bays deep; all faced in stone, with large arched openings on the ground floor for commercial activity; then a mezzanine and two principal upper floors. In the eighteenth century it became a hotel, the Aquila Nera; Mozart stayed here in 1770. Opposite, on the N side, extending along Via Zannetti, is **Palazzo Martelli**, originally early sixteenth century, but in 1627 it was joined to adjacent houses in the same ownership. In 1668–9 the block along Via Zannetti was restructured by Bernardino Ciurini. See also p. 203.

On the next block W (S side) is **Santa Maria Maggiore**. On the homonymous little piazza. One of the oldest foundations in the city; established before the eleventh century, but rebuilt for the Vallombrosians, a Benedictine congregation, in the later thirteenth century. A simple stone façade: a Gothic portal and a high-level oculus. Inside: an aisled nave with pointed Gothic arches on square piers; a rib-vaulted ceiling. At the E end: square chancel flanked by side chapels. The interior was partially modernised by Gherardo Silvani in the early seventeenth century, perhaps from a proposal by Buontalenti. In the eighteenth century further decoration was added. Restorations in 1912–13 removed some of the Baroque decorations, and inserted a new high altar. Inside the façade, and on the adjacent pilaster: frescoes attributed to Mariotto di Nardo, 1390–95. The inner façade was modernised by Cigoli in 1595–6.

Third right chapel: stucco and fresco vault decoration attributed to Bernardino Poccetti. Altarpiece: *St Francis Receiving the Stigmata* by Piero Dandini. In the lateral niches: *St Zanobius* and *St Bartholomew* by G.B. Caccini, very early seventeenth century. On the chancel side walls are detached frescoes of the *Massacre of the Innocents* attributed to Jacopo di Cione, 1395–1400. Adjacent are two fifteenth-century marble tabernacles.

Third left chapel: in front is a fresco by Volterrano, 1642. Second left chapel: *Ecstasy of St Maria Maddalena de' Pazzi* by Onorio Marinari, *circa* 1675.

Behind the church is a small sixteenth-century cloister, part of the monastic buildings; two frescoes (1607): *St Albert*, by Bernardino Poccetti and the *Madonna della Misericordia* (*Virgin of Mercy*) by Nicodemo Ferrucci.

Directly opposite the church, at no. 1, is the so-called **Palazzo delle Cento Finestre**; its four façades do contain almost 100 windows. Also known as the Palazzo del Centauro, because the sculpted *Hercules and* *the Centaur* by Giambologna (now in the Loggia dei Lanzi) once stood nearby, in Via dei Cerretani. The first palace was late fifteenth century, but the present building is *circa* 1720. Four storeys, with seven bays to the E façade, and eleven to the longer N façade. Rusticated quoins, aediculed windows to the *piano nobile* and rusticated surrounds to the portals. Balconies in the centre of the façades, added by Giuseppe Poggi. Much of the interior dates from after 1810, when it was bought by Elizabetta Gannucci: neo-Classical decoration by Luigi Catani.

Take Via dei Vecchietti S from the church. On the corner of Via dei Pecori, at nos. 6–8, is the imposing **Palazzo Gondi 'di Francia'**, or Palazzo Orlandini del Beccuto. Alessandro Gondi acquired the site in 1495. His brother Guidobaldo married in France and became the banker of Caterina de' Medici and King Henri II of France; hence the affix. The present palace was built by Girolamo Gondi (late sixteenth century), but was extensively modernised by Antonio Maria Ferri in 1679. Neo-Classical but with Mannerist elements, in the style of Buontalenti. A long south-facing main façade, eleven bays; three orders, all generous, plus an attic. Two large ground-floor portals, surmounted by balconies. All the lower windows are aediculed, with sills on corbels. The ground floor has squared rustication, the upper floors plain render; the upper windows have rusticated frames, those to the *piano nobile* with broken pediments. Inside the *piano nobile* are frescoes by Piero Dandini, Alessandro Gherardini and Antonio Domenico Gabbiani. The Stanza delle Grottesche is decorated by Bernardino Poccetti. Since 1913 the building has been the seat of the Monte dei Paschi di Siena; restored 1970–73 by Italo Gamberini.

On the next block S on Via dei Vecchietti (no. 6) is **Palazzo Ricci Altoviti**, incorporating the **Torre degli Agli**, identifiable in the N corner. Most of the present fabric is from 1528, for the Ricci; these works included the filling in of the Loggia degli Agli and building over a *vicolo* (alley). The relatively long, low façade is rendered, with irregular fenestration; prominently rusticated quoins and main portal. It was later owned by the Altoviti and more recently by the Banca San Paolo.

Returning N to the junction with Via dei Pecori, turn right, and then right again, into Via dei Brunelleschi. Wrapping around the corner is the heavy pile of **Palazzo Pola e Todescan**, sometimes called Casa Paggi, which occupies the whole side of Via dei Brunelleschi S to Via del Campidoglio. Designed by Giuseppe Paciarelli and built 1901–3; idiosyncratic, with elements of the new 'Liberty' style mixing with heavy nineteenth-century neo-Classicism. It was originally a department store, hence the name, but is today mostly occupied by banks. Rich, chunky decoration including ceramic tiles, wrought iron and stone sculptures. The long principal façade has a ponderous colonnade rising through the ground floor and mezzanine; this axis extends S down the full length of Piazza della Repubblica. Above: three upper storeys with rectangular aediculed lights. At the S end of the block, turn right into Via del Campidoglio and left down Via dei Vecchietti.

At no. 4 Via degli Strozzi and no. 2 Via dei Vecchietti, is **Palazzo Vecchietti del Diavolino**. The two façades are of different dates; that to Via degli Strozzi is nineteenth century and was re-faced in conjunction with the local road 'improvements' (1829, by Leopoldo Pasqui). That to Via dei Vecchietti, though, is by Giambologna, 1573–8, for Bernardo Vecchietti; four bays, with pedimented windows and the date on the architraves: MDLXXIII. On the corner are the Vecchietti arms, also by Giambologna, and a copy of his *Diavolino* ('little devil', in fact a satyr); the original is in the Museo Bardini. The satyr was originally paired with a horse (the devil), now lost. The figures referred to a local legend of St Peter Martyr, in which the saint slew the devil, in the form of a horse, in front of a host of supplicants (1243). The Via degli Strozzi entrance gives access to a fifteenth-century courtyard, with a *sgraffito*-decorated loggia.

Directly S, with its main façade onto Via Sassetti, is **Palazzo Sassetti**. The Sassetti were an important pro-Medici family, some of whose members, notably Francesco, were managers of the Medici bank. The building is fourteenth century, with later enlargements. All faced with stone, four orders, and six bays along the original main façade; severe and reticent, with large stone arches to the ground floor and simple arched windows above. The uppermost order may have been crenellated, and it was later modified with brickwork. On the façade: fresco of the family arms.

Return to the corner of Via degli Strozzi, continue E under the Arcone and into:

2 PIAZZA DELLA REPUBBLICA AND VICINITY

Today one of the hubs of city life, surrounded by large late nineteenth-century developments, all built following the destruction of the Mercato Vecchio. On the N side: the seat of **Fondiaria Assicurazione** by Giuseppe Boccini (1893). An elegant, restrained neo-Renaissance block,

63 Via dei Cerretani: north side towards the west

64 Santa Maria Maggiore: detail of the Gothic west portal

65 Piazza della Repubblica: the Arcone from the east, by Vincenzo Micheli, 1895

66 Palazzo dell'Arte dei Beccai (foreground), early fourteenth century, with the cathedral campanile, from the Orsanmichele bridge

67 Calimala towards the north, with the Palazzo dell'Arte della Lana, right

68 Palazzo dell'Arte della Lana, seat of the guild since 1308: detail of the *Agnus Dei*, emblem of the guild

with four orders. The equivalent block on the S side, less successful, is by Torquato del Lungo. On the E side, corner of Via dei Speziali: **Hotel Savoy** by Vincenzo Micheli. Neo-Renaissance, with a giant order of pilasters to the ground floor and mezzanine; then a continuous balcony to the *piano nobile*, which has seven bays. Two upper storeys and then a big crowning cornice; a very plain attic above. The corner bays are emphasised by rusticated quoins and large arched openings. Adjacent is **Palazzo del Trianon** by Luigi Buonamici, later a department store. In the centre of the Piazza was placed Emilio Zocchi's figure of *Vittorio Emanuele II*, later (1932) transferred to the entrance of the Cascine.

The most flamboyant block is that on the W side, where the point at which Via degli Strozzi enters the piazza is marked by a vast monumental arch, the **Arcone**, by Vincenzo Micheli, 1895. The Arcone is 65 flanked by two lower blocks, each colonnaded, and with two orders, Doric and Ionic, plus an attic, all deeply modelled. The arch itself is flanked by two orders of paired columns projecting forwards; above is a bold cornice. In the centre of the deep crowning entablature is an inscription, celebrating the *risanamento* – restoration to health – of the city's heart; the inscription became notorious, since to many the Arcone represented not restoration, but the destruction of the city's ancient core.

The final element in the piazza is the Colonna dell'Abbondanza, the only physical survivor from the Mercato Vecchio; on top is a copy by G.B. Foggini of the figure of *Abundance*, replacing the original by Donatello, which had deteriorated beyond repair.

Calimala and Por Santa Maria: Via Calimala, or usually simply Calimala (named after the merchants' guild) runs S from the SE corner of Piazza della Repubblica; beyond the Mercato Nuovo it becomes Por Santa Maria, continuing to the Ponte Vecchio.

Off the E side is Via Orsanmichele. At no. 4 is the **Palazzo dell'Arte dei Beccai**. A rendered façade, with stone surrounds to the openings. 66 Four bays and four storeys; the ground floor is asymmetrical, with a large, square, off-centre portal and a smaller doorway on the left. The second floor is the *piano nobile*, with arched windows; the roof has a deep overhang. On the external angle onto Piazza dei Tre Re: coat of arms of the guild. The guild of *beccai* (butchers) transferred here in 1318, converting the former tower-house of the Macci, which had also been used by the Capitani or officers of the adjacent Orsanmichele. Since 1784 it has been the seat of the Accademia delle Arti del Disegno, established by Cosimo I de' Medici two centuries earlier. Inside: a

Crucifixion and a *Virgin and Child*, both by Pontormo; and a *Virgin and Child Enthroned* by Mariotto di Nardo, *circa* 1395.

Almost in front is a bridge (1569) connecting Orsanmichele with the

Palazzo dell'Arte della Lana: Guildhall of the wool workers, one of the most wealthy and influential of the *arti*. Originally the fortified early medieval house of the Compiobbesi, the palace became incorporated into the seat of the guild in 1308 (plaque). In 1770, following the suppression of the guilds, it became the *canonica* for the adjacent Orsanmichele. It was acquired in 1890 by the *comune* and in 1903 ceded to the Società Dantesca, which radically transformed it, including the addition of the tabernacle. The modernisation, in a rather eclectic neo-medieval manner, was undertaken by Enrico Lusini, 1905. Today the building has four elements. The first is the restored original rectangular thirteenth-century Compiobbesi block facing Calimala, three bays wide and with two upper orders above the ground-floor shops and workshops; crowning crenellations on bold corbel arches. On the Calimala façade are two images of the *Agnus Dei*, emblem of the guild. This element has its E façade towards Orsanmichele, also of three bays. The second element is an additional, lower wing along the S side, Renaissance, only one bay wide, with two orders and a portal onto Calimala. This was added for Cosimo I by Buontalenti in 1569. The third is the little open Gothic loggia on the NW corner, with *bifore* to the upper floor. Finally there is the remaining fabric along the N side, stone-faced, two bays, with the tabernacle on the NE corner.

This last is that of Santa Maria della Tromba, fourteenth century, reassembled here from the lost homonymous church, formerly in the Mercato Vecchio. Within the tabernacle: image of the *Virgin and Child Enthroned*, restored 1991. Above is the *Coronation of the Virgin* by Pietro Gerini, 1380–85.

Inside the original block: cross-vaulted ceilings and notable fourteenth-century frescoes (perhaps by Lippo di Benivieni) to the ground floor (inside the shops on Calimala) and the Sala dell'Udienza on the first floor. One depicts the stages in the working of wool. Some are *circa* 1310–20, others *circa* 1340.

Continuing S down Calimala, on the W side, just past Via Porta Rossa, is the

Loggia di Mercato Nuovo: By Giovanni Battista del Tasso, 1547–51, under the direction of Cosimo I. One of many urban improvements instigated by Cosimo; there had been a market on the site previously, but Cosimo intended this robust new structure to house the sale of goods of high value and prestige: gold, jewellery and fine fabrics. Originally each bay specialised in one type of product. Today it houses a lively general market, selling mainly Tuscan leather goods.

The rather heavy structure is of *pietra forte*, with colonnades, three bays by four; massive square piers at the outer corners and substantial arched openings between. Inside: simple plastered vaults supported by Composite columns. On the outer faces of the corner piers are aedicules, today containing nineteenth-century statues. Within these corner piers are narrow spiral staircases leading up to an attic, which was to contain an archive for the traders and their contracts. In the centre of the floor, a marble wheel marks the site where the *carroccio* (cart), symbol of republican freedom, was located before the city went into battle. On the S side is the well-known bronze *Cinghiale* (boar), ordered by Ferdinando II and made by Pietro Tacca in 1612, based on a Hellenistic marble original in the Uffizi. Popularly known as 'il porcellino', the piglet.

Continue S down Por Santa Maria. Almost all the earlier, mostly medieval buildings here were destroyed by the retreating Germans in 1944, and were replaced by a collection of new structures attempting to replicate the spirit of the medieval urban form. Reconstruction in the 1950s brought to light the remains of the Roman city gate (corner of Via Vaccereccia). Among the rare survivors is the tall narrow **Torre dei Baldovinetti**, just around the corner of Borgo Santi Apostoli (no. 4r). The **Torre degli Amidei** (nos. 9–11r), a massive rectangular tower, was largely rebuilt, with mostly symmetrical fenestration. Pointed arches to the lower mezzanine and semicircular arches to the upper-floor windows. Two lions' heads at second-floor level gave it the nickname Torre dei Leoni.

Off the W side of Por Santa Maria are two streets, Borgo Santi Apostoli and Via delle Terme, the former one of the most complete surviving medieval streets in the city.

3 BORGO SANTI APOSTOLI AND VICINITY

No. 6 is **Palazzo Buondelmonti**, with its tower, after 1300 owned by the Acciaioli; the house itself has five bays and three orders; restrained late sixteenth century. At no. 9 (S side) is **Palazzo Acciaioli,** later

Usimbardi; two adjacent thirteenth-century houses joined together. In the centre is a long hallway or *androne*, formerly a *chiasso* (lane). Seriously damaged in 1944, but the Borgo façade survived. Adjacent, at no. 10 is another Acciaioli house, typically sixteenth century, with five bays, ground floor, mezzanine, *piano nobile* and attic. The *piano nobile* has arched rusticated window surrounds. Opposite, the **Palazzo del Gran Siniscalco** is at no. 8. Also known as the Palazzo della Certosa, with a tower (*circa* 1280) on the corner of the Chiasso delle Misure. The tower is one of the tallest that survive. Originally owned by the Buondelmonti, then in the fourteenth century by Niccolò Acciaioli, the Gran Siniscalco (seneschal) of the kingdom of Naples, and founder of the Certosa (Charterhouse) at Galluzzo; Acciaioli gave this house to the Certosa; hence the coat of arms on the façade: two lions holding a flag. It remained in their possession until the Napoleonic dissolution. An austere façade: four bays and four orders; simple arched lights and big arched ground-floor portals (3 + 1).

A little further along the s side is **Palazzo Rosselli del Turco** (nos. 17–19). A notable house, probably by Baccio d'Agnolo, *circa* 1517, for Pier Francesco Borgherini, who bought the site from the Altoviti. It was completed *circa* 1530. The site was too constrained for the conventional central courtyard, so it has a modest atrium instead. In 1530 the family bought some land across the street for a garden, which still survives. The building was bought by the Rosselli in 1750; it is still owned by their descendants. A long, restrained but refined façade; nine bays and three orders. Its simplicity is said to reflect the influence of sobriety of the republican period in the city (1494–1512). Rusticated quoins in *pietra forte*, and much plain render. The lowermost order has arched portals with rusticated surrounds. On the *piano nobile*: a row of large arched windows, again rusticated. The uppermost order contains two storeys: rusticated arches with small square lights set into them (altered), above which is a very low attic and boldly projecting eaves on corbels. In the internal atrium: surviving decoration, still fifteenth century in style. A fine contemporary fireplace, by Benedetto da Rovezzano, is today in the Bargello. Another, probably by Baccio, remains *in situ*. Some *piano nobile* rooms conserve their original coffered timber ceilings. The w end wall (three bays) faces the little Piazza del Limbo; relief of the *Virgin and Child* by Benedetto da Maiano. Unbaptised babies were once buried here, hence the name, based on the hypothesis that they could not enter Paradise unless baptised.

On the piazza is the little church of

69 Mercato Nuovo, by Giovanni Battista del Tasso, 1547–51: detail of the colonnade

70 Mercato Nuovo: corner pier, with statue of *Giovanni Villani* by Gaetano Trentanove, 1890

71 Mercato Nuovo: the *Cinghiale* or 'Porcellino' by Pietro Tacca, 1612

72 Por Santa Maria: the lower west side, all rebuilt after war destruction in 1944

Santi Apostoli: Probably founded in the late eleventh century, and restored in the fifteenth, sixteenth (by the Altoviti) and eighteenth. In the 1930s further restoration attempted to return the church to its original Romanesque character. Valuable surviving material inside, including marble columns and capitals. The plan is a traditional basilica, with a central vessel and two lower side aisles.

The façade: a typically tripartite form, all stone, with two flanking lower wings to the aisles. A large square central portal, sixteenth century, perhaps by Benedetto da Rovezzano, above which is an eleventh-century *bifora*. The side wings have small arched portals and single arched windows, and the façade is capped by a cornice on *archetti*.

Inside: two colonnades with green Prato marble columns and rich Composite / Corinthian capitals; the first two are Roman, spoils from the adjacent site of the baths. The nave roof of timber trusses is from the 1930s, but medieval in style. The lateral chapels are fifteenth and sixteenth century. A mosaic floor, in which are set numerous tomb monuments. Terminating the chancel is a semicircular apse (rough stone walling), with a hemispherical vault. The church was badly damaged by the floods of 1966.

Right aisle, second chapel: on the left wall: monument to Piero del Bene, 1530. At the end of the nave, above the doorway into the canons' residence: monument with figures, perhaps by Ammannati. The chancel was patronised by the Altoviti, who lived nearby; decoration by Giovanni Antonio Dosio, 1573. Among the other monuments is that to Archbishop Antonio Altoviti, perhaps by Caccini. At the end of the left aisle: large tabernacle in vitrified terracotta by Giovanni della Robbia, containing stones from the Holy Land brought back by Pazzino de' Pazzi after the First Crusade; below is the monument to Donato Acciaioli, 1333. On the adjacent wall: monument to Oddo Altoviti by Benedetto da Rovezzano, *circa* 1510. Fourth left chapel: side wall: *Archangel Raphael with Tobias and St Andrew* by Maso da San Friano, *circa* 1560. Second left chapel: eighteenth-century frescoed vault by Matteo Bonechi. Adjacent to the first chapel: sepulchre of Anna Ubaldi by Foggini, 1696.

Adjacent to the church is the fifteenth-century canons' residence with the family arms of the Altoviti, by Benedetto da Rovezzano, *circa* 1512.

On the Borgo, at nos. 18 and 25 (N side), corner of Via delle Bombarde, is **Palazzo Altoviti**; fourteenth century, typical of the era. Fairly tall and narrow, all faced with stone. On the ground floor: large arched portal and two side lights. Above: four orders, each of four regular lights, arched to the *piano nobile*.

Return to Por Santa Maria, walk N and turn left into Via delle Terme. On the right:

Palazzo dei Capitani di Parte Guelfa: Formerly the seat of the Guelph faction, who, following their defeat of the Ghibellines (1289), became an important magistracy, governed by Capitani. The building has been altered and extended several times. The original structure is perhaps thirteenth century, but was extended in the fourteenth, when the Guelphs were the de facto rulers of the city, and this became their power base. This fourteenth-century meeting hall is on the first floor, with workshops below, and approached by an external stair. It is capped by crenellations, and the upper hall is lit by a large Gothic *bifora*. At the end of the fourteenth century the first order of the loggia in the courtyard was built, as was the basement order of the block between Via delle Terme and Via di Capaccio. Construction of this wing necessitated demolition of part of the adjacent church of Santa Maria sopra Porta. After *circa* 1420 Brunelleschi extended this wing upwards by building a second large hall; it was continued, but modified, by Francesco della Luna, and finally completed by Vasari in 1589. On the Via di Capaccio is a further extension by Vasari (*circa* 1589); on the façade: an elegant loggetta, with a Medici symbol by Giambologna. In 1921–7 the whole complex was heavily restored in a neo-medieval manner. The covered external stair was also built in this period, based on original medieval drawings.

The building's complex plan represents these centuries of adaptation and enlargement. Brunelleschi's Salone is a large rectangular hall, four bays by two, with four tall arched windows down the long side and two on the end façade; directly above are oculi, later filled in. Inside, the coffered ceiling was added by Vasari. Above the doorway: lunette with *Virgin and Child* in glazed terracotta by Luca della Robbia, from the lost church of San Pier Buonconsiglio. The original fifteenth-century Sala dell'Udienza (audience chamber) has a timber ceiling and a frieze of trilobate arches.

Immediately adjacent, Via di Capaccio no. 3, is the fourteenth-century **Palazzo dell'Arte della Seta**, with a square off-centre portal; guild symbol above the architrave. A tall, plain ground floor, above which are two storeys, both with four arched lights, all simple and restrained. In the meeting hall are fourteenth-century frescoes. Two blocks further W along Via delle Terme (corner of Via del Fiordaliso) is **Palazzo dei Nobili**. Sixteenth century, with the side façade supported on *sporti*. An arched portal to the main façade, square lights to the mezzanine and stone arched windows to the *piano nobile*. No. 29 is **Palazzo Scali Ricasoli**. Seventeenth century, with a simple façade and three principal orders. A large rusticated arched portal. Plaque to Guglielmo Marconi, who studied at a technical institute here. Return to the Palazzo Guelfa.

Just to the N, in the little Piazza di Parte Guelfa: **Palazzo Giandonati**: fourteenth century, with two storeys above a rusticated ground floor. Modernised in the fifteenth century. Adjacent, no. 3 is **Palazzo Canacci**, mid-fifteenth century, two upper orders of arched windows. The architect is unknown. The longest façade is to the narrow Chiasso San Biagio: four orders and six bays. The ground floor has two large portals; two *piani nobili*, each with six arched lights. A full-width loggia on the top floor; a narrow side wing on *sporti*. During the nineteenth-century modernisations, the building was joined with Palazzo Giandonati. Palazzo Canacci was restored in 1902, when Giuseppe Castellucci reopened the top-floor loggia and added the *sgraffito* decoration. Restored again *circa* 2000, when it became the property of the *comune*.

Opposite, abutting the Palazzo di Parte Guelfa: the former church of **Santa Maria sopra Porta**; rebuilt in the mid-thirteenth century, but suppressed in 1785. A very simple stone façade with a central oculus at high level. Today it houses the Biblioteca Comunale di Palagio di Parte Guelfa, opened in 1987.

From the Piazza di Parte Guelfa, walk N along Via Pellicceria. Beyond the crossroads with Via Porta Rossa, on the left is the vast mass of the **Palazzo delle Poste e Telegrafi**, 1906–17, in a neo-Renaissance style. The roundels on the façade were made by the Cantagalli company. Opposite the Poste façade is Via San Miniato. At the corner of this street and Via dei Cavalieri is the **Palazzo dei Catellini**, fourteenth century, incorporating *torri* of the Castiglione *consorteria*. Clad with stone, with large arched lights to the upper floors. Return down Via Pellicceria to the junction of Via Porta Rossa and walk a short distance W. The street takes its name from a small gate in the Roman walls, which, unusually, was of red brick rather than stone. On the S side is

Palazzo Davanzati: One of the finest medieval houses in the city. Built by the Davizzi, wealthy merchants, *circa* 1350, it passed to the Bartolini in 1516, and then (in 1578) to Bernardo Davanzati. It remained in the family's ownership until 1838. It was threatened with demolition in a

73 Palazzo Rosselli del Turco, by Baccio d'Agnolo, *circa* 1517: detail of west façade

74 Borgo Santi Apostoli: local shop built into the base of an early medieval tower

75 Palazzo dei Capitani di Parte Guelfa, originally thirteenth and fourteenth centuries: north courtyard

76 Palazzo Davanzati, *circa* 1350: the north façade in the early morning

77 The fourteenth-century Torre dei Foresi: façade detail

proposal to widen Via Porta Rossa, but was bought by Elia Volpi, an artist and antiquarian, in 1904. Volpi restored the interior in a neo-medieval manner and in 1910 opened it to the public as a museum of medieval Florentine life; in 1916 its contents were sold, but Volpi refurnished the house and it reopened in 1920. Since 1951 the palace has been the property of the Italian state and houses a collection of medieval and later fittings from many sources.

76   The façade, in *pietra forte*, is severe but refined: three principal orders above the ground floor. The right side extends over the *chiasso* (lane) on *sporti*. On the ground floor: three bays with large arched openings; three small square lights above. The three principal upper floors all have five bays, with single arched windows; the tall crowning loggia was added by Bernardo Davanzati *circa* 1580, to replace the original crenellation, with stone columns supporting a timber trabeation. In the same period the large, ostentatious Davanzati coat of arms was added to the façade. The original fourteenth-century ironwork includes rings for tethering horses, brackets for torches (flanking the windows) and horizontal rails for drying washing and displaying tapestries and banners.

Inside the entrance is a three-bay, transverse, cross-vaulted atrium, originally used for commercial purposes. Holes in the ceiling allowed the occupants to repel any aggressors in the atrium below. Beyond is the picturesque courtyard, which was originally open to the sky; the staircase and balconies are largely the work of Volpi. Octagonal stone columns with rich capitals support groin vaults. The stair rises to three floors of open galleries; on each upper floor is a single large room across the front of the house, the *sala madornale*, with smaller service rooms towards the rear: dining room, bedroom, study and bathroom. Several upper rooms contain fine original fireplaces. The house was extremely unusual in having toilets built into the external walls at each floor, with a waste pipe in the thickness of the wall, together with a well in the courtyard, and a shaft for bringing water up to each floor.

On the first *piano nobile*: three principal rooms; the *sala madornale* has a richly decorated ceiling. Adjacent is the Sala dei Pappagalli (originally the dining room), with important fourteenth-century decoration. The lower register has illustrations of parrots (*pappagalli*), the upper one trees and columns. Adjacent is a small *studiolo*. At the rear, approached by the balcony, is the Salone dei Pavoni (peacocks), the bedroom, again richly frescoed, including a high-level frieze with family arms of the Davizzi and others to whom they were related. Adjacent is the bathroom and toilet.

On the second floor, only one room conserves its original finishes, the bedchamber. Its other functions repeat those of the floor below. The third floor (not generally accessible) contains a large kitchen, and a collection of historic domestic artefacts.

Piazza Davanzati was formed at the end of the nineteenth century by the demolition of houses belonging to the Davanzati and the Cavalcanti loggia. On the corner, no. 15 Via Porta Rossa, is the **Torre dei** 77 **Foresi**. The Foresi are first recorded in 1197, and were Guelphs, fighting at Montaperti in 1260. There are two elements: the house itself, facing the piazza, and the adjacent tower on the corner. The tower was reduced in height, and now has five storeys, rising only slightly higher than the house; both are massively and impressively detailed in a very similar manner.

Continuing w, no. 13r is the **Torre degli Strozzi**, on four levels; again its height has been reduced. No. 19 is **Palazzo Torrigiani**, originally Bartolini, but it passed to the Torrigiani in 1559. It was completed *circa* 1500, perhaps by Baccio d'Agnolo, architect of the nearby Palazzo Bartolini at Santa Trinità. The palace incorporates the ancient **Torre dei Monaldi**, one of the most imposing surviving towers. It became a hotel in the mid-nineteenth century, as it remains. The central part of the façade is cantilevered forward on stone corbels; the carved poppies are the symbols of the original owners.

Return to Por Santa Maria and continue s to the bridgehead of the Ponte Vecchio. Turn w (right) along the Lungarno degli Acciaiuoli. On the right (corner of Vicolo dell'Oro) is the **Torre dei Consorti**, eleventh century, but rebuilt after 1944. A solid, square tower now annexed to an adjacent hotel. There follows a series of buildings constructed in the 1950s and 1960s to replace those lost in 1944. Halfway along the quay, no. 8 is by Italo Gamberini; at no. 14 is the **Albergo Berchielli**, once used by many notable visitors to the city. At the w end, the quay reaches a junction, with Ponte Santa Trinità bridging the Arno, left.

4 SANTA TRINITÀ, VIA DEI TORNABUONI AND PALAZZO STROZZI

To the right begins Via dei Tornabuoni, one of the most important streets in the city centre for its monuments. On the corner is the prominent mass of **Palazzo Spini Ferroni (Feroni)**. 78

The site, controlling the bridgehead, had great strategic importance during the periods of Guelph–Ghibelline strife. It was built for the Spini after 1289; they were a wealthy clan of financiers, at one time bankers to the papacy. It has been attributed to Arnolfo di Cambio or Lapo Tedesco. The building was modified after a disastrous flood of the Arno in 1299, and consisted of two parts for different branches of the clan. The N section remained in the ownership of the descendants of Geri degli Spini until 1651. Later owners included the Pitti and Francesco Antonio Feroni (from 1674); it was a hotel, 1834–46, and later housed the city's government, 1861–71. In 1881 it was ceded to the Cassa di Risparmio di Firenze. Finally, in 1938 it was bought by Salvatore Ferragamo, who established his famous shoe manufactory and showroom here; it is still owned by the Ferragamo, with a small museum of footwear inside (opened 1995).

The building is all of *pietra forte*, with a ground floor, three upper floors and a prominent crenellation on stone corbels on all four sides. Its plan is a long rectangle, only two bays across at the S end, and formerly extending to the river's edge, with a covered passageway underneath it; the length was reduced in 1824 when the bays adjacent to the river were demolished to widen the Lungarno. The ground-floor shops date from the mid-nineteenth century. The regularly spaced upper-floor windows have shallow arched heads. Inside: some rooms conserve sixteenth-century decoration; a private chapel is decorated by Bernardino Poccetti, 1609–12.

On the W side, opposite, is one of several palaces of the Gianfigliazzi; the others stand adjacent, on the Lungarno Corsini. **Palazzo Gianfigliazzi** (Piazza Santa Trinità no. 1) is roughly contemporaneous with Palazzo Spini; it was built after 1260, when the previous tower-house on the site was destroyed by the Ghibellines, following the battle of Montaperti. Its appearance is part-way between a true *torre* and a fortified *palazzo*, with a relatively tall, narrow façade of only three bays; shallow arched window openings and a boldly projecting row of corbels supporting the crenellation (rebuilt 1841), which returns (without the corbels) down the N flank. The house was owned by the Pietroboni until the fifteenth century, when it was acquired by the Gianfigliazzi and linked to their other adjacent properties.

Immediately adjacent is

Santa Trinità: Founded *circa* 1092 by monks from Vallombrosa. Part of the earliest Romanesque church can be seen inside the façade, and remains in the crypt also date from the original construction. A new, larger church was begun in 1250–60, although work continued well into the fourteenth century, perhaps under Neri di Fioravante. The church was enclosed by the city walls of 1172–5. The first phase of fourteenth-century construction was *circa* 1300–30; following a hiatus resulting from the devastating plague of 1348, work recommenced *circa* 1365 and continued to the end of the century. The adjacent monastery to the W was completed at about the same time. The present façade was added in 1593–4 by Bernardo Buontalenti.

This façade is all in *pietra forte*, with three bays and two orders; the 79, 80 wider central bay represents the central vessel of the nave. A giant order of broad, square Composite pilasters to the lower register, in which are set two orders of openings. In the lower one: a square-headed pedimented central portal; in the outer bays: smaller portals with segmental pediments. In the upper order, the two outer bays have rectangular lights with split pediments. A broad entablature divides the lower order from the upper; a square central bay again framed by broad Composite pilasters and capped by a large pediment; a central oculus; modest flanking volutes to the two outer bays.

Inside: a complex plan, basically a Latin cross, a nave of five bays flanked by side aisles, beyond which is a series of lateral chapels, added in the fifteenth century. The nave bays are rectangular, while those to the aisles are square. A square crossing, with transepts corresponding to the depth of the aisles plus the chapels; a square chancel beyond, flanked by shallow rectangular chapels on each side.

A main arcade of stout square piers with pointed arches and attached shallow pilasters rising to a simple rib vault. The crossing is less austere, with striped stone arches to the transepts. A single large traceried window of two lights to the chancel, while the nave is lit by high-level clerestory windows.

Right side, first aisle chapel: modernised *circa* 1630, although frescoes (*circa* 1400) attributed to Cenni di Francesco have survived. They depict *St Benedict* and *Eight Apostles*. Second chapel: Baroque decoration, *circa* 1640. Altarpiece: *St John the Baptist* by Francesco Curradi, 1649. Third chapel: *Virgin and Child with Saints* by Neri di Bicci. On the left wall: *Virgin and Child*, fresco by Spinello Aretino, *circa* 1390. Fourth chapel: the only one to retain its fifteenth-century appearance. Comprehensively frescoed by Lorenzo Monaco, 1420–25, with episodes from the *Life of the Virgin*. The altarpiece is the *Annunciation*, also by Lorenzo. Fifth chapel: frescoes both inside and on the outer face are by Giovanni Toscani, *circa* 1423. Marble altar by Benedetto da Rovezzano, 1505–13.

Right transept: at the far end is a lobby or anteroom with six Gothic tomb monuments, later fourteenth century. The portal at the end, onto Via del Parione, is a good fifteenth-century work.

Just beyond the right transept is a small doorway to the sacristy. A long room, three bays, with a rib-vaulted ceiling; formerly the Strozzi chapel. Built in 1418 by Lorenzo Ghiberti. At the far end (left) is the tomb of Onofrio Strozzi, now generally recognised as an early work of Michelozzo, *circa* 1425.

Back in the church: two chapels to the right of the chancel: the first (right) is that of the Sassetti, with a renowned cycle of frescoes by Domenico Ghirlandaio, 1483–6. They were commissioned by Francesco Sassetti, and depict *Scenes from the Life of St Francis*; they are notable for many naturalistic scenes of contemporary Florentine life. They also portray many of Ghirlandaio's contemporaries, including Lorenzo il Magnifico de' Medici (a close friend of Sassetti), Poliziano and the families of both Lorenzo and Sassetti. The altarpiece is the *Adoration of the Shepherds*, again by Ghirlandaio. On the two flanking walls: tomb monuments of Francesco and his wife, Nera Corsi, both attributed to Giuliano da Sangallo.

The next chapel to the left: the fresco on the outer wall surface is *Christ in Glory*, attributed to Giovanni del Ponte, 1430. Right side: panel painting of the *Virgin and Child*, by Bernardo di Stefano Rosselli, very late fifteenth century.

81 The chancel was originally comprehensively decorated with *Old Testament* scenes by Alessio Baldovinetti, 1471–7; most were destroyed in 1760, but fragments survive. The high altar is partly composed of elements by Desiderio da Settignano. On the right flank wall: triptych of the *Holy Trinity* by Mariotto di Nardo, 1416.

Left transept: the first chapel past the chancel arch: modernised by Cigoli in 1628. Contemporary frescoes by Matteo Rosselli and Fabrizio Boschi. On the front outer face: frescoes by Giovanni del Ponte, 1434. In the next chapel to the left: frescoes again by del Ponte, including *St Bartholomew* on the front outer face; *Evangelists* on the vault; and two further frescoes of *St Bartholomew* on the inner side walls. On the left wall: marble tomb monument of Benozzo Federighi, bishop of Fiesole; a notable work, surrounded by polychrome terracotta, by Luca della Robbia, 1454. At the far end of the left transept is the small square

78   Palazzo Spini Ferroni, after 1289, with Ponte Santa Trinità in the foreground

79   Santa Trinità: upper order of the façade, by Bernardo Buontalenti, 1593–4

80   Santa Trinità façade and (beyond) Palazzo Gianfigliazzi

81   Santa Trinità: stained-glass window in the chancel

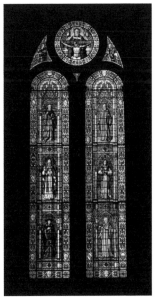

Cappella delle Reliquie di San Giovanni Gualberto, designed by Caccini and frescoed by Passignano, 1594.

Left side aisle: fifth chapel: altarpiece: wooden figure of the *Magdalene* by Desiderio da Settignano, *circa* 1455, based on the same subject by Donatello today in the Museo dell'Opera del Duomo. Fourth chapel: above the entrance arch: *St John Gualbert*, fresco by Lorenzo di Bicci, *circa* 1460. On the wall above and behind the altar: fresco of *St John Gualbert in Glory* by Neri di Bicci, 1455. On the right wall: *Annunciation* by the same artist. Third chapel: originally frescoed with the *Story of St Catherine of Alexandria* (1340); fragments survive. On the left wall: tomb monument of Giuliano Davanzati, attributed to Bernardo Rossellino. Altarpiece: *Coronation of the Virgin* by Bicci di Lorenzo, *circa* 1430. Second chapel: modernised by Matteo Nigetti in 1635. First chapel: modernised by Caccini, *circa* 1600, who also made the statues; frescoed vault by Poccetti. Altarpiece: *Annunciation* by Jacopo Chimenti, 1603.

Outside the church, down Via del Parione, at no. 7 is the entrance to the cloisters; a Doric colonnade, 1584–93, designed by Buontalenti and executed under Alfonso Parigi. The adjacent refectory has seventeenth-century frescoes.

Piazza Santa Trinità: In the irregularly shaped square is the Colonna della Giustizia, a granite monolith taken from the Baths of Caracalla in Rome. It was given by Pope Pius IV to Cosimo I in 1560, who erected the column to commemorate Florence's victory over Siena at Marciano (1554). On top: porphyry figure of *Justice* by Francesco del Tadda, 1581.

Via dei Tornabuoni, west side: Walking N, on the corner of Via del Parione, no. 3 is the substantial **Palazzo Minerbetti**, originally fourteenth century, and originally three separate structures (4 + 2 + 2 bays); a long rusticated stone façade. The ground floor has seven portals, that on the left being the original entrance; the tall central portal marks a lost *vicolo* (alley). Above: a low mezzanine, then two storeys of eight shallow-arched windows and an attic, a filled-in *altana*. No. 6 is **Palazzo Medici Tornaquinci Altoviti**, again originally two fourteenth-century houses, one of four bays, one of two; they were joined *circa* 1430, and extended upwards in the sixteenth century by an additional storey and a loggia. The ground floor retains four stone arched openings; four lights to the *piano nobile*.

At the corner of Via della Vigna Nuova, no. 2, corner of Via della Spada, is the **Palazzo del Duca di Nortumbria**, late sixteenth century, but radically modernised in 1912. The plan has an unusual wedge shape, with its strongly articulated single-storey 'prow' towards Via dei Tornabuoni and main façades, with four orders, to Via della Vigna Nuova and Via della Spada. It was largely rebuilt by Orazio Rucellai in the early 1580s. His sons sold it to the Englishman Robert Dudley, duke of Northumberland, in 1614. It later passed by heredity to Marchese Paleotti di Bologna and in 1912 to Francesco Navone, who had his architect, Adolfo Coppedè, cut off the sharp corner towards Via dei Tornabuoni and form the prow instead, with a terrace on top.

Further up, no. 15 is **Palazzo Viviani della Robbia**, rebuilt in 1693–6 by G.B. Foggini. An impressive structure, Foggini's only known *palazzo*, built for one of Cosimo III's courtiers. A boldly rusticated ground floor and three upper storeys, capped by a heavy cornice. In the centre of the broad façade is a Serliana with a large balcony. This tripartite central bay is flanked by three bays on each side; all the windows are pedimented, and recessed into rectangular openings. A six-bay return façade at the S end to Via della Spada. On the corner at high level: coat of arms of the Viviani. Inside, on the *piano nobile*, is a great hall richly decorated with stucco, fresco and busts. No. 17 is the **Palazzetto Tornabuoni**, with a broad façade of four orders. A central stone portal, flanked by lesser doorways. On the main upper floors: nine bays of arched windows.

Adjacent, no. 19 is **Palazzo Larderel** or **Lardarelli**, built by Giovanni Antonio Dosio in 1580 for the Giacomini Tebalducci. Broadly modelled on Palazzo Bartolini at the S end of the street; three bays and three orders, all *alla romana*. Rusticated quoins and a heavy roof cornice; a central pedimented portal flanked by two large rectangular aediculed windows; the upper openings also pedimented aedicules. Impressive but rather cold and mechanical. On the outer corner: small family coat of arms; below is the larger arms of the French family Larderel, who acquired the house in 1839.

A little further N, the street widens into Piazza Antinori. On the W side (no. 1), opposite San Gaetano, is the modest **Palazzo Beccanugi**, mainly eighteenth century. A little further N on the W side is **Palazzo Antinori**, a fine example of a fifteenth-century Florentine noble house. 83 Built in 1461–6, probably by Giuliano da Maiano for Giovanni Buoni; sold to Lorenzo de' Medici in 1475, it passed to Niccolò Antinori in 1506, whose descendants still own the building. Niccolò made some alterations, including the addition of the garden façade, perhaps by Baccio d'Agnolo. An austere, reticent but elegant public façade, entirely faced with *pietra forte*, all fine ashlar with recessed joints. Three orders and boldly projecting roof eaves. The ground floor is a little irregular, with an off-centre portal, but the *piani nobili* are regular, with six bays of arched windows. The internal courtyard has refined colonnades of *pietra serena* on three sides; a fine della Robbia coat of arms of the Antinori. Inside is a cantina, where the public may sample the famous Antinori wines. The attractive small garden has a colonnaded loggia along the N side.

Via dei Tornabuoni, east side (from S to N): Opposite Santa Trinità, on the corner of Via delle Terme, is

Palazzo Bartolini Salimbeni (Piazza Santa Trinità no. 1): By Baccio d'Agnolo for Giovanni Bartolini, 1520–23. A notable, highly original and imposing High Renaissance façade *alla romana*, influenced by Raphael. The site was acquired by Bartolomeo Bartolini from the Dati, and the building remained in family ownership until 1839, when it became a hotel, and was later subdivided. For a time it housed the French consulate; it was restored in 1961.

84, 85   The façade has three bays and three orders, defined by string courses, framed by rusticated quoins, and the whole surmounted by a massively overhanging dentilled cornice. Baccio used three types of stone: *pietra forte* for the main W façade, *pietra serena* and *pietra bigia* (pale grey) to the flank on Via Porta Rossa. In the lower order: a large central pedimented portal flanked by smaller aediculed windows. The second order has three large pedimented windows, alternating with shallow niches, and the third repeats the second, although the pediments to both are alternated. On the third order: square recesses between the windows instead of niches. All the main windows are divided into four panels by stone transoms and mullions. The house was much criticised on completion for its 'foreign-ness' (i.e., its Roman character), provoking Baccio to add above the portal the Latin phrase CARPERE PROMPTIUS QUAM IMITARI ('it is easier to criticise than imitate').

The barrel-vaulted entrance hall leads to a small courtyard, three bays square, and colonnaded on three sides. The walls are richly decorated with grotesques in *sgraffito*. Within the frieze above the arches are oculi, intended to have reliefs; further oculi above the *piano nobile* windows; the principal upper windows repeat the transom-and-mullion design of the main façade. On the uppermost level is an elegant *liagò*.

82   Via dei Tornabuoni: lower west side, with Palazzo Minerbetti

83   Palazzo Antinori: detail of the façade, 1461–6, probably by Giuliano da Maiano

84   Palazzo Bartolini Salimbeni: general view of the west façade, by Baccio d'Agnolo, 1520–23

85   Palazzo Bartolini Salimbeni: detail of the second order of the façade

Palazzo Buondelmonti (Piazza Santa Trinità no. 2): Originally owned by the Cambi, who sold it in 1517 to Lorenzo and Leonardo Buondelmonti. It was then extensively modernised, with a new façade, perhaps by Baccio d'Agnolo (*circa* 1525), originally decorated with *chiaroscuro* (black, white and grey) frescoes. A square façade with four orders; a very tall ground floor faced with *pietra forte* ashlar, and incorporating a mezzanine; a central rusticated arched portal. Two upper orders of seven bays with arched windows. The upper loggia, also of seven bays, was reopened at the end of the twentieth century, but is now fully glazed. On the façade: plaque recording that Ludovico Ariosto stayed here several times when it was owned by Zanobi Buondelmonti. For some time after 1820 the influential literary and scientific society Gabinetto Vieusseux met here under the auspices of Jean-Pierre Vieusseux; attendees included Manzoni, Dumas, Stendhal and Leopardi; a second plaque.

Continuing up the E side, at no. 5 is **Palazzo Strozzi del Poeta**, or Giaconni, the former title derived from the fact that in the late sixteenth century it was owned by Giovanni Battista Strozzi, the writer. A major modernisation of an earlier house, the façade is by Gherardo Silvani (1626), elegant, restrained Florentine Baroque; four orders and five bays. On the ground floor: two pairs of pedimented openings flank the central entrance arch. On the *piano nobile*: five large pedimented windows, the central one with a balcony; the second floor is similar but a little more modest; a simple attic.

At no. 7 is the **Palazzo del Circolo dell'Unione**, seat of a noble association founded by Anatolio Demidoff and based here after 1853. Also known as the Palazzo della Commenda di Castiglione. The house was acquired from the Ughi by Simone Corsi in the 1550s, and in 1573 he commissioned Vasari to design a new façade: simple but refined, with six bays and four orders; an off-centre portal surmounted by a balcony; above the portal: bust of *Francesco I de' Medici* attributed to Giambologna. Flanking windows now replaced by shop fronts; large rectangular lights to the first *piano nobile*; those to the second, smaller, have Mannerist split pediments. The façade was originally frescoed, one of the first in the city. It remained Corsi property until 1780, when it passed to the Uguccioni. Next, nos. 10–14, is **Palazzo Altoviti Sangalletti**, modernised in 1835. Large rusticated stone arches to the ground floor; three orders of rectangular lights above. From Italian Unification until the Second World War it was occupied by the famous Caffè Doney.

Next is **Palazzo Gherardi Uguccioni**, an imposing structure, nine bays long; façade by Roberto Franceschi, 1831. Heavy stone rustication to the ground floor and mezzanine, with a massive arched portal. Two orders of rectangular lights plus an attic above, with a long balcony above the portal and smaller balconies to the two outermost bays.

Palazzo Strozzi: Occupies the block bounded by Via dei Tornabuoni, Via degli Strozzi, Piazza degli Strozzi and Vicolo degli Strozzi. One of the largest and most massively impressive palaces in the city; broadly modelled on Michelozzo's Palazzo Medici. The Strozzi were exiled by the Medici in 1434, but allowed to return in 1466. Land was acquired for the new building in stages over twenty years. It was begun in 1489 by Benedetto da Maiano for the merchant Filippo Strozzi, but Benedetto left for Naples as soon as work on site had begun; the building is broadly based on a surviving wooden model, made for Strozzi in 1490 by Giuliano da Sangallo, and usually on display inside. The final design as built differs in some respects from the model, notably in the increased overall height and the roof cornice. Work on site continued under Il Cronaca. Strozzi died in 1491, but construction continued under his eldest son, Alfonso. Il Cronaca completed the second floor by 1495, the top floor by 1498, the massive crowning cornice (1502), and the elegant internal courtyard (1503).

Construction was suspended from 1504 to 1523, but then began again, only to be halted permanently in 1538. The remainder of the roof cornice was never completed. The palace was confiscated by the Medici in the same year, but returned to the Strozzi thirty years later. It remained in their ownership until 1937–8, when it passed to the Istituto Nazionale delle Assicurazioni. Today it houses a number of cultural bodies including the Istituto Nazionale di Studi sul Rinascimento and the Gabinetto Vieusseux. It is frequently used for exhibitions and conferences.

The plan is rectangular, nine bays by thirteen, with the long axis E–W. The façades have three very tall orders, each faced with 'cushion' rusticated stonework, diminishing in boldness with each storey. The 86 lowermost order has a central arched portal to each of the three main façades, flanked by rows of small, square, high-level windows. Other than the rustication, the upper floors are almost identical, with arched *bifore* at regular intervals. Each storey is demarcated by a string course at sill level. On the external corners are the original wrought-iron torch holders and lanterns designed by Benedetto da Maiano. 87, 88

The plan centres on the courtyard, five bays by three, with a spacious ground-floor colonnade on all sides. The stonework is *pietra serena*, with 62 wall surfaces in plain white render. The lowermost order has elegant Corinthian colonnades; the second has large arched windows, one per bay; the top floor has an open colonnaded loggia. The principal suite of rooms on the first floor consists of a single enfilade wrapping around the courtyard, divided into two apartments, east and west; two staircases on the S side. In his will, Filippo left the western half of the palace to one of his sons, Alfonso, and the eastern half to his other two sons, Lorenzo and Filippo the younger.

Turning right briefly down Via degli Strozzi, at no. 2 Piazza degli Strozzi (SE corner) is the **Palazzo dello Strozzino**, built for another branch of the same clan. It was begun *circa* 1457; the rusticated ground floor has been attributed to Michelozzo, the second order to Giuliano da Maiano, who also began the (uncompleted) courtyard. The ground-floor exterior is heavily rusticated, with three large portals; the top floor was added in the nineteenth century. In the 1920s the building was adapted by Marcello Piacentini, in the Art Deco style (very rare in Florence), to become a cinema, the Odeon, with the auditorium in the former courtyard. The splendid auditorium has a notable coloured glass cupola. It retains many Art Deco fixtures and sculptures inside, including three gilded wood *Muses* above the screen. Also noteworthy is the faceted lantern on the outer corner of Via dei Sassetti and Via degli Anselmi, with eight bronze nudes. Return to Via dei Tornabuoni.

No. 16 (right) is **Palazzo Corsi**, formerly Tornabuoni, and later the Banca Commerciale, occupying the block from Via degli Strozzi to Via dei Corsi. First built in the mid-fifteenth century by Michelozzo, whose internal courtyard has survived. Modernised by Cigoli *circa* 1606, who also rebuilt the loggia, then at the SW corner. The palace was extensively rebuilt in 1736 by Ferdinando Ruggieri, including the **Loggia dei Tornaquinci**. In 1857–67 Via dei Tornabuoni was widened, and the building was given a new façade by Telemaco Bonaiuti; he also relocated the reassembled loggia at the NW corner, where it remains; a rich elaborate work, Doric, all in stone, with a central arch carried on free-standing columns. Michelozzo's original façade had eighteen bays, whereas the rebuilt main façade now has eleven bays and three orders, the lowermost rusticated, and all the windows large rectangular lights; balconies in the central bays.

On the adjacent Via dei Corsi (no. 1), corner of Via dei Pescioni, is **Palazzo Sertini**. The Sertini had owned property here since the fourteenth century, but the present house, for Andrea and Tommaso Sertini, is from 1490, probably by Baccio d'Agnolo. The later sixteenth-century

86   Palazzo Strozzi: detail of portal and first-floor windows, mostly *circa* 1490–98, by Giuliano da Sangallo and Il Cronaca

87   Palazzo Strozzi: detail of torch holder

88   Palazzo Strozzi: detail of lantern at the outer corner of the façades

89   Palazzo dello Strozzino, mid-fifteenth century, later the Cinema Odeon: detail of lantern by Marcello Piacentini, 1922

90   San Gaetano: upper part of the façade, by Pier Francesco Silvani, 1648

91   San Gaetano: detail of the central part of the façade

sgraffito decoration is by Andrea Feltrini. Both façade and *sgraffito* are very similar to Palazzo Lanfredini on the Lungarno Guicciardini, again by Baccio and Feltrini. A square portal, off-centre, with three bays on one side, two on the other; *piano nobile* with six rectangular lights, and a very modest attic.

Return to Via dei Tornabuoni, which opens into Piazza Antinori. Dominating the E side is the façade of

San Gaetano: Formerly dedicated to both San Michele Berteldi and San Gaetano. First recorded in the eleventh century; the dedication to San Michele Berteldi dates from 1192. Following a modernisation proposal by Buontalenti, the work, for the Theatine fathers, was begun by Matteo Nigetti (1604–30), who completed the choir and transepts; he was succeeded by Gherardo Silvani, who rebuilt the nave on a larger scale, and then in turn (after 1639) by Silvani's son Pier Francesco; the last began the façade in *pietra forte* in 1643, although it took several decades to complete. It was given parochial status by Grand Duke Leopoldo II.

90, 91 The Baroque façade is one of the most notable in the city; three bays and two orders, defined by fluted Corinthian pilasters in pairs flanking the central bay, and square at the outer corners. Above the pedimented portal and the flanking openings: sculpted groups of the Theatine symbol and allegories of *Hope* and *Poverty* by Balthazar Permoser. Above the side openings: niches containing statues of *St Gaetano* and *St Andrew Avellino* (by Anton Francesco Andreozzi, 1690). The marble statues contrast strongly with the *pietra forte* stonework. The upper order is confined to the central bay, with a rich central oculus (above: the Medici arms), paired Corinthian flanking pilasters and a bold crowning pediment; volutes flanking the upper order.

Inside: an intact Florentine Baroque interior, of which few survive unaltered. The plan is a Latin cross, with chapels flanking the nave, three down each side; the order is again Corinthian, with a barrel-vaulted ceiling. At high level at the sides of the chapels: fourteen statues of the *Evangelists* and *Apostles*, with a relief depicting the life of each one. The cycle was begun by Antonio Novelli in the 1640s, and completed by many different artists including G.B. Foggini and Gioacchino Fortini. Contributions of both artistic input and funding were provided by Giovanni de' Medici, architect and intellectual, and a relative of Cosimo II.

Right aisle, first chapel: glazed terracotta *Virgin and Child* by Andrea della Robbia, 1470–80. Vault frescoes by Ottavio Vannini, 1642–3.

Second chapel: frescoes by Angelo Michele Colonna, *circa* 1640. Side walls: paintings by Jacopo Vignali. Third chapel: altarpiece of *St Gaetano di Tiene* by Matteo Rosselli, 1640. The frescoes in both arms of the transepts are by Filippo Maria Galletti (vaults) and Jacopo Chiavistelli (walls). Galletti also frescoed the cupola: *St Gaetano in Glory*, 1678.

To the right of the high altar is the Cappella della Natività: frescoes and two canvases by Matteo Rosselli, 1631. In the choir: bronze Crucifix by Giovanni Francesco Susini, 1634–5. In the sacristy: stucco decoration by Carlo Marcellini, 1702. Vault fresco by Piero Dandini. To the left of the high altar is the chapel of Sant'Elena: frescoes by Jacopo Vignali and Giovanni Bilivert. Altarpiece by Matteo Rosselli, *circa* 1644.

Left aisle: third chapel: decoration by Lorenzo Lippi (1642–4); stucco work by Antonio Novelli. Second chapel: altarpiece: *Martyrdom of St Lawrence* by Pietro da Cortona, 1637, the most notable work in the church. Vault and lunette frescoes by Angelo Michele Colonna, 1643. First chapel: decoration by Galletti and Vignali.

To the left of the church is the Antinori chapel, rebuilt in 1634 by Gherardo Silvani. Inside: early sixteenth-century altar with panel paintings from the school of Filippo Lippi.

At the N end of Piazza Antinori, Via dei Rondinelli continues NE to meet Via dei Cerretani. No. 1 is **Palazzo Adorni Braccesi**, fifteenth century, but radically modernised in the nineteenth. A façade of four orders; the ground floor strongly rusticated, with three large arched openings; the upper floors each with five rectangular lights. A *sgraffito* frieze on the second floor, and the Adorni coat of arms on the outer corner. At no. 2 is **Palazzo Pasquali**, a radical early seventeenth-century modernisation of a sixteenth-century house, perhaps by Cigoli. Four orders, with mezzanine between the *piano nobile* and the top floor. A prominent Pasquali coat of arms on the rusticated outer corner (by Antonio Novelli, *circa* 1620s). In 1685 Cosimo Pasquali also bought the adjacent house at no. 4, **Palazzo Portigiani**, built a few decades earlier; they were joined internally and fresco decoration added to the principal rooms. No. 3 is **Palazzo Franceschi**, sixteenth century, the top floor added in the nineteenth; only three bays wide with arched windows with *pietra serena* surrounds. At no. 7: **Palazzo Ginori**, rebuilt in the nineteenth century; plaque to Carlo Lorenzini (Collodi), creator of *Pinocchio*, who lived here.

The *Quartiere* of Santa Croce

The *Quartiere* of Santa Croce

I   LUNGARNO GENERALE DIAZ, THE PONTE ALLE GRAZIE AND VICINITY

The Lungarno runs E from Piazza dei Giudici to the Ponte alle Grazie; it then becomes the Lungarno delle Grazie. Just past Piazza dei Giudici is the neo-Classical **Camera di Commercio (Palazzo della Borsa)**, by Michele Maiorfi and Emilio de Fabris, 1858–60. Three elements: two simple, restrained side wings (four bays, three orders), with rectan-   93
gular neo-Renaissance lights and plain render to the walls; and a central section, faced with *pietra serena* and a five-bay pedimented Doric temple front, also restrained but rather imposing.

Continue E along the Lungarno. To the left, just after Piazza Mentana, is the oratory of **Santa Maria delle Grazie** by Vittorio Bellini, 1874. Continue E to the

Ponte alle Grazie: First built in 1237, with nine stone arches, by the *podestà* Rubaconte da Mandello, thus also known as the Ponte Rubaconte. It survived for centuries; on top accumulated a number of chapels, workshops and tabernacles, much like the Ponte Vecchio. It was widened in 1876 to permit its use by trams, but was destroyed by the Germans in 1944. The present bridge is from 1957, by Giovanni Michelucci, Edoardo Detti and others, winners of a competition launched in 1945. Simple detailing, with five shallow arched spans, supported by four narrow stone piers in the river.

Turn inland along Via dei Benci. No. 1 (left) is **Palazzo Alberti-Malenchini**, originally fourteenth and fifteenth centuries. The impressive main façade is to Via dei Benci: three orders and nine bays. It was added for Giovan Vincenzo Alberti in 1760–63, in a *quattrocento* Renaissance manner, to unify the disparate structures behind it. The neo-Classical river façade was added by Vittorio Bellini, 1849–50, who also set out the adjacent garden. On the other corner, with one façade to the Lungarno (no. 28), the other to Via dei Bardi (no. 4), is **Palazzo Bardi Tempi**, modernised *circa* 1610 by Matteo Nigetti. Refined, monu-   94
mental façades, seven bays towards the river, nine to Via dei Benci; four orders. Central portals surmounted by balconies. Ground- and first-

floor windows all aediculed, with triangular pediments below, segmental above. Coats of arms of the Alberti and others. A little further N we reach the crossroads with Corso dei Tintori. On the right is the

Museo Horne (Palazzo Corsi Alberti), no. 6 Via dei Benci. Built towards the end of the fifteenth century (1489?) for the Corsi, on the site of an earlier house of the Alberti. Attributed to Giuliano da San-gallo or (more likely) Il Cronaca. Three orders, and four bays on each of the two external façades. They are rendered, but with rusticated stone to the quoins, the portal and the window surrounds, that to the quoins graded in the manner of Palazzo Gondi and others. The two upper orders have large single arched lights; a boldly projecting 'Tuscan' overhanging roof. Inside: the plan is a 'C', wrapped around an attractive small courtyard, with a colonnade along two sides and a loggia above; refined capitals in *pietra serena* by Andrea Sansovino; *sgraffito* decoration to the loggia balcony. The palace was acquired in 1912 by Herbert Percy Horne, a British architect and art collector, who restored it (1912–14). Horne bequeathed the building to the *comune*. It was badly damaged in the 1966 floods. Today it houses a museum based on his collections, chiefly Florentine art of the fifteenth and sixteenth centuries, recreating the interior of a typical noble house of the Renaissance. As well as paintings (by Giotto, Masaccio, Gozzoli, Bernardo Daddi, Ammannati and others), there are small collections of ceramics, glass, coins and textiles.

On the NE corner of the crossroads of Via dei Benci with Borgo 95 Santa Croce is the **Torre degli Alberti**, thirteenth century, with an unusual plan and three façades, fitted onto the prominent corner site. In the fifteenth century the small loggia was added at the base. Oppo-96 site Palazzo Horne, no. 5 Via dei Benci is **Palazzo Busini Bardi**, attributed by Antonio Manetti (Brunelleschi's biographer) and Vasari to Brunelleschi; datable to *circa* 1430, with rendering inscribed with *sgraffito* to imitate ashlar. Built for the Busini but bought by the Bardi in 1482. An imposing street façade, eight bays, with a tall ground floor incor-porating a mezzanine, and two very similar upper floors, each with eight arched lights. The off-centre portal has a rusticated stone sur-round. Inside: an elegant central colonnaded courtyard, three bays square, Corinthian, probably the earliest Renaissance *cortile* in a private *palazzo* in the city. Remains of an earlier structure along the S flank.

97 Continuing N, no. 20 Via dei Benci is **Palazzo Mellini Fossi**, very early sixteenth century. Many houses on the street were originally

93   Palazzo della Borsa by Michele Maiorfi and Emilio de Fabris, 1858–60

94   Palazzo Bardi Tempi: façade to Via dei Benci

95   Torre degli Alberti, thirteenth century, with fifteenth-century loggia at the base

96   Palazzo Busini Bardi, *circa* 1430: detail of the portal, attributed to Brunelleschi

97   Via dei Benci: general view towards the south, with Palazzo Mellini Fossi, left

owned by the Alberti, recorded here since 1236; in 1456 Duccio Mellini bought this site from Francesco Alberti. A typical façade of the period, perhaps by Baccio d'Agnolo: symmetrical, five bays, with rusticated surrounds to the big central portal and the upper windows; iron grilles to the square ground-floor windows; boldly projecting roof eaves. The frescoes (late sixteenth century, restored 1996) were designed by Francesco Salviati, and executed by Giovanni Stolf, a Dutch painter. They depict mythological scenes, including *Perseus and Andromeda*. Following the Mellinis' extinction (1634), the palace eventually passed to Marchese Federico Fossi. On the left side of Via dei Benci is **San Jacopo tra i Fossi**, established perhaps in the eleventh century, although today little remains other than the nave; a Methodist church since 1849.

98   **Borgo Santa Croce** runs diagonally NE from the Torre degli Alberti towards the homonymous church; several houses of interest. No. 6 is the impressive **Palazzo Antinori Corsini**, built by the Serristori; very early sixteenth century, passing to the Corsini in 1587 and later, in 1886, to the Antinori. Sometimes attributed to Giuliano da Sangallo. An austere, rendered façade: three orders and an off-centre portal. A refined internal courtyard, rectangular, all in *pietra serena*, with Composite colonnades on three sides and cantilevered vaults on the fourth. No. 8 is the **Casa Vasari**, former home of the artist and writer Giorgio Vasari; the Salone is frescoed by him. No. 10 is **Palazzo Spinelli**, built *circa* 1470 for Tommaso Spinelli, who also patronised a chapel in Santa Croce and funded the second cloister. A sober fifteenth-century façade, with central rusticated portal; square ground-floor windows, the upper ones arched. Rich *sgraffito* decoration to the courtyard as well as the façade; the former has colonnades on two sides. Sometimes attributed to Bernardo Rossellino (who designed the Santa Croce cloister) and (less likely) to Brunelleschi. No. 19 is **Palazzo Morelli**, with a façade again decorated with *sgraffito*. At the NE end of the Borgo, turn sharp right down Via Magliabechi, which at the far end meets the Corso dei Tintori. No. 13 (with a façade to the Lungarno) is the nineteenth-century **Palazzina Brogi**, built as a studio for the photographer Giacomo Brogi. The elegant Lungarno façade has four bays, with four huge arched windows to the *piano nobile* studio. Turning E, we reach the Piazza dei Cavalleggeri, in front of the impressive

Biblioteca Nazionale: Occupies the block between Via Magliabechi (W), the Lungarno and the conventual buildings of Santa Croce (N). Built in 1911–35 by Cesare Bazzani. The institution itself dates from the period when Florence was briefly capital of Italy (1865–70), but the original nucleus of its collection was the Fondazione Angelo Magliabechi, consisting of approximately 30,000 volumes, established in 1714; first opened to the public in 1747. It was greatly enlarged by subsequent donations, and today contains more than a million books, manuscripts and incunabula. The present building is the result of a competition (1902). A grandiose, self-confident neo-Renaissance pile, with a tall, spacious three-bay loggia in the centre, flanked by square, chunky towers; the more modest side wings each have four bays and two orders; large rectangular multi-light windows.

On the W corner of the Piazza (Corso dei Tintori no. 7 and Lungarno delle Grazie no. 2) is **Palazzo Riccioli**, or Guasconi. It was once the Hotel Jennings Riccioli. Rebuilt in the nineteenth century in a rather eclectic manner, with a new façade unifying two or three different structures. Five bays and four floors plus mezzanine; the longer river façade has seven bays.

Continue E along the Lungarno della Zecca Vecchia. This quay was constructed in 1870, continuing the Lungarno delle Grazie, but necessitating the demolition of medieval walls and towers along the river bank. The apartment blocks and villas along the quay are thus mostly late nineteenth century.

At the E end is Piazza Piave, in the centre of which is the **Torre della Zecca**, which survived the nineteenth-century demolition of the outer city walls. It was built *circa* 1324, and matches the Torre San Niccolò on the other bank (q.v.); relatively tall and narrow. A little beyond the tower, on the Lungarno Pecori Giraldi, is the large block of the **Caserma di Cavalleria Baldissera**, 1909.

2 BORGO DEI GRECI AND VICINITY

A small, densely developed district between the Palazzo Vecchio and Santa Croce. The main axis is the Borgo itself.

Begin at the SE corner of the Palazzo Vecchio, in the little Piazza del Grano. On the SE side is the **Loggia del Grano**, built on Cosimo II's orders in 1619, to a rather eclectic design by Giulio Parigi; bust and coat of arms in the centre of the façade. Grain was sold under the colonnades, and was stored in the upper floor. The loggia measures three bays by two, with tall semicircular arches; above is a low mezzanine and then the *piano nobile*, with tall arched windows. At the end of the nineteenth century it was acquired by Tommaso Salvini, an actor, who enlarged it and converted into a theatre. In the late twentieth century it became a cinema.

North-east of the Loggia, Via dei Neri contains a number of early houses and vestiges. Immediately adjacent to the Loggia (S side) at no. 35 is **Palazzo Fagni da Diacceto**, early fourteenth century, a substantial stone structure five bays wide. Three arched portals, and three upper orders. No. 23 is **Palazzo Soldani**, and no. 25 is **Palazzo Bagnesi**, the latter with a fifteenth-century courtyard. Further E, nos. 4 and 6 are respectively **Palazzo Grifoni** and **Palazzo Nori**, both again fourteenth century in origin. The latter is mostly early fifteenth century, with a tall rusticated stone lower façade (arches for workshops); three orders above. The *piano nobile* has large arched windows, partly filled in. Halfway down Via dei Neri, the short Via dei Rustici (left) leads to **San Remigio**. Founded in the eleventh century, and based on a hostel for French pilgrims on their way to Rome, it is dedicated to the patron saint of Reims. Rebuilt in the late thirteenth century and the early fourteenth, in a simple Gothic style. The façade is almost devoid of decoration. Inside: nave and two side aisles, of equal height, rather like German 'hall churches'. Octagonal piers of *pietra forte* and simple rib vaults.

Following extensive damage in the 1966 floods, the four lateral altars were removed for restoration, bringing to light fourteenth-century frescoes. Right chancel chapel: thirteenth-century *Virgin and Child* by the otherwise unknown Master of San Remigio. In the adjacent canons' residence: monochrome frescoes, fourteenth to fifteenth century. Further fourteenth-century frescoes, in the manner of Uccello, were uncovered after 1966 in the upper part of the small adjacent cloister (*chiostrino*).

From the NE corner of San Remigio, take Via dei Rustici NE; nos. 4–6 is **Palazzo Visconti**, with a simple but impressive fifteenth-century façade; three orders and eleven bays, with portals near each end. No. 5 is **Palazzo Peruzzi**, one of many once in their ownership in this area. Today of eighteenth-century appearance, but originally fourteenth century. A simple façade with rectangular lights. No. 7 is **Palazzo Venerosi Pesciolini**, adjacent to the Torre Peruzzi. A stone-clad ground floor with arched openings for workshops and a later portal; two upper orders with arched lights (altered). No. 8 is **Palazzo Borgianni**, sixteenth century; a very simple façade with five bays and four orders. Continue NE into the unusual curved form of Via Bentaccorti. The buildings along this street, and its NE continuation, Via Torta, are all constructed directly

98 Courtyard of a house on Borgo Santa Croce

99 The Biblioteca Nazionale from Piazzale Michelangelo, by Cesare Bazzani, 1911–35

100 Palazzo Peruzzi, late thirteenth century

101 Palazzo Cocchi Donati Serristori, Piazza Santa Croce; perhaps *circa* 1470, attributed to Baccio d'Agnolo or Giuliano da Sangallo

on the remains of the ancient Roman amphitheatre, built in the second century AD. The overall plan took the form of an ellipse.

Turning right at the junction between Via dei Rustici and Via Bentaccorti, the latter terminates in Piazza Peruzzi. The famous Peruzzi banking dynasty owned most of the properties in this area. The most important is **Palazzo Peruzzi** itself, Borgo dei Greci no. 3, occupying the block bounded by the Borgo, Piazza Peruzzi and Via dei Benci. The principal façade is to Piazza Peruzzi, simple and austere, curving to follow the shape of the amphitheatre below. It was originally two separate buildings, later joined together. Inside, the courtyard shows traces of the original building: square columns of *pietra forte*; brick arches. Around Piazza Peruzzi are other houses formerly in the family's ownership, including no. 2 (eighteenth-century façade), later owned by the Salutati; at no. 3 was the family's loggia, demolished in 1778. At no. 4 (corner of Via dei Bentaccordi): a house incorporating the remains of an early medieval tower.

Taking the N section of Via dei Bentaccordi, cross Borgo dei Greci. At nos. 8–22r of the Borgo, nos. 29–31r Via dell'Anguillara and nos. 4–12r Via dei Bentaccordi is the **Palazzo di Ubaldino Peruzzi**, named after its nineteenth-century owner. The original nucleus is fourteenth century, but was radically modernised by Gherardo Silvani in the eighteenth for Ludovico Peruzzi. Its long principal façade has a fine portal by Silvani. In 1771 the original family house (Borgo dei Greci no. 3) was sold and this became their main residence. Ubaldino was a leading Risorgimento figure and sometime mayor. Continuing around the curved plan of the amphitheatre, at no. 17 Via dell'Anguillara is a small restored fourteenth-century house; nos. 19–21 is **Palazzo Ginori**, late eighteenth century. No. 23 is **Palazzo Baccelli**. A little further to the W is **Palazzo d'Anghiari**; Balduccio d'Anghiari was the *conte* (count) of Anguillara; hence the name of the street.

The E ends of both Borgo dei Greci and Via dell'Anguillara open out into the extensive rectangular **Piazza Santa Croce**. This zone was just outside the early medieval walls (1173–5), but was settled in the following decades, notably after the foundation of Santa Croce itself by the Franciscans in 1226. The square was formally set out as an atrium for the church and to accommodate the huge numbers who came to hear the friars' sermons. It has also always been associated with public festivities and spectacles. The Medici used the square for pageants and horse races, and for centuries it has been used for playing football; annual games between the city's *contrade* (districts) are still played here in the medieval manner. Most of the surrounding houses are small to medium-sized *palazzetti*, mainly seventeenth or eighteenth century, although some are older but modernised.

At the W end (no. 1) is **Palazzo Cocchi Donati Serristori**, originally attributed to Baccio d'Agnolo, but today often given to Giuliano da Sangallo. Perhaps built *circa* 1470 (although it has been dated as late as the 1520s) on the fabric of an earlier fourteenth-century house, originally owned by the Peruzzi, but which passed to the Cocchi Donati in the mid-fifteenth century. In 1892 it was sold to the *comune* by the Serristori, who had inherited it by marriage from the Cocchi; it remains communal property today. The fourteenth-century structure survives in the rusticated ground-floor piers. The *alla romana* façade, three bays and three orders, has unusual features, including the prominent jetties at the outer corners, and the pilasters, paired in the outer bays, within which the arched secondary orders are set. Three large arched openings to each of the first and second orders, large rectangular lights to the third, the whole capped by massively overhanging eaves. Inside: a number of eighteenth-century frescoes, perhaps by Atanasio Bimbacci.

On the S side of the piazza (no. 21) is the unusual **Palazzo dell' Antella**. Its site was earlier occupied by houses of the Gondi and others. The long, regular façade is by Giulio Parigi, 1619, and was a major modernisation of earlier, sixteenth-century structures, perhaps by Buontalenti: ground floor, two *piani nobili* and a low attic. The upper floors are supported on *sporti* at first-floor level. Thirteen bays of single arched windows to the main floors, the spacing of which is closer towards the church, to heighten the perspective; small square lights to the attic. Much of the façade is frescoed, 1619–20, commissioned by the patron, Niccolò dell'Antella, and executed by thirteen different artists under the direction of Giovanni da San Giovanni. The frescoes depict *putti*, allegorical figures and flowers. To the S is a small garden.

3 SANTA CROCE

One of the most important historic monuments in the city, both for its architecture and for the works of art and artefacts within it. It contains tombs and monuments to many of Florence's greatest sons. Franciscans had settled in the city before 1226, establishing their first church outside the confines of the city walls; this church was enlarged in 1252. With the construction of the final circle of walls in the 1280s and '90s, however, the site was now within their protection. The present church was begun in 1295, and is traditionally ascribed to Arnolfo di Cambio. It is one of the largest in Italy, and is said to be the biggest Franciscan church in the world. By the time of Arnolfo's death in 1302, the chancel, transepts and their chapels were probably complete; work continued on the vast nave and aisles until 1385; it was finally consecrated in 1443 by Pope Eugenius IV.

The Exterior

The façade remained incomplete for centuries, and was eventually added in 1853–63, by Nicola Matas. As with the cathedral façade, it followed considerable stylistic discussion, and triggered a historicist debate that has remained highly controversial ever since. The style is a very literal Florentine neo-Gothic, the three unequal bays representing the nave and the lower narrow aisles. Prominent pilasters define the bays, each of which has a large portal, with a pointed tympanum over the doorway and a triangular gable. The side bays are capped by triangular pediments, while the central bay has an upper order with a large central oculus, and is again capped by a larger triangular pediment. The entire façade is clad with polychrome marble, much of it in rectangular panels, based on the baptistery of San Giovanni.

The campanile (1847), towards the E end, is by Gaetano Baccani, again neo-Gothic, this time in *pietra forte*.

The Interior

The plan of the church has the overall shape of a T or tau, sometimes called an Egyptian cross. The dominant requirement of the interior, as with all the great medieval mendicant churches, was for a very large open nave to preach to huge congregations. Its overall length is 115.43 m (approx. 379 ft). The nave is flanked by two much narrower side aisles, and has seven bays, the eighth bay forming the cross axis of the transepts. Beyond the crossing, the relatively small chancel projects E with a polygonal apse. On the east face of the transepts are ten tall, narrow chapels, five on each side.

The overall impression is of severe solemnity, simple and rational, although magnificently refined. The octagonal nave piers of *pietra forte* support large pointed arches, above the heads of which is a prominent walkway on corbels. Flat pilasters continue up to define the upper order, the clerestory, which has one arched window per bay. The nave is completed by a massive timber open-truss roof, described by Ruskin (in *Mornings in Florence*, 1875–7) as 'the roof of a farm-house barn'. The eighth bay is formed by the larger transept arches, beyond which is the pierced screen defining the chancel; this screen has a tall pointed chancel arch flanked by smaller, lower arches, which are surmounted by tall, slender, two-light traceried windows. The narrower side aisles are articulated by transverse arches, each bay being lit by a large traceried light, many filled with fine stained glass. Until 1566 the nave was subdivided at the east end of the fifth bay by a choir screen. It was removed by Vasari to conform to the liturgical requirements of the Counter-Reformation. The side altars in the aisles were added in the same period, to a standard design by Francesco da Sangallo. Their altarpieces also have a common theme in the story of the *Passion*.

Principal Works of Art and Monuments

Right aisle
First bay: altarpiece: *Crucifixion* by Santi di Tito, 1568. Between the first and second altars: tomb of Michelangelo, designed by Vasari but executed by others. Second altar: altarpiece: *Ascent to Calvary*, by Vasari. Next: cenotaph monument to Dante Alighieri, by Stefano Ricci, 1829. Third altar: altarpiece: *Ecce Homo* by Jacopo Coppi, 1576. Next: monument to Vittorio Alfieri, a fine neo-Classical work by Antonio Canova, 1810. In front, attached to the third nave column, is the pulpit, by Benedetto da Maiano (1472–6), a magnificent work whose octagonal form echoes the shape of the main arcade piers; decorated with refined scenes of the *Life of St Francis*. Fourth altar: altarpiece: *Flagellation* by Alessandro Fei, late sixteenth century. Next: tomb of Niccolò Macchiavelli by Innocenzo Spinazzi, 1787. Fifth altar: altarpiece: *Prayer in the Orchard* by Andrea del Minga, late sixteenth century. Next: monument to Luigi Lanzi by Giuseppe Belli, 1810. Adjacent is an aedicule in gilded and polychrome *pietra serena* containing a splendid *Annunciation* by Donatello, *circa* 1435, commissioned by Niccolò Cavalcanti, and carved in exceptionally high relief from a single piece of stone. Next: lateral portal into the adjacent cloister. Beyond the portal: monument to Leonardo Bruni, a harmonious and important work by Bernardo Rossellino, 1444–5. Next: tomb of Gioacchino Rossini, by Giuseppe Cassioli, 1900. Sixth altar: altarpiece: *Entry of Christ into Jerusalem* by Cigoli, 1603–4. Adjacent: sepulchre of Ugo Foscolo, by Antonio Berti, 1939.

Right (south) transept

Off the W side of the transept is the Castellani chapel; a notable fresco cycle by Agnolo Gaddi and assistants, depicting the *Lives of St Nicholas of Bari, St John the Baptist, St John the Evangelist and St Anthony Abbot*, *circa* 1380. Also in the chapel: statues of *St Francis* and *St Dominic* by the della Robbia. At the S end of the transept is the Baroncelli chapel, with fine frescoes of the *Life of the Virgin* by Taddeo Gaddi, 1332–8. Altarpiece: *Coronation of the Virgin* by Giotto (and perhaps Taddeo). The stained glass is also by Taddeo.

Adjacent is a corridor, the Androne del Noviziato, built by Michelozzo (*circa* 1445) for Cosimo il Vecchio. To the left is the **sacristy**, a large square room, built *circa* 1340 by the Peruzzi; contemporaneous wall frescoes by Niccolò di Pietro Gerini (*Ascension* and *Resurrection*), Spinello Aretino (*Road to Calvary*) and Taddeo Gaddi (*Crucifixion*). Fine fifteenth-century cupboards with intarsia decoration. On the E side of the sacristy is the Rinuccini chapel: entirely frescoed by Giovanni da Milano, a follower of Giotto, 1363–6; the cycle illustrates the *Life of the Virgin* and the *Life of St Mary Magdalene*.

At the S end of the *androne* is the **Medici chapel** or **Cappella del Noviziato**. A simple rectangular hall, three bays long, with a vaulted ceiling, also by Michelozzo, 1440s. It contains a terracotta altarpiece of the *Virgin and Child with Angels* by Andrea della Robbia, *circa* 1480.

Return to the S transept of the church. Along the E wall are five very tall, narrow chapels. From S to N, they are:

Velluti chapel: fourteenth-century frescoes by a follower of Cimabue, illustrating the life of *St Michael the Archangel*;

Riccardi chapel: frescoes by Giovanni da San Giovanni, early seventeenth century;

Giugni chapel: contains the tombs of Giulia and Carlotta Bonaparte, the latter the niece of Napoleon;

Peruzzi chapel: a superb cycle of frescoes by Giotto, 1320–25, dedicated to scenes from the *Life of St John the Baptist* (left wall) and *Life of St John the Evangelist* (right wall). In the archivolt: eight heads of *Prophets*; in the vault itself: *Symbols of the Evangelists*;

Bardi chapel: another fine fresco cycle by Giotto, of roughly contemporary date, depicting scenes from the *Life of St Francis*. On the altar: a panel painting with twenty scenes from the saint's life, by a thirteenth-century artist.

Chancel

The east wall is polygonal, with a very strong vertical emphasis: three extremely tall lancet windows, radiating vaulting ribs above. The surfaces are entirely frescoed by Agnolo Gaddi, depicting *Christ*, the *Evangelists* and the *Legend of the Finding of the True Cross*. The altarpiece is a polyptych composed of pieces by different artists, assembled in 1869; the central *Virgin and Child* is by Niccolò Gerini.

Left (north) transept

Again five chapels; from S to N, they are:

Spinelli chapel: redecorated in 1837 by Gaspare Martellini;

Capponi chapel: in 1926 it was rededicated to the mothers of those lost in battle;

Ricasoli chapel: scenes from the *Life of St Anthony of Padua* by Luigi Sabatelli, mid-nineteenth century;

Pulci Berardi chapel: frescoes by Bernardo Daddi of the *Lives of St Lawrence and St Stephen*, circa 1330;

Bardi di Vernio chapel: frescoes by Maso di Banco, a follower of Giotto, circa 1340, showing the *Life of St Silvester*.

Adjacent to the NE corner of the transept is the Niccolini chapel, by Giovanni Antonio Dosio, circa 1580; cupola frescoes by Volterrano, 1652–64. Next to it is the second Bardi di Vernio chapel: the metal gates are from 1335. On the altar: a notable wooden Crucifix by Donatello, 1412–13. Off the west side of the transept is the Machiavelli or Salviati chapel.

Left aisle

Return W down the N aisle. On the column at the crossing of nave and transept: monument to Leon Battista Alberti, by Lorenzo Bartolini, nineteenth century.

Sixth altar: altarpiece: *Pentecost* by Vasari. A little further along: monument to Carlo Marsuppini by Desiderio da Settignano; a splendid, richly decorated early Renaissance work, 1453–64. Left of the organ: fresco of the *Annunciation*, attributed to Agnolo Gaddi, late fourteenth century. Fifth altar: altarpiece: *Ascension* by Giovanni Stradano, sixteenth century. Adjacent: *Pietà* by Bronzino, circa 1569. Set into the floor: tomb of Lorenzo Ghiberti and his son Vittorio. Fourth altar: altarpiece: *Incredulity of St Thomas* by Vasari. Third altar: altarpiece: *Supper at Emmaus* by Santi di Tito. Second altar: altarpiece: *Resurrection*, also by Santi; both sixteenth century. Adjacent is the eighteenth-century tomb of Galileo Galilei; bust by G.B. Foggini. On the wall nearby: fresco attributed to Mariotto di Nardo, late fourteenth century or very early fifteenth. First altar: altarpiece: *Deposition* by Giovanni Battista Naldini, late sixteenth century.

Conventual buildings: The conventual buildings all lie to the S of the church, built around two cloisters. They are usually reached by the doorway in the S aisle. The first, larger one, itself originally consisted of two; the removal of the colonnade between the two cloisters resulted in the present L-shaped plan. It was built in the late fourteenth century, with a ten-bay colonnade along the S flank of the church. Between it and the second, southern cloister are the main surviving conventual buildings, now forming the Museo dell'Opera (see below). At the E end of this first cloister is the famous **Pazzi chapel**, one of the pivotal works of the early Renaissance; designed by Brunelleschi for Andrea de' Pazzi, begun 1429–30. It was intended as the friars' chapter house as well as the family chapel. Economic difficulties resulted in slow progress, and it was still not complete in 1445, when Pazzi died, or in the following year, when Brunelleschi died. The cupola and the vaults were finished in 1459, perhaps by Michelozzo, the portico in 1461.

The unusual façade has a large central arched portico, flanked on each side by a Corinthian colonnade of two smaller, narrower bays, with *pietra serena* columns, above which is a tall attic, divided into square panels; the central arch breaks through the attic. Above again is a transverse six-bay loggia, behind which rises the cupola, on a drum pierced by small oculi. The colonnade is roofed with a rich coffered barrel vault, broken in the centre by a small hemispherical cupola, and with terracotta decoration by Luca della Robbia. The colonnade was added after the chapel was built, and it may not have formed part of Brunelleschi's original intention; it was perhaps built by Giuliano da Maiano or Bernardo Rossellino.

The interior is a development from Brunelleschi's Sagrestia Vecchia at San Lorenzo, completed a few years earlier (see p. 196). Here, though, the main space is rectangular, not square, with its axis at right angles to the entrance, and the central square bay, surmounted by a cupola, is flanked by two fairly narrow rectangular barrel-vaulted bays. On axis on the E side is a small square chancel, itself surmounted by a small cupola. The articulation is all in *pietra serena*, with fluted Corinthian pilasters rising from a continuous low-level bench, the latter used for meetings of the chapter. The cupola has twelve radiating ribs rising

102 Santa Croce: west façade to the piazza, by Nicola Matas, 1853–63

103 Santa Croce: the Pazzi chapel from the west, begun by Brunelleschi in 1429–30, completed perhaps by Bernardo Rossellino or Giuliano da Maiano, 1459–61

104 Santa Croce: the Pazzi chapel: right side of the façade

105   Santa Croce: the Pazzi chapel: detail of the narthex or portico

106   Santa Croce: the Pazzi chapel: detail of roundel of *St John the Evangelist*, perhaps by Brunelleschi

107   Santa Croce: the south or second cloister, after 1453, probably by Bernardo Rossellino

from the drum, with small oculi in each facet around the base. At high level in the wall bays are roundels of the *Twelve Apostles*, in glazed ceramic, by Luca della Robbia. In the pendentives of the cupola: four more roundels, the *Evangelists*, perhaps by Brunelleschi himself. 106

Museo dell'Opera: The principal hall is the former refectory. Among the works are: a remarkable Crucifix by Cimabue, badly damaged in the 1966 floods, but painstakingly restored; on the end wall: a large fresco by Taddeo Gaddi (1333), of the *Tree of Life*, an allegorical Cross, the *Last Supper* and four narratives of *St Benedict*, *St Francis*, *St Louis of Toulouse* and *Christ and the Pharisees*. On the side walls: six fragments of fresco by Orcagna, depicting *Hell* and the *Triumph of Death*. Other works include frescoes or fragments by Gaddi and others. On the south side is the gilded bronze statue of *St Louis of Toulouse* by Donatello (1424), formerly in one of the tabernacles of Orsanmichele.

Room 2 contains stained glass and fresco fragments. Room 3 (former Cerchi chapel): frescoes and fragments from the della Robbia shop. Room 4: fourteenth- and fifteenth-century frescoes. Room 5: sculpture fragments, mostly fourteenth century.

Adjacent to the end room is the entrance to the second cloister, 107 reached through a rich portal by Benedetto da Maiano. The simple, elegant cloister (after 1453) is strongly influenced by Brunelleschi, and is probably by Bernardo Rossellino. All in *pietra serena*, with a lower cloister of arched colonnades, and roundels containing coats of arms in the spandrels; above is an upper loggia with a trabeated arcade.

4 VIA GHIBELLINA FROM THE BARGELLO TO THE CITY WALLS

From the corner of Via del Proconsolo walk E. On Via dei Giraldi (left) is the church of **San Procolo**, founded in the thirteenth century. Deconsecrated, with an eighteenth-century interior (1739–43); the church was dedicated to the guild of *beccai* (butchers), whose patron was St Peter.

On the second block, N side, is **Palazzo Borghese** (no. 110), a rare 108 example of a neo-Classical *palazzo*, occupying the whole block back to Via dei Pandolfini. It stands on the site of a fifteenth-century house by Michelozzo for the Salviati. In 1632 it was radically modernised by Gherardo Silvani for Vincenzo Salviati; of these works, the staircase and atrium survive. Michelozzo's loggia was also incorporated. At the end of the eighteenth century the Salviati became extinct and it became the property of Marcantonio Borghese. After 1821 the building was enlarged and transformed by Gaetano Baccani for Prince Camillo Borghese. An exceptionally broad façade, grandiose but restrained, with three wings and slightly projecting outer corners. The central wing is more richly detailed and projects slightly, with a strongly rusticated first order. In the centre of the *piano nobile* is a seven-bay row of Ionic semi-columns supporting a continuous entablature; deep niches at each end. In the attic: three semicircular lights, the central one flanked by angels in high relief. The outer wings are simpler, five bays each, with tall rectangular windows. Family coat of arms on the skyline. Inside: magnificently rich apartments, forty rooms in all; the most notable, on the *piano nobile*, include the Salone degli Specchi (with gilded mirrors, stucco and huge chandeliers) and the Galleria Monumentale, 35 m (approx. 115 ft) long; rich nineteenth-century decoration by Giuseppe Bezzuoli, Gasparo Martellini, Nicola Benvenuti and others.

Opposite Palazzo Borghese (no. 125) with a façade also to Via della Vigna Vecchia (nos. 7–9) is **Palazzo Covoni**, originally medieval (some frescoes survive on the first floor), but now mostly fifteenth century. A simple rendered façade.

Continuing E along Via Ghibellina, we reach Via Palmieri. On the corner is **Palazzo Salviati Quaratesi** (no. 102), early fourteenth century, built for the Salviati, with large ground-floor arches. An early semi-fortified *palazzo*. Six bays to the main façade, which has prominent rustication to the ground floor and mezzanine. Doorways with rusticated surrounds, and two upper floors with arched windows. Above is a later colonnaded *liagò*. Salviati coat of arms on the outer corners. On the other side of the street, this block was formerly occupied by notorious prisons, known as Le Stinche, built in 1301. They were surrounded by high blank stone walls and a moat, forming an 'island', hence the Via dell'Isola delle Stinche. They were demolished in 1838 and the present **Teatro Giuseppe Verdi** built on the site. Originally known as the Teatro Pagliano, its present name dates from 1901. Designed by Telemaco Bonaiuti for Girolamo Pagliano; the original theatre had stalls and six tiers of boxes, with a total capacity of 4,000. It was inaugurated on 10 September 1854 with Verdi's *Rigoletto*. Damaged by fire in 1865, but restored. It was comprehensively modernised in 1950 for Raffaello Castellani, and restored again after the 1966 floods. The theatre has also been used as a cinema, with (after 1966) the largest screen in Italy. It was damaged by fire again in 1984 but reopened four years later. The present capacity is around 1,600. The exterior is neo-Classical and restrained, with a rusticated lower order, and three upper orders of tall rectangular windows. The auditorium has a classic horseshoe plan, relatively deep, with gold and white decoration.

Briefly diverting down Via dell'Isola, on the right is **Palazzetto Salviati** (nos. 11–15r), originally fourteenth century, with jetties supporting the upper floors and a ground floor of *pietra forte*.

A little further down is the tiny Piazza San Simone; **Santi Simone e Giuda** is on the E side. Originating in a Benedictine oratory and documented since 1192, it was enlarged *circa* 1243, when it was given parish status. In 1621 it became a priory. Modernised by Gherardo Silvani in 1630, notably the interior. The work was patronised by Bartolomeo Galilei, a Knight of Malta. The façade is very simple; a sixteenth-century portal, capped by a semicircular arch; fresco in the lunette. Inside: an aisle-less hall, with perimeter articulation by two orders of *pietra serena* pilasters. Within the bays of the lower order are altars, five down each side; in the upper order a window to each bay. A richly decorated and gilded coffered ceiling, 1670, also funded by Galilei. A large triumphal arch to the chancel, which is surmounted by a very small cupola. The lateral altars have altarpieces by Jacopo Vignali, Onorio Marinari and others. Between the fourth and fifth left lateral altars is a glazed terracotta tabernacle by Andrea della Robbia, in which is a fourteenth-century bust of *St Ursula*.

On the diagonally opposite (NW) corner of the piazzetta is **Palazzo da Cintoia**, fourteenth century, built for the da Cintoia, and bought by Salviati *circa* 1430. Three orders, with both façades clad with *pietra forte*; the right façade has notable *sporti* carrying the upper floors.

Return to Via Ghibellina, continuing E. Via dei Pepi crosses it at right angles. At no. 7 is **Palazzo Pepi Ferri**, a substantial early fifteenth-century house, enlarged in the later fifteenth century and early sixteenth. Owned by the Strozzi and Pucci, in 1653 it was bought by the Pepi. Most of the façade remains fifteenth century, although the large aediculed ground-floor windows were added in the seventeenth. Inside: extraordinarily rich *sgraffito* decoration on the S wall of the courtyard. Executed in 1570, it remains in excellent condition.

Back on Via Ghibellina, no. 88 is **Palazzo Gherardi**, with a severe, rendered fifteenth-century façade; three orders, with the arched portal offset and flanked by square lights (3 + 4). The two upper orders have simple arched windows, two rows of ten, with continuous cornices as sill level. Inside: a small courtyard with filled-in arches.

Continue further E; no. 70 is the **Casa Buonarroti**, originally three houses bought by Michelangelo in 1508, and where he lived in 1516–25. He left them to his nephew Leonardo, who joined the houses together. The simple, restrained façade has three orders and seven bays, all rendered. Inside is a small attractive *cortile*. Leonardo's son, another Michelangelo, adapted part of the property to form a gallery dedicated to Michelangelo's work. Today it houses a small but interesting collection, established in 1868, and illustrates the development of the family house over more than two centuries. Cosimo Buonarroti left the house to the city in 1858. The museum was reordered in 1965. Ground floor: Etruscan and classical Roman works, as well as paintings and sculptures based on Michelangelo's works. First floor: two notable early reliefs by Michelangelo: *Battle of the Centaurs* and *Madonna della Scala*, both *circa* 1492, when he was only around seventeen.

In the other first-floor rooms: model for the completion of the façade of San Lorenzo, by Michelangelo, 1516, but never executed; in the same room: wooden model for a river god, *circa* 1524, probably for one of the tomb monuments in the Sagrestia Nuova at San Lorenzo; a small collection of his drawings. A suite of four rooms is decorated in celebration of Michelangelo's life, with works by Artemisia Gentileschi, Jacopo da Empoli and others; bronze head of *Michelangelo* based on his death mask, by Daniele da Volterra, 1564–6.

Directly opposite is **Palazzo Guicciardini Salviati** (no. 73). Late seventeenth century, by Pietro Paolo Giovanozzi, with window surrounds derived from Buontalenti.

Continuing E, out towards the former walls: on the N side, at no. 28 Via delle Conce, is **Palazzo Vivarelli Colonna**; built in the 1560s by the Gaburri, it passed to the della Stufa in the later eighteenth century, and to Michele Giuntini in 1808. The twelve-bay façade was partially modernised, as was the interior of the *piano nobile*, in the 1820s and 1830s, by artists including Gasparo Martellini and Giuseppe Bezzuoli. The fine garden was also remodelled in the same period, with a fountain and statues.

On the S side, nearly opposite, is the former church of **Santi Jacopo e Lorenzo**, late sixteenth century, by Antonio Lupicini, but long deconsecrated. It was occupied by Franciscan Poor Clares until 1808.

Further E is the former **Carcere delle Murate**. The site was originally occupied by a nunnery (established in 1424), whose occupants

108   Palazzo Borghese, 1821–2, by Gaetano Baccani: detail of upper façade

109   Palazzo Ramirez de Montalvo by Bartolomeo Ammannati; detail of the Medici arms, 1568–62

110   Palazzo Altoviti: detail of the herm depicting Donato Acciaioli, by Giovanni Battista Caccini, *circa* 1600–04

had previously lived in small cells ('le Murate') on the Ponte alle Grazie. The nunnery was rebuilt in 1471 and dedicated to St Catherine and the Annunciation. It was rebuilt again a century later, after floods. Suppressed by Napoleon in 1808, the site was then redeveloped as a prison (1832–1983). It fills the block between Via Ghibellina and Via dell' Agnolo; in 2002 it was converted to house the Faculty of Architecture, a museum and public housing. Bold balconies were added to the original structure, supported by tall steel tubes. Set within the perimeter wall (at no. 6) is the late sixteenth-century façade of the chapel of the **Madonna della Neve**.

South of Via Ghibellina: Between Via Ghibellina and Santa Croce are several parallel streets, all of them reaching Via di San Giuseppe and Largo Bargellini at their S end. Many retain their popular character.

Via delle Pinzochere (opposite Casa Buonarroti): at no. 3 is **Palazzo Bargellini**, formerly da Verrazzano. Said to stand on the site of the house of the humanist Poggio Bracciolini. Rebuilt *circa* 1505 for the da Cepparello, perhaps by Baccio d'Agnolo. In 1578 it was sold to the Alamaneschi, then in 1650 to the dell'Antella, and in 1662 it was bought by the senator Andrea da Verrazzano, a relative of the navigator. Today owned by the Bargellini; Piero Bargellini was mayor at the time of the 1966 floods. Three orders, the façade rendered, but with flat rusticated arches to the window and door openings. The internal courtyard was formerly colonnaded on two opposite sides, although one is lost. A small, attractive garden.

Three blocks further E is Via dei Macci; no. 11 is the little church of **San Francesco**, founded by the dei Macci in 1335, and occupied by Poor Clares, who also administered the adjacent hospital. It was rebuilt in 1704 by G.B. Foggini, with funding from Cosimo III. Fresco decoration by Piero Dandini. At the S end of Via dei Macci we reach Via di San Giuseppe. Turning left, after a very short distance is the deconsecrated

Santa Maria della Croce al Tempio: Fourteenth century in origin, the tiny oratory contains a large fifteenth-century fresco by Bicci di Lorenzo and Stefano d'Antonio. After 1424 it was the base of a confraternity, the Battuti Neri, which escorted condemned prisoners to their deaths at the Porta della Giustizia; suppressed in 1785. The church still contains the cross carried in these processions.

Further E along Via San Giuseppe, corner of Via delle Conce, is

San Giuseppe: Built in 1519, also for the Battuti Neri, by Baccio d'Agnolo. They remained until 1583, when it passed to the Minims of St Francesco da Paola. In 1784 it was made a parish foundation. Badly damaged in the 1966 floods. The façade is from 1759, late Baroque (rather neo-Classical) with three bays, the larger central one capped by a heavy pediment, and flanked by broad pilasters. A central portal with split pediment, and above it, a single rectangular light. The outer bays are much lower, very plain, linked to the central bay by volutes.

Inside: a nave flanked by lateral chapels, rather like the slightly earlier San Salvatore al Monte, by Il Cronaca, who was Baccio's teacher. Flat Composite pilasters define the nave bays, with semicircular arches to the side chapels; large clerestory lights above the nave entablature. The decoration is mostly late Baroque. Frescoes to the nave and chancel vaults by Sigismondo Betti, 1754. First right aisle chapel: by Gaetano Baccani, with nineteenth-century frescoes by Antonio Marini. Second chapel: decorated by Atanasio Bimbacci, 1705; fourteenth-century trip-tych by Taddeo Gaddi, and a fifteenth-century Crucifix. Third chapel: again by Baccani; on the altar: *Nativity* by Santi di Tito, 1564. On the high altar: painted Crucifix, early fifteenth century. The organ is mounted above and behind the altar, supported by a rich Baroque balcony. Chancel canvases by Jacopo Vignali and Francesco Bianchi Buonavita. Second left chapel: a venerated early sixteenth-century *Madonna del Giglio* by Raffaellino del Garbo.

The street continues E as Via dei Malcontenti. Extending as far as Viale della Giovine Italia and the line of the city walls were two monastic houses, Montedomini and Monticelli; both suppressed by Napoleon. The **Deposito di Mendicità**, a home for the poor, was established on the sites in 1808, and was designed by Giuseppe del Rosso. Simple neo-Classical façades. On the restoration of the house of Lorraine in 1815, it was reformed and took the name of **Pia Casa di Lavoro**, housing the poor, the disabled and the old and infirm. Today it still houses the old and infirm, but also supports students and con-valescents recovering after surgery.

5 VIA DEI PANDOLFINI AND BORGO DEGLI ALBIZI

Via dei Pandolfini runs E–W one block north of Via Ghibellina; it terminates at its west end at Via del Proconsolo. Although originally medieval, the street has a largely sixteenth-century character today.

At its E end (corner of Via Giuseppe Verdi) is the oratory of **San Niccolò del Ceppo**, built by the homonymous confraternity. Founded in the fourteenth century, it moved to this site in 1561–2; it survived the general suppression of 1785. Renaissance portal in *pietra serena*. Inside the hall (restored 2009): sail vaults with frescoes by Giovanni Domenico Ferretti and others. The altarpiece is a seventeenth-century *Crucifixion* by Francesco Curradi.

The next section of the street W is lined by fourteenth-century houses, mostly modernised in the sixteenth century. No. 12 is **Palazzo Arrighi**; no. 16 is **Palazzo Medici Tornaquinci**; no. 18 is **Palazzetto Rittafè**, still of fourteenth-century appearance (restored). No. 20 is the most notable, **Palazzo Galli-Tassi**, built for the Valori in the early sixteenth century, over an earlier structure; acquired by the Galli-Tassi in 1623. The ground floor retains the fourteenth-century structure, but the aediculed windows were formed in the sixteenth, as was the top-floor loggia (later filled in) and the *sgraffito* decoration. The courtyard has medieval elements, including characteristic fourteenth-century octagonal columns. The neo-Classical staircase was added in 1762–3 by Gaspare Maria Paoletti. Inside are 1620s frescoes.

Further W again is the long N flank of Palazzo Borghese (see Via Ghibellina, above). On the next corner is San Procolo (see also above). Just beyond, Via dei Pandolfini reaches Via del Proconsolo.

Borgo degli Albizi: The Borgo, formerly Borgo San Pier Maggiore, extends E beyond the former inner circle of medieval walls, an extension of the ancient Roman *cardo*, the present Corso. Like Via Ghibellina and Via dei Pandolfini, it became enclosed by the second communal walls of 1173. Although the street line is medieval, most of the buildings are sixteenth century. Start at the corner of Via del Proconsolo, although the numeration runs from E to W.

No. 28 (N side), just after Palazzo Nonfinito, is **Palazzo Pazzi della Colombaria**, the affix deriving from the eighteenth-century literary society of that name, which met here. Although the house is late fifteenth century, the façade was rebuilt for the Pazzi; often attributed to Ammannati, although undocumented. Boldly modelled, with a pedimented portal, three aediculed ground-floor windows, and four pedimented windows to the *piano nobile*, decorated with the family coat of arms. The Accademia was founded here in 1735 by Giovanni Girolamo de' Pazzi.

Nos. 23–7 is **Palazzo Tanagli**, or dal Borro, once owned by the *condottiere* Alessandro dal Borro. No. 26 is **Palazzo Ramirez de Mon-**

talvo. By Ammannati, *circa* 1568, and built for Antonio Ramirez, a Castilian nobleman in the service of Cosimo I. The property had been acquired ten years earlier, and the present house was formed by the unification of several structures, hence the off-centre portal (Ramirez coat of arms above). In the centre of the ground floor there is instead a large aediculed window; big rectangular lights with rusticated surrounds to the *piani nobili*, each of five bays. Directly above the central first-floor window is an ostentatious Medici coat of arms. The *sgraffito* 109 decoration of the *Virtues*, in four orders, now badly deteriorated, is by Poccetti, to a design by Vasari.

No. 18 is the imposing **Palazzo Altoviti**, on the site of three earlier houses, of which the central one was owned by the Albizi. It was modernised by Baccio Valori, who employed Caccini (*circa* 1600–04) to unite the three with a new façade. Above the portal: bust of *Cosimo I de' Medici*. Large rectangular lights to the upper floors. The façade is decorated with fifteen marble herms with portraits of notable Florentines, also by Caccini, 1600–04; they include *Marsilio Ficino, Francesco Guicciardini, Alberti, Dante, Petrarch, Donato Acciaioli* and *Boccaccio*. In 1687 the 110 palace passed to the Guicciardini, then by marriage to the Altoviti.

No. 15 is another Albizi house, **Palazzo degli Alessandri**. Badly damaged by fire during the Ciompi riots in 1378, it was owned by Alessandro and Bartolomeo Albizi, who changed their surname to Alessandri. Restored *circa* 1400, as one of the most notable houses in the city, with three portals and an eight-bay façade. The detailing is in *pietra forte*, and the lower order is rusticated. In the early nineteenth century it was owned by the senator Giovanni degli Alessandri, patron of Canova; the house contains a collection of his and other neo-Classical works. It incorporates one of several towers of the Donati.

No. 14 is another Albizi house, also based on a truncated thirteenth-century tower, and conserving some fourteenth-century material; family coat of arms. It is contiguous with no. 12, **Palazzo degli Albizi**. From the thirteenth century the family owned many properties in this street, from the Canto dei Pazzi as far as the Canto alle Rondini. This was their principal residence, modernised *circa* 1500, with a new façade attributed to Il Cronaca. Three storeys, with square windows with stone frames to the ground floor, arched to the two upper floors, with rusticated surrounds. Extensively modernised internally by Gherardo Silvani, 1625–34.

Continuing E, no. 11 is **Palazzo Tassinari** (also Albizi Donati), which incorporates another tower, also formerly of the Donati; Corso Donati was leader of the Black Guelphs at the time of Dante. The building was re-faced in the seventeenth century, with a rather Mannerist façade; four bays and four orders. We now reach Piazza San Pier Maggiore. No. 35 is the **Torre dei Corbizi** or Donati; the attached Corbizi house has stone *sporti* supporting the upper floors. The tower is tall and narrow, with six floors. It had an important strategic location, controlling access into the city from the E.

The only surviving element of the former ancient church of **San Pier Maggiore**, founded in the eleventh century, is the large three-bay loggia or narthex on the SE side of the piazza. Three arches and a bold entablature, all in *pietra serena*. The church was rebuilt by Matteo Nigetti in 1638, but was demolished in 1783 because it had become structurally dangerous. A roadway now passes through the central arch.

6 VIA PIETRAPIANA AND SANT'AMBROGIO

Via Pietrapiana continues the axis of Borgo degli Albizi E, extending as far as the city's former outer walls. The zone between Via dell'Agnolo, Via Pietrapiana, Via Giuseppe Verdi and Borgo Allegri was demolished by the Fascists in the mid-1930s, but the planned rational redevelopment never took place, and after 1945 it was rebuilt in a piecemeal manner.

Via Pietrapiana starts at Piazza Salvemini. On the S side, occupying the whole block, is the **Sede Provinciale delle Poste e Telegrafi** by Giovanni Michelucci, 1959–67. A rather complex form, with the façade planes at different angles. The plan is a U, based around a double-height central space for the public, treated as an internal street. The main hall has a roof of reinforced concrete parabolas. Above are the regional offices of the post service. On the N side of the street, no. 32 is **Palazzo Fioravanti**, with a strongly modelled façade sometimes attributed to Ammannati; coat of arms above the portal.

Continuing E, we reach Piazza dei Ciompi (right), one of the Fascist-era clearances, and named after the medieval wool workers who rebelled in 1378; many lived and worked in this area. Along the N edge is the **Loggia del Pesce**, relocated from its original site along the W side of the Mercato Vecchio, as part of the nineteenth-century 'improvements' that formed the Piazza della Repubblica; it was reassembled here in 1951, but was given no definable function. Designed by Vasari (1567), it has a double colonnade of square columns, nine bays, sup-

111 San Pier Maggiore: remains of the façade, by Matteo Nigetti, 1638

112 The Loggia del Pesce, by Giorgio Vasari, 1567

113 Sant'Ambrogio: campanile from the east

porting semicircular arches. In the spandrels are polychrome terracotta roundels, depicting fish and sea creatures; coat of arms of the grand dukes on the outer corners. Opposite the Loggia is **Palazzo Pascolutti**, sixteenth century.

On the E side of the piazza is a sixteenth-century tabernacle; and at no. 11 is the house and workshop once owned by Lorenzo Ghiberti. Running down the W side of the piazza is Via Buonarroti. **Palazzo Gerini** (no. 10) was once owned by the Fioravanti, but bought by the Gerini in 1451. The main façade has three orders and seven bays. In 1941 the Centro Didattico Nazionale was established here, and the interior was comprehensively modernised by Giovanni Michelucci and Leonardo Ricci. Public gardens to the N and S.

At the E end of Via Pietrapiana is Piazza Sant'Ambrogio, and the church of

113 **Sant'Ambrogio**: One of the oldest foundations in the city, documented in 988, when it was a Benedictine house. Rebuilt at the end of the thirteenth century, and again *circa* 1486, when the Cappella del Miracolo and the lateral altars were added. The last major modernisation was in 1716 by G.B. Foggini. At the SE corner is the campanile, probably from the reconstruction of 1486.

The simple rendered façade appears Gothic but was largely rebuilt in the nineteenth century. Inside: a broad square nave, with an open timber trussed roof, and prominent side altars, five down each side. At the east end: triumphal arch to the chancel, capped by a pediment and flanked by curved side wings with choir balconies, all modified by Foggini. The chancel is flanked by two lateral chapels. In the twentieth century the original Gothic windows on the right side were reopened.

Inside the façade: *Deposition* by Niccolò di Pietro Gerini. Right side: first altar: badly damaged fourteenth-century fresco. In the floor: tomb of the architect Il Cronaca (Simone del Pollaiolo). Second altar: *Virgin and Child Enthroned* by Matteo di Pacino, late fourteenth century. Third altar: *Crucifix with Four Saints*, late fifteenth century.

The left chancel chapel is the Cappella del Miracolo: beautiful marble tabernacle by Mino da Fiesole, 1481, commemorating a eucharistic miracle; the relics, said to have saved the city from plague in 1340, are still venerated there. Mino is buried in the floor adjacent. On the back wall: fresco by Cosimo Rosselli (*circa* 1486) depicting a procession with the chalice in front of the church; vault frescoes also by Rosselli. Fourth left altar: altarpiece by Raffaellino del Garbo, early sixteenth century; in the floor: tomb of Andrea del Verrocchio, 1488. Third altar: *Virgin and Child in Glory* by Cosimo Rosselli, 1498–1501. Second altar: *Visitation* by Andrea Boscoli, 1597. Adjacent to the first altar: tomb of the painter Francesco Granacci (+1543).

Adjacent to the church, at no. 36 Borgo La Croce is the little **Oratorio dei Santi Crispino e Crespianino**, dedicated to two early Christian martyrs. Now used as a mortuary chapel. The lively Borgo continues E as far as the former city walls (see below).

Taking Via dei Macci s of the church, then left into Via del Verrocchio, we reach the **Mercato Sant'Ambrogio**, 1873; one of three built contemporaneously, all by Giuseppe Mengoni, the second being the central market of San Lorenzo (q.v.) and the third, since demolished, at San Frediano. A simple, functional rectangular structure, smaller than the Mercato Centrale, with the long axis N–S.

7 THE NORTH-EAST CORNER OF THE *QUARTIERE*

This zone is bounded to the NE by the line of the city walls, to the W by Borgo Pinti and to the s by Via Pietrapiana and Borgo La Croce.

From Sant'Ambrogio take Via dei Pilastri NW and then Via Farini N. On the right, behind impressive railings, is a synagogue, the

Tempio Israelitico: An imposing pile by Vincenzo Micheli, Marco Treves and Mariano Falcini, 1874–82, patronised by David Levi. Restored *circa* 2005. An eclectic mixture of Moorish and Byzantine elements, but also using the local tradition of alternating bands of different coloured marbles. The exterior is clad with travertine from Colle Val d'Elsa and *pomato* from Assisi. The principal façade has three orders; the lowermost is an elegant portico, with paired columns. The second order (the level of the women's gallery) has three bays, each with a *bifora*; the third order also has three bays, but with a central *trifora* flanked by single lights. The whole is crowned by a large sweeping semicircular arch, above and behind which rises a tall, bright green, copper-clad cupola on a drum. The façade is flanked by paired towers of Moorish inspiration, and with miniature copper 'onion' cupolas. The interior is as rich and polychromatic as the exterior; painted decoration by Giovanni Panti.

Continue to the end of Via Farini; to the NE is an extensive rectangular square, **Piazza Massimo d'Azeglio**. One of several large-scale works of modernisation planned by Giuseppe Poggi, it was to form the heart of this district, known as Mattonaia. It was set out in 1864–6, largely on the grounds of the lost Villa Ginori. The piazza is laid out as a garden. Surrounding it are fairly homogeneous blocks of apartments, most early twentieth century, mostly four or five storeys, and mostly neo-Classical, although some are *quattrocento* Renaissance in style. Some are rather more eclectic: for example, **Villino Uzielli** (nos. 38–9), by Paolo Emilio Andree. No. 28 is **Palazzo Wilson Gattai**, designed for himself by the British artist Frederick Wilson, *circa* 1870. A rusticated ground floor and neo-Renaissance *piano nobile* with arched lights; a large balcony. On top is a covered loggia. The interior is in the Liberty style by Eugenio Gattai.

One block E of Piazza d'Azeglio is Via della Mattonaia, in which is the former Carmelite convent of **Santa Teresa d'Avila**. Founded in 1628, after the general suppression it was converted to a prison in 1866, and after the 1966 flood was converted for other uses. The stone rotunda of the church survives.

Back in the piazza, from the SW corner, take Via Colonna a short distance NW. The street was cut through the middle of the convent of Santa Maria Maddalena de' Pazzi, in conjunction with the setting out of Piazza d'Azeglio. To the left is the **Liceo Classico Michelangiolo**, which contains the convent's cloisters of 1542. At the next junction turn left onto Borgo Pinti. A short way along (left), no. 58 is

Santa Maria Maddalena de' Pazzi: Founded in 1257, together with the adjacent Benedictine convent. After 1265 it was occupied by the Convertite, an order suppressed by Pope Eugenius IV in 1442, when it passed to the Cistercians; in 1520 it was occupied by nuns of Santa Maria degli Angeli of San Frediano, one of whose members was Caterina de' Pazzi, who took the name Maria Maddalena; she was canonised in 1609, after which the site became a pilgrimage destination. From 1628 to 1888 it was occupied by Carmelites. After 1928, in turn, it was occupied by French Augustinians. Extensively restored after the 1966 floods.

The principal architectural interest is the work commissioned in 1479 by the Cistercians from Giuliano da Sangallo; he transformed the church, *circa* 1480–1500, with funding from Bartolomeo Scala, whose own palace he also designed (see below). Said to be Giuliano's first architectural work, the church is approached by an *androne* and then a square colonnaded atrium or cloister, *circa* 1490, funded by the Salviati: a work of great simplicity and refinement: Ionic colonnades supporting

114 The Tempio Israelitico (synagogue): west façade; by Vincenzo Micheli, 1874–82

115 Santa Maria Maddalena de' Pazzi: the entrance cloister by Giuliano da Sangallo, *circa* 1480–1500

116 Piazza Cesare Beccaria: detail of one of the enclosing blocks, by Giuseppe Poggi, 1865–74

a continuous flat trabeation, four bays on each side of the central approach arch on both the outer entrance wall and the identical arch on the opposite face; the first time flat trabeation had been used in this way in the Renaissance. The two arches are the only features breaking its continuity; both are on axis with the church itself, the simple façade of which rises above and behind.

The church interior resembles the contemporaneous San Salvatore al Monte, by Il Cronaca: a central nave, with six deep rectangular chapels down each side, and each side bay approached by an arch in *pietra serena*. The chapels have sail vaults, while the nave is covered with a richly painted fresco by Jacopo Chiavistelli. After 1480 the interior was elaborated with paintings and altarpieces by Botticelli, Perugino and others, today dispersed.

Right side chapels: works by Francesco Curradi and others.

The principal feature is the chancel, which is a mausoleum to the saint. Rich and robust Roman Baroque, designed by Ciro Ferri (a Roman colleague of Pietro da Cortona) and supervised by Pier Francesco Silvani, 1675–7; complex cladding and decoration; columns of red and yellow marble. The cupola is frescoed by Piero Dandini, 1701, depicting the saint ascending to heaven; the altarpiece is the *Virgin and St Mary Magdalene* by Ferri; two lateral pictures by Luca Giordano.

Left side chapels: works by Raffaellino del Garbo, Santi di Tito and Curradi.

From the sacristy, via an underground passageway, we reach the former Sala Capitolare (chapter house). The principal work, occupying the whole end wall, is a beautiful frescoed *Crucifixion* by Perugino, 1493–6; a triptych framed by the three arched bays of the structure, well preserved and highly refined.

The line of the former city walls: Take Borgo Pinti N (the street forms the boundary between the *quartieri* of Santa Croce and San Giovanni). For Borgo Pinti itself, see pp. 181, 220. At the far end, we reach Viale Matteotti, on the line of the former city walls. To the right is the large oval open space, Piazzale Donatello, occupied by the

Cimitero degli Inglesi: Also known as the Cimitero dei Protestanti, established in 1828 just beyond the site of the former Porta Pinti, and modified by Giuseppe Poggi in his master plan for the city. Among those buried here is Elizabeth Barrett Browning. Continuing S along Viale Antonio Gramsci, we reach **Piazza Cesare Beccaria**, another of the large open squares laid out by Poggi, retaining the medieval **Porta alla Croce** in the centre. The piazza is named after the marchese della Beccaria (1738–94) a notable Enlightenment figure who tried to reform the judicial system; his views of 'equality for all before the law' were highly influential. The gate is from *circa* 1284, when the outer walls were built. The site was the traditional place for public executions; prisoners were brought here from the nearby Stinche prisons. The piazza, elliptical on plan, was the first of Poggi's to be set out (1865–74). Monumental neo-Classical blocks define the space, some with a rusti- 116 cated ground floor and a giant order of Corinthian semi-columns to the two *piani nobili*, capped by a strong cornice. Above is a low attic behind a balustrade. Others blocks are simpler, in a *quattrocento* Renaissance manner, with tall arched ground-floor colonnades and two orders of regularly spaced pedimented windows.

From the S end of the piazza two major streets lead towards the Arno: Viale della Giovine Italia and Viale Giovanni Amendola. In the large triangular plot between the two is the **Archivio di Stato**, by Italo Gamberini, Franco Bonaiuti and others, 1978–86, following a competition in 1971. The basic form consists of two long rectangular blocks; that along Viale Amendola contains six levels of archive storage, with floors that cantilever progressively up the building. Along Viale della Giovine Italia, instead, is a series of glazed circulation routes and staircases, with blocks containing administration and laboratory functions. Down the centre between the two blocks is a linear atrium. The archive, previously at the Uffizi, is one of the richest and most important in Europe. Also on Viale Amendola, adjacent to Piazza Beccaria: **Nostra Signora degli Angeli**, neo-Gothic, occupied by Camaldolesi until 1938; inside, a single nave with open timber roof.

Adjacent, at Viale della Giovine Italia no. 4, is the headquarters of *La Nazione* newspaper, by Pier Luigi Spadolini, 1961–6. A complex of elements, fragmented, each containing different functions, and mostly clad with precast concrete panels.

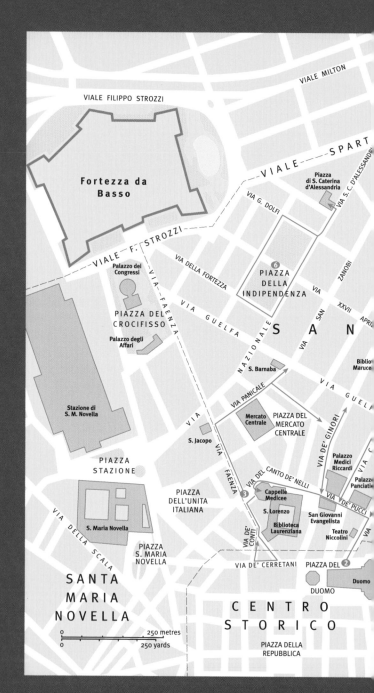

The *Quartiere* of San Giovanni Battista

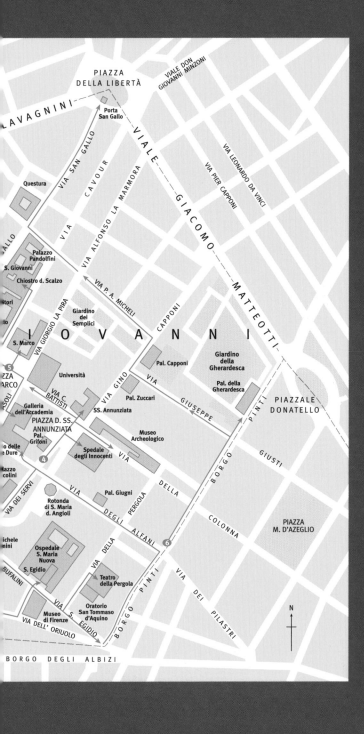

The *Quartiere* of San Giovanni Battista

This series of walks covers the north-central section of the city, that is, the *quartiere* of San Giovanni, named after the baptistery in its S corner. The walks generally proceed from the centre outwards, and from E to W. The innermost zone, centred on Palazzo Medici and San Lorenzo, is intimately identified with the Medici, whose influence over the development of the district was considerable.

I SANTA MARIA NUOVA AND VICINITY

This walk covers a compact rectangle bounded by Via dell'Oriuolo (S), Borgo Pinti (E), Via dei Servi (W) and Via degli Alfani (N). The Arcispedale di Santa Maria Nuova is in the centre.

Via dell'Oriuolo: Runs SE from the SE corner of the Piazza del Duomo to meet Borgo Pinti at Piazza Salvemini. Nos. 37–9 is the imposing pile of the Banca d'Italia, built 1865–9, when Florence was briefly the Italian capital. By Antonio Cipolla, in a robust late sixteenth-century neo-Renaissance style. A long façade, eleven bays, with the three at each end projecting slightly. Rusticated quoins. A tall rusticated ground floor, with a three-bay colonnade to the central wing, supporting a balcony. Two upper floors, with pedimented windows, and a monumental cornice. Next door, no. 35 is **Palazzo Bastogi**, mid-eighteenth century, the seat of the Archivio Storico del Comune. A boldly articulated façade, six bays and three orders, with a large portal surmounted by a balcony. Aediculed ground-floor windows; Baroque pediments to the *piano nobile*. Rich early nineteenth-century neo-Classical interiors.

Continue to the E end of Via dell'Oriuolo, where it meets Via Sant'Egidio at a sharp angle. In the angle is **Palazzo Busini** or the Palazzo degli Sporti, from the notable *sporti* that run down both main façades; none on the three short bays at the E end. The principal façade has seven bays with two upper orders of square lights. The design has been associated (without documentation) to Michelangelo.

Return back down Via dell'Oriuolo. No. 24 (N side) is the entrance to the **Museo di Firenze com'era**, within a group of structures also containing the Biblioteca Comunale Centrale and the Archivio Storico di Firenze.

The museum is housed in former conventual buildings of the Suore Oblate. The attractive entrance garden is bounded on two sides by fifteenth-century colonnaded wings, with octagonal columns and loggias above. The small museum has two wings, one archaeological, the other containing a collection of historic maps, plans and views of the city. Among the exhibits are: a scale model of the Roman city; a well-known series of lunettes depicting the Medici villas by Giusto Utens, 1599; a model of the Mercato Vecchio prior to its destruction; a copy of the famous 'della Catena' view of the city originally painted in 1470; and a series of views of the city by Giuseppe Zocchi, published in 1754.

Along the W side of the Museo is Via Folco Portinari, named after the man who founded the Arcispedale Santa Maria Nuova (see below) and the father of Dante's Beatrice.

Via Portinari terminates at Piazza Santa Maria Nuova. To the left is Via Maurizio Bufalini; no. 6 is the **Cassa di Risparmio di Firenze**; its origins lie in **Palazzo Pucci**, nos. 10 and 12, late sixteenth century, of which only the façade now remains. One of the Pucci descendants, Giuseppe (1782–1838), was a founder of the Cassa di Risparmio, as was Piero Guicciardini, a later owner of the palace. In 1865 it was sold to the new bank; the original front block was modernised by Antonio Cipolla, 1869, but was radically transformed in 1953–7 with a large new rear extension by Michelucci. The principal element is the spacious public hall, with a central axis (characteristic of his work), with administrative offices on one side and public banking activities on the other. The hall has an elegant exposed concrete roof, with inverted trough beams. Nearby is **Palazzo Compagni**, rebuilt by Zanobi del Rosso, mid-eighteenth century. Five large bays, with a central portal surmounted by a balcony; tall aediculed lights in *pietra serena* to the upper floors.

At the W end of Via Bufalini, corner of Via dei Servi, is

San Michele Visdomini, popularly San Michelino. The original church stood further SW, but was demolished in 1363 to build the E parts of the cathedral. It was transferred here, where it replaced an earlier structure. In 1552 it was acquired by the Celestine order, which rebuilt it (*circa* 1560), and established a number of chapels. It was further restored after being badly damaged in the 1966 floods; fourteenth-century frescoes were identified in the transept.

A very simple façade with the arms of the Visdomini, and a short inscription.

Inside: a single nave with five chapels down each side. First right altar: altarpiece: *Nativity* by Jacopo da Empoli, early seventeenth century. Second right altar: altarpiece: *Virgin and Child with Saints*, a 'Sacra Conversazione', by Pontormo, 1518. At the end of the right transept: *Birth of the Virgin* by Agostino Ciampelli, 1593. In the adjacent sacristy: rare fifteenth-century stalls with intarsia decoration. Right chancel chapel: frescoes attributed to Spinello Aretino, late fourteenth century. Left chancel chapel: fourteenth-century wooden Crucifix and frescoes.

At the end of the left transept: *Resurrection* by Francesco Morandini (Poppi), late sixteenth century; third left altar: altarpiece: *Immaculate Conception*, also by Poppi. Second left altar: *St John the Baptist Preaching* by Passignano. First left altar: altarpiece: *Virgin and Child*, again by Poppi. Cupola frescoes by Niccolò Lapi, late seventeenth century.

Return SE down Via Bufalini into Piazza Santa Maria Nuova.

Arcispedale di Santa Maria Nuova: The oldest hospital in Florence, 118 founded in 1288 by Folco Portinari. It was expanded greatly to cope with the devastating plague of 1348, and consisted of three elements; a wing for men to the E, one for women to the SW (on the present Via Folco Portinari), and the church of Sant'Egidio (San Gilio), W of the men's wing. In the fifteenth century it was modernised and further enlarged, with the cloister of the Medicherie, by Bicci di Lorenzo, 1420. The church was also enlarged in the same period, with a grand altarpiece of the *Coronation of the Virgin* by Lorenzo Monaco, now in the Uffizi. The new choir was frescoed by Piero della Francesca, Domenico Veneziano and Andrea del Castagno. The cycle was almost entirely lost in a further modernisation at the end of the sixteenth century, by Buontalenti, completed after his death by Giulio Parigi.

This modernisation included the imposing colonnade across the front and the E wing. The detached fourteenth-century women's wing was replaced by a new W wing, built in 1660, to a cruciform plan, similar to that for men. In the Napoleonic era, many works of art from suppressed monasteries were assembled here.

Buontalenti's impressive façade has two orders, with an arched colonnade to the lower one; five bays on each side of the central portal, divided by flat Corinthian pilasters. The portal is emphasised by free-standing columns and is surmounted by a balcony. This colonnade was completed after 1612 by Giulio Parigi; the upper order did not follow until the early eighteenth century. It has large aediculed windows; simple triangular pediments, except to the central bay, with a more elaborate split pediment. The two projecting end wings were part of the original proposal; they extend forward three bays, detailed in the same way as the main central wing, with broad paired pilasters at the outer corners. The right wing was built in 1707–10, but the matching W wing was finally added only in 1960.

Sant'Egidio is reached directly from the central portal. Inside: late sixteenth-century modernisation by Buontaleni. A shallow vaulted ceiling with frescoes by Matteo Bonechi, early eighteenth century. Right wall: remains of the fourteenth-century tomb of Folco Portinari. First left altar: *St Louis of France* by Volterrano, *circa* 1665. Second left altar: *Deposition* by Alessandro Allori, 1579.

Immediately E of the church is the Chiostro delle Medicherie, with an early sixteenth-century *Pietà* by Giovanni della Robbia. On the opposite (W) side of the church is a loggia, beyond which is the Chiostro delle Ossa (burial ground); from the cloister, stairs rise to the hospital's administrative offices. A number of paintings and sculptures are kept here, including works by Alessandro Allori, Andrea del Castagno and Andrea della Robbia.

At the SE corner of the hospital, **Via della Pergola** runs NE. A short distance along on the right (no. 8) is the **Oratorio di San Tommaso d'Aquino** by Santi di Tito, 1568–73; the adjacent *ospizio* is mostly lost. Inside: barrel-vaulted frescoed ceiling and a high altarpiece of *St Thomas Aquinas Presenting his Work to the Crucified Christ*, also by Santi di Tito. Immediately adjacent (nos. 12–30) is the long façade of the **Teatro della Pergola**. The second oldest theatre in the city; first built (in timber) in 1656 by Ferdinando Tacca for the Accademia degli Immobili. Later, it became the official theatre of the grand duchy, but was opened to the public for the first time in 1718. It was rebuilt more permanently in 1755 by Giulio Mannaioni, but was modernised again by Bartolomeo Silvestri in 1828. It was the first theatre in Italy to have superimposed layers of galleries and boxes, rather than the historic, classical raked auditorium. The neo-Classical foyer, vestibule and café are by Gaetano Baccani, 1857. Major structural restoration was necessary after the 1966 floods. The elegant horseshoe-shaped auditorium is richly carved and decorated, and contains three tiers of boxes above the stalls; above the boxes is a continuous upper-level colonnade. In the centre is the grand ducal box.

Return to Via Sant'Egidio and turn left (SE), continuing to the junction with Via dell'Oriuolo. Then turn left (N) along

Borgo Pinti: The Borgo defines the E boundary of the *quartiere* of San Giovanni and extends in a straight line NE as far as the former city walls; it was formerly the main route to Fiesole, and terminated at the lost Porta Pinti (*pinti* = penitents). No. 13, opposite Via di Mezzo, is **Palazzo Roffia**, from the family who acquired the site in 1646. Late seventeenth century, by G.B. Foggini, with an attractive façade; the portal surmounted by a balcony, and coat of arms in the tympanum. The *piano nobile* has alternating pediments: triangular and segmental; a rich, ornate cornice. Inside: decoration by Giovanni Domenico Ferretti and others. No. 26 is **Palazzo Bellini** or Quaratesi, a house allocated by the grand duchy to official court sculptors. It was given by Ferdinando I to Giambologna, who lived and worked here until his death in 1608, as – later – did G.B. Foggini and others. On the façade: bust of *Ferdinando I de' Medici* (1603), attributed to Giambologna. No. 27 is **Palazzo Marzichi Lenzi**, sixteenth century, on the site of a fourteenth-century structure. Four bays, with rusticated surrounds to the portal and upper windows. No. 33 (corner of Via Nuova dei Caccini) is **Palazzo Caccini Ferrantini**, originally early fifteenth century but modernised in the late sixteenth. A long, thirteen-bay façade, with ground floor, mezzanine and two upper floors. The loggia to the rear garden is frescoed by Bernardino Poccetti, late sixteenth century. A notable garden was established by Matteo Caccini in the late sixteenth century, but only a small part survives. At no. 56, near the junction with Via dei Pilastri, is the former **Liceo Regio**, by Giuseppe del Rosso, 1812–13, who incorporated the former convent of Santa Maria di Candeli. A neo-Classical façade. The church was modernised by G.B. Foggini in 1703, and has a rich late Baroque interior. Vault fresco of the *Assumption* by Niccolò Lapi. Today it houses the Carabinieri headquarters. At the junction with Via degli Alfani, turn left. Continue W, crossing Via della Pergola.

No. 48 (N side) is the notable **Palazzo Giugni**, by Ammannati, *circa* 1577. His patron was the banker Simone da Firenzuola. A simple but refined and imposing façade, with rusticated quoins; three orders and five bays. The central bay, containing the portal, is further emphasised by a balcony and a prominent coat of arms. Plain rendered wall surfaces, with stone string courses. The prominent ground-floor windows are aediculed, while the first and second floors have large rectangular windows surrounded by flat rustication. On top is a square loggia, not visible from the street, with views in all directions.

Inside: a colonnaded rectangular Doric courtyard in *pietra serena*. Above: first-floor loggias (Ionic) on two sides (E and W), with *pietra serena* pilasters. The courtyard gives direct access to the garden. The rear façade resembles that of a villa; on the top floor is a three-bay loggia, with paired colonnettes. At the far end of the garden is a Mannerist fountain, with a figure of a *Giant*, crushed by a landslide of rocks from a mountainside. The palace passed to Simone's daughter, Verginia, who married into the Giugni; it remained in Giugni ownership until 1830, when it was sold to the Doria Colonna and della Porta; it then passed to the Fraschetti, who still own it.

Opposite, at no. 39 (left), is the former church of **Santa Maria degli Angioli.** A simple façade; portal surmounted by a 'thermal' window and the whole capped by a triangular pediment, probably sixteenth century.

Inside: frescoes by Alessandro Gherardini, *circa* 1700. Attached (S side) is a cloister, by Gherardo Silvani, 1628, with lunettes originally frescoed by Poccetti. At the corner of Via del Castellaccio is the **Rotonda del Brunelleschi** or **di Santa Maria degli Angioli.**

The latter is the formal dedication, since on this site was established a Camaldolesian convent, founded in 1295 by the Knights of Malta. It was suppressed in 1810 and its conventual buildings were annexed to the nearby Arcispedale di Santa Maria Nuova. Most is now considerably altered, but the Rotonda was designed by Brunelleschi and begun in 1433–4. It remained incomplete as a result of lack of funding, and the upper part was finally completed, perfunctorily, only in 1936. The upper octagonal drum and facetted pitched roof do not follow Brunelleschi's original design. Today it is occupied by the university.

The Rotonda was sponsored by Andrea and Matteo Scolari, to an octagonal plan; it was to form the choir for the adjacent church, and marked an important stage in Brunelleschi's development of centralised three-dimensional forms. The external envelope has sixteen facets, originally defined by alternating niches and windows. The interior is an octagon, and each of the eight facets terminates around the perimeter with a chapel. The chapels have a rectangular plan, but with little semicircular apses to left and right. The choir was intended to be roofed by an octagonal cupola, like that on Santa Maria del Fiore, standing on an octagonal drum. Each of the external facets was to have been crowned by a triangular pedimented gable.

To the E of Piazza Brunelleschi, itself a rather formless space, is the **Chiostro Grande** of the former monastery; early seventeenth century, by Matteo Nigetti. The second cloister, the Chiostro degli Angeli, is by Gherardo Silvani, 1628; arched colonnades on all four sides; lunettes frescoed by Poccetti, *circa* 1601. The third cloister, the Chiostro dei Morti, is adjacent to the Via degli Alfani entrance, and again has four colonnades surmounted by a covered loggia.

From the Rotonda, continue NW on Via degli Alfani past the junction with Via dei Servi; on the right (no. 78) is the **Opificio delle Pietre Dure**. The Opificio was founded in 1588 by Ferdinando I, as a workshop specialising in rich, complex, inlaid work in many types and colours of marble, known as *pietra dura*. The workshops were originally at the Casinò Mediceo (q.v.), but later moved to the Uffizi, and finally here in 1796 into the palace originally built by Ammannati in 1577. They remain a renowned centre for the manufacture and restoration of these works. The decoration of the Cappella dei Principi at San Lorenzo was made by the Opificio; former directors included Buontalenti and Nigetti. Further W, no. 84 is **Palazzo Baldi** (seventeenth century?), five bays and three orders, with a large off-centre rusticated arched portal.

Return E back to the junction with Via dei Servi, and turn S (right), back towards the cathedral; fine views of the cupola. On the right, no. 15 is **Palazzo Niccolini,** formerly **Montalto**. Originally built for Bastiano Ciaini on the site of five houses, acquired in 1548. Attributed to Domenico di Baccio d'Agnolo and Giovanni Antonio Dosio, 1548–50. After Bastiano's death (1552), the house and the family villa were both bought by Giovanni Niccolini. The façade was frescoed *circa* 1660 by Volterrano and Vincenzo Meucci. Four orders and six bays; a notable similarity to the Ginori palace on Via dei Ginori of thirty years earlier (by Baccio). The off-centre portal has an arched rusticated surround. Pronounced rustication to the quoins, but only on the two lower orders. The first and second *piani nobili* are almost identical, except for the rusticated window surrounds to the former. On top: a full-width covered *liagò*. The refined courtyard is attributed to Baccio; Doric colonnades on three sides, with columns and arches in *pietra serena*. Beyond is a garden, with a nineteenth-century layout by Francis Sloane.

Continuing towards the cathedral, no. 12 (corner of Via del Castellaccio), is **Palazzo Sforza Almeni**, built for Piero di Antonio Taddei, *circa* 1510–20. The house was later confiscated by Cosimo I, and given to Giovanni Battista Ricasoli, but Cosimo repossessed it in 1546 and gave it to Sforza Almeni, a loyal supporter. Almeni added the Medici and Toledo arms on the corner and inserted the ground-floor windows (perhaps by Ammannati). He also added *sgraffito* decoration, designed by Vasari, on the façade; it was executed by Cristofano Gherardi, but no trace remains. Six bays and three orders; a big arched portal and prominent corner rustication. No. 11 is **Palazzo Buontalenti**, sixteenth century, so named because it was bought by the descendants of the architect in the seventeenth century. Two large stone arched portals, surmounted by balconies, and nine bays in all. Nineteenth-century neo-Classical decoration to some internal rooms. On the corner of Via dei Servi and Via (Maurizio) Bufalini is **Palazzo Pasqui**, mostly late sixteenth century, but with an earlier tall lower order of rusticated stone, in which are set arches with a mezzanine above.

2 SAN LORENZO AND THE MEDICI QUARTER

This itinerary covers the area immediately around San Lorenzo; it extends from Via dei Servi (E) to Via Faenza (W) and from the cathedral precincts (S) to Via Guelfa / Via degli Alfani (N).

Via Ricasoli: Off the N side of the Piazza del Duomo, one block W of Via dei Servi and roughly parallel to it. A short distance up on the left is the **Teatro Niccolini**, the oldest in the city, established in 1652 as the Teatro al Cocomero (Coconut). Radically modernised in 1830 and again in 1859; the latter modernisation also changed its name, in honour of the tragedian Giovanni Battista Niccolini. Nearly opposite (no. 9) is **Palazzo Ricasoli,** once owned by Bettino Ricasoli (1809–1880), former mayor and governor of Tuscany, and head of the government during Florence's brief term as capital city. Largely rebuilt by Angelo Ricasoli in the late seventeenth century; prominent coat of arms on the outer corner.

A little further N is the junction with Via dei Pucci. On the NE corner is

Palazzo Pucci: Nos. 2–6 Via dei Pucci, occupying the whole N side between Via dei Servi and Via Ricasoli. Three distinct structures, but collectively one of the largest palaces in the city. Twenty-three bays in all; the central house has five, the two flanking houses nine each. The core (no. 4) was bought *circa* 1450 by Antonio Pucci. The present façade is probably by Ammannati, *circa* 1565–70. His patrons were Roberto and Lorenzo Pucci. Considerably richer than the side wings, it has a rusticated ground floor, with a large portal surmounted by an elaborate Serliana to the first *piano nobile*; the flanking aediculed lights are simpler. The second *piano nobile* is relatively simple, but with a split pediment to the central bay. No. 6 (the W wing) was originally by Baccio d'Agnolo, although the façade is the later work of Paolo Falconieri, *circa* 1688, who modernised the façades of both flanking houses to create a more unified whole. The E element (no. 2) has central paired rusticated portals separated by a large square window. The two main upper orders are simply detailed with aediculed rectangular lights. Interiors: each element is built around a courtyard; the first (W) is eighteenth century and neo-Classical. The second, central one is the oldest, partly sixteenth century (Tuscan order), partly eighteenth. The third (E) has an impressive atrium with paired columns in *pietra serena*. Part of the palace is still owned by the Pucci.

Opposite no. 2 (S side), corner of Via dei Servi, is **Palazzo Incontri**, designed by Ludovico Incontri and Paolo Falconieri, *circa* 1676; the style fuses the late Florentine Renaissance with Roman Baroque. An imposing but asymmetrical façade, with three principal orders and nine bays; the heavily rusticated portal is in the fourth bay, surmounted by a balcony. Heavy rustication also to the ground-floor windows and quoins; pediments to the *piano nobile*. The courtyard (Composite) is colonnaded on three sides. An earlier house on the site was decorated by Botticelli and Piero di Cosimo.

Continuing N up Via Ricasoli, nos. 40 and 42 are the two **Palazzi Gerini**. Originally fifteenth century; modernised in the late sixteenth. The original house was acquired by the Ginori in 1455, who also bought adjacent properties; it was sold to the Salviati in 1579, who had the façade modernised, probably by Ammannati or Buontalenti, generally as we see it now: the main body of the façade has nine bays, with large rusticated pedimented portals at each end; seven large aediculed windows in between; the *piano nobile* is much simpler, with arched rusticated window surrounds; the second floor is simpler still; boldly projecting eaves. The Salviati owned the house until 1650, when it was sold to Carlo Gerini; it was then modernised again by Gherardo Silvani. At the end of the eighteenth century yet another adjacent house was bought, at the corner with Via Guelfa, but was not fully integrated with the earlier houses until the late nineteenth century, by Giuseppe Poggi, who also radically altered the interior and incorporated a ballroom. The house is still owned by the Gerini.

Via dei Ricasoli now enters Piazza San Marco; see p. 213. Turn left along the S side of the piazza and left again into the S section of Via Cavour.

Via Cavour: south section: Known for centuries as the Via Larga for its generous width, the name was changed in 1861 shortly after Cavour's death. The numeration has odd numbers on the W side, even on the E. At no. 50r (E) is the **Teatro della Compagnia**, a conversion of the former Cinema Modernissimo (1921). By Adolfo Natalini and others, completed 1987. The theatre has a highly adaptable interior, capable of configuration from traditional proscenium to a classical cavea. Ingenious planning on a narrow site between Palazzi Bastogi and Panciatichi. The exterior and interior are clad with pink Santafiora stone. In the last few years it has been used again as a cinema. No. 43 (W) is the **Biblioteca Marucelliana**, by Alessandro Dori, 1748–52. The library originates from the collections of Abbot Francesco Marucelli (+1703). It was opened to the public in 1752 and today contains more than half a million books. A rather eclectic façade, the central section with three bays and three orders, the central bay projecting slightly and with giant pilasters to the upper floors. In the centre at high level: inscription surmounted by a broken pediment; a bold cornice on corbels.

Nos. 37–9 is **Palazzo Dardinelli**, later Fenzi, by Santi di Tito, late sixteenth century, with four orders and seven bays. The articulation is conventional but the wall surfaces are covered with panels of complex *sgraffito* decoration. Two family arms in the central bay. No. 31 (also W side) is the fourteenth-century **Palazzo di Bernardetto de' Medici**.

On the E side, no. 26 is **Palazzo Vettori**, nineteenth century; three orders, the first rusticated. Nos. 22–4 is **Palazzo Bartolommei** by Gherardo Silvani, mid-seventeenth century; a broad nine-bay façade, with two prominent portals surmounted by balconies. Three big aediculed windows to the ground floor. Still on the E side, no. 18 is **Palazzo Capponi**, later Bastogi, originally by Ferdinando Ruggieri, 1740, but largely rebuilt by Poggi in the nineteenth century. An exceptionally long twelve-bay façade, with central balcony and rusticated ground floor.

Back on the W side, no. 13 is **Palazzo Ginori Conti**, rebuilt for the Ughi (mid-eighteenth century) on the site of earlier houses of the Medici. Arms above the portal. Rebuilt again in the nineteenth century by Telemaco Bonaiuti; for a short time it was owned by the composer Gioacchino Rossini (plaque).

118 Arcispedale di Santa Maria Nuova: detail of the upper order of the east wing; by Giulio Parigi, early eighteenth century

119 Palazzo Pucci: detail of the western part of the façade, by Paolo Falconieri, *circa* 1688

120 Biblioteca Marucelliana: façade by Alessandro Dori, 1748–52

121 Palazzo Fenzi Dardinelli, by Santi di Tito: detail of façade with graffito decoration

On the E side again, no. 4 is **Palazzo Covoni** and no. 6 is **Palazzo Capponi**, the former modernised by Gherardo Silvani in 1623, perhaps to an earlier design by Buontalenti. The impressive façade has five bays and three orders; large rectangular windows, all aediculed, with a central portal surmounted by a balcony. Inside: courtyard and upper loggia by Clemente Orlandi, 1734. The adjacent house, no. 6, with four bays and an off-centre portal, was bought in 1729 by Marchese Ruberto Capponi; it had been built in the sixteenth century for the Milanesi. The two houses were then joined by Orlandi, although the façades were unchanged.

The last house on the E side, corner of Via dei Pucci, is **Palazzo Panciatichi** (no. 2), late seventeenth century, by Carlo Fontana. A long W façade of eleven bays with three orders; the central bay has a large arched portal surmounted by a balcony. The first order is badly altered, but the upper ones survive, all with regular rectangular lights. Inside: monumental staircase by Francesco Fontana, *circa* 1696; and several rooms with contemporaneous fresco decoration by Vincenzo Meucci and others.

On the NW corner of the junction looms the vast, imposing mass of

Palazzo Medici Riccardi: Commissioned by Cosimo de' Medici il Vecchio (*pater patriae*) and designed by Michelozzo di Bartolomeo; it remains the archetypal Florentine Renaissance *palazzo*, the earliest and still one of the largest. Cosimo returned to Florence from exile in Venice in 1437; work began in 1444 and was completed before 1462. Its original extent consisted of ten bays along both principal façades, with three orders. It remained the family seat until 1540, when Cosimo I transferred first to the Palazzo Vecchio and then to Palazzo Pitti; Palazzo Medici remained occupied by other members of the family until 1659, when it was sold to the Riccardi, who extended it by a further seven bays along the Via Larga. In 1814 it passed to the house of Lorraine, and from 1865, when Florence was capital of Italy, it was the interior ministry. In 1871 it was bought by the provincial government, whose administration remains here, together with the Prefettura.

Before the Riccardi extension, the basic form of the palace was a 'hollow cube' with a central courtyard. The principal façades have three orders, with graduated stone facing, all in *pietra forte*: powerful rough 'cushion' rustication to the first order, squared ashlar with prominent joints to the second, and smooth ashlar to the third. Each order is

122   Palazzo Medici Riccardi: general view of the west façade; begun by Michelozzo, 1444; extended northwards by G.B. Foggini, 1685

123   Palazzo Medici Riccardi: detail of rustication to the south flank

124   Palazzo Medici Riccardi: upper south-east corner with the family coat of arms

125   Palazzo Medici Riccardi: detail of the south-east corner window, by Michelangelo, 1517

126   Palazzo Medici Riccardi: detail of the courtyard, by Michelozzo, begun 1444

defined by a prominent string course at sill level, and the façade is capped by a monumental cornice on corbels. At the corner, the Canto de' Medici, are two large rusticated arches, originally forming an open loggia, which was 'reclaimed' in 1517 by Michelangelo, who inserted 125 the two large aediculed windows. Other than the portal, detailed in the same way as the lost loggia, the ground floor has simple square lights. The *piani nobili* both have similar fenestration: *bifore* set below a larger arched opening. On the corner at the first-floor *piano nobile* is a large Medici coat of arms; smaller coats of arms in the *bifore* above the window heads. The Riccardi extension continues the same façade treatment but with their own arms above the windows.

The original entrance leads through the *androne* into a square court-126 yard, Corinthian, three bays by three. Above the colonnade is a frieze in which are set twelve roundels containing reliefs of copies of classical sculptures from the Medici collections; *circa* 1450, and attributed to Bertoldo di Giovanni, from the circle of Donatello. The *piano nobile* is faced with flat false rustication, and has *bifore* like those to the external façades, while the second floor has a loggia, originally probably open but today filled with glazed screens. In the eighteenth century the courtyard housed the Riccardi's rich collection of classical sculptures. Directly beyond the central courtyard is a second one, with a loggia along one side and enclosed by high boundary walls. It was replanned as a garden in 1911.

The main stair rises on the right of the courtyard, and is by G.B. Foggini, 1685. At the top is the Medici chapel, known as the **Cappella dei Magi**, after the rich fresco decoration by Benozzo Gozzoli. The chapel itself is by Michelozzo, and is one of very few original internal elements to survive: a rectangular space, with a small tribune at the end for the altar. Around the walls: richly detailed wooden choir stalls, *circa* 1465, perhaps by Giuliano da Sangallo. The ceiling is of timber, carved, painted and gilded, to a design by Michelozzo. The floor has decorative geometrical motifs in porphyry and coloured marbles.

The walls are entirely covered by Gozzoli's fresco cycle, considered his *capolavoro* (masterpiece), 1459–60; restored to their rich original coloration in 1992. The principal theme is the procession of the Magi to Bethlehem. The paintings incorporate numerous contemporary allusions and illustrations, including portraits of Giuliano de' Medici (Lorenzo il Magnifico's brother), Piero il Gottoso, Lorenzo himself, Galeazzo Maria Sforza of Milan and many others. The altarpiece is a *Nativity*, a contemporary copy of a work by Filippo Lippi.

The interior was extensively modernised by Gabriello Riccardi after 1670. Work continued under his son Francesco, and concluded *circa* 1720. In the first phase, a new wing on Via dei Ginori by Pier Maria Baldi included a library and exhibition gallery. After 1685, in a second phase, Foggini added the N wing on the Via Larga, a new staircase and principal reception room. The whole is richly decorated Baroque; the Galleria, especially, has a barrel-vaulted ceiling frescoed by Luca Giordano, 1682–3. The library has fine wooden bookcases; the reading room again has a frescoed ceiling by Giordano. It was first opened to the public in 1715.

On the SW corner of the junction stands **San Giovanni Evangelista** or San Giovannino degli Scolopi, with an adjacent convent; on the site of an ancient oratory, founded by Giovanni di Lando Gori (1351). In 1557 it passed to the Jesuits. The present church is by Ammannati (begun 1579), and completed by Alfonso Parigi the younger. In 1775 it passed in turn to the Padri Scolopi (Piarist fathers), a teaching order founded in 1617 by Giuseppe Calasanzio; they remained until 1878. Ammannati's façade was altered by Parigi, then partly restored in 1843 by Leopoldo Pasqui. Two orders, with a square central portal and a large rectangular light above; they are both flanked by paired Corinthian columns set into niches, Parigi's alterations. The outer bays have round-arched niches. This lower order is wider than the upper one, and the outer corners have further pairs of recessed Corinthian columns; modest volutes link the two orders. The façade is capped by a large pediment.

Inside: a rich, spacious, aisle-less hall, in the characteristic Jesuit manner; four chapels down each side. *Circa* 1660 Parigi also altered the interior, substituting the vaulted ceiling with a new flat one, and adding sumptuous decoration, including ceiling frescoes by Agostino Veracini. Towards the end of the century, the high altar was added by Carlo Marcellini. Further decoration added in the eighteenth century included the vault depicting the *Triumph of St Francis Xavier* by Piero Dandini; the niches with stucco figures of the *Apostles*; and richly carved wooden confessionals. The second left altar has an altarpiece of *Christ and the Woman Taken in Adultery* by Alessandro Allori.

The broad, busy Via dei Martelli continues S back to the baptistery. It is named after the Martelli family, who owned houses on the W side. That at no. 9 was absorbed by the adjacent Jesuit convent in the sixteenth century. After 1836 it became the Liceo Classico. On the exterior: a fifteenth-century marble tabernacle.

From Palazzo Medici walk W along Via dei Gori to Piazza San Lorenzo. Leading off the NE corner is **Via dei Ginori**, with several palaces of note. No. 7 is **Palazzo Neroni**, built in 1463–5 for Nigi Neroni; later owned by the Donati. The ground floor is heavily rusticated, modelled on the nearby Palazzo Medici, hence attributions to Michelozzo. On both sides, the rustication is incomplete, leading to the conclusion that since both adjacent sites were also owned by the Neroni, the intention was to unify and modernise all three in the same manner. Four bays and three orders. No. 9 is **Palazzo Barbolani di Montauto**. Built for the Neroni in the late 1440s. An imposing eight-bay façade, rusticated stone to the lower order, two orders above. Also attributed to Michelozzo. The long *androne* leads into a Renaissance courtyard with four-bay loggias at the two ends, one (W) more refined (later?) than the other. No. 10 is the W (garden) entrance to Palazzo Medici. No. 11 is **Palazzo Ginori**: early sixteenth century, with typical features of the era: rusticated quoins to the ground floor and ashlar quoins to the upper floors; a six-bay façade, asymmetrical, with portal offset to the right. Arched windows with rusticated surrounds to the first and second floors and a colonnaded loggia across the full width at the third floor; boldly projecting eaves. It was built in 1516 for Carlo di Leonardo Ginori on a site bought from the Ubaldini. Like so many of the period, it is perhaps by Baccio d'Agnolo. A rear façade to the W, on Via della Stufa, modernised (*circa* 1691–1701) by Lorenzo Merlini and Antonio Maria Ferri, who also modernised the interior; rich stucco decoration. Another Carlo Ginori later established the famous porcelain works at Doccia in 1737. The palace was linked to Palazzo Taddei in the early nineteenth century. It remains in Ginori ownership today.

Adjacent, no. 15 is **Palazzo Taddei**, early sixteenth century. The Taddei owned several houses in this area, such that the Via del Bisogno was renamed Via Taddea. The palace was built for Taddeo Taddei, a humanist and art collector, perhaps by Baccio d'Agnolo, in the early 1500s. Similar to several others of the era: five bays and three orders; square ground-floor windows, rusticated surrounds to the portal and the upper windows, string courses at each level, boldly projecting roof eaves. Raphael lived here for a time *circa* 1505 (plaque erroneously located at no. 17). The house was sold to the Giraldi in 1542. In 1847 it was bought by the Ginori Lisci.

Nos. 19 and 23 were both also originally owned by the Taddei. The first, no. 19, was later known as **Palazzo Tolomei Biffi**; perhaps once again by Baccio, 1503–4. It originally had three orders and only five bays; the three large aediculed ground-floor windows were inserted in the following century, when it was extended by a further two bays. In 1564 it was sold to the Baglioni, and in 1584 to the Galli. In 1743 it was acquired by the Tolomei. In 1644 the adjacent house at no. 23, **Palazzo Tolomei Garzoni**, was also bought by the Tolomei and rebuilt as we see it today. A narrow but symmetrical façade of three bays and three orders plus an attic; large arched windows to the *piano nobile*.

Back in Piazza San Lorenzo, in the NE corner is the monument to *Giovanni dalle Bande Nere* (de' Medici), by Baccio Bandinelli, 1540. The continuation of the square along the N side of the church, until recently filled with market stalls, is the Via del Canto dei Nelli. Along the N and E sides: a number of medium-sized palaces, mostly fifteenth and sixteenth century, and with three to five bays and four orders. The most notable is **Palazzo Lotteringhi della Stufa** (no. 4), of medieval origin. The Lotteringhi were recorded here since 1281, and built their first house in 1292. In 1665 they acquired an adjacent property towards Via dei Ginori, and Gherardo and Pier Francesco Silvani provided a unified façade for the whole. Today the left part retains fourteenth-century stonework on the ground floor, with five arched bays; two intermediate floors, each of five bays, and on the third floor a spacious fifteenth-century *liagò* across the top. Also fifteenth century is the fine coat of arms in *pietra serena* on the left façade. The right section remains very simple. The Lotteringhi owned the palace until 1946.

On the E side of the piazza, opposite the church façade, at no. 6 is the **Osservatorio Ximeniano**, named after a Jesuit, Leonardo Ximines, who founded an astronomical observatory here in 1756. It is housed at the top of the adjacent medieval (but much altered) Torre dei Rondinelli (Borgo San Lorenzo no. 26), adapted for the purpose. The observatory has kept meteorological and seismographic records since 1813.

San Lorenzo: One of the most important churches in the city, its origins probably lay in the arrival of Christianity in Florence. Said to have been founded in the fourth century, it later became the patronal church of the Medici, whose famous legacy it has become. Built on a slight eminence adjacent to the Mugnone stream (later diverted), it was consecrated as the cathedral of Florence in 393 by (St) Ambrose, archbishop of Milan. The site lay outside the ancient Roman walls and the first communal walls (*circa* 1078), but was enclosed by the second communal walls of 1173–5. Ambrose's cathedral was rebuilt by Bishop Gherardo da Borgogna and reconsecrated in 1059, when Gherardo became pope (Nicholas II). In 1418 the Medici decided on a radical modernisation, to make it their family church and mausoleum. The commission was given to Brunelleschi, whose design is from 1421. Construction probably began at the liturgical E end (in fact, the W end); the sacristy (the present Sagrestia Vecchia) was complete by 1429, although the church itself was not completed until 1461 (fifteen years after Brunelleschi's death), by Antonio Manetti, who made some alterations to Brunelleschi's design.

The façade: a competition was launched by the Medici pope Leo X (r. 1513–21); proposals were submitted by Michelangelo (his wooden model is in the Casa Buonarroti), Raphael, Jacopo Sansovino, Baccio d'Agnolo and Giuliano da Sangallo. In 1516 Michelangelo was given the commission, but it was never executed, and was formally abandoned in 1519.

The plan of the church is a Latin cross, with an eight-bay nave and two side aisles, both flanked by rows of shallow rectangular chapels. The whole interior is based on simple geometrical forms and mathematical proportions. On plan these are all represented by large squares, derived from the square plan of the crossing, as well as smaller squares; four of the latter make one of the former. Thus: the nave is four large square bays in length, and its central vessel is twice the width of the aisles, which in turn are twice the depth of the side chapels. The square forming the crossing is repeated in each transept arm and the chancel; the chancel's flanking chapels are small squares, the same size as the nave aisle bays.

The Interior

The interior has a calm, imposing harmony, light and spacious. Its principal materials are *pietra serena* for all architectural elements and plain white plastered surfaces to the flanking walls and the aisle vaults. The nave has tall monolithic Corinthian columns, supporting dosserets (short sections of entablature), which in turn support semicircular arches; above the cornice is a simple clerestory with arched windows. The nave has a rich, flat, coffered ceiling, white with gold detailing. Its side aisles have simple sail vaults and high-level oculi. The lateral chapels are approached by three steps, and are framed by semicircular arches flanked by Corinthian pilasters.

127   San Giovannino degli Scolopi: façade begun by Bartolomeo Ammannati, completed by Alfonso Parigi, *circa* 1665

128   San Lorenzo: north side of the piazza, with market stalls

129   San Lorenzo: upper part of the unfinished façade

130   San Lorenzo: the fifteenth-century first cloister, and, beyond, the crossing of the church and the cupola of the Cappelle Medicee

131   San Lorenzo: the fifteenth-century first cloister; and beyond it, the *ricetto* of Michelangelo's Biblioteca Laurenziana, begun 1524

Principal monuments and altars

The inner face of the façade is by Michelangelo. First right aisle chapel: *Martyrdom of St Sebastian* by Jacopo da Empoli. Second chapel: *Marriage of the Virgin* by Rosso Fiorentino, 1523. Third chapel: *St Lawrence* by Niccolò Lapi. Fourth chapel: *Assumption* by Michele di Ridolfo del Ghirlandaio. At the corner of the aisle and right transept: altar of the Sacrament by Desiderio da Settignano, highly refined, with three elements: a *Pietà*, two angels holding candelabra and, at the summit, the *Child Blessing*, 1461. In front, at the side of the nave, the first of two magnificent bronze pulpits, the last works of Donatello, *circa* 1460, completed by his pupils Bertoldo di Giovanni and Bartolomeo Bellano. Now raised on Ionic columns (*circa* 1560). On this pulpit: *Resurrection*, *Ascension* and *Pentecost*. On the matching pulpit on the left side: scenes from the Passion: *Mocking of Christ*, *Marys at the Tomb* and *Descent into Limbo*.

Right transept, right chapel: chapel with a Roman sarcophagus. Right transept, end chapel: chapel dedicated to the Blessed Sacrament. Adjacent is the Sagrestia Nuova (New Sacristy), usually reached via the Cappella dei Principi (see below). On the E side of the transept: two chapels, the first with a monument to Bernardo Cennini, who printed the first book in Florence (1471); the other has a triptych of the *Annunciation* by Puccio di Simone, 1350s?.

Crossing: in the floor: monument to Cosimo il Vecchio (+1464). The cupola is frescoed by Vincenzo Meucci, 1742. In the centre: *Florentine Saints in Glory*; in the pendentives: *Fathers of the Church*.

Left transept: right chapel: fourteenth-century *Virgin and Child* in polychrome wood. Left chapel: *St Anthony, with St Lawrence and St Julian*, from the workshop of Domenico Ghirlandaio. At the end of the transept: Cappella delle Reliquie, with wooden cabinets containing relics of St Lawrence. Adjacent, off the left side of the transept, is the Martelli chapel; on the wall: monument to Donatello (by Dario Guidotti and Raffaello Romanelli, 1896), who is buried in the vault below. The adjacent monument to Niccolò and Fioretta Martelli, *circa* 1464, is by Donatello. On the altar: *Annunciation* by Filippo Lippi, *circa* 1450, one of his best works. Above the altar: polychrome wooden Crucifix, fifteenth century. On the aisle wall outside is a huge fresco of the *Martyrdom of St Lawrence* by Bronzino, 1565–9.

In the right corner of the transept is the entrance to the **Sagrestia Vecchia** (Old Sacristy), a notable work of the early Renaissance, by Brunelleschi, 1421–6. The earliest part of the church to be rebuilt under the patronage of the Medici, specifically that of Giovanni di Bicci, who is buried here. A long, careful restoration (1989) revealed the original colours of the friezes and stuccowork. The sacristy is a cube, with the same dimensions as the crossing square, surmounted by a hemispherical cupola, divided into panels by 'umbrella' ribs, and supported on pendentives. Most of the decoration is by Donatello. All the stonework is *pietra serena*; the perimeter articulation is by fluted Corinthian pilasters, above which is a frieze containing roundels of cherubim and seraphim, by Donatello. In the centre of the nave is the tomb of Giovanni di Bicci, by Buggiano (Andrea Cavalcanti), *circa* 1433. On the left side wall: fine bronze and porphyry sarcophagus of Piero il Gottoso and Giovanni de' Medici, sons of Cosimo il Vecchio, commissioned by Lorenzo il Magnifico from Verrocchio in 1472. At high level on the walls are four roundels of the *Evangelists*. In the pendentives supporting the cupola: four more roundels with scenes from the *Life of St John the Evangelist*, all by Donatello. Opposite the entrance is the tiny chancel, a miniature version of the sacristy itself, surmounted by a hemispherical cupola; it has a dark blue fresco representing the night sky, showing the sun and stars; from their locations it has been identified as 4 July 1442. The altar is also from Donatello's workshop, carved by Buggiano and Pagno Portigiani. Above is a polychrome Crucifix by Simone Ferrucci. Flanking the chancel are side chapels; above the doorways: reliefs of *St Cosmas and St Damian* (right) and *St Lawrence and St Stephen* (left), again all by Donatello, as are the two pairs of bronze doors. The left door depicts ten scenes from the *Lives and Deaths of Early Christian Martyrs*, while the right door depicts the *Apostles*, *Fathers of the Church* and the *Baptist*. Within the left chapel is an elegant lavabo, commissioned by Piero il Gottoso de' Medici in 1467.

Nave left aisle: above the door to the cloisters: organ loft, *circa* 1460. Sixth chapel: twentieth-century altarpiece by Pietro Annigoni; fifth chapel: altarpiece by Giovanni Antonio Sogliani, 1521. Fourth chapel: fifteenth-century wooden Crucifix of German origin.

A doorway in the corner of the left transept leads to the first cloister, but access is usually from the SW corner of the piazza outside. Clearly derived from Brunelleschi, but by Antonio Manetti, 1457–62. Two superimposed orders, with Ionic colonnades. The second cloister is 130 beyond the first; smaller, rectangular, five bays by two, and built in the fourteenth century.

At the NW corner of the first cloister is the entrance to the

Biblioteca Laurenziana: A famous, remarkable work by Michelangelo, begun in 1524 to house the notable collection of books and manuscripts originally assembled by Cosimo il Vecchio, and further enlarged by Lorenzo. After various vicissitudes, the library was brought back to Florence from Rome in 1523, and Pope Clement VII commissioned Michelangelo to build the new library. After his death (1564), it was completed by Vasari and Ammannati, closely following Buonarroti's intentions.

The design addressed several constraints, including the existing canons' accommodation down this side of the cloister, which were retained and the library built directly above them. The space available for the entrance lobby was also highly restricted by the left transept of the church. The library thus consists of two principal elements; the first is the *ricetto*, the tall square lobby containing the staircase, at the top of which is the second element, the long rectangular reading room itself. The internal walls of the *ricetto* are treated as façades and are highly articulated in *pietra serena*. Above the tall basement are two superimposed orders, three bays to each face, articulated with paired columns. The detailing is highly Mannerist: some of the windows are blind; the paired columns are 'pushed' back into niches; below them are exaggeratedly elongated console brackets that do not support the columns at all; and the stair itself has an extraordinary plastic quality. It was built by Ammannati, following Michelangelo's model, and fills much of the lobby. Its unique form has a broad central flight with curved steps and heavy balustrading, and flanked by two narrower rectangular outer flights that join the central one at a half-landing before rising in a single flight to the portal; the outer flights have no perimeter balustrades.

The library itself is a long rectangular hall, fifteen bays, and considerably more rationally detailed than the *ricetto*. Down each side are two rows of reading desks and bookcases. The articulation, *pietra serena* again, consists of a basement (obscured by the fittings); a principal order of flat pilasters, between which are large rectangular lights; and a modest attic of simple blind square 'window' panels. The rich, flat, coffered carved wooden ceiling is by G.B. del Tasso and Antonio Carota, and its patterning echoes that of the equally rich tiled floor. The original benches and fittings, designed by Michelangelo, all survive. Halfway down the W side, a lobby leads to a circular hall, the Tribuna d'Elci; a neo-Classical design by Bernardino Poccetti, to hold manuscripts and incunabula left by Angelo Maria d'Elci in 1841. The original

132   Biblioteca Laurenziana: detail of the stairs in the *ricetto*

133   Biblioteca Laurenziana: the reading room

134   Biblioteca Laurenziana: detail of stained-glass window, perhaps by Giovanni da Udine, 1568

135   Cappella dei Principi (Cappelle Medicee) from the south, begun by Matteo Nigetti, 1604, completed by Giuseppe and Ferdinando Ruggieri

stained-glass windows are perhaps by Giovanni da Udine. The library itself contains a priceless collection of books and manuscripts, including the only surviving manuscript copies of works by Horace, Cicero and Tacitus.

Back in the first cloister, a doorway in the NW corner leads to steps down to the crypt, below the church's chancel, where the sepulchre of Cosimo il Vecchio is located. Generally attributed to Verrocchio, 1465–7, and decorated with panels of green marble. Adjacent is the tomb of Donatello, as well as a number of others, reorganised after the floods of 1966.

The remaining elements of the Medici complex of San Lorenzo are reached by leaving the church, walking down the long N flank wall to the Via del Canto dei Nelli, around the far end of the massive Cappella dei Principi and entering the **Cappelle Medicee** through a doorway in the SW wall.

135   The **Cappella dei Principi** is capped by a large octagonal cupola, a conscious re-evocation of that of the cathedral. The chapel was first conceived by Cosimo I *circa* 1568, but commissioned by Ferdinando I, and begun in 1604. Traditionally ascribed to Buontalenti, it was probably designed and certainly executed by Matteo Nigetti, with contributions from Giovanni de' Medici. Nigetti (who died in 1644) was assisted and succeeded by G.B. Foggini, Ferdinando and Giuseppe Ruggieri and others. Work proceeded rapidly up to the base of the cupola (1625), but much more slowly thereafter. The Ruggieri completed the external cladding of *pietra forte* and white marble, and the rather bizarre windows in the cupola, as late as 1736–48. Ruggieri's wooden model of the chapel (*circa* 1740) has survived. The last elements to be completed were the frescoes inside the cupola (1836), the rich marble floor (1874) and the altar (1934).

The floor plan is an irregular octagon, 28 m (approx. 92 ft) across, with four long sides and four shorter ones. The upper order, though, with the clerestory and cupola, is a regular octagon. Access to the main chapel is usually via the extensive crypt, in which are tombs of many members of the Medici dynasty and a display from their treasury. It has a sail-vaulted roof on very short, stout, square piers. Around the perimeter are four niches (corresponding to the monuments in the chapel above) containing the remains of the grand dukes and their close relatives, including Giovanni dalle Bande Nere and Anna Maria Luisa (+1743), the last Medici. A stair rises up into the chapel itself, a vast, gloomy but extremely richly decorated hall; a true mausoleum.

All the wall surfaces are clad with *pietre dure*, marbles of many types and colours. The famous Opificio delle Pietre Dure was founded by Ferdinando I in 1588 specifically for the project (see p. 183). Around the lower walls: inlaid coats of arms of the sixteen Tuscan bishoprics subject to Medici-ruled Florence. On tall plinths around the walls are the monuments to the Medici princes: clockwise they are: Ferdinando II, Cosimo II, Ferdinando I, Cosimo I, Francesco I and Cosimo III. Set in aedicules above and behind the marble sarcophagi were to be statues of the grand dukes: only two were realised: *Ferdinando I de' Medici* by Pietro Tacca (1626–32) and *Cosimo II de' Medici* by Pietro and Ferdinando Tacca, *circa* 1642.

A small corridor on the E wall leads into the **Sagrestia Nuova**, a 117 masterpiece by Michelangelo and his first significant architectural project. It was commissioned by Pope Leo X and his cousin, Cardinal Giulio de' Medici (later Pope Clement VII), in 1520, to serve as the funerary chapel for the two brothers Lorenzo il Magnifico and Giuliano, the latter assassinated by the Pazzi in 1478. It was also to house the monuments to Lorenzo, duke of Urbino (Lorenzo il Magnifico's grandson), and of Giuliano, duke of Nemours, Lorenzo's third son.

Work proceeded from 1520, but was interrupted in 1524 until 1530, when construction continued until 1533. When Buonarroti left the city permanently for Rome in 1534, it was still incomplete, although the sculpted figures had been carved. It was finally completed by Vasari and Ammannati in 1554–5, who located Michelangelo's statues in place.

The basic plan and dimensions match and balance Brunelleschi's Sagrestia Vecchia, on the opposite side of the church, but its treatment is quite different. The structure itself may have been begun by Giuliano da Sangallo, but Michelangelo raised its height by inserting an additional order above the principal one and below the springing of the cupola, thus accentuating its verticality.

The articulation is in dark *pietra serena*, with flat fluted Corinthian pilasters supporting a two-part entablature. Above the principal order is the lower clerestory order, with large rectangular aediculed windows (some blind) in a narrow bay near each corner. Above again are semicircular lunettes, between which rise the pendentives supporting the cupola. The cupola itself is decorated with *trompe l'oeil* coffering, inspired by the Pantheon in Rome.

To the right of the entrance is the simple slab monument to Lorenzo il Magnifico (+1492) and his brother Giuliano. The only part executed is Michelangelo's unfinished *Virgin and Child* (his last *Madonna*), flanked by figures of *St Cosmas* by Giovanni Angelo da Montorsoli, *circa* 1537, and *St Damian* by Raffaele di Montelupo, 1531.

On the right wall is Michelangelo's monument to Giuliano, duke of Nemours, depicted as a captain of the army, seated, with his baton, and with the figures of *Day* (right) and *Night* (left) below him, on the sepulchre; the former is unfinished, although the latter is one of his finest figure sculptures. Directly opposite is the monument to Lorenzo, duke of Urbino, 1533. The figure is in the form of a *condottiere*, again seated, and deep in thought. On the sepulchre below are two further figures, *Dawn* (*Aurora*) and *Dusk* (*Crepuscolo*), both from 1531–2. Behind both monuments are rich screens of white marble, the central bay of which contains the memorial statue, flanked by paired Corinthian pilasters and outer bays containing blind aedicules.

The sixteenth-century altar has two marble candelabra, also said to be by Michelangelo; on the altar: a bronze Crucifix attributed to Giambologna. To the left, a small doorway gives access to a little room in which some of Michelangelo's lost original charcoal sketches were discovered in 1978; some are preparatory studies for the Medici monuments.

Piazza della Madonna degli Aldobrandini: The little square to the SW of the Cappella dei Principi. No. 4, W side, is **Palazzo Benci 'della Stufa'**, later Mannelli Riccardi. The Benci had owned a house here since 1469, but it was rebuilt in the mid-sixteenth century. Above the portal: bust of *Francesco I de' Medici*. On the façade: remains of painted allegories, perhaps from the shop of Allori or Poccetti, *circa* 1575. It was one of five such façades, the first in the city decorated in this manner; Benci coat of arms in the centre. In the SW corner of the piazza, no. 1, corner of Via dell'Amorino, is **Palazzo Gaddi**, originally fourteenth century, modernised in the sixteenth, with impressive *sporti*; the English poet John Milton once stayed here. No. 8 is **Palazzo Aldobrandini**, eighteenth century, with two façades enclosing the corner of the square, one of five bays, the other of four.

In the nearby Via del Giglio, corner of Via del Melarancio (no. 1), is **Palazzo Arrighetti Gaddi**, sixteenth century, with eight bays and three orders; *piano nobile* rooms frescoed by Luca Giordano and others. No. 13 Via del Giglio is the eighteenth-century **Palazzo Gaddi**.

Off the SE corner of the piazza is Via dei Conti, leading to Via Zanetti, with a small triangular piazza at the junction. Nos. 4–5 Via dei Conti is the imposing eighteenth-century **Palazzo Conti**, with aediculed windows. Turning into Via Zanetti, no. 8 is **Palazzo Martelli**, early sixteenth century in origin. In 1627 it was extended by annexing other properties belonging to the same family, and in 1668–9 further modernisations were made by Bernardino Ciurini. In 1738 still more alterations were made for the archbishop, Giuseppe Maria Martelli, and at the end of the century the important art collection was systemised by Marco Martelli. The last Martelli, Francesca, gave the palace to the curia in 1986, which in turn gave it the state in 1998. After a long restoration, the present museum was opened in 2009. Among the paintings are works by Luca Giordano, Piero di Cosimo and a disputed *David* by Donatello. On the façade: a marble tabernacle containing a *Virgin and Child* in the style of Mino da Fiesole, *circa* 1460s. Return to the piazza.

3 VIA FAENZA AND THE MERCATO CENTRALE

To the NW is the long, narrow Via Faenza, marking the border with the *quartiere* of Santa Maria Novella. Few notable works of architecture, but an attractive scale and some smaller vernacular houses. One block down, Via Sant'Antonino crosses it at right angles. On the left, no. 11 is the bizarre seventeenth-century Baroque **Palazzo dei Cartelloni**, so called for the large cartouches on the lower façade (1693–4). Within them are Latin epigraphs in honour of Galileo and Louis XIV of France. It was designed by G.B. Nelli for Vincenzo Viviani, a mathematician and close colleague of Galileo. Above the portal: bust of *Galileo*, in a Mannerist surround, by G.B. Foggini. Also on Via Sant'Antonino is the little oratory of **San Giuseppe**, 1646, with a simple façade; inside, the ceiling decoration (1717) depicts *Eleonora Ramirez de Montalvo Presenting her Congregation of the Minime Ancelle to the Virgin*. Returning to Via Faenza and continuing NW, one block further down on the left side is

    San Jacopo in Campo Corbolini (Corbellini): Founded in 1206, and occupied after 1256 by the Knights Templar, then in succession by the Knights of Rhodes and of Malta. On the street façade is a rare surviving medieval portico, late thirteenth century, three bays long and one bay deep, with semicircular arches on robust cushion capitals with coats of arms on the shields and octagonal stone piers. Inside the portico: simple groin vaults. On the external corner: a large coat of arms of the Knights of Malta in *pietra serena*. Today the church is deconsecrated and attached to the adjacent art school. The interior:

136

137

mostly late thirteenth or early fourteenth century. Two rib-vaulted bays; a single nave with a small terminal apse. Various tombs and inscriptions of the priors of the order. Restored in the seventeenth century, and again after the 1966 floods.

One block further NW along Via Faenza is Via Nazionale; on the other side is the monumental **Tabernacolo delle Fonticine**, a complex work incorporating fountains and a *Virgin and Child Enthroned*, by Giovanni della Robbia, 1522. Nearby, at nos. 87–95, is the BICA building, by Italo Gamberini, 1957, with a highly articulated façade incorporating brises-soleil. Continuing NW along Via Faenza, on the right (no. 40) is the ex-**Convento delle Monache di Foligno**. Originally an Augustinian foundation (1316), it later passed to Franciscan tertiaries. It was completed in 1429, when it was frescoed by Bicci di Lorenzo. Suppressed by Napoleon in 1800, it became a girls' school. The refectory can be visited; it contains a notable *Last Supper*, by collaborators of Perugino, to his design; very late fifteenth century. The refectory also contains the detached frescoes by Bicci.

Returning SE down Via Faenza, take the short Via Zannoni, left, to reach the busy Via dell'Ariento. This is the central market district, and these streets are filled with stalls. The **Mercato Centrale** occupies a large rectangular block, bounded by Via Panicale (NW) and the Piazza del Mercato (NE). The hall is by Giuseppe Mengoni, 1870–74, based on the lost Les Halles in Paris. All of iron and glass, its internal structure has a tripartite form, with a taller central nave and lower side aisles, later compromised by inserting an intermediate floor. The main façades have thirteen bays, four to each of the side aisles, five to the 'nave'; the block is eleven bays deep. Shallow copper roofs with a clerestory to the 'nave'. Despite the advanced internal structure, the lower part of the external envelope is traditional, with rusticated stone arches, and the iron structure decorated with neo-Classical columns and pilasters.

Take Via Panicale NE. In Via Taddea (right) no. 8 is the **Palazzetto dei Serragli**, a relatively small early sixteenth-century house, with typical rusticated portal. Continue up Via Panicale to the junction with Via Guelfa; on the W corner is **San Barnaba**.

Rebuilt *circa* 1309–22 by Augustinians; it was patronised by the Arte dei Medici e Speziali (physicians' and pharmacists' guild). It then passed to the reformed Carmelite nuns, who partially modernised it in 1521, and remained until 1808. A simple façade with a Gothic portal with two coats of arms: the red cross of the *popolo* and the *Eagle Devouring the Dragon* (Guelph). The inset polychrome terracotta *Virgin and Child*

136 Palazzo dei Cartelloni by Giovan Battista Nelli, 1693–4

137 San Jacopo in Campo Corbolini: twelfth- to thirteenth-century portico from the south-east

138 Mercato Centrale: detail of the upper clerestory, by Giuseppe Mengoni, 1870–74

is from the della Robbia workshop, *circa* 1520; above is a sixteenth-century oculus. Inside: a notable carved eighteenth-century ceiling. Contemporaneous stucco decoration to the chancel apse. On the left side wall: remains of an extensive fourteenth-century fresco. A Baroque organ above the *barco* or nuns' choir, itself carried on four columns.

Immediately to the E, the block bounded by Via Taddea, Via Panicale, Via Guelfa and Via Sant'Orsola is occupied by an extensive complex, originally the nunnery of **Sant'Orsola**. Suppressed in 1810, it was then redeveloped as a tobacco factory. In the 1980s it was to be converted for the Guardia di Finanza, but the project was abandoned and the complex stood empty until 2010, when work began to restore it as a mixed development, including residential and commercial market functions.

4 ON AND AROUND PIAZZA DELLA SANTISSIMA ANNUNZIATA

This zone is a small, compact rectangle, bounded by Via degli Alfani (S), Borgo Pinti (E), the university buildings (W) and Via Giuseppe Giusti (N).

The Piazza della Santissima Annunziata is best approached from Via dei Servi to the S. This was the axial approach intended by Brunelleschi when he planned the piazza, one of the most significant pieces of urban intervention of the early Renaissance. Although it had existed as an open space since the later thirteenth century, when it was used for a weekly market, Brunelleschi began to transform it into a formal, symmetrical 'ideal' city square. The process began with the loggia of the Ospedale degli Innocenti on the SE side (begun 1419), although its matching loggia on the NW side was not built until 1516, by Antonio da Sangallo the elder and Baccio d'Angolo. In the centre of the piazza, on axis with Via dei Servi, is Giambologna's equestrian statue of *Ferdinando I de' Medici*, 1601, completed by Pietro Tacca in 1608; on each side are two fountains with sea monsters, also by Tacca, 1629. In the SW corner is

Palazzo Grifoni Budini Gattai: Built in 1563–74 by Baccio d'Agnolo and Ammannati for Ugolino di Jacopo Grifoni. The site was bought from the Ricci in 1549. Baccio is said to have been responsible for the plan, Ammannati for the façade. The overall volume is a cube, with five bays on each side. Uniquely, the principal material is red facing brickwork, although *pietra forte* is used for the rusticated quoins, door and window surrounds and the ponderous roof cornice. All the detailing is Mannerist. The more prominent N façade is almost symmetrical, although the portal, with rusticated surround, is offset to the right and its place taken by a large window, with a massive rusticated surround. The Via dei Servi façade is more disciplined, again five bays, symmetrical, this time with a central portal, again with a heavy arched, rusticated surround and also surmounted by an Ionic Serliana. Fenestration: large, rectangular windows, treated as aedicules, but differently to each storey: triangular pediments to the ground floor, curved broken pediments to the first, flat cornices to the second. The rear façade has a loggia facing a garden, in which is a Mannerist fountain by Giovanni Bandini. 139

The E side of the piazza is occupied by the

Ospedale degli Innocenti: An early masterpiece in the history of the Renaissance in the city, and one of Brunelleschi's most important urban contributions; it epitomises the civic aspects of Florentine life in the period. Begun in 1419, and sponsored by the Arte della Seta (silk workers' guild) as a foundling hospital for abandoned babies, who were to be housed, cared for and educated here. Between 1419 and 1427 the celebrated colonnaded portico was built, together with two wings behind and at right angles to it, one containing the chapel, the other accommodation for boys. They are separated by a square colonnaded cloister. Construction recommenced in 1436 under Francesco della Luna, who completed the third wing, towards the SW, for young girls, and the smaller cloister between it and the boys' wing. In 1445 the whole complex was inaugurated. The building's condition deteriorated seriously in the eighteenth and nineteenth centuries, but was comprehensively restored in 1966–70. Currently under restoration again (2015).

The spacious, elegant loggia to the piazza is the most notable feature; nine arched bays set above the pavement on nine stone steps. This was the first time that such a device had been used to 'front' a major public building on this scale, presenting a harmonious façade to the rather heterogeneous functions behind it. The order is a rich Ionic / Corinthian composite, all in *pietra serena*, and each bay is a precise cube; the portico is vaulted with simple white sail vaults. In 1487 roundels were added to the spandrels; eight terracotta roundels, blue and white, depicting an infant in swaddling clothes, by Andrea della Robbia. In the lunettes at each end of the colonnade: frescoes by Poccetti. 140 141

The second order, above the colonnade, was added by Francesco della Luna in 1438–9; in each bay is a small pedimented rectangular light.

Entering through the central bay, a short corridor leads on axis to the first cloister, five bays square, with elegant semicircular arches; by della Luna, 1445, but completed in 1470 by Stefano Rosselli. Above the colonnades: again a lower first floor, with simple rectangular lights alternating with panels decorated with geometrical motifs. Taking the stairs in the NW corner, above Brunelleschi's portico is a long hall, now an art gallery, with works by Luca della Robbia, Botticelli and others. Towards the SW is the second, smaller cloister, also by della Luna: narrow and rectangular, two bays by ten, with fine Ionic capitals to the colonnades.

The church, Santa Maria degli Innocenti, is reached by a doorway in the second left bay of Brunelleschi's colonnade. The plan is a long narrow rectangle. Radically modernised by Bernardo Fallani in 1786, with vault fresco by Sante Pacini. A rich high altar in *pietre dure* (seventeenth century), from the lost church of San Pier Maggiore. The font, late fourteenth or early fifteenth century, is based on that in the baptistery at Parma.

Loggiato dei Serviti: On the NW side of the piazza, and begun in 1516 by Antonio da Sangallo the elder and Baccio d'Agnolo. It faces Brunelleschi's Ospedale, with a loggia of similar dimensions and detailing; flat Corinthian pilasters define the corners. The three bays at the S end are filled in and occupied by the seat of the Compagnia di San Filippo Benizzi by Filippo Baglioni, 1599. The two loggias are not quite parallel to each other but converge slightly towards the church on the N side of the piazza.

Santissima Annunziata: Founded in 1250 by Servite friars, initially as a small oratory, but enlarged and modernised on several occasions. Most of the present underlying fabric is from 1444–77, by Michelozzo. His first work was the atrium or narthex, known as the Chiostrino dei Voti, three bays by two, followed by the larger main cloister (Chiostro dei Morti) to the NW. His most radical and controversial intervention, though, was the insertion of a circular choir, surrounded by chapels, and modelled on Brunelleschi's nearby (uncompleted) Santa Maria degli Angioli. Following great controversy over its design, in 1455 Ludovico Gonzaga, the patron, dismissed Michelozzo, who was replaced

139   Palazzo Grifoni (Budini Gattai):
detail of north façade, by Baccio
d'Agnolo and Bartolomeo Ammannati,
1563–74

140   Ospedale degli Innocenti, begun by
Filippo Brunelleschi, 1419; completed by
Francesco della Luna after 1436: detail of
colonnade, with terracotta roundels by
Andrea della Robbia, 1487

141   Ospedale degli Innocenti: detail of
the colonnade

142   Santissima Annunziata: detail of the
colonnaded portico, by G.B. Caccini, 1601

first by Antonio Manetti and later by Alberti. In 1477–81 the nave walls were raised in height.

Further radical modernisations took place after 1601, first with the present portico, by G.B. Caccini; after 1605 the choir, too, was remodelled in the Baroque manner. Final interventions included the Colloredo chapel by Matteo Nigetti (1643–52) and the Feroni chapel by G.B. Foggini, 1691–3.

Although it completes the urban composition begun by Brunelleschi and continued by Sangallo, Caccini's portico is considerably heavier than the first two, the seven-bay colonnade terminating with large square Corinthian pilasters at the outer corners, and capped by a heavy, boldly projecting cornice. Above the column capitals are dosserets, from which the arches spring, again different from the first two loggias.

The central bay leads, on axis, into the Chiostrino dei Voti, now with a glass roof, and so called for the *ex voti* placed here by pilgrims. On the walls: important frescoes, late fifteenth and early sixteenth centuries. Anti-clockwise, around the right end are works by Rosso Fiorentino (1517); Pontormo (1514–16); Franciabigio (1513); two works by Andrea del Sarto (second corner, 1514); to the left of the door into the church: Baldovinetti (1460) and Cosimo Rosselli (1476). All were detached after the 1966 floods, restored and then repositioned. At the left end of the portico, a doorway leads to the Cappella della Madonna, with a fragment of fresco said to be by Botticelli. At the other, right end of the portico, another doorway leads to the Oratorio di San Sebastiano, built with funding by the Pucci in 1452; perhaps by Michelozzo. Partly modernised in 1608 by G.B. Caccini. Vault frescoes by Poccetti.

The church interior: now of seventeenth- and eighteenth-century appearance. The overall appearance is a richly detailed Baroque, but extremely gloomy. A broad five-and-a-half-bay nave, flanked by rows of deep side chapels, five down each side, followed by a narrower bay and then the cross axis of the transepts. Beyond is the chancel arch and the circular choir / chancel.

Nave right side chapels: first chapel, of San Niccolà; fresco by Matteo Rosselli, 1623. Altarpiece: *Virgin and Child with Saints* by Jacopo da Empoli, 1628. Second chapel: altarpiece by Piero Dandini, 1677. Left wall: Crucifix by Antonio Sangallo the elder and Giuliano da Sangallo, 1483. Third chapel, of the Colloredo; by Matteo Nigetti, 1643–8. Cupola frescoed by Volterrano, 1650. Fourth chapel: altarpiece by Cosimo Ulivelli, 1679. Fifth chapel: frescoes by Ulivelli, 1677. Left flank wall: monument to Orlando de' Medici by Bernardo Rossellino, 1456.

Right transept: Blessed Sacrament chapel by Ferdinando Fuga, 1768. On the left wall, towards the chancel: small chapel with a *Pietà* by Baccio Bandinelli, who is buried here.

Chancel: an impressive circular space, with four semicircular chapels around each of the left and right sides; at the far end is the larger, square chapel of the Madonna del Soccorso. Above the arches of the principal order is a tall drum, with rectangular arched clerestory windows. The appearance today is largely G.B. Foggini's Baroque decoration, early eighteenth century.

The chapels, anti-clockwise from the right: third chapel: by Passignano. Frescoes by Ottavio Vannini, early seventeenth century. Fourth chapel: *Martyrdom of St Lucy* by Jacopo Vignali, 1649. Next is the chapel of the Madonna del Soccorso: reordered by Giambologna, who also made the Crucifix and the six reliefs of the *Passion*. Sixth chapel: altarpiece: *Resurrection* by Bronzino, *circa* 1550. Seventh chapel: early sixteenth-century altarpiece: *Virgin and Child with Saints* by Perugino. Ninth chapel: *Birth of the Virgin Mary* by Allori, 1602.

Back in the nave, left side chapels: in front of the first chapel is the rich, ornate Cappella dell'Annunziata, in the form of a *tempietto*, built for Piero il Gottoso by Maso di Bartolomeo (1447), with a later Baroque baldacchino. Beyond, in the chapel itself: rich tabernacle by Matteo Nigetti, 1617. Second chapel: the Feroni chapel, by G.B. Foggini, 1691–3; on the altar: fresco by Andrea del Castagno, 1455–6. Third chapel: altarpiece: another fresco by Castagno, 1454. Fourth chapel: altarpiece: *Crucifixion* by Giovanni Stradano. Fifth chapel: *Assumption* by Perugino, 1506.

In the left transept: Cappella del Santissimo Crocifisso, with terracotta *St John the Baptist* by Michelozzo. Off the N side of the transept is the sacristy, a large rectangular hall, two bays long, with a good marble doorway, 1459.

Adjacent is the doorway to the main cloister, the Chiostro dei Morti. Rectangular, six bays by five, by Michelozzo, 1444–77. Slightly flattened arches, with columns on square plinths; simple groin vaults. Within the lunettes: fresco cycle of episodes from the *Lives of Servite Saints* by Poccetti and others, including the fine *Madonna del Sacco* by Andrea del Sarto (1525). Above the colonnades: two orders of the friars' accommodation, all with small square windows. Off the N side of the cloister is the chapel of the Compagnia di San Luca, the painters' confraternity, founded in the fourteenth century; in 1563 it was transformed by Cosimo I into the Accademia delle Arti del Disegno, based here until

1784, when it transferred to the Palazzo dei Beccai. Inside: works by the della Robbia, Luca Giordano, Vasari, Bronzino and Antonio da Sangallo the elder.

Back in the piazza, a covered way in the NE corner leads into Via della Colonna. Adjacent, on Via Gino Capponi, almost on the corner, is the new entrance to the **Museo Archeologico**, now subject to many years of refurbishment. It consists of three elements, a smaller western part (for temporary exhibitions), a long linking gallery running along the N edge of the garden, and finally, at the E end, the substantial **Palazzo della Crocetta,** built in 1620 by Giulio Parigi for Maria Maddalena, grand duchess of Austria, sister of Cosimo II. She was born severely disabled, and high-level bridges were built to link the building to the Santissima Annunziata, to the Ospedale degli Innocenti, and two others across Via Laura to the Convento della Crocetta. The palace was modernised (late eighteenth century), but the garden façade retains the original superimposed loggias. The long rectangular garden, parallel to the street, was set out in the mid-eighteenth century. The Museo Archeologico was established here in 1880. It contains a fine collection of Etruscan artefacts, as well as outstanding works from ancient Egypt. The upper floors of Palazzo Crocetta were modernised and reopened in 2010.

Further E along Via della Colonna, is **Santa Maria degli Angiolini**, founded in 1507 as a nunnery. It was suppressed in 1784. A simple little church externally, but with rich mid-seventeenth-century Baroque decoration inside. Return to Piazza della Santissima Annunziata, and turn N. At no. 4 Via Capponi, just past the Museo Archeologico, is the **Oratorio di San Pierino**, with a sixteenth-century terracotta relief of the *Annunciation*, by Santi Buglioni, in the lunette above the portal. Inside: late sixteenth-century cloister with fresco decoration by Poccetti and others, 1585–90; badly damaged in 1966 but detached and restored. A little further SE along the adjacent Via Laura is the former **Convento della Crocetta**, with the two bridges noted above. Founded in 1515, it housed Dominican nuns, but was suppressed in 1808 and became a girls' conservatory.

Back in the piazza, take Via Cesare Battisti out of the NW corner. At nos. 10–12 (right) is the **Istituto Geografico Militare**, the national body responsible for mapping the country, housed in former monastic buildings of the Santissima Annunziata. The Istituto contains a fine library and map collection.

Another compact area, bounded by the Galleria dell'Accademia and other museums to the SE, the Corte d'Appello and San Marco to the N and Sant'Apollonia to the W. Most of the significant buildings surround Piazza San Marco. The attractive tree-planted square is also a busy bus terminus; buses to Fiesole, Settignano, etc. leave from here. In the centre: monument to *General Manfredo Fanti* by Pio Fedi, 1873.

On the NW side, no. 51, corner of Via degli Arazzieri: the **Palazzina** or **Casinò della Livia**, formerly attributed to Buontalenti, but now given to Bernardo Fallani, 1775, and thus an unusual example of late *cinquecento* revival. Once the seat of public offices, but in 1786 was given by Pietro Leopoldo to the ballerina Livia Malfatti Raimondi, and became her home. The short main (E) façade has three bays and two orders; rusticated quoins and a heavy cornice; a central pedimented portal flanked by pedimented windows. Above the flanking windows: roundels with dolphin decoration. The upper order: three pedimented windows, the central one with a balcony. The flank to Via degli Arazzieri, also of three bays, is more restrained.

On the SE side of the piazza, no. 4 is the **Università degli Studi**, the headquarters of the university; once the grand ducal stables. It originated with the Studium Generale founded by the republic in 1321, and in 1364 became the Università Imperiale under Emperor Charles VII. The university was transferred to Pisa by the Medici in 1473, although it returned here (1497–1515), after which it was again transferred to Pisa. It was permanently re-established in Florence after 1859, although the title of university was regained only in 1923.

South of the junction with Via Cesare Battisti, façade to Via Ricasoli, is the **Galleria dell'Accademia**. The Galleria, together with the adjacent institutions of the Accademia itself, the Conservatorio Musicale, the Opificio delle Pietre Dure and the Museo degli Strumenti Musicali Antichi, all occupy the former Ospedale di San Matteo and the Ospedale di San Niccolò di Cafaggio.

The oldest element is the front loggia, 1388–1410, within which are three portals, each surmounted by a terracotta lunette by the della Robbia. The teaching academy was founded by Cosimo I in 1563, but in 1784 was transferred to the Palazzo dell'Arte dei Beccai, when Pietro Leopoldo established the galleries here. The entrance is at no. 58 Via Ricasoli. It was radically reorganised in 1980, after a number of works had been transferred to Palazzo Pitti and the new Museo

143

di San Marco. The Galleria is world-famous for its works by Michelangelo. The entrance leads first to the Sala dell'Anticolosso, then the Sala del Colosso. The latter contains early sixteenth-century paintings by Fra Bartolomeo, Perugino and Filippino Lippi. In the centre is the full-size gesso model for Giambologna's *Rape of the Sabines*, in the Loggia dei Lanzi. From here (left) we reach the main gallery, in which the principal works are Michelangelo's four massively impressive *Prisoners* or *Slaves* (*circa* 1530), intended for the base of the mausoleum of Pope Julius II in St Peter's, Rome. Never completed, they were given by Michelangelo's nephew Leonardo to Cosimo I. They were located in Buontalenti's grotto in the Giardino di Boboli until 1909, when they were transferred here. Also here is Michelangelo's *St Matthew* (1505–6), again incomplete, and intended to be one of a series of *Twelve Apostles* for the exterior of the tribune of the cathedral. At the far end of the gallery is the Tribuna, by Emilio de Fabris, 1882, built to house the famous *David* (1502–4); carved from a single block of Carrara marble, the figure itself is 4.10 m (approx. 13 ft 6 in.) high. It, too, was probably intended for the exterior of the cathedral, but was instead positioned outside the Palazzo Vecchio until it was brought here. To the left of the Tribuna is a room leading to the Salone, now called the Gipsoteca Bartolini, and formerly the ward of the Ospedale di San Matteo. Today it contains plaster models of works by Lorenzo Bartolini (1777–1850), set out in 1985. The four rooms on the first floor contain an important collection of works by Lorenzo Monaco.

Adjacent, to the S, with its entrance at no. 2 Via degli Alfani, is the **Conservatorio di Musica Luigi Cherubini**, established in 1849 and formally rendered autonomous in 1860. It contains a fine library and an exceptional collection of historic musical instruments, today reached from the Accademia galleries.

San Marco: The church façade occupies the NE side of the piazza, with the conventual buildings to the right and behind. Originally built by the Sylvestrines, a reformed Benedictine community; by 1300 the church also had parish functions. Around 1418 the congregation was accused of decadence and was evicted, to be replaced in 1435 by reformed Dominicans. Two years later, under Cosimo il Vecchio, Michelozzo was commissioned to enlarge and modernise the complex. It was reconsecrated in 1443 by Pope Eugenius IV. Under Medici patronage, San Marco became a centre of cultural and intellectual life.

The church façade is by Fra Giovanni Battista Paladini, and was 144 added in 1777–8. Two principal orders and three bays; a central pedimented portal, and niches to the outer bays, containing statues. The second order has a single central pedimented window; the façade is crowned by a triangular pediment, flanked by volutes. Inside: a single, broad, spacious rectangular nave, with three altars down each side; remains of formerly extensive wall frescoes, *circa* 1370–1420; notably the *Crucifixion* on the inner façade above the portal and the *Annunciation* (right side, 1371). Partly modernised in 1579–1600, including the lateral chapels, to conform to the liturgical requirements of the Counter-Reformation. The tribune was modernised again after 1679. A carved and gilded timber ceiling, with an *Assumption* by Giovanni Antonio Pucci, 1725. A square chancel, approached by a large semicircular arch carried by detached columns; beyond is a polygonal apse, both by Michelozzo. Above the chancel: cupola by Angelo Ferri, with frescoes by Alessandro Gherardini, 1717. To the right of the chancel is the small sacristy, also by Michelozzo; it contains a marble sarcophagus of St Antonino (+1459), archbishop of Florence and a Dominican friar, with bronze effigy by Giambologna.

To the left of the chancel, a portal leads to the Serragli or Blessed Sacrament chapel, 1590s, with decorations all in honour of the Sacrament; works by Santi di Tito and Poccetti.

Off the left side of the nave is the large Salviati or St Antonino chapel, with access from Via Cavour by a passage along one side. The chapel stands above a crypt, and is by Giambologna, with decoration by Alessandro Allori (1588) and G.B. Naldini. Left nave chapels: paintings by Cigoli, Passignano and Gabbiani.

Conventual Buildings and Museum

The conventual buildings are ranged around two cloisters, one, that of St Antonino, to the SE of the church; the other, larger, of St Dominic, to the NE, beyond the church apse. The former are now the Museo di San Marco, established in 1866–9, while the northern buildings remain occupied by Dominicans. The whole complex is the work of Michelozzo, mostly 1439–44, and has a refined, elegant simplicity and consistency of detailing. Among those who lived here were Fra Angelico (see below), Fra Antonino (later canonised) and Savonarola. After 1922 most of the other surviving paintings by Fra Angelico were collected here. The Chiostro di Sant'Antonino is five bays square, with simple groin vaults, and surrounded by former monastic buildings. S side: Sala dell'Ospizio, a long narrow hall, with three groin-vaulted bays. Works by Fra Angelico include the notable *Deposition*, 1432, and the *San Marco Altarpiece*, *circa* 1440. At the end of the hall is the *Tabernacle of the Linaiuoli* by Lorenzo Ghiberti, *circa* 1433–4.

The visitors' sequence continues with the Sala del Capitolo (chapter house) on the N side of the cloister; a square hall with a fine frescoed *Crucifixion* by Fra Angelico on the main wall, 1442. A door in the NE corner of the cloister leads first to the Sala del Lavabo, forming an antechamber to the refectory. This wing is fourteenth century, thus pre-dating Michelozzo's interventions. The Sala del Lavabo contains further works by Angelico. In the impressive refectory are works by Giovanni Antonio Sogliani, including the huge frescoed *Crucifixion* (above) and the *Supper of St Dominic* (below), on the S end wall (1536). Returning to the Sala del Lavabo, a corridor (N) leads to the Sala di Alessio Baldovinetti, formerly the kitchen, and now containing Baldovinetti's badly deteriorated standard of St Antonino. To the W of the Sala del Capitolo a corridor leads N towards the larger Chiostro di San Domenico, by Michelozzo, seven bays square, and with similar detailing to the first cloister. Visible through the gateway, but not publicly accessible. In the centre: sculpture of *St Dominic* by Andrea Baratta, 1700. Off the SE corner of the large cloister is the Sala del Cenacolo, or smaller refectory (currently the bookshop), with the splendid frescoed *Last Supper* by Domenico Ghirlandaio, *circa* 1480. Adjacent, along the E side of the large cloister, is the Foresteria, where guests were accommodated; currently used to display archaeological finds and other lapidary fragments.

Behind the Sala del Capitolo are the stairs to the first floor. The friars' cells wrap around three sides of the cloister; they are famous for the wonderful series of frescoes by Fra Angelico and assistants, *circa* 1442–5, all on devotional themes, and totalling thirty-eight works. Most cells are decorated, as are parts of the corridor walls. At the head of the staircase is the notable *Annunciation*, *circa* 1442, and opposite is the *Crucifixion with St Dominic*. The E wing was the first to be decorated, with a row of eleven cells down the left (E) side and ten down the other. The S wing is mostly undecorated, other than the three rooms at the W end, which were the prior's apartments. They also contain memorabilia associated with Savonarola. The N wing contains a further thirteen decorated cells. Adjacent to the stairs, a doorway leads into Michelozzo's library, a long rectangular hall divided into three aisles by two rows of Ionic columns of *pietra serena*. A light, refined and harmonious space, it

143   Palazzina della Livia by Bernardo Fallani, 1775–80

144   San Marco: façade to the piazza, by Giovanni Battista Paladini, 1777–8

145   Casinò Mediceo: detail of window on the east façade, by Bernardo Buontalenti, 1568–74

146   San Giovannino dei Cavalieri: detail of façade, *circa* 1550

is one of the earliest purpose-built libraries of the modern era; it was open to the public from its establishment, and is thus said to be the oldest public library in Europe since antiquity. Today it contains a display of invaluable manuscripts from the San Marco collection.

Via Cavour: north section: Via Cavour continues N from the NW side of the piazza. On the next block (NW side), opposite the conventual buildings of San Marco, is the

Palazzo della Corte d'Appello, the former **Casinò Mediceo** (no. 57). Intentionally located on the same street, but some distance from Palazzo Medici and the courtly activities there. It was used as a workshop, study and laboratory for Francesco I's interests in natural history, science and alchemy.

Its site, as far S as Via degli Arazzieri, had been occupied earlier by Medici orchards, and Cosimo il Vecchio established his Accademia degli Orti Medicei here, later continued by Lorenzo. The Accademia amassed an exceptional collection of classical statues and antiquities; among those who studied here were Donatello, Michelozzo, Michelangelo and Verrocchio. The Accademia was later transferred by Cosimo I to the present Accademia di Belle Arti.

On Cosimo I's death, Francesco I established his own offices here, but in 1568 he commissioned Buontalenti to build a new structure for workshops and foundries. The Opificio delle Pietre Dure was also based here after 1588. The overall plan is a U, wrapped around a courtyard and with the two wings facing W. The Via Cavour façade is very long (eleven wide bays), but restrained, other than the quirky ground-floor windows. The more interesting internal (W) façade is more eclectic, with a projecting central section; three bays and three orders, with rusticated quoins and a large arched, rusticated central portal flanked by aediculed windows. Above: three rectangular windows and above them a rather odd attic with two tiny windows and a central clock. The side wings are similar but more conventional. After Cosimo III the building deteriorated rapidly and its collections were dispersed. In the period of Florence's role as capital it was used by the finance ministry and its interiors largely destroyed. Thereafter it became the appeal court and the Corte d'Assise (assize court).

Opposite the Casinò, no. 146 is the **Antica Farmacia di San Marco**, founded in 1436, like the friary, by St Antonino. Many historic fittings and ceramic pieces from the della Robbia workshop.

Further NE, left, no. 69 is the early sixteenth-century **Chiostro dello Scalzo**, the former base of the Compagnia di San Giovanni Battista, and so called because the members walked barefoot (*scalzi*), carrying a Cross in procession. A simple street façade, with imitation ashlar render, and a portal surmounted by a split pediment, containing a glazed terracotta *Christ* flanked by two members of the order. The principal surviving element of the convent is the elegant courtyard (now roofed) with single and paired columns supporting semicircular arches. On the walls: notable monochrome frescoes by Andrea del Sarto of the *Life of St John the Baptist*, 1507–26.

Returning to Piazza San Marco, this time take Via degli Arazzieri NW to its intersection with Via San Gallo. On the NE corner is the **Oratorio di Gesù Pellegrino**, rebuilt by Giovanni Antonio Dosio, 1584–8, under the patronage of Cardinal Alessandro de' Medici (later Pope Leo XI). A simple façade with pedimented portal. Inside: a rectangular hall with timber beamed roof; around the walls: a cycle of frescoes and canvases by Giovanni Balducci, *circa* 1590, with scenes of the *Life of Christ*. On the diagonally opposite corner (SW) is the former Benedictine **Monastero di Sant'Apollonia**, founded in 1339. Most is now occupied by the university. The principal interest is the refectory, with splendid frescoes by Andrea del Castagno filling the west wall. At low level is the *Last Supper*, one of the earliest and finest of the Renaissance, 1447. Directly above: *Resurrection, Crucifixion* and *Deposition*, all by Andrea, all badly damaged in the 1966 flood, but restored. Smaller fragments of other frescoes by Domenico Veneziano and Piero della Francesca. The monastic church has its portal on Via San Gallo, reputedly by Michelangelo. Its cupola is frescoed by Bernardino Poccetti, late sixteenth century. Three cloisters survive, the biggest, from 1442 (reached from no. 25 Via San Gallo), one of the largest in the city, with Ionic colonnades on three sides of the lower order and plain columns to the upper one; a smaller one, the Chiostro del Silenzio, towards the N; the third is that of the novices.

Directly opposite, at no. 10 Via San Gallo, is **Palazzo Marucelli Fenzi**, on the site of earlier cottages of the Castelli. Designed for them by Gherardo Silvani, 1634, one of the most imposing of the period; in 1659 it passed to the Marucelli. In the early eighteenth century Sebastiano and Marco Ricci decorated the interior extensively, with frescoes of the *Labours of Hercules* (*circa* 1707). Other rooms were richly decorated with stucco by Cosimo Ulivelli. Francesco Marucelli amassed a notable library, which, on his death in 1703 was to be housed in a new building constructed on land that he had also acquired nearby (see p. 186). Today it is occupied by the department of philosophy of the university. The main façade has seven bays and three orders, strongly modelled, with a rich, impressive portal flanked by satyrs and surmounted by a balcony; aediculed windows to the ground floor, pedimented to the *piano nobile*; a simple attic.

Continuing N on Via San Gallo, on the right, past the junction with Via degli Arazzieri, is the **Loggia dei Tessitori**, early sixteenth century, with five bays. Next is the church of **San Giovannino dei Cavalieri**, on the site of a fourteenth-century oratory dedicated to St Mary Magdalene. It was transformed after 1550 when it became the base of the Knights of St John of Jerusalem. A rather bizarre Mannerist three-bay façade with three pedimented portals and swirling decoration to the central bay. Inside: an entrance lobby, beyond which is a rectangular nave with side aisles, three bays long, with timber beamed ceiling. It retains elements of the fourteenth-century structure; paintings by Neri di Bicci, Lorenzo Monaco, Palma il Giovane and Santi di Tito.

146

6 THE NORTHERNMOST ZONES OF THE *QUARTIERE*

This zone, just inside the line of the old city walls, is characterised by the continuation of the same street pattern as the slightly more central zones – large rectangular blocks and parallel streets generally oriented SW–NE – but it is less densely developed and contains two large open spaces.

Borgo Pinti, north of Via degli Alfani: No. 64 is the former **Monastero di San Silvestro**, founded 1530 as a Benedictine nunnery. Suppressed in 1808; more recently a school, and then the seat of the Sovereign Order of the Knights of Malta. A simple three-storey façade with arched lights to the *piano nobile*. A little further, on the other side, at no. 87, the nineteenth-century neo-Classical **Casa Bartolini**, built by the sculptor Lorenzo Bartolini.

Opposite, corner of Via Giusti, is **Palazzo Ximines da Sangallo**, nos. 66–8, incorporating part of an earlier house built by Giuliano and Antonio da Sangallo the elder, *circa* 1498, for their own residence. It was complete before 1510, by which date it housed the Sangallo collection of Roman antiquities. In 1603 it was sold by Giuliano's descendants to Sebastiano di Tommaso Ximines d'Aragona, a Spanish noble. It was then radically modernised by Gherardo Silvani in the late seventeenth century. The rendered façade has five bays, with Mannerist aediculed windows to the ground floor, and a big arched portal. In 1816 the last Ximines left the house in his will to the Panciatichi. A fine garden was then laid out and the house further modernised and enlarged.

Crossing Via Giuseppe Giusti and continuing NE, we reach **Palazzo della Gherardesca** (nos. 95–9). Originally the summer *casinò* of Bartolomeo Scala, chancellor of the republic, it was built in 1472–7 by Giuliano da Sangallo; it then passed to Alessandro de' Medici (later Pope Leo XI), in 1585, who gave it to his sister, who married into the Gherardesca. A notable early example of the *casinò di delizie*, or semi-rural villa. Of Sangallo's original house, only the fine square courtyard survives, with twelve reliefs of allegorical subjects around the walls. The chapel is late sixteenth century. In 1713–20 the building was enlarged and reordered by G.B. Foggini (and perhaps Antonio Maria Ferri). The extensive gardens were set out by Guido Alberto della Gherardesca, *circa* 1820, with a rich collection of rare species, and a circular *tempietto* by Giuseppe Cacialli. Its N boundary was radically altered when Poggi's new road was set out along the line of the city walls, and the gardens were then enclosed with a new wall and gates by Poggi. The palace has been extensively restored and since 2001 has been a hotel.

A little further is **Palazzo Salviati Larderel** (no. 80), built by Gherardo Silvani in the late seventeenth century but radically altered and modernised in the nineteenth century. A very broad façade: three orders plus an attic, a cross between a *palazzo* and a *casinò di delizie*. A projecting stone portal but very simple fenestration.

Return to the junction with Via Giuseppe Giusti and turn right (NW) along the street towards its junction with Via Gino Capponi. At no. 43 (S side) is the highly eclectic façade of

Palazzo Zuccari: Designed by the artist Federico Zuccari for himself in 1579, when he settled in the city (and began the frescoes in the cupola of the cathedral). It was intended primarily as a studio. The tall, fairly narrow, symmetrical Mannerist façade is one of the most truly bizarre in Florence; on the lower part are small square windows set into the façade surface, which itself is partly flat ashlar and partly rusticated, with relief decoration also set into it. In the centre of the upper part is a huge plain rectangular panel. The entire composition appears wilfully dissonant, with stone and plaster intermingled. Inside, the ground-floor hall giving onto the rear garden is elaborately frescoed, 1577.

147

Back on Via Capponi, no. 22, on the corner, is the house built for himself by Andrea del Sarto, 1520. It was bought by Zuccari in 1577, who lived here while building the adjacent palace. The two buildings shared a common garden. A little further on Via Capponi, no. 9 is the **Palazzina dei Servi**, a neo-Classical building (1810) by Luigi de Cambray-Digny, built to house the French archbishop during the Napoleonic occupation. A very long façade and a central colonnade. Returning N, just past the junction with Via Giusti, at no. 26, is the important

Palazzo Capponi Farinola (di Gino Capponi): An imposing *palazzo* by Carlo Fontana for the senator Marchese Alessandro Capponi, 1699–1716. One of the most notable of the last generations of palaces; its first-floor salon is said to be the largest in a private palace in the city. Designed by Fontana while in Rome, the drawings were then sent to Florence, and work was supervised on site by Alessandro Cecchini, possibly with the young Ferdinando Ruggieri. The plan takes the form of a U, with a long street façade, and the relatively short rear wings built around a courtyard, open on the SE side to the gardens. The street façade, nineteen bays, is majestically imposing, if rather monotonous, with two outer wings each of five bays and a central section of nine bays, taller and set slightly forward. The garden façade is more highly articulated; three storeys, with the windows to the *piano nobile* capped by idiosyncratic Mannerist pediments. The central bays are further articulated with full-height pilasters, arched windows and balconies. In 1716 Alessandro left the palace to his two sons, who decorated the interiors lavishly. The splendid staircase is decorated with statuary and fountains. Around 1840 it passed to Gino Capponi, a notable intellectual who made the palace a centre of Florentine cultural life. Later again, after 1945, it passed to the senator Alessandro Contini Bonacossi, whose heirs own the house today.

From the N end of Palazzo Capponi, take Via Pier Antonio Micheli W. At no. 2 is the unusual **Palazzo Guadagni** or **di San Clemente**. Built *circa* 1640, perhaps by Gherardo Silvani. Something between a city *palazzo* and a suburban villa. The street façade is articulated into three sections: two projecting side wings, linked by a single-storey central bay containing a strongly modelled portal. Above is a terrace, behind which is the recessed central section of the main house. Rusticated quoins and chunky aedicules to the windows. Towards the garden (N) is a three-bay colonnaded loggia, with a terrace above. After 1777 it

147 Palazzo Zuccari: detail of façade, by Federico Zuccari, 1579

148 Palazzo Capponi Farinola: central window and balcony to west façade, by Carlo Fontana and others, begun 1699

149 Palazzo Pandolfini: detail of first-floor windows, by Raphael, begun 1520

was owned by Charles Edward Stuart, the 'Young Pretender' to the English throne. Recently used by the university.

No. 3 (S side) is the entrance to the Natural History Museum and the

Giardino dei Semplici or **Orto Botanico**: Founded by Cosimo I in 1550; one of the most notable botanic gardens in Italy. Originally laid out by Niccolò Tribolo, it has been altered several times, notably at the beginning of the nineteenth century (by Ottaviano Targioni Tozzetti) and again towards the end of the century. Although its present extent is that of Cosimo's foundation, many of the trees date from Targioni's interventions. The Museo Botanico, housed in twelve rooms along the N edge of the site, was founded in 1842, and is again one of the most notable in Europe.

Continuing NW along Via Micheli, at the corner of Via La Marmora is the **Chiesa Valdese**. Built in 1890 by Frederick Bodley for the Anglican community, in a Perpendicular Gothic manner, with a prominent bell-tower with Gothic tracery. A spacious interior, with marble English Gothic piers and a flat coffered painted ceiling. It passed to the Valdese community in 1967. After crossing Via Cavour, Via Micheli becomes Via Salvestrina. At the junction with Via San Gallo is the important

Palazzo Pandolfini: Via San Gallo no. 74. Built for Giannozzo Pandolfini, bishop of Troia, a town in Puglia, to a design by Raphael, probably *circa* 1513–14; it was begun in 1520, the year in which Raphael died. His only work of architecture in Florence, construction was supervised initially by Giovanni Francesco da Sangallo, until his death in 1530, and thereafter by his brother Aristotele. The palace is still owned by the Pandolfini. An impressive structure *alla romana*, with two distinct elements; the larger, towards the N, has a C-shaped plan built around a courtyard, open towards the S. The second, smaller element is a narrower wing along Via San Gallo towards the S; the upper order of this wing was never completed. In the centre, at the junction of the two elements, is a huge rusticated portal. The principal N wing has four bays and two orders, with rusticated quoins and large rectangular windows treated as aedicules with alternating curved and triangular pediments; Ionic semi-columns to the upper windows. A massive, boldly projecting cornice. An inscription below the cornice, with large, elegant Roman lettering, records the construction following the issue

149

of a papal bull by Leo X. The substantial garden was reordered in the eighteenth century, when the *limonaia* (orangery) was also built. It was transformed into a garden *all'inglese circa* 1830–40.

Continuing N along Via San Gallo, on the W side is the

Former Ospedale di Bonifacio or **di San Giovanni Battista**: Occupies a whole square city block between Via delle Ruote and Via delle Mantellate. Named after its founder, Bonifacio Lupi, who established it in 1377; rebuilt in 1787 by Giuseppe Salvetti for Pietro Leopoldo. He also added the impressive portico, modelled on that of the Spedale di Santa Maria Nuova. A single *piano nobile* with aediculed windows above the colonnade. The long façade originally terminated with the churches of San Luca and San Giovanni Battista at each end (both now lost). It survived as a hospital until 1877. In 1928 it was acquired by the provincial government; ten years later it became the seat of the Questura. A little further NE is the church of **Sant'Agata**, now the chapel of the adjacent Ospedale Militare (military hospital). Founded in 1211 and occupied by a series of orders of nuns including the Camaldolese order of the Donne di Bibbiena, after 1289. Modernised and reconsecrated in 1569. A rather Mannerist façade of three bays and three orders; rusticated quoins and large niches for statues. The high altarpiece is the *Marriage at Cana* by Alessandro Allori.

Via San Gallo terminates at the spacious Piazza della Libertà (1865–73), set out where it meets the line of the old city walls. The large rectangular piazza was formed by Giuseppe Poggi at the point where no fewer than six streets and three avenues converge. It is defined by four identical blocks, again by Poggi, in a refined neo-Renaissance manner, with generous ground-floor colonnades and two upper orders. On axis with Via San Gallo is the **Porta San Gallo**, one of the oldest surviving medieval city gates (1284–5). A massive simple central arch, all of stone, with a large platform above, from which the city could be defended. On the same axis, a little further NE, is the **Arco di Trionfo**, built by the French architect Jean Nicolas Jadot, for Francesco Stefano di Lorena, to celebrate the arrival into Florence of the eighth grand duke (20 January 1739). Three bays, Corinthian, with a large central arch and two much smaller flanking arches. Its original simplicity was lost when the over-elaborate sculpture was added in 1744.

The north-west corner of the *quartiere*: This district, known as Barbano, is defined by Via Faenza to the SW, Viale Spartaco Lavagnini to the NW and Via Santa Reparata to the NE. The district was laid out in 1844–55, the first of several major nineteenth-century urban developments. The principal feature is the vast **Piazza dell'Indipendenza**, occupying two city blocks, and bounded by Via della Fortezza (SW), Via Nazionale (SE) and Via Giuseppe Dolfi (NE). Set out after 1850, it was dedicated to Princess Maria Antonia Lorena, but was renamed at Unification. The attractive central garden was set out in 1869. The surrounding housing is mostly of three storeys, and largely neo-Classical, although with considerable local variation: there is no grand unifying theme as there is with the later interventions of Poggi.

One block SW of the piazza is the W end of Via Guelfa; at no. 79 is the **Istituto di Sant'Agnese**, an extensive complex, founded as an orphanage by the Compagnia del Bigallo in 1438. It remains in use today for sheltered housing. A long two-storey street façade, seventeenth century, with two pedimented portals and tall arched windows.

Back in the piazza, off the NE corner is Via **Santa Caterina**, with the homonymous church. Founded in 1310 as an Augustinian convent, the present church was begun in 1848 by Gaetano Baccani, to serve the new residential quarter. Shortage of funding resulted in a hiatus, and work restarted in 1856 to a new design, on a considerably increased scale, by Giuseppe Maria Martelli. Construction ceased in 1863. In 1904 it was acquired by missionaries of the Sacro Cuore, and rededicated accordingly. The design is neo-Classical, with a nave and two side aisles, the former with a barrel vault, the latter with flat coffered ceilings. A semicircular tribune terminates the east end; the intended rich internal decoration was never completed, nor was the main façade. In front: two rich columns of *pietra serena* intended for the façade loggia. Further NE on the other side is the mid-nineteenth-century **San Giuseppe**, in a very simple neo-Gothic style, with a neo-Renaissance portal. On the same street, nos. 33–4 is an office building, the **Centro Leasing**, built for Olivetti in 1968–72 by Alberto Gagliardi and others. An elegant block, with a highly articulated façade; a rectilinear grid of concrete elements set well forward of the fully glazed façade itself. Four storeys cantilevered above the ground floor. At no. 14 is the **Palazzo della Cassa di Risparmio**, built in 1953 as the offices for *Il Mattino* newspaper. The architect was Giorgio Giuseppe Gori; a simple rhythmic façade, with brick cladding and recessed windows.

150   Palazzo Pucci: a rather time-worn *stemma* of the Medici

The *Quartiere* of Santa Maria Novella

The *Quartiere* of Santa Maria Novella

This is the third of the three *quartieri* on 'this' (N) side of the Arno. It covers the NW sector of the historic centre, and is bounded on the E by the long, narrow Via Faenza, and then the medieval heart; to the S it is defined by the Arno, while its outer limit is defined by the course of the lost medieval walls. Its most prominent monument is the monastic complex of Santa Maria Novella itself.

I THE INNERMOST ZONE: PALAZZO RUCELLAI, PALAZZO CORSINI AND SAN PANCRAZIO

A small, roughly wedge-shaped district, bounded by the former Roman *castrum* (Via dei Tornabuoni) to the E, the river to the S and Via del Moro to the NW. Proceed from the SE corner towards the N.

Ponte Santa Trinità: One of the oldest bridges, first built in 1252, in timber. Destroyed by floods seven years later, it was reconstructed in stone, but was again badly damaged by the disastrous flood of 1333. Rebuilt once again by Taddeo Gaddi, this time with five arches, it survived until 1557, when it collapsed into the floodwaters once more. The replacement was built by Ammannati (1567–70) on the instructions of Cosimo I, and possibly to a design by Michelangelo, with three broad, shallow but extremely elegant polycentric arches. In 1608 four symbolic statues were added to the two bridgeheads, representing the four seasons: *Spring* (*Primavera*) by Pietro Francavilla and *Summer* (*Estate*) by G. B. Caccini (N bridgehead); *Autumn* (*Autunno*), also by Caccini, and *Winter* (*Inverno*) by Taddeo Landini (S bridgehead). The bridge was blown up by the retreating Germans on 4 August 1944, but was rebuilt in 1952 as accurately as possible, using some original material. 152

Lungarno Corsini: The Lungarno follows the N bank from Ponte Santa Trinità to the Ponte alla Carraia. Turning the corner of Via dei Tornabuoni, with five bays towards Palazzo Spini and four towards the

151   The new Teatro dell'Opera Lirica by Paolo Desideri and Studio ABDR

river (no. 2r), is one of several Gianfigliazzi houses, also known as **Palazzo Piccioli**. A much-altered ground floor, then three orders with rusticated arched window heads, the top one added in the nineteenth century; a prominent rusticated quoin. After a narrow infill building, no. 2n is **Palazzo Gianfigliazzi**, later Masetti, fourteenth century, but modernised by Gherardo Silvani in the seventeenth. Four orders and seven bays; in recent times the British consulate. Plaque to Vittorio Alfieri, who died here in 1803. No. 4 is a second Gianfigliazzi house, significantly larger but also many times modified and modernised. These houses collectively form the longer arm of an 'L', of which the shorter arm is the wing onto Piazza Santa Trinità. No. 4 became the main family residence. In 1457 it was sold to the Tegghiacci from Siena, but bought back again only two years later, when it was modernised. A big square façade with a very tall ground floor and mezzanine; a large central portal, flanked by small windows. A generous first floor, originally with seven bays (now eight), with tall arched lights; a full-width loggia across the top. Plaque to Alessandro Manzoni. In 1825 the palace was bought by Louis Bonaparte, Napoleon's brother. At nos. 32–40r is the **Palazzo dei Vallombrosani**, attached to the adjacent church of Santa Trinità. Five bays and four orders; probably by Buontalenti. Immediately adjacent, no. 10 is the imposing

Palazzo Corsini al Parione: One of the largest private palaces in the city, with an exceptionally long river façade, and occupying the block back to Via del Parione. On the site of former houses of the Altoviti, which were sequestered by the Medici and in 1649 given to Maria Maddalena Machiavelli, widow of Filippo Corsini. Construction of the present palace took place over some decades, and under several different architects, finally concluding *circa* 1737. The completed complex is unusual for Florence and has a distinctly 'Roman' appearance (c.f. Carlo Maderna's Palazzo Barberini). Initial restoration of an original *casinò* was by Alfonso Parigi; work then continued under Ferdinando Tacca until 1671. In 1679 construction began again, this time under Gherardo Silvani, to whom is usually attributed the U-shaped plan, with the courtyard towards the river. Silvani also designed the 'spiral' staircase inside, in *pietra serena*, in 1683. In 1685 a further phase was begun for Filippo di Bartolomeo Corsini, again mostly on the S side, and incorporating an adjacent house formerly owned by the Guadagni. The principal staircase and Salone are by Antonio Maria Ferri, 1694–7, as are the courtyard elevations.

The long river façade has three orders; the main W wing has only four bays, but the much longer E wing has ten, the two groups of five representing the original extent and later eastward extension. Between the wings is the courtyard, at the rear of which are two superimposed five-bay loggias. The main wings are joined by the long single-storey screen wing along the front (by Ferri), above which is a terrace, which continues to left and right as a balcony for the two side wings. In the low single-storey wing is a portal, with six bays to one side and seven on the other. The detailing is all rich but restrained. The equally rich internal decoration is by Piero Dandini, Tommaso Gherardini and others. The ballroom is decorated by Alessandro Gherardini, 1693. The palace contains the most important private art collection in Florence, including works by Luca Giordano, Salvator Rosa, Filippino Lippi, Luca Signorelli and Giovanni Bellini.

Terminating this section of the Lungarno is

Palazzo Ricasoli: Piazza Goldoni no. 2 (E side). Begun *circa* 1480 for Ranieri and Lorenzo Ricasoli, but completed *circa* 1500; attributed to Michelozzo or Baccio d'Agnolo. In 1580 a tunnel was built under the street to connect the palace with a large garden towards the NW. A substantial building: three orders, with an eight-bay façade to the river and a five-bay return façade to the piazza; both refined but restrained. The tall ground floor has rusticated arched portals to both façades and aediculed rectangular windows. Above: two orders of single-arched windows. The façade to Via del Parione has *sporti*.

From Piazza Goldoni (monument to the playwright Carlo Goldoni by Ulisse Cambi, 1873) take Via della Vigna Nuova NE towards Via dei Tornabuoni. Halfway down is the small, triangular Piazza Rucellai, formed by Leon Battista Alberti in conjunction with the adjacent

Palazzo Rucellai: No. 18. The palace itself was built, or reordered, in stages, mainly in 1446–51; the façade, too, was built in phases, the first *circa* 1455–8 and the second *circa* 1465–70. The completed building unified a number of existing properties behind this new façade. The patron was the wealthy banker Giovanni di Paolo Rucellai. Its highly refined façade, all in *pietra forte*, was designed by Alberti, but executed under Bernardo Rossellino. It probably originally had just five bays, later extended to seven, but was never completed as intended, since the adjacent property to the right was not acquired; consequently, the eighth, and perhaps ninth, bays were never built, and the façade terminates arbitrarily. It has great importance as the first attempt in the Renaissance to apply the classical orders to the façade of a *palazzo*, and is in marked contrast to the massively powerful façades of Palazzo Medici and Palazzo Strozzi. Three orders, defined by flat pilasters: respectively Doric, Ionic and Corinthian. Dividing the orders are elegant entablatures, containing the Rucellai and Medici symbols. The entire façade is clad with flat rustication. On the first order: large square portals in the third and sixth bays, and small square windows at high level. The two upper orders are nearly identical, with *bifore* set within rusticated arched heads; the façade is capped by a bold overhanging cornice. Part of the building is still occupied by the Rucellai. The plan remains irregular, with a courtyard towards the rear; two sides are now filled in but the remaining elegant colonnade has Corinthian capitals.

On the opposite corner is Alberti's

Loggia Rucellai, 1463–6, built to accommodate the wedding celebrations of Bernardo Rucellai and Lucrezia (Nannina di Piero) de' Medici in 1466, but used subsequently for many family events and to display the family's produce; rather grandiose for the very small square. Three bays by one, with robust square corner piers and circular columns to the main façade; semicircular arches, and the Rucellai family symbol (a stylised sail) along the frieze. The colonnade was walled up in 1677 but reopened and filled with glazing in 1963.

Take the narrow Via dei Palchetti, left of Palazzo Rucellai, then right into Via dei Federighi. After a short distance, it opens into the small Piazza San Pancrazio.

San Pancrazio: Recorded since the ninth century; rebuilt by the Vallombrosan order between 1370 and 1454. Medieval remains in the crypt and the nave vault. The church was under the patronage of the Rucellai, who in 1465 commissioned Alberti to modernise it. It was further radically modernised by Giuseppe Ruggieri in 1751–4, but deconsecrated in 1808. Many alterations were made thereafter, including the closure of the access into the adjacent Rucellai chapel (see below), while the columns that Alberti had added to link the church and the chapel were relocated on the main façade. Extensive restoration was concluded in 1988; today it contains a museum of the works of the sculptor Marino Marini (1901–1980).

152 Ponte Santa Trinità: statue of *Spring* by Pietro Francavilla, 1608, and the Ponte Vecchio beyond

153 Palazzo Corsini al Parione: general view from the south-east, by Antonio Maria Ferri and others, 1655–99

154 Palazzo Rucellai, by Leon Battista Alberti, 1446–51: detail of first-floor windows

155 Palazzo Rucellai: detail of portal

156 Loggia Rucellai, by Leon Battista Alberti, 1463–6: detail of arches and frieze

To the right (S) side are the remains of the monastic buildings, with a small cloister from *circa* 1447; after 1933 occupied by a barracks.

Adjacent on the N side is the

Rucellai chapel: Today reached directly from Via della Spada, since the link to the church was bricked up. The original structure is fourteenth century, but was transformed by Alberti; a rectangular plan, three bays long, with a barrel-vaulted roof. The internal articulation is by rich fluted Corinthian pilasters, which rise to an elaborate entablature. The long right-hand side of the chapel had been opened by Alberti so that it linked directly with the church itself; the two columns at present on the church façade originally stood here, supporting a long, continuous entablature.

In the centre of the chapel is Alberti's tomb monument to Giovanni di Paolo Rucellai (completed 1467), and based on an impression of the Holy Sepulchre in Jerusalem: a rectangular free-standing reliquary casket, with a semicircular apse at one end, and entirely clad with beautifully finished marble. Articulation is again by fluted Corinthian pilasters, and the cladding incorporates geometric patterns and motifs. Around the entablature: a fine frieze with an elegant Roman inscription from St Mark's Gospel; the tomb is capped by a rich, rather complex crenellation of stylised lilies, the symbol of Florence, but also representing the Annunciation, to which the chapel is dedicated.

Via della Spada: on the W section (nos. 13–15r), with a second façade to Piazza Ottaviana, is **Palazzo Niccolini**, early sixteenth century, built for the Bourbon, later (1863) acquired by the Niccolini. Four orders, and four bays on the façade to Via della Spada; all with simple, seg-mental-arched openings. The wall surface has imitation rustication throughout. Taking Via della Spada in the other direction, SE, we reach Via del Sole and Via delle Belle Donne.

No. 11 Via del Sole is **Palazzo da Magnale**, with two street façades, the principal with five bays, the other with three. Earlier modest houses on the site were bought in 1443 by the Minerbetti, who joined them into one. The property then passed to the Bonsignori and the Torna-buoni. In 1540 it passed to the Bernardo who rebuilt it as we see today; refined façades, with aediculed ground-floor windows. Three orders, the lowest faced with stone, plus an attic. No. 9 Via del Sole (corner of Via del Moro) is **Palazzo Farinola**, a simple seventeenth-century structure with pedimented portal (bust of *Cosimo I de' Medici* above) and three upper orders.

Turn N up Via delle Belle Donne. On the right is the late sixteenth-century **Palazzo Larderel**, originally Giacomini, with another façade to Via dei Tornabuoni (see p. 129). Continue N to the junction with Via del Trebbio. Several streets meet here at the Croce al Trebbio (= *trivio*, 'three ways'). In the centre: a granite column, erected in 1338 to record a confrontation that took place in 1244 between orthodox Catholics and heretics. Continue up Via delle Belle Donne; it enters the extensive Piazza Santa Maria Novella on the E corner.

2 PIAZZA SANTA MARIA NOVELLA, CHURCH AND FRIARY

The piazza, one of the largest in the city centre, was set out in 1287 by the *comune*, and was completed *circa* 1325. In the centre: two marble obelisks, erected in 1608, standing on top of little bronze tortoises by Giambologna; they defined the course of the chariot race (Palio dei Cocchi) that took place here from 1563 to the mid-nineteenth century, at the instigation of Cosimo I. The piazza was paved until 1933, when the central section was grassed and a pond added. It was replanned *circa* 2008–9; in the centre: a series of parallel benches, of mixed materials (wood, glass and steel), with inscriptions from the writings of Alberti. Along the SW side is the elegant **Loggia dell'Ospedale di San Paolo**, 157 its design based on Brunelleschi's Ospedale degli Innocenti. The Ospedale di San Paolo was first recorded in 1208; after 1222 it was taken over by Franciscan tertiaries. In the fifteenth century it was patronised by both the guilds of Medici e Speziali (physicians and pharmacists) and of Giudici e Notai (judges and lawyers); it reached its peak of importance and physical extent in the later fifteenth century, with extensive modernisations by Michelozzo (*circa* 1459), including the loggia, the Chiostro degli Uomini and the Chiostro delle Donne. The hospital was suppressed in 1780, after which (*circa* 1830s) it became a school managed by the Leopoldine order. The oldest surviving element is a long dormitory hall, the Corsia, reached from Via Palazzuolo. The loggia (1489–96) has nine bays, with spacious semicircular arches supported by Corinthian columns. In the spandrels: terracotta medallions of Franciscan saints by Andrea della Robbia, 1489–96; in the centre: bust of *Ferdinando I de' Medici* by Pietro Francavilla, *circa* 1594. In the right end bay, above the portal that gives into the church, is a fine lunette depicting the *Meeting of St Francis and St Dominic*, again by della

Robbia. As at the Innocenti, the loggia forms a unifying element, screening the heterogeneous functions behind it; from SE to NW they are: the men's quarters and cloister; the Corsia and its chapel; the women's refectory and women's cloisters. The latter are considerably larger than the men's: five bays square, with a Composite colonnade supporting simple groin vaults and a covered gallery above.

On the corner of Via della Scala is a large fifteenth-century tabernacle with a copy of the *Virgin and Child with Saints* by Francesco d'Antonio, late fifteenth century. Off the E side of the piazza is Via dei Banchi, which, at its E end, joins Via dei Cerretani. On the N side, no. 2 is **Palazzo Doni**. The site was acquired by Niccolò Doni in 1546, and the palace was probably built by Mario Doni, a senator, *circa* 1599; a second façade to Via dei Panzani (altered in the nineteenth century when the street was widened). It was attributed to Buontalenti by Ferdinando Ruggieri. The Via dei Banchi façade has two portals and six aediculed windows to the ground floor; eight bays and two orders above, classical and restrained. In 1667 it was sold to Cosimo Venturi, whose family owned the adjacent house. One first-floor room is frescoed by Poccetti, late sixteenth century. Towards the piazza, no. 4 is **Palazzo Venturi**, with a second façade to Via del Giglio.

On the other side: no. 5 is **Palazzo Lapaccini**, then **Palazzo Buontalenti** and finally **Palazzo Giraldi**. At no. 4, corner of Via del Giglio, is **Palazzo Mondragone**, or Ricasoli di Meleto, probably by Ammannati. By 1567 the Spanish nobleman Fabio de Arazzo, marchese di Mondragone, and tutor of Francesco de' Medici (son of Cosimo I), had bought several houses from the Cini, and commissioned Ammannati to rebuild. By 1572, though, Mondragone had been disgraced and exiled, and it was returned to earlier owners, the Carnesecchi. The main façade has three orders; large coat of arms of the Ricasoli on the short façade towards the piazza.

Santa Maria Novella: Together with Santa Croce, the most important friary foundation in the city. It originates from 1221, when Dominicans obtained the use of a church called Santa Maria delle Vigne, which had been built in the eleventh century. The earlier church was oriented E–W and its foundations have been located below the present crossing and transepts. New conventual buildings were then begun, and in 1278 a new church was also started; it has a different orientation from the older one, with the liturgical E end now facing N. The great new church was largely complete by the mid-fourteenth century, as was its campanile, although it was not consecrated until 1420. The nave and most of the conventual buildings are said to be by Jacopo Talenti, one of the friars.

The Façade

The famous piazza façade was begun in the Gothic era, but not completed. Proposals were sought in 1439–42, and when Alberti was commissioned by Giovanni di Paolo Rucellai, he had to integrate much of the lower order, including the six flanking Gothic arches and the two outer portals, as well as a large oculus in the upper order. Work began *circa* 1458. The result is an ingenious, complex and extremely elegant composition, all in white and greenish-black marble. It draws on the Florentine tradition of geometrical cladding but interprets it in a radically new manner.

The broad lower order is defined by the width of the nave and side aisles. Alberti's imposing central portal, with a semicircular arch, is flanked by two monolithic Corinthian columns, a second pair of which define the outer corners. On each side of the portal: four tall bays of round-arched decoration, the lower parts incorporating Gothic niches. Set into the bases of the niches are tombs, with family arms on the front faces. At the outer corners the Corinthian columns are flanked by stout square pilasters of striped marble.

The broad entablature contains the Rucellai sail symbol, but above it is a much larger, deeper frieze, with a row of fifteen square marble panels. The real tour de force is the upper order, treated as a temple front; the central bay incorporates the Gothic oculus, with flanking paired pilasters and a wall cladding of refined decorated marble panels; the order is capped by a richly detailed triangular pediment, in the centre of which is a radiant sun, symbol of the Dominicans. On each side of this central upper order are two massive, richly detailed volutes, which unite the narrower upper order with the much broader lower one. The entire surfaces of the volutes and pediment are clad with rich, complex, patterned marble, treated almost like intarsia.

The Interior

The interior is monumental, light and spacious: 99.2 m (approx. 325 ft) long, 61.4 m (approx. 201 ft) across at the transepts. Like Santa Croce, the plan is a T, an Egyptian or tau cross, with a long, spacious nave of

157 Loggia di San Paolo: detail of the colonnade, 1489–96

158 Via dei Banchi, towards the cathedral cupola, with Ammannati's Palazzo Mondragone, 1567, left

159 Santa Maria Novella: façade, mostly by Alberti, 1439–42

160 Santa Maria Novella: the façade from the south-east

161   Santa Maria Novella: central part of the façade, with oculus

162   Santa Maria Novella: upper order of the façade

163   Santa Maria Novella: the Chiostro Verde, by Jacopo Talenti, 1332–50

164   Santa Maria Novella: entrance to the historic pharmacy on Via della Scala

six rectangular bays, flanked by shallow aisles; at the crossing is a large square bay, while the transepts are also square. The four nave bays towards the façade are longer than the remaining two; the difference may have been linked to the location of the screen that once separated the nave from the choir. It was removed *circa* 1571 by Vasari on instructions from Cosimo I. Light derives from high-level oculi in each of the nave bays and tall lancets to the side aisles. Beyond: a square-ended chancel, with three lancets, flanked on each side by pairs of smaller rectangular chapels. Pilasters and columns are of *pietra forte*, Corinthian, while the vaults are defined by pointed arches and rib vaults of striped white Carrara and green Prato marble.

Monuments and chapels

Inner façade: in the oculus: stained-glass *Coronation of the Virgin* designed by Andrea di Buonaiuto, *circa* 1367. In the lunette above the portal: *Nativity* fresco, school of Botticelli.

Right aisle

First chapel: *Martyrdom of St Lawrence* by Girolamo Macchietti, 1573. Second chapel: tomb of Blessed Villana de' Botti, by Antonio and Bernardo Rossellino and Desiderio da Settignano, 1451. Altarpiece: *Nativity* by Giovanni Battista Naldini, 1573. To the left: tomb of Blessed Giovanni da Salerno, with replacement figure by Vincenzo Danti, in *quattrocento* style. Third chapel: *Presentation at the Temple* by Naldini, 1577. Fourth chapel: *Deposition*, again by Naldini, 1572. Fifth chapel: *St Vincent Ferrer Preaching*, with *Christ the Redeemer* at high level, sixteenth century, by Jacopo Coppi. Off the sixth bay is the Cappella della Pura: built for the Ricasoli in 1473 to house a refined marble *tempietto*, in which is a miracle-working image of the Virgin Mary. Internal decoration, nineteenth century, by Gaetano Baccani. On the altar: thirteenth-century English Crucifix. In the sixth chapel: altarpiece: *St Raymond* by Jacopo Ligozzi, 1620–23.

Right transept

On the right wall: three tomb monuments: above, tomb of Tedice Aliotti (+1336), attributed to Maso di Banco. Left: tomb of Fra Aldovrando Cavalcanti (+1279). Below: tomb of Joseph II, patriarch of Constantinople (+1440). Off the end wall of the transept, raised about 1.5m (approx. 5 ft) above the floor level, and approached by a large Gothic arch: Rucellai family chapel: rib-vaulted, decorated with gold stars on a blue ground. Altarpiece: marble *Virgin and Child* by Nino Pisano, mid-fourteenth century. Left wall: *Martyrdom of St Catherine* by Giuliano Bugiardini, *circa* 1540. In the centre of the floor: tomb of Fra Leonardo Dati, general of the Dominican order, bronze, by Ghiberti, 1425–6.

Two chapels off the liturgical E side of the transept: right chapel, of the Bardi: also known as that of the Blessed Sacrament or of St Dominic: a complex eighteenth-century iron screen. It originally housed Duccio's *Rucellai Madonna*, today in the Uffizi. On the right pilaster: high relief of *St Gregory*, thirteenth century. On the walls: further remains of thirteenth-century decoration. Altarpiece: Vasari's *Our Lady of the Rosary*, 1570. To the left is the Strozzi chapel: frescoes of the *Lives of St Philip and St John the Evangelist* by Filippino Lippi, *circa* 1494–1502. On the end wall: tomb of Filippo Strozzi by Benedetto da Maiano; *Virgin and Child* in a roundel (*tondo*) supported by four angels. *Chiaroscuro* frescoes also by Lippi.

Chancel

Dedicated to the Assumption, and to the Tornabuoni family: originally frescoed by Orcagna; some survive, now in the adjacent museum. On the walls: a celebrated fresco cycle by Domenico Ghirlandaio, assisted by his brothers Davide and Benedetto, and patronised by Giovanni Tornabuoni, 1485–90. The various scenes, from the *Life of the Virgin* on the left wall and the *Life of St John the Baptist* on the right, are enlivened by portraits of many contemporary Florentines. Below the frescoes: wooden choir stalls, with intarsia decoration by Baccio d'Agnolo, 1485–90. The choir was reordered by Vasari in 1566. On the altar: bronze Crucifix by Giambologna. The rich marble high altar is by Enrico Romoli, 1860.

Left transept

Chapels: right chapel, of the Gondi family: the chapel itself is a restrained work by Giuliano da Sangallo, 1503, clad with geometric patterns in black and white marble and porphyry. In a niche on the altar wall: a noted polychrome wooden Crucifix by Brunelleschi, his only known work in this medium. In the vault: remains of thirteenth-century frescoes. To the left is the Gaddi chapel, modernised in 1574–7 by Giovanni Antonio Dosio and decorated with *pietra dura*, one of the first examples of this technique. Vault frescoes by Alessandro Allori and stucco by Dosio.

At the end of the left transept, elevated, is the Strozzi di Mantova chapel, dedicated to St Thomas Aquinas. Adjacent to the access steps: fourteenth-century fresco in the manner of Orcagna. The chapel itself, 1335, has a notable fresco cycle by Nardo di Cione, Orcagna's brother, *circa* 1350–57, said to have been commissioned by Tommaso Strozzi to atone for the sin of usury. On the left wall is *Paradise*, on the end wall is the *Last Judgement*, on the right wall are *Purgatory* (above) and *Inferno* (below). In the vault: *St Thomas Aquinas* and the *Four Cardinal Virtues* in roundels, all by Giovanni del Biondo. The fine altarpiece is *Christ the Redeemer Giving the Keys to St Peter and the Book of Knowledge to St Thomas*, by Orcagna, 1357. The stained-glass window above the altar is also by Nardo: *Virgin and Child* (above) and *St Thomas Aquinas* (below).

Giving off the S wall of the transept is the sacristy, formerly the Cavalcanti chapel; fourteenth century, modernised in the seventeenth, reached via a Mannerist portal by Federico Boschi, 1629. The Gothic rib vaults are by Jacopo Talenti, although the decoration is mostly nineteenth century. A rather heavy three-light window in *pietra serena*, with stained glass by Niccolò di Pietro Gerini, 1386. Adjacent to the doorway: polychrome terracotta lavabo by Giovanni della Robbia, 1498, his first documented work. On the end wall: splendid *armadio* (cupboard), attributed to Buontalenti, 1593. Wall paintings include a painted Crucifix by Giotto.

Left aisle

Sixth chapel: *St Hyacinth of Poland* (+1257) by Alessandro Allori, 1596. Fifth chapel: *Stories of St Catherine of Siena* by Bernardino Poccetti. Fourth chapel: *Resurrection* by Vasari. Third chapel: a famous fresco of the *Holy Trinity* by Masaccio, *circa* 1427, one of the most notable works of the Florentine *quattrocento*. To the left: *St Lucy* by Davide Ghirlandaio. On the adjacent pilaster: marble pulpit made by Andrea Cavalcanti to a design by Brunelleschi, for the Rucellai. Second chapel: altarpiece: *Christ and the Samaritan Woman at the Well* by Alessandro Allori, 1575. To the right of the first altar: monument to Antonio Strozzi, 1524, by Andrea Ferrucci and assistants. First chapel: *Raising of Lazarus* by Santi di Tito, 1576.

Conventual buildings

The extensive conventual buildings stand to the W of the church, and are built around three cloisters of different sizes. Within these buildings is the museum. It is generally reached by a doorway in the piazza, adjacent to the church façade. The Chiostro Verde stands immediately W of the church; built by Fra Jacopo Talenti, 1332–50. Five bays square, with colonnades of robust octagonal columns supporting slightly depressed arches of green and white striped marble; simple rib vaults. Within the vaults are fourteenth-century frescoes of Dominican saints, set in roundels. Around three sides of the cloister is a celebrated series of frescoes by Paolo Uccello and his workshop, *circa* 1425–30, some in very poor condition. Each bay has an upper and lower illustration of *Scenes from Genesis*, on a background of *terra verde* (giving the cloister its name). They were removed after the 1966 floods, restored and replaced in 1983. The cycle begins in the NE corner adjacent to the door into the church. Off the N side of the cloister is the equally celebrated Cappella degli Spagnoli or Spanish chapel. Built as the friars' chapter house by Talenti, *circa* 1343–55, it was assigned by Eleanora di Toledo, wife of Cosimo I, to the Spanish community of the city, *circa* 1540. In the architrave of the entrance: *Martyrdom of St Peter Martyr*, attributed to Talenti. Inside: a simple rectangular hall, with a rib vault, and octagonal semi-columns at the corners. On the N wall: a small square chancel with altar. The hall is comprehensively frescoed with a series of monumental works by Andrea di Buonaiuto and his workshop, 1367–9. The theme is the glorification of the Dominican order. In the vaults are: the *Navicella* (the 'Ship of the Church'), *Resurrection*, *Ascension* and *Pentecost*. On the wall opposite the entrance: *Road to Calvary*, *Crucifixion*, *Descent into Limbo*. On the entrance wall: *Preaching*, *Martyrdom* and *Miracles of St Peter Martyr*. On the right wall: the notable *Church Militant* and *Church Triumphant*; in the right foreground: portraits of Petrarch, Dante, Giotto, Cimabue and Boccaccio. On the left wall: *Triumph of St Thomas Aquinas*; in the lower register are *Personifications of the Arts and Sciences*, represented by their most illustrious representatives: Aristotle, Cicero, etc. Within the *scarsella* or chancel: altarpiece by Allori, 1592. Wall and vault frescoes also by Allori.

Also giving off the N side of the Chiostro Verde: a corridor leading to the much smaller Chiostrino dei Morti (not usually accessible). It dates from the pre-Dominican church but was rebuilt *circa* 1340–50. Colonnades on two sides, again with octagonal columns and depressed arches. The upper floor also has loggias on two sides. To the left: funerary chapel of the Strozzi, with two walls frescoed with a *Nativity* and a *Crucifixion*, attributed to the Cione, *circa* 1350. To the right are small chapels: the chapel of Sant'Anna, with frescoes in the manner of Nardo di Cione, *circa* 1345–55; and that of San Paolo, with frescoes of *St Dominic* and a *Crucifixion*, badly deteriorated.

Back in the Chiostro Verde, a doorway in the NW corner leads into the W wing, housing the museum. A small hall with four doors leads into the ante-refectory: *Prophets*, frescoes in the style of Orcagna, removed from the Tornabuoni chapel. The refectory: a long spacious hall, four bays, with rib-vaulted ceiling, again by Talenti, *circa* 1353. It contains a fourteenth-century fresco of the *Virgin and Child with Saints*, and other frescoes by Allori, 1584–97. Back in the small hall of the four doors: a doorway on the W side leads to the Chiostro Grande, not generally accessible. A very spacious, rectangular cloister, the largest in the city, with fourteenth-century colonnades on octagonal piers and, on the N side, an upper-level loggia, added in the fifteenth. Many frescoes in the lunettes, mostly sixteenth century and badly deteriorated; they depict the *Life of Christ* and *Dominican Saints*, and are by Santi di Tito, Allori and Poccetti. The cloister is surrounded by the fourteenth-century conventual buildings, including the imposing three-aisled dormitory on the N side, with two rows of tall octagonal columns with Corinthian capitals, and a stone rib-vaulted roof. Following the inundation of 1333, a new dormitory was built on the first floor. In 1419 the upper dormitory on the west side of the cloister was converted to a *foresteria* (guest accommodation), the imposing Salone dei Papi (hall of the popes), and a chapel, the noted Cappella dei Papi, decorated in 1515 by Pontormo and Ridolfo del Ghirlandaio. On the S side of the cloister a doorway and steps lead to the ancient pharmacy, accessible from Via della Scala (no. 16), and attached to the convent until 1866. The dispensary is the former chapel of San Niccolò and contains neo-Gothic fittings as well as a fine collection of seventeenth-century apothecaries' jars and equipment.

The church campanile stands NW of the liturgical east end. It was built in 1332–3 on earlier foundations from *circa* 1250. Its tall, slender form is enhanced by the series of openings that increase in size and number towards the top; it is roofed by a tall spire.

To the E of the church is the irregular rectangle of the Cimitero degli Avelli, enclosed by a Gothic wall; in a series of niches are monuments to notable Florentine families, together with their arms and a cross representing the Popolo.

Immediately NE of the walls enclosing the cemetery is the Piazza dell'Unità Italiana. Its site was the ancient Piazza Vecchia; it took its present form at the beginning of the twentieth century, when the Grand Hotel Baglioni was built. The very long façade of **Palazzo dei Cerretani** (nos. 1–2) originally consisted of only the six-bay central wing with the upper colonnaded loggia; the side wings were added later. In 1625 an earlier house on the site was acquired by the Cerretani from the Scarpa, and a major modernisation was begun. As well as the loggia, it included a *salone* on the *piano nobile*, one of the largest in the city, with rich Baroque fresco decoration by Vincenzo Meucci, 1743. Following a serious fire in 1714, the building was restored and extended, by buying an adjacent house on Via Valfonda. A grandiose new stair was also added. In 1763 the Cerretani became extinct; the palace passed to the Capponi and Gondi. In 1937 the building was radically altered and enlarged further in connection with the urban works to the adjacent piazza.

At no. 6 Piazza dell'Unità is the **Grand Hotel Baglioni**, constructed by Prince Carrega di Lucedo in the late nineteenth century, following the widening of Via dei Panzani. Initially a palace for himself, it was converted to a hotel in 1903. The façade is in a simple Tuscan Renaissance style. On the NE side of the piazza is the **Albergo Majestic**, by Lando Bartali, 1974; although the scale is appropriate for the prominent site, the façade is rather fussy. Currently unoccupied.

Further NW, and contiguous with the Piazza dell'Unità, is the Piazza della Stazione.

Stazione centrale di Santa Maria Novella: The city's principal railway station, and often considered the most notable twentieth-century building in the city. It was built in 1933–5, following a competition (1932), and was designed by the self-styled Gruppo Toscano, of whom Giovanni Michelucci was perhaps the most remarkable member. The principal façade addresses the N (liturgical E) end of the homonymous church, and is all of *pietra forte*. Its design is uncompromisingly modern, with its *pietra forte* cladding broken by a 'waterfall' of glazing to the ticket hall, which also descends to the *porte-cochère*. The interior is dominated by the broad, spacious main concourse, the Galleria di Testa, which links Via Alamanni (W) with Via Valfonda (E); it is floored with

165

white Calacatta marble and stripes of red Amiata marble, heightening the perspective. The concourse, 109 m long and 22 m wide (approx. 358 × 72 ft), has a 'folded' concrete roof structure, the N facet of which is fully glazed. Between the concourse and the S façade is the tall, imposing, rectangular ticket hall, with yellow Siena marble to the walls and columns, bronze fittings, and flooring in Serpentino delle Alpi. Most of the original fittings have survived.

Outside the E end of the Galleria di Testa, on Via Valfonda, stood a **bus station**, by Cristiano Toraldo, 1990; built for Italy's hosting of the World Cup. Highly controversial, its form and materials both appeared out of context, with the long structure terminating with drum-like pavilions of striped marble. It was demolished in 2010.

Attached to the E side of the station, further N along Via Valfonda, on Piazza Adua, is the **Palazzina Reale**, 1934–5, again by Michelucci, probably with Italo Gamberini. A simple volume, clad in marble, with tall narrow bands of glazing; it is approached via a courtyard within the station and by the portico of honour onto Via Valfonda. Attached to the latter façade is a sculpted group representing the Arno and its valley by Italo Griselli. The pavilion was restored in 1990 and conserves most of its original internal fittings, with simple but sumptuous decoration in white Carrara and green serpentine marble. Also along this flank, further N again, is a more recent entrance, added in 1990 by Gae Aulenti and others, with a pedestrian bridge flanked by towers.

On the NE side of Piazza Adua, and extending along Via Cennini, is the imposing **Palazzo degli Affari**, by Pier Luigi Spadolini, 1975; the building makes considerable use of pre-cast elements. At no. 9 is **Palazzo Riccardi di Valfonda**, originally built by Baccio d'Agnolo for Giovanni Bartolini Salimbeni in 1520; in 1589 it passed to the Riccardi, who later employed Gherardo Silvani to modernise and extend it. The Via Valfonda façade is very long and simple, with two orders and eleven bays to the *piano nobile*. A central rusticated arched portal; oculi to the attic. The garden façade is more attractive, with a spacious, elegant, nine-bay colonnade across the full width, surmounted by a terrace, and the outer bays raised to form short *torreselle*, small towers or turrets. Some of the richly decorated interiors survive. The notable garden extended SW towards Via della Scala, but most was lost when the station and its tracks were built.

Palazzo dei Congressi: On the NE side of Via Valfonda is a garden, formerly attached to the adjacent nineteenth-century neo-Classical

Villa Contini Bonacossi. The Palazzo, also by Spadolini, was built here in 1964–9, a large hall seating 1,200, with an elliptical plan, much of which is below ground level.

At the NW end of Via Valfonda is the extensive

Fortezza da Basso (di San Giovanni): Built by Antonio da Sangallo the younger in 1534 on the instructions of Alessandro de' Medici. Construction was extraordinarily rapid, and was complete in only six months. Its function was to provide additional defence to the city against attackers approaching from the NW, but could also be used, if necessary, against popular uprisings within the city itself; to this end, there are gun emplacements on the SE face. It stands on the line of the medieval walls, which were thus broken on each side of it; the extensive fortress, covering 10 ha, incorporates the medieval Porta Faenza, on axis with Via Faenza. The plan is pentagonal and symmetrical, with the longest face towards the city, and with massive bastions at the corners. Its original height was 12 m (approx. 39 ft), although the only section that retains this height is that towards the station.

The most imposing, SE part of the outer defences is clad with *pietra forte* (the rest is in simple brickwork), and is rusticated, with a pattern of diamonds and hemispheres; the latter may refer to the famous Medici *palle* (the six balls on their coat of arms).

Within the walls are a number of buildings. The most notable of the original structures is the octagonal Corpo di Guardia, with a tile-clad cupola. Near the W side are workshops used by the Opificio delle Pietre Dure; towards the E side is a large rectangular hall (1978) used for trade exhibitions. Adjacent are the nineteenth-century *polveriera* (powder store) and *scuderia* (stables).

4 SOUTH-WEST OF SANTA MARIA NOVELLA

A small, compact area defined by Via dei Fossi (SE), Via della Scala (NE), the Lungarno Vespucci (SW) and Via Finiguerra (NW). Begin at Piazza Goldoni, which reached its present form in 1854, when the Lungarno Vespucci was built.

Ponte alla Carraia: First built in 1218, it was the second crossing of the Arno after the Ponte Vecchio. Destroyed by floods in 1274, it was rebuilt and survived until 1304, when it collapsed under the weight of a crowd watching a spectacle on the Arno. Destroyed again by the disastrous floods in 1333, it was further damaged in 1557. Two years later it was rebuilt by Ammannati on the instruction of Cosimo I. This time it survived until it was destroyed by the retreating Germans in 1944. In 1948 it was rebuilt by the architect Ettore Fagiuoli, with five arches, a similar form to that of Ammannati.

From Piazza Goldoni take Borgo Ognissanti NW. No. 20 is the former **Ospedale di San Giovanni di Dio**. Founded by Simone Vespucci in 1382, in 1587 it passed to the Brothers Hospitallers of St John of God. Largely rebuilt in 1702–13 by Carlo Andrea Marcellini. This work also encompassed the house where Amerigo Vespucci was born in 1454; the façade was rebuilt to take account of this enlargement. The most interesting element is the entrance hall, 1735, which contains a rich Baroque curvilinear double-branch staircase, wrapping around the portal into the convent itself. At the foot of the stairs (left and right) are figures of *Faith* and *Hope*, by Girolamo Ticciati; on the upper landing is a large marble group of *St John of God with Gabriel and a Poor Man Genuflecting*, also by Ticciati, 1737. The paintings to the vaulted ceiling are by Vincenzo Meucci and Rinaldo Botti. The church itself was completed in 1702. It has a rectangular plan and four lateral altars.

No. 9 Borgo Ognissanti is the impressive **Palazzo della Marescialla**, with a strongly modelled Baroque façade. A bold portal surmounted by a balcony; three orders, all the windows aediculed, but with different pediments: curved to the ground floor, triangular to the first, curvilinear to the second. Just beyond the Ospedale (no. 26) is the unusual **Casa Galleria Vichi**, 1911, by Giovanni Michelazzi for Argia Marinai Vichi. A splendid example of Art Nouveau (or the Liberty style), the only one in the city centre. A tall, narrow façade, with strong verticality but with the superimposition of curvilinear transverse elements in reconstructed stone. Behind the plastic forms of the outer layer is a façade of steel and glass. The two richly ornamented lower floors were for commercial use, with a more restrained three-storey residence above.

A little further NW is Piazza Ognissanti, which in its present form again dates from the formation of the Lungarno Vespucci. On the NW side is **Palazzo Lenzi**, originally perhaps *circa* 1430, although some claim as late as 1470; sometimes attributed to Michelozzo, and (wrongly) to Brunelleschi, but much altered later; in 1765 it passed to the Quaratesi. The main façade is to the piazza, with three orders. The first is a little asymmetrical, with arched openings surrounded by rustication.

168

165   Stazione centrale di Santa Maria Novella from the south-east

166   Stazione centrale di Santa Maria Novella: the ticket hall by the Gruppo Toscano, 1933–5

167   Fortezza da Basso, by Antonio da Sangallo the younger: central bastion (1534), with the Porta Faenza behind

168   Casa Galleria Vichi, Borgo Ognissanti, by Giovanni Michelazzi, 1911: doorway detail

169   Ognissanti: façade towards the Arno, by Matteo Nigetti, 1637

The upper two orders each have nine bays of large arched windows; the northernmost bay is the result of the dramatically cantilevered *sporti* on the Borgo façade. On both façades, *sgraffito* was added by Andrea Feltrini, 1885. Immediate adjacent, on the corner of the Lungarno, is **Palazzo Giuntini**, built as a hotel in the late nineteenth century. Impressive and neo-Renaissance, with rusticated ground floor and four orders above. Carefully restored 1974–86; it remains a hotel today.

Dominating the piazza is the façade of **Ognissanti**, founded in 1251 by the Umiliati order. The church was built in the fifteenth century, and in 1554 passed to the Franciscans. In 1627–37 it was rebuilt by Bartolomeo Pettirossi. The tall fourteenth-century campanile and three octagonal cloister columns are the only significant survivors of the medieval monastic complex. The present fine Baroque façade is by Matteo Nigetti, 1637. It was reassembled in 1827 according to the original design, in the same Travertine marble; richly modelled, with three bays and two principal orders. The large, complex portal was adapted to incorporate a relief of the *Coronation of the Virgin*, attributed to Giovanni della Robbia, set into the lunette. Flanking the central bay, the outer bays have large aediculed niches. The lower order terminates in a bold cornice, which rises in the central bay to form a segmental pediment. In the upper order: three bays divided by flat Corinthian pilasters, the central bay containing an aediculed niche; the outer two have windows with reversed split pediments at their heads. Rising above the second order is a boldly modelled attic, flanked by half-pediments, all three elements capped by vigorous cornices.

Inside: the plan is a Latin cross, with a spacious aisle-less nave and deep transepts. Rich seventeenth- and eighteenth-century decoration throughout. The side altars are of *pietra serena*, set into bold arched surrounds. Second right altar: *Pietà*, a fresco by Domenico Ghirlandaio, *circa* 1480. Third altar: *Virgin and Child with Saints* by Santi di Tito, 1565. Adjacent is *St Augustine in his Study*, a notable detached fresco by Botticelli, *circa* 1480. The seventeenth-century pulpit has two marble reliefs of the *Story of St Francis* from the school of Benedetto da Rovezzano, early sixteenth century. In one of the right transept chapels, a disc in the floor marks the tomb of Botticelli. Transept decorations by Matteo Bonechi and Jacopo Ligozzi. High altar in *pietra dura*, again by Ligozzi, 1593–5. Seventeenth-century bronze Crucifix by G. B. Cennini. In the sacristy: remains of fourteenth-century frescoes, including a *Crucifixion* by Taddeo Gaddi. Back in the church: left aisle altars; between the third and fourth altars: fresco of *St Jerome in his Study* by Domenico Ghir-

169

landaio, 1480. Beyond the cloisters, the former refectory has a fine *Last Supper* fresco by Ghirlandaio, 1480.

Adjacent to the Galleria Vichi, take Via del Porcellana NE to the junction with Via Palazzuolo. Two churches: San Paolino, a short distance SE, and San Francesco, a little further NW.

San Paolino is said to have been founded as early as 335, but the definitive establishment was around 1000; it passed to the Dominicans in 1217, after which it was occupied by canons from the cathedral (Angelo Poliziano was the prior in 1480); and then in turn, after 1618, by Carmelites, who rebuilt it in 1669–93, to a design by Giovanni Battista Balatri. A simple façade with a terracotta lunette by the della Robbia; early sixteenth century, with the Pandolfini arms, directly above which are those of Pope Leo X. The other two are of the canons of the cathedral and of Cardinal Giulio de' Medici, later Pope Clement VII. The interior: a Latin cross, with a single barrel-vaulted nave; lateral chapels, each with a small cupola; transepts, and a large chancel. The late seventeenth-century altars are of rich polychrome marble. First right chapel: monument to Luca and Gerolamo degli Albizi by G. B. Foggini, *circa* 1700, incorporating the sepulchre of Maso degli Albizzi (+1417). Altarpiece by Giovanni Domenico Ferretti. Second chapel: altarpiece by Sogliani, early sixteenth century. Also on Piazza San Paolino, opposite the church, is the **Monte di Pietà**, a charitable institution providing cheap loans for the poor. Founded in 1495, there were originally three, one at Santo Spirito, one in Via Monalda and a third in Via del Proconsolo.

No. 17 is **San Francesco dei Vanchetoni**, a restrained work by Giovanni and Matteo Nigetti, 1602–20. It was built for the Congregation of Christian Doctrine, known as the Vanchetoni. The church is approached via a narthex, added *circa* 1620 and funded by the Grand Duchess Maria Maddalena (coat of arms). Interior: a rectangular hall, the ceiling of which has seventeenth-century paintings by Giovanni Martinelli, Volterrano and Lorenzo Lippi; high-level frescoes, in poor condition. A large Baroque altar.

Taking Via del Porcellana one block further NE, we reach the long, straight Via della Scala. At No. 9 is the oratory of **Santi Filippo e Giacomo**, formerly attached to a hospital, now lost. The church is by Matteo Nigetti, 1626, and contains a cycle of ten paintings of *Works of Charity* by Cosimo Ulivelli. No. 6 is **Palazzo dal Borgo**, 1550–60, with a façade decorated with *sgraffito* (now deteriorated) of the *Triumph of David*. No. 16 is the noted **pharmacy** of Santa Maria Novella (see above).

A good deal further NW is the **Ospedale della Scala**, no. 79, founded in 1313 by the Pollini. It was suppressed in 1531 and converted for the nuns of San Martino a Mugnone. After 1873 it became the Centro di Rieducazione dei Minorenni (centre for the rehabilitation of minors). The church of San Martino della Scala survives, with a fourteenth-century portico, as do the cloisters. A little further, left, no. 85 is **Palazzo Venturi Ginori**, the site of which was acquired by Bernardo Rucellai and his wife Lucrezia (Nannina di Piero) de' Medici in 1481; a *casinò* and gardens were then built here. After the exile of the Medici in 1494, the Accademia Platonica, which formerly met at Villa Medici at Careggi, was transferred here and renamed the Accademia degli Orti Oricellari (a corruption of Rucellai). By 1573 the *casinò* was owned by Bianca Cappello, the lover of Francesco I de' Medici. When they married (1579), Bianca gave the palace to Francesco's son from his earlier marriage, Don Antonio. In the seventeenth century the palace was rented by Cardinal Giovanni Carlo de' Medici, brother of Ferdinando II. He reordered the garden and had the building frescoed by Pietro da Cortona. It later passed to the Ridolfi, who, in 1679, had it enlarged by Pier Francesco Silvani. In 1861 it passed to Gregorio Orloff, a Russian prince, who employed Poggi to modernise the interior. In 1890 the garden was much reduced in size, but it was then acquired by Ipollito Venturi Ginori, who restored both house and garden. The typical long, low façade of a Florentine *casinò di delizie*: nine bays and two storeys plus a low attic. Balcony and Ridolfi coat of arms above the central portal.

On the other side, at no. 62, is the former church of **San Jacopo di Ripoli**, once attached to a Dominican nunnery, more recently a barracks. In the lunette of the portal is a *Virgin and Child with St James and St Dominic* by Giovanni della Robbia, 1522.

5 THE NORTH-WEST CORNER OF THE *QUARTIERE*

This zone is defined by the Lungarno Vespucci (SW), the line of the old medieval walls (Via Fratelli Rosselli), Via Finiguerra (SE) and Via della Scala (NE).

The Lungarno Vespucci continues NW as far as Piazzale Vittorio Veneto and the SE end of the Cascine (see below). Just beyond Piazza Ognissanti is the Pescaia di Santa Rosa, a weir, located where the Macinante stream met the Arno. Opposite its junction with Via Melegnano is the **Ponte Amerigo Vespucci**. The bridge was built in 1957, although it had been planned since 1896; a simple, elegant form by Riccardo Morandi and others. Despite the intermediate support, the impression is of a broad, gently curved single arch. The next section of Lungarno Vespucci contains two significant works by Giuseppe Poggi. On the corner of Via Curtatone (no. 38) is **Palazzo Calcagnini Arese**, built for Marchese Manfredi Calcagnini Estensi, 1857–77. A substantial free-standing neo-Renaissance *palazzo* with three orders; seven bays to the main façade, three to the return façades at the ends. The ground floor is rusticated; in the centre of the *piano nobile* is a long balcony; Ionic pilasters define the bays, while a bold cornice divides the second order from the third; this is again defined by flat pilasters, with simple rectangular lights. Rich stucco decoration, gilded and polychrome, to the *piano nobile* apartments. Recently it has housed the US consulate.

On the next corner, in the centre of its garden, is the **Villa Favard**, 1857–8, again by Poggi. Another refined neo-Renaissance work. Two orders, with a symmetrical façade, in the centre of which is a two-storey loggia, Doric below, Ionic above. Three bays, with paired columns at the outer corners. Rich interior decoration by Annibale Gatti. In between the two buildings: statue of *Giuseppe Garibaldi* by Cesare Zocchi, 1890.

A little further inland from the Lungarno, almost parallel to it, is Corso Italia. Halfway down, on the right (nos. 12–16), is the **Teatro Comunale**, by Telemaco Bonaiuti, 1862. The largest in the city, with a capacity of 2,000. Owned by the *comune* since 1929. The long façade retains its rather heavy neo-Classical appearance, with a rusticated ground floor and seven tall arched bays to the upper floor. Badly damaged by bombing in 1944, but restored. A major modernisation in 1957–61 by Corinna Bartolini; restored once again after the 1966 floods. The auditorium is surrounded by lateral boxes, above which are two upper galleries. Attached is a smaller auditorium, the Ridotto Comunale, capacity approximately 500. The theatre is the principal centre for the famous Maggio Musicale music festival, inaugurated in 1933.

Corso Italia terminates at the huge, open Piazza Vittorio Veneto. To the NW, towards Le Cascine: equestrian monument to *Vittorio Emanuele II* by Emilio Zocchi, 1890. The **Ponte della Vittoria** crosses the Arno here; the first bridge was a suspension bridge built in 1835 for Grand Duke Leopoldo II. The present three-arched bridge was built in 1946 to replace an earlier bridge (1925) destroyed in 1944.

The broad boulevard of Viale Fratelli Rosselli runs NE following the line of the lost medieval walls. To the left is the old railway station of **Porta al Prato**, by Enrico Presenti, 1844–8. It was the terminus of the earliest railway in the grand duchy, which ran from the city to Pisa and Livorno, but it was only in use for twelve years, since in 1860 it was converted into an exhibition hall; later still, it became a goods depot.

Immediately SW of the former Leopolda station is the imposing new **Teatro dell'Opera Lirica**, or **Opera House**, by Paolo Desideri and Studio ABDR. Opened in December 2012, it contains a main auditorium with 1800 seats, a second hall of 1000 seats, and an open air amphitheatre on the roof.

It is approached by a long grassed piazza. The simple, box-like central wing is framed by two broad external *scaloni d'onore* which rise up towards the west, where they meet 'around the back', and give access to the rooftop amphitheatre. The rather futuristic interior of the main theatre has superb acoustics.

Halfway along, junction with Via il Prato, is the **Porta al Prato**, one of the surviving medieval gates (1284), massively imposing. Inside: a sixteenth-century fresco of the *Virgin and Child* attributed to Michele Ghirlandaio. This was the only major point in the *circonvallazione* (the circumference) where Giuseppe Poggi did not create a formal urban set piece.

Leading SE from the Piazzale Porta al Prato is Via il Prato, which continues back towards the city centre as Borgo Ognissanti. At no. 12 Via il Prato is the neo-Gothic **Studio Villa**, by Ignazio Villa, *circa* 1850, a rare example of nineteenth-century neo-Gothic in a private house. At no. 58 is **Palazzo Corsini al Prato**, begun by Bernardo Buontalenti for Alessandro Acciaioli, *circa* 1591; it was intended to be a *casinò*, with extensive gardens. Three years later Acciaioli lost a fortune when the Ricci bank failed, and work was halted. In 1621 it was sold by Caterina Acciaioli to Filippo Corsini, and was completed for him by Gherardo Silvani. The street façade has five bays and two orders, with a prominent aediculed portal and flanking lights. It was extended *circa* 1860 with a new six-bay wing to the left, much heavier in style, with rustication and an exceptionally long balcony. The main feature of the garden façade is a tall, spacious, three-bay loggia. Most of the extensive gardens have survived.

At the far end of Via il Prato is the **Loggia Reale**, 1820–30, by Luigi de Cambrai-Digny, built for the grand dukes in connection with the horse races that were held here. In the adjacent 'island', on the fork between Borgo Ognissanti and Via Palazzuolo, is the **Rotonda Bar-betti**, *circa* 1847, originally built to house a panorama of the city.

Return to the Piazzale Porta al Prato. The next section of Viale Fratelli Rosselli terminates just before the railway lines leading out of Santa Maria Novella; the road continues NE in a long underpass. Just before it, left, is Via delle Ghiacciaie; between the road and the railway lines are the **Cabina Comandi** and the **Centrale Termica** (1929–34) by Angiolo Mazzoni, together with the adjacent Palazzina della Squadra Rialzo. The Centrale Termica is a highly articulated 'Constructivist' work, with each element clearly and separately expressed.

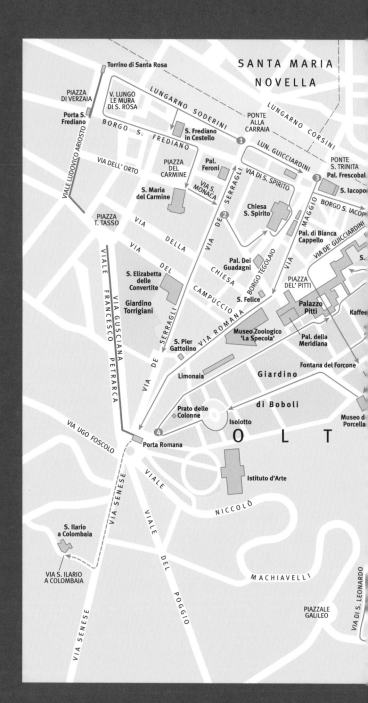

The Oltrarno

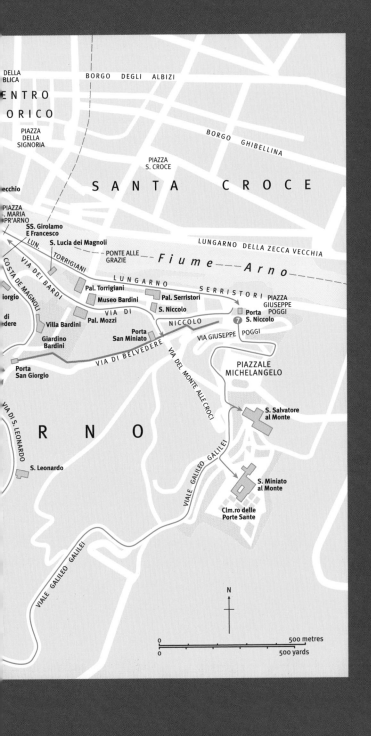

DELLA
BLICA

ENTRO
ORICO

PIAZZA
DELLA
SIGNORIA

ecchio

PIAZZA
. MARIA
PR'ARNO

SS. Girolamo
E Francesco

S. Lucia dei Magnoli

LUN.
TORRIGIANI

VIA DEI BARDI

COSTA DE MAGNOLI

iorgio

di
dere

Villa Bardini

Giardino
Bardini

Porta
San Giorgio

VIA DI S. LEONARDO

S. Leonardo

RNO

BORGO   DEGLI   ALBIZI

BORGO   GHIBELLINA

PIAZZA
S. CROCE

SANTA   CROCE

LUNGARNO DELLA ZECCA VECCHIA

PONTE ALLE
GRAZIE

Fiume ——— Arno

LUNGARNO

SERRISTORI

PIAZZA
GIUSEPPE
POGGI

Pal. Torrigiani

Museo Bardini

Pal. Mozzi

VIA DI

Pal. Serristori

S. Niccolo

Porta
San Miniato

NICCOLO

VIA DI BELVEDERE

Porta
S. Niccolo

VIA GIUSEPPE   POGGI

VIA DEL MONTE ALLE CROCI

PIAZZALE
MICHELANGELO

S. Salvatore
al Monte

VIALE GALILEO GALILEI

S. Miniato
al Monte

Clm.ro delle
Porte Sante

VIALE GALILEO GALILEI

N

0 _____ 500 metres
0 _____ 500 yards

The Oltrarno

The Oltrarno was not settled in antiquity, since the Roman city stood exclusively on the N bank of the Arno. Nor was it enclosed by the first communal ('Matildine') walls of 1078. When the second communal walls were built (1173–5), however, they were extended to embrace a small extent of settlement on the S side of the river, bounded by Via dei Serragli, Via Sant'Agostino and its continuation, Via Mazzetta, turning NE along Via dei Guicciardini towards the river. They then continued SE, parallel to the Arno, before turning N and terminating at the Ponte alle Grazie.

A major enlargement took place in 1258, shortly before the last great city walls were built on the N bank. This expansion enclosed the sites of the later Palazzo Pitti and half of the future Giardino di Boboli, before turning E to meet the Arno at the Lungarno Serristori. When the final medieval city walls were built in 1284–1333, the E part of this section was retained, but the new walls now extended considerably further S, as far as the surviving Porta Romana, and W to the Porta San Frediano. Substantial tracts of this wall have survived, in addition to the city gates noted above.

Initially, settlement on this bank was thus confined to a small area immediately adjacent to the river, and centred on Santo Spirito, founded in 1250; after 1343 the Oltrarno was known as the *quartiere* of Santo Spirito. The most densely developed areas were those immediately adjacent to the bridgeheads of the Ponte Vecchio and Ponte Santa Trinità. Later settlement remained concentrated in a larger triangular zone, defined by the hills of Monte Uliveto and Bellosguardo to the SW and that of Boboli to the SE. Unlike the N bank, these hills were significant constraints to wider expansion. Even today, there is very little urban development beyond the last medieval walls, except for modern housing projects a good deal further downstream (Pignone, Isolotto) and upstream (Ricorboli, Gavinana).

For convenience, the walks are divided into two zones, covering the W and E parts of the Oltrarno respectively. The districts beyond the walls are discussed later.

170 Palazzo Pitti: detail of upper order window in the courtyard, by Ammannati, 1558–70

The W part centres on the churches of San Frediano and Santa Maria del Carmine. The section of the Lungarno W of Ponte alla Carraia is the Lungarno Soderini. At no. 5 is the **Galleria dell'Antiquariato Bellini**, early twentieth century, by Adolfo Coppedè, characteristically eclectic. No. 15 is **Palazzo Capponi**, its present also rather eclectic appearance the result of modernisation by Marchese Vincenzo Maria Capponi after 1769. A U-shaped plan, open towards the river, with two wings linked by an elegant three-bay loggia. The façades are finished with *sgraffito* render in imitation of brickwork. At no. 19 is the **Seminario Maggiore**, the simple former monastic buildings attached to San Frediano.

A little further W the Lungarno opens into Piazza di Cestello. On the SW side is the incomplete façade of

San Frediano in Cestello: Begun in 1670 for the Cistercians; the original design was by Gherardo Silvani, and construction continued until 1674, when Silvani was dismissed. His proposal had a long nave, the completion of which would have necessitated the demolition of some of the recently completed monastic buildings. A new architect was appointed, the Roman Giulio Cerruti, and in 1679 Silvani's work was demolished and a new church begun; it was completed in 1689 under Antonio Maria Ferri. The drum and cupola were added in 1698. The exterior is tall but very plain, and remains unfinished, other than the tall, elegant drum and cupola, one of the distinctive landmarks of the Oltrarno. Around the drum are large rectangular windows, with alternating triangular and segmental pediments. At one side is a small Baroque campanile.

The plan: a Latin cross, with three chapels down each side of the nave, each with a small cupola. The tall nave has extensive eighteenth-century decoration, including rich stucco, extending into the lateral chapels. The fresco in the cupola is *St Mary Magdalene in Glory* by Antonio Domenico Gabbiani, 1702–18; that to the pendentives is by Matteo Bonechi. Right lateral chapels: first chapel: frescoed vault, again by Bonechi. Altarpiece: *Ecstasy of St Maria Maddelena de' Pazzi* by Giovanni Camillo Sagrestani, 1702. Third chapel: frescoed vault by Alessandro Gherardini; altarpiece: *Birth of the Virgin*, also by Gherardini. Chancel: the eighteenth-century high altar is of *pietre dure*. Left lateral chapels: third chapel: frescoed vault by Piero Dandini, 1689. On the

171

172

altar: fourteenth-century polychrome wood figure of the *Virgin and Child* (*Madonna del Sorriso*).

On the NW side of Piazza di Cestello is the former **Granaio di Cosimo III**, by G.B. Foggini, 1695–7, extending a full block along the Lungarno. A simple symmetrical façade to the piazza: three bays and two orders, with an arched central portal and a rich Medici coat of arms above the first-floor central window. The long river flank is austere and repetitive.

The Lungarno continues NW past the Ponte Vespucci to reach the fourteenth-century city walls at the **Torrino di Santa Rosa**. Turning left along the Via Lungo le Mura, we reach Piazza di Verzaia. To the left, in the corner, is Via Bartolini; no. 4 is the **Antico Setificio Fiorentino**, a silk-weaving factory relocated here in 1786. Between Via Bartolini and Borgo San Frediano is the former **Monastero dell'Arcangelo Raffaele**, founded by Benedictines in 1531, but suppressed in 1748, after which it became a hospice, then a barracks and then the studio of the sculptor Lorenzo Bartolini (1777–1850). The piazza is dominated by the massive **Porta San Frediano**, the largest surviving city gate. It was built in 1332–4 and has been attributed to Andrea Pisano; it stands at the start of the road to Pisa, and retains its original great wooden doors (height 13.22 m / approx. 43 ft), with hinges and ironwork. To the SE, Borgo San Frediano, the main street of the *borgo* (area formerly outside the walls), is lined with artisans' workshops. Few palaces, but a good selection of more modest houses. Parallel to the Borgo, one block further S, is Via dell'Orto, in which is the former church of **San Francesco di Sales**. Built in 1700 by Antonio Maria Ferri; a three-bay street façade with a central arched portal. Take Via di Camaldoli S from Via dell'Orto. On Piazza Torquato Tasso is the former monastery of **San Salvatore a Camaldoli**, founded in 1102; the present simple, elegant façade is by Giulio Parigi, 1621. Return NE along Via del Leone and then right into Piazza Piatellina, which leads into **Piazza del Carmine**, an ill-defined square, reduced to a car park. At the SW corner: a fourteenth-century tabernacle. Another tabernacle on the SE corner, at the junction of Via Santa Monaca, in *pietra serena*, late fifteenth century; and a third on the corner towards Borgo San Frediano, representing the *Holy Family*.

On the S side is the tall, unfinished façade of

Santa Maria del Carmine (I Carmini): Founded in 1268 by the Carmelites, it was completed only in 1475, although in a fourteenth-century manner. It was partly modernised in the sixteenth and seventeenth centuries, but was seriously damaged by fire in 1771; most of the interior reflects the late eighteenth-century restoration, begun by Giuseppe Ruggieri and completed by Giulio Mannaioni in 1775. The celebrated Brancacci and Corsini chapels were damaged, but survived the fire.

The internal plan is a Latin cross, with a long, broad, barrel-vaulted nave flanked by shallow lateral chapels, five down each side. A tall, stately nave, articulated by flat Corinthian pilasters. The chapels have altars decorated with stucco, and alternate with aediculed confessionals. On the nave ceiling: *trompe l'oeil* decoration by Domenico Stagi, in which are frescoes by Giuseppe Romei. The crossing is capped by a cupola, also decorated by Romei. It is flanked by short, square transepts and terminates in a square chancel. Right nave chapels: third chapel: *Crucifixion* by Giorgio Vasari. Fourth chapel: *Visitation* by Aurelio Lomi, *circa* 1620.

At the end of the right transept is the famous Brancacci chapel, now generally reached from the Porta del Martello (right of the main entrance) and then down the left flank of the cloisters. The chapel was patronised by the Brancacci from the later fourteenth century until 1780, when patronage passed to the Riccardi. Its decoration was begun in 1423, under Felice Brancacci, and the famous frescoes by Masaccio and Masolino were executed from 1424 to 1427 or 1428. In 1436 Brancacci, an enemy of the Medici, went into exile with the decoration uncompleted. It was finished after 1480 by Filippino Lippi, who adapted his style to accord with the earlier work of Masaccio and Masolino. The chapel was restored in 1983–90.

The frescoes:

Upper row, right wall: two works showing *Miracles of St Peter* by Masolino. To the right of the altar: *St Peter Baptising* by Masaccio. Left of the altar: *St Peter Preaching* by Masolino. Left side: the *Tribute Money* by Masaccio, probably his finest work. Entrance arch: *Expulsion of Adam and Eve from Paradise* by Masaccio, another masterpiece.

Lower row: right side wall: *St Peter and St Paul before the Proconsul* and the *Crucifixion of St Peter*, both by Filippino Lippi. Right of the altar: *St Peter and St John Distributing Alms* by Masaccio. Left of the altar: *St Peter Healing the Sick with his Shadow, with St John* by Masaccio. Left side wall: *St Peter Enthroned as Bishop of Antioch* by Masaccio, his final work. The adjacent panel of *St Peter Raising the Son of the Prefect of Antioch, Theophilus* was begun by Masaccio but completed by Filippino Lippi. Entrance arch: *St Peter in Prison Visited by St Paul* and *St Peter Released from Prison*, both by Filippino.

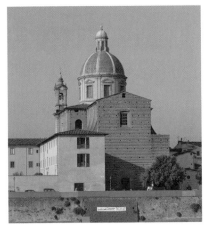

171 San Frediano in Cestello from the Lungarno Vespucci; cupola by Antonio Maria Ferri, 1698

172 The Ponte alla Carraia and San Frediano

173 Porta San Frediano: detail of the city gate, 1332–4

174 Santa Maria del Carmine: the main cloister, 1597–1612

On the E side of the right transept is the Manetti chapel; decoration by Domenico and Giuliano Ruschi, 1781. On the W side is the Alamanni Uguccioni chapel; stucco decoration also *circa* 1780.

The chancel, with the choir, was patronised by the Nerli, Soderini and Serragli. Within the choir, right wall (usually inaccessible): rich monument to Piero Soderini by Benedetto da Rovezzano, 1512–13.

Left transept: to the right and left, two chapels matching those on the other side; to the right (E) is that of the Crucifix, again decorated by the Ruschi; to the left that of the Buonaccorsi-Salvi. At the far end of the transept is the notable Corsini chapel, commissioned in 1675 by Marchese Bartolomeo Corsini, and designed by Pier Francesco Silvani. A sumptuous late Baroque work, in the Roman manner. A square plan, with fluted Corinthian pilasters and a cupola on pendentives. The latter is decorated by Luca Giordano, 1682. Opposite the entrance: monument to St Andrea Corsini, with a deep relief in marble of *St Andrea Corsini in Glory* by G.B. Foggini; set in an aedicule, flanked by pink marble columns. On the two side walls are monuments to the cardinals Pietro and Neri Corsini, to similar designs, all by Foggini.

The conventual buildings stand to the right of the church, and are reached by the Porta del Martello. The simple cloisters (1597–1612) are seven bays square, with flattened arched colonnades; in some of the lunettes are seventeenth-century frescoes by Domenico Bettini, Cosimo Ulivelli and others. Some of the monastic quarters are not publicly accessible, but they include the thirteenth-century Sala Capitolare (chapter house), in the centre of the S side. Adjacent is the Sala del Cenacolo (refectory), also thirteenth century, with a *Last Supper* by Alessandro Allori (1582). In the corner is the fourteenth-century Sala della Colonna, with a collection of fragments of fourteenth- and fifteenth-century frescoes, by Filippo Lippi and others, formerly in the old cloisters. The second refectory (seventeenth century), west wing, is known as the Sala Vanni (fresco by G.B. Vanni, 1645), and is used for concerts and conferences.

Leaving the church, take Via Santa Monaca out of the SE corner of the piazza. No. 6 is **Santa Monaca**; a very simple façade with a fifteenth-century portal, and, inside, a nave vault frescoed by Cosimo Ulivelli. The house was founded in 1440 by Ubertino de' Bardi, but was suppressed by Napoleon. Now deconsecrated. At the corner of Via dei Serragli, no. 2 is **Palazzo Mazzei**, seventeenth century, modernised in the eighteenth. Simple façades of three orders; balcony above the portal.

Enter Via dei Serragli, one of the principal streets of the Oltrarno, which runs in a straight line from the Ponte alla Carraia to the Porta Romana. Named after the Serragli family, who founded San Firenze. On the section (left) between the junction with Via Santa Monaca and the Ponte alla Carraia, at no. 8 is **Palazzo Amerighi Feroni**, *circa* 1469, for the del Pugliese, on the site of several smaller houses; the façade is more typical of the early sixteenth century. In 1770 it was acquired by Marchese Giuseppe Feroni, and modernised and enlarged by Zanobi del Rosso. Zanobi extended the palace around a large central courtyard; colonnaded loggias on two sides, blind arcades on the others. Feroni also bought several other properties, so that eventually he owned the entire urban block. Much was turned into an extensive botanical garden. An imposing main façade, with ground-floor rustication; nine arched bays to the two upper floors.

Opposite, nos. 7–9 is **Palazzo Antinori di Brindisi**, originally fifteenth century, but partly modernised in the nineteenth by Giuseppe Poggi. A very long but simple façade; three orders.

No. 17 is **Palazzo Rosselli del Turco**; no. 19 is **Palazzo Palavicini**; façade by Gherardo Silvani, with three orders and five bays, probably mid-seventeenth century. A stone balcony above the arched portal. Pedimented aedicules to the *piano nobile*. No. 21 (corner of Via Sant'Agostino) is **Palazzo Baldovinetti**; early sixteenth-century façade with five bays and four orders. Stone arched lights to the principal floors. No. 44 is **Casa Antonio Meucci** and no. 49 is the seventeenth-century **Palazzo Ricasoli Salviati**, by Gherardo Silvani, who unified several discrete properties; a long façade of three orders. After the 1920s it housed the Istituto Emily Gould.

Continuing SW down Via dei Serragli, at the corner of Via della Chiesa is a tabernacle with a fresco of *St Philip Neri* by Cosimo Ulivelli, late seventeenth century. Diverting briefly W along Via della Chiesa, we reach the former monastic buildings of **San Salvatore**, or the Nunziatine. Founded in 1517; a long, very simple two-storey façade. Recently used as a school. Back in Via dei Serragli, no. 104, corner of Via del Campuccio, is the former nunnery of **Santa Elizabetta delle Convertite**, more recently the Istituto degli Artigianelli; on the façade another tabernacle, with a *Crucifixion* by Bernardino Poccetti, late sixteenth century. The nunnery was founded in 1330, and in 1624 expanded to annexe the house where (St) Philip Neri was born in 1515. Inside the church: ceiling fresco by Alessandro Gherardini, eighteenth century. In 1837 the nunnery transferred to Via dei Malcontenti, and the buildings were deconsecrated, although the church itself was restored by Giuseppe Castellucci.

On the other side (no. 99) is the former nunnery of **Santa Chiara**, founded in 1356, but suppressed by Napoleon. The conventual buildings were converted to various uses in the early nineteenth century, including the Teatro Goldoni (later a cinema; see below); in 1842 the church became the studio of the artist Pio Fedi (1815–1892).

Some way further down Via dei Serragli, at no. 146 (W side) is the entrance to the extensive **Giardino Torrigiani**. Among the largest in the city, the gardens extend W to Viale Petrarca, along the city walls. Today reached from no. 53 Via del Campuccio. They were begun towards the end of the eighteenth century by Pietro Guadagni Torrigiani, and were extended (1802–17) by Luigi de Cambrai-Digny, succeeded by Gaetano Baccani, in the Romantic manner. In 1824 Baccani also built the neo-Gothic **torrino**, an early example of the style, with a small observatory at the top. Rusticated masonry, with diminishing orders, the lower ones with bold machicolation. The *palazzo* itself has the character of a villa, with a broad façade, three orders and a spacious colonnaded loggia to the garden. The gardens contain a number of other eclectic structures, including a grotto and a Palladian *tempietto*.

2 SANTO SPIRITO AND SURROUNDINGS

Return N down most of the length of Via dei Serragli, and turn sharp right into Via Sant'Agostino. Here is the seventeenth-century former **Oratorio di San Carlino**, which in 1843 passed to the Padri Scolopi (Piarist Fathers) and later (1890) became a gymnasium. An attractive neo-Classical façade in stucco and *pietra serena* by Leopoldo Pasqui, 1838. After two blocks, the street opens out into the long rectangular Piazza Santo Spirito, with the homonymous church at the far (N) end. The attractive tree-lined piazza is the social centre of the district, with a small market. A simple fountain in the centre, and a statue of *Cosimo Ridolfi* by Raffaello Romanelli, 1896. Most of the surrounding houses are fifteenth century, of fairly modest appearance, but in the S corner (no. 10) is the imposing **Palazzo Dei Guadagni**, one of the most notable in the Oltrarno. Built for Riniero di Bernardo Dei, a wealthy silk merchant, in 1503–6, and usually attributed to Il Cronaca. Its simple, undecorated appearance was the model for a number of later palaces by both Il Cronaca and Baccio d'Agnolo, and reflects the 'age of austerity' of the

175

republican government, following the expulsion of the Medici in 1494. In 1683 the Dei became extinct and the building was acquired by Donato Maria Guadagni. The piazza façade is rigorously symmetrical: four orders and seven bays. The first order is clad with *pietra forte*, with the outer angles and the portal rusticated; six small rectangular lights flank the portal. The next two orders are treated similarly, with seven arched lights; those to the first floor, though, have rusticated surrounds, while the upper order has smooth ashlar; the wall surface is plain render. The fourth order has a generous seven-bay loggia with a continuous flat architrave, and surmounted by massively overhanging eaves. The central courtyard has been altered more than once; two colonnades down the sides, with depressed Baroque arches, but supported on Renaissance columns. A monumental internal stair (nineteenth century) by Poggi. Outside, on the corner between the two façades was a coat of arms of the Dei (now gone); an iron lantern survives.

Opposite is Via delle Caldaie; on the corner of Via dei Preti is **Palazzo Settimanni**, sixteenth century, with a seven-bay façade; a single *piano nobile* with an attic lit by oculi.

Back in the piazza, at the NE end is the second principal ecclesiastical monument of the Oltrarno,

Santo Spirito: A simple eighteenth-century façade finished with plain render; three portals, and an oculus in the centre of the upper part, which is linked to the broader lower order by large, plain volutes. Founded by Augustinians in 1250, but rebuilt by Brunelleschi after 1444. His first proposal (*circa* 1436) reversed the church's orientation, with a façade towards the N, facing a broad piazza extending as far as the Arno, but nothing came of this scheme. On Brunelleschi's death, two years after work began on the present church, it was continued and concluded by Antonio Manetti, with Giovanni da Gaiole and Salvi d'Andrea, who made some alterations to Brunelleschi's proposal; these included the external cladding of the fabric with a flat continuous wall surface, rather than Brunelleschi's intended external expression of the semicircular chapels that surround the perimeter of the structure.

The internal plan is a Latin cross; like San Lorenzo, the whole interior is based on simple proportions and mathematical ratios, all using multiples of 11 *braccia*, the Florentine unit of length (approx. 58 cm, or nearly 2 feet). The plan itself is based on a simple module of a square, used singly for the perimeter aisles, doubled for the width of the nave and the other three arms off the crossing. The outer chapels have a semicircular plan, set within half of a square module. In general, the interior resembles San Lorenzo, but some details are richer and more complex. The overall dimensions of the interior are: 97 m (approx. 318 ft) in length and 58 m (approx. 190 ft) across the transepts. All the structural stonework is *pietra serena*, the other surfaces plain plaster. The nave has nine bays, Corinthian, with monolithic columns on attic bases, and the capitals surmounted by dosserets. These in turn support the semicircular arches of the nave colonnade. Above is a tall clerestory with a single arched light to each bay. The nave is finished with a flat, coffered ceiling, replaced in the nineteenth century.

Flanking the nave are the side aisles, each bay square on plan, with plain plastered vaults. At the end of the nave is the square crossing, flanked by transepts, each one two bays across and three bays deep. Above the crossing: a hemispherical cupola on a drum on pendentives, planned by Brunelleschi but executed by Salvi d'Andrea, 1479–81. The high altar is located in the centre of the crossing; a complex, Baroque, free-standing work with a heavy baldacchino, decorated with *pietre dure*, by Giovanni Battista Caccini, assisted by Gherardo Silvani and Agostino Ubaldini, 1599–1607.

Beyond is the choir, again square on plan, with the same configuration and bay arrangement as the transepts. One of the most remarkable features is the series of semicircular chapels that wraps around the entire perimeter of the Latin-cross plan, forty in all, and each one originally with a small altar with a fifteenth-century altarpiece. Several survive in the sanctuary and the left transept.

Inner face of the façade: designed by Salvi d'Andrea with the *Descent of the Holy Spirit* by Perugino in the oculus. Right nave aisle: first chapel: *Disputation on the Immaculate Conception* by Pier Francesco Foschi, 1544–6. Second chapel: marble *Pietà* by Nanni di Baccio Bigio, 1545, a copy of that by Michelangelo in St Peter's in Rome. Third chapel: polychrome wooden statue of *St Niccolò da Tolentino* attributed to Nanni Unghero, sixteenth century. Fourth chapel: *Jesus Ejects the Merchants from the Temple* by Giovanni Stradano, 1572. Fifth chapel: *Coronation of the Virgin* by Alessandro Gherardini, 1694. Seventh chapel: *Martyrdom of St Stephen* by Passignano, 1602. Eighth chapel: *Raphael and Tobias*, marble altarpiece by Giovanni Baratta, *circa* 1690.

Around the right transept: first chapel: *Crucifixion* attributed to Francesco Curradi (or Piero Dandini), mid-seventeenth century. Second chapel: *Transfiguration* by Foschi, 1545. Third chapel: *Madonna del Soccorso*, panel attributed to the 'Maestro della Natività', 1475–85. Fourth chapel: within an architectural context by Buontalenti: small wooden Crucifix, fourteenth century. Fifth chapel: *Virgin and Child with Saints*, a panel by Filippino Lippi, 1493–4, in a rich contemporary frame. Sixth chapel: seventeenth-century decoration, with a copy of Felice Ficherelli's *Apparition of the Virgin to St Bernard*, 1655–6. Seventh chapel: *Marriage of the Virgin* by Giovanni Camillo Sagrestani, 1713. Behind a bronze grille: marble tomb of Neri di Gino Capponi, attributed to Bernardo Rossellino, 1458. Eighth chapel: *St Nicholas of Bari* by Giovan Gaetano Gabbiani, mid-eighteenth century.

Main apse, first chapel: panel painting: *Virgin and Child with St Matthew and St Jerome*. Second chapel: *Virgin and Child with Four Saints*, polyptych by Maso di Banco, *circa* 1345. Third chapel: *Adoration of the Magi* by Aurelio Lomi, *circa* 1608. Fourth chapel: *Martyred Saints* by Alessandro Allori, 1574. Fifth chapel: the *Woman Taken in Adultery*, also by Allori, 1577. Sixth chapel: *Blessed Clare of Montefalco* by Jacopo Vignali, 1629. Seventh chapel: *Annunciation* by Pietro di Donzello. Eighth chapel: *Nativity Crib* by Giuliani Bugiardini, *circa* 1495.

Left transept, continuing anti-clockwise: first chapel: *Virgin and Child with St Bartholomew and St John the Evangelist*, late fifteenth century. Second chapel: *St Monica*, attributed to Francesco Botticini, *circa* 1460–70, in a contemporary frame. Third chapel: *Virgin and Child Enthroned* by Cosimo Rosselli, 1482. Fourth (Corbinelli) chapel: the architecture and fittings all by Andrea Sansovino, 1492. *Altar of the Sacrament*: a fine work. In the central niche, treated as an aedicule: *Risen Christ Flanked by St James and St Matthew*. Above: roundels of the *Annunciation*. In the predella: *Last Supper*. Fifth chapel: *Holy Trinity Adored by St Catherine and St Mary Magdalene* attributed to Donino and Angelo Mazzieri. Sixth chapel: *Virgin and Child Enthroned with St Bartholomew and St Nicholas*, also by the Mazzieri workshop. Seventh chapel: *Virgin and Child Enthroned* by Raffaellino del Garbo, *circa* 1501–5. Eighth chapel: *Road to Calvary*, attributed to Antonio del Ceraiolo, early sixteenth century.

Left nave chapels, from the transept corner: eighth chapel: *Virgin and Child with Saints*, school of Fra Bartolomeo. Seventh chapel: *Virgin and Child with Saints*, copy of a work by Rosso Fiorentino, today in the Pitti. Sixth bay: entrance to the sacristy (see below). Fifth chapel: *Virgin and Child with Saints* by Ridolfo and Michele del Ghirlandaio. Fourth chapel: *St Tommaso di Villanova* by Rutilio Manetti. Third chapel: *St John of San Facundo* by Giuseppe Nasini, 1691. Second chapel: *Risen Christ* by Taddeo Landini, 1579. First chapel: *Resurrection* by Foschi, 1537.

The sixth left aisle bay gives access to the sacristy, a notable work by Giuliano da Sangallo. It is approached by a doorway below the organ, and a transverse vestibule, built by Il Cronaca (1492–4) to Sangallo's design; a rich, coffered, barrel-vaulted ceiling, supported by twelve Corinthian columns. Set into the coffers are *Mythological Scenes*. The sacristy itself is a significant Renaissance work, 1489–92, with an octagonal plan, and all in *pietra serena* and white stucco, simple but refined. It is roofed with a faceted cupola with a lantern, by Antonio Pollaiolo and Salvi d'Andrea. Two superimposed orders, articulated by flat fluted Corinthian pilasters, the upper order shorter and with smaller pilasters than the lower one. In the lower order: each facet has a large blind semicircular arch. Above the continuous double entablature, the second order has a single rectangular aediculed window on each facet, with a triangular pediment. On the main altar: altarpiece of *St Fiacre* by Alessandro Allori, 1596.

At the left end of the vestibule a doorway gives access to the first cloister, not generally accessible; seven bays square, early seventeenth century, by Alfonso and Giulio Parigi, with lunettes frescoed by Cosimo Ulivelli and others. On the side adjacent to the sacristy is the Sala Capitolare (chapter house); on the W side is the Refettorio Nuovo (new refectory), sixteenth century, with frescoes by Bernardino Poccetti. Beyond is the second cloister, an elegant work by Ammannati, 1564–9, of the same dimensions as the other; Doric colonnades. Off the far side is the Corsini chapel, originally fourteenth century, but rebuilt 1698–1704 and frescoed by Stefano Fabbrini, 1787–91.

The fourteenth-century refectory, on the S side of the first cloister, is reached directly from the piazza at no. 29; the only part of the medieval monastery to survive largely unaltered. One of the end walls is almost entirely covered by a fresco of the *Last Supper*, with a *Crucifixion* above; both in very poor condition. Both are *circa* 1360–65, attributed to Orcagna. The hall itself contains a collection of sculptures, architectural fragments and archaeological finds, and includes pieces by Jacopo della Quercia, Ammannati and attributions to Donatello.

The campanile was begun in 1490, but completed by Baccio d'Agnolo after 1503; above the shaft is a tall, elegant, bell chamber, with Serlianas on all four faces, and volutes at the outer corners. The crowning pyramidal roof is from 1541.

From the piazza, take Via del Presto (NE corner) into Via dei Coverelli, to reach

Via di Santo Spirito: The narrow street runs parallel to the Arno, one block to the S. From the E end (Piazza dei Frescobaldi), no. 3 is **Casa Vettori**, with a coloured family coat of arms by Luca della Robbia and Maso di Bartolomeo (1450); no. 4 is the rear façade of **Palazzo Capponi** (see below).Very narrow, only two bays, with paired aediculed windows. No. 6 is **Palazzo Segni Reali**. Mid-sixteenth century with a restrained eighteenth-century neo-Renaissance façade of five bays; three orders plus mezzanine. At nos. 5–7 (S side) is **Palazzo Machiavelli**, with jetties on the left flank. Built *circa* 1427, with a stone-faced ground floor (two arched portals) and three upper orders. Niccolò Machiavelli lived here for a time. At nos. 11–13 is **Palazzo Frescobaldi**, originally late fifteenth century, but enlarged on several occasions. Several earlier buildings were unified in 1621–44 under Matteo Frescobaldi; a reticent neo-Classical façade. The *androne* leads to a small courtyard, beyond which is a second *androne* leading to the extensive garden, abutting the campanile of Santo Spirito. Adjacent, on the N side, are the rear façades of Palazzo Lanfredini and Palazzo Guicciardini (see below). No. 15 (S side) is **Casa Pitti**, later Bucciolini, sixteenth century, formerly frescoed by Poccetti; remains are conserved inside the atrium. Three bays, with a large square central portal. No. 17 is **Palazzo Rosselli del Turco**, with an impressive but restrained Baroque façade. Three orders, eight bays and a big rusticated portal. No. 23 is **Palazzo Manetti**, first built in the fourteenth century; today with a fifteenth-century façade (and a huge nineteenth-century portal), incorporating the remains of the early medieval **Torre dei Lanfredini**, corner of Via dei Geppi.

Further W, no. 32 is the former house of Francesco Ferrucci, 1489–1530 (plaque), a defender of Florentine republican liberty. No. 58r is **Palazzetto Medici**, a small, attractive façade, late seventeenth century, in the style of Gherardo Silvani. Three bays and three orders, with a stone portal surmounted by a balcony. Nos. 39–41 (S side) is **Palazzo Rinuccini**, occupying an entire block and comprising two different structures. The first is attributed to Cigoli or G.B. Caccini, but was modernised in 1733–44 by Pietro Paolo Giovanozzi, who added a new staircase; it was further enlarged by Giulio Mannaioni (1753), who extended it towards Via Maffia. The second element, no. 41, was rebuilt by Pier Francesco Silvani towards the end of the seventeenth century. An imposing eighteenth-century façade unites the two. Inside: frescoes by Poccetti, Giuseppe Zocchi and others. It also contains a fine private archaeological collection, rich internal decorations and a small theatre.

Turning right into Piazza Nazario Sauro, and right again, we reach the

Lungarno Guicciardini: Extends from the bridgehead of the Ponte alla Carraia to that of Ponte Santa Trinità. Starting at this W end: nos. 19–21 is **Palazzo Medici Soderini**, modernised in 1765 in conjunction with the construction of the adjacent Scottish Presbyterian church. No. 9 is **Palazzo Lanfredini**, early sixteenth century, with a façade generally said to be by Baccio d'Agnolo; five bays, sober and restrained, with two floors above a very tall basement. Slightly later *sgraffito* decoration by Andrea Feltrini. Inside: a refined courtyard, with loggias on two sides of the *piano nobile*.

At no. 7 is **Palazzo Guicciardini**, originally owned by the Bardi, rebuilt in the seventeenth century; it was bought by the Guicciardini in 1810 and modernised again by Poggi (1840). The restrained, symmetrical river façade has three orders (plus mezzanine) and seven bays. On the corner of Via dei Coverelli is **Palazzo Coverelli**; the long side façade is the most interesting, clad with monochrome *sgraffito* decoration; a portal gives access to the central courtyard, also with *sgraffito*. A narrow three-bay façade to the river, with ground-floor rustication and a top-floor loggia. Almost at the E end is the **Palazzo di Ludovico Capponi**, no. 1, originally fifteenth century but enlarged and altered on several occasions. The site was originally occupied by houses of the Vettori, to whom the Capponi were closely related. Enlarged and modernised by Ludovico Capponi after 1560, when he married Maddalena Vettori; further modernisations in 1583–90 under Bernardino Poccetti. The *piano nobile* hall is frescoed by Poccetti, 1585. The main N façade has eight bays and an off-centre portal, surmounted by a balcony. The S façade towards Via Santo Spirito (no. 4) is attributed to Buontalenti: only two bays, four orders, with rusticated outer quoins and rustication around the arched windows to the first and second floors.

We have now reached Piazza Frescobaldi, with Ponte Santa Trinità to the left, and the important axis of Via Maggio to the right.

3 PIAZZA FRESCOBALDI, BORGO SAN JACOPO, VIA MAGGIO AND VIA ROMANA

On the E side of the piazza, corner of Borgo San Jacopo, is the imposing pile of **Palazzo Frescobaldi** (nos. 1, 2 and 3r). Probably first built in the thirteenth century, at this important strategic location adjacent to the bridgehead, and opposite the equally fortified Palazzo Spini Feroni on the other bank, the two together forming a gateway into the city centre. Parts of the fourteenth-century house have survived, but the rest was lost when the Palazzo delle Missioni was built. The building was comprehensively restored in 1921. The ground-floor loggias (originally open) were later filled in with shops and workshops. At the SE corner of the piazza with the Borgo (junction with Via dello Sprone) is an elegant little fountain, attributed to Buontalenti; above: an attractive loggetta with the Medici arms. On the NE corner of the piazza, at no. 1 is the **Palazzo dei Padri delle Missioni**, once part of 176 the adjacent monastic house of the Scopetini. The imposing Baroque five-bay piazza façade is by Bernardino Radi, 1640; five orders, all the openings surrounded by rich frames of stone; a monumental central portal capped by a broken pediment. The four flanking window bays have Mannerist surrounds; above the mezzanine windows are four niches containing busts of the grand dukes. Tall rectangular lights to the *piano nobile* and small arched lights to the upper mezzanine. The long river façade has two elements, the left one plainer than the other.

Walking E along the Borgo, we reach **San Jacopo sopr'Arno** 177 (N side) originally tenth century, but many times modernised and rebuilt. On the street façade is an elegant three-bay portico, twelfth or thirteenth century, from the lost church of San Donato in Scopeto, destroyed in 1529 during the siege of the city. It was reassembled here by Piero il Gottoso de' Medici in the late 1460s. Inside: nave and two side aisles, generally eighteenth-century Baroque, all white and gold; the Romanesque colonnade had been encased in Baroque piers, but was revealed during restorations after the flood of 1966, which had badly damaged the church. The eighteenth-century modernisations involved the demolition of the Ridolfi chapel, with a cupola by Brunelleschi, said to have been a model for that of the cathedral. Most of the altarpieces to the side altars are also eighteenth century. The campanile is by Gherardo Silvani, 1660. Today the church is used by the Greek Orthodox community.

No. 30 (left) is the **Torre degli Angiolieri**, early medieval but with the upper parts rebuilt. No. 14, a little further E, is the **Torre dei Barbadori**. At no. 17 (right) is the **Torre dei Marsili**, with an *Annunciation* in polychrome terracotta from the della Robbia workshop above the portal (now replaced by a copy); two small angels in the outer 178 flanking niches. A little further on: more medieval towers; at no. 9, set

back on the right, is the **Torre Belfredelli** and behind it (Via Ram-
iglianti no. 9r) is the **Torre Ramaglianti**; on the other side of the
Borgo, no. 14 is the second **Torre dei Barbadori**. The eastern tract of
the Borgo is occupied by relatively modern structures (*circa* 1955) built
to replace those destroyed in 1944. Finally, the Borgo reaches the
southern bridgehead of the Ponte Vecchio. On the corner is the **Torre
dei Rossi Cerchi**, thirteenth century, like most, although partly rebuilt
after 1944. At its base is the **Fontana del Bacchino**, with a good statue
attributed to Giambologna.

Via Maggio (a corruption of Maggiore, principal street) is indeed
the most important axis of this district, running S from the Ponte Santa
Trinità to Piazza San Felice, where its orientation and name change,
and it continues as the Via Romana to the city gate. Start at Piazza dei
Frescobaldi. Although of ancient origin, much of the street today is of
late sixteenth-century appearance. This is the result of the transfer of
the Medici court to Palazzo Pitti in 1549, after which Via Maggio
became the street housing many of the Medici's courtiers.

On the W side, no. 2 is **Palazzo Pitti**, with Pitti and Manelli coats
of arms, and a bust of *Cosimo I de' Medici* in a niche, attributed to
Baccio Bandinelli. Tall and narrow, two bays by four, on a very confined
site; originally fourteenth century, with rusticated stone below, arched
windows above. No. 6 is **Palazzo Agostini**, generally attributed to
Baccio d'Agnolo; four orders (including mezzanine) and four bays,
with stone arched windows to the *piani nobili*. A large coat of arms
(Calimala?). **Palazzo Ricasoli Firidolfi,** no. 7, with characteristically
restrained façade, is also given to Baccio. Built *circa* 1520 for Giovanni
Francesco Ridolfi. Six bays, with an off-centre rusticated arched portal
(coat of arms above), flanked by five (later) aediculed lights, two and
three. Above: two orders of six arched windows with rusticated surrounds. Inside: an attractive courtyard with loggias on three sides, a
balcony on the fourth. Oculi to the upper mezzanine. The *piano nobile*
contains eighteenth-century frescoes.

On the E side, no. 9 (corner of Via dei Velluti) is **Palazzo Martellini**,
with another reticent sixteenth-century façade. Twin arched portals in
the centre, flanked by two later aediculed lights. Seven regular bays of
arched lights to the two *piani nobili*. Rusticated quoins and a bold roof
overhang. Next, no. 11 is **Palazzo Michelozzi**, rebuilt in the later sixteenth century, on the site of a house of the Corbinelli; probably built
for Giovanni Battista Michelozzi (1523–1604). The house is perhaps by
Caccini, who designed the high altar in the adjacent Santo Spirito, also

175   Palazzo Dei Guadagni: façade to Piazza Santo Spirito by Il Cronaca, 1503–6

176   Palazzo dei Padri delle Missioni: façade to the Arno, by Bernardino Radi, 1640–50; on the right: Ponte Santa Trinità by Bartolomeo Ammannati, 1567–70 (rebuilt)

177   San Jacopo sopr'Arno: apse towards the river and campanile

178   Torre dei Marsili: copy of a sixteenth-century terracotta group of the *Annunciation*

179   The Oltrarno: post-war reconstruction between the Arno and Borgo San Jacopo, by Italo Gamberini and others, after 1950

funded by Michelozzi. A simple, refined façade; an arched portal flanked by (later) aediculed lights, three and two. Above: two orders of six bays of plain arched windows. Inside is an earlier fifteenth-century courtyard, surviving from the Corbinelli house, with Tuscan colonnades of *pietra serena* on two sides. No. 18 is the **Anglican church of St Mark**, established here in 1880, in a converted palace; a neo-Classical façade; inside: a colonnaded nave with vaulted ceiling, and side aisles, all 'expatriate' Victorian neo-Gothic. Opposite Palazzo Michelozzi, no. 24 is a four-bay late medieval house, stone clad. Next to it (no. 26) is the unusual

Palazzo di Bianca Cappello: Originally a fifteenth-century house owned by the Corbinelli; extensively modernised, probably *circa* 1570–74, by Buontalenti, his first major architectural commission. Bianca Cappello (b. 1548) was the daughter of a Venetian noble family, who fled to Florence with a Florentine bank clerk, Pietro Bonaventuri, and later became first the lover and then the wife of Francesco I de' Medici. When Bianca became grand duchess (1579), she gave the house to the Ospedale di Santa Maria Nuova. The façade is notable for the remark-181 ably rich and complex *sgraffito* decoration added by Bernardino Poccetti, 1579–80. Most is monochrome, but the Medici coat of arms is in colour. Four orders, the ground floor having a rusticated portal flanked by two large aediculed windows, inserted by Buontalenti. The two principal floors have simple arched single-light windows; above is a low attic lit by four oculi. Buontalenti and Francesco shared interests in alchemy and the occult, and the decoration incorporates a wide variety of masks, fauns, monsters and other imaginary creatures.

No. 28, next door, is **Palazzo Peruzzi de' Medici**, sixteenth century, on the site of houses also formerly owned by the Corbinelli; modernised by Gherardo Silvani in the seventeenth century. In this period it was bought by the Pannocchieschi, who retained it until the mid-nineteenth century, when it passed to the Peruzzi de' Medici. A long, flat, ten-bay façade with portals at each end.

Opposite, no. 13 is **Palazzo Zanchini**, late sixteenth century, perhaps by Santi di Tito. Again originally owned by the Corbinelli, it was rebuilt for Girolamo Zanchini and was complete by 1585 when it was sold to the Sangalletti. A typical late sixteenth-century façade, with a large portal; six bays and three orders. Inside: an attractive fifteenth-century courtyard with two loggias. The chapel, of the same date, is contiguous internally with no. 15, **Palazzo di Cosimo Ridolfi**, sixteenth century, three bays, with a rusticated stone ground floor.

No. 17 is **Palazzo Firidolfi**, with a coat of arms of the Ridolfi family by Jacopo Sansovino. No. 30 is **Palazzo Biliotti**, with fourteenth-century rustication to the ground floor and arched *sporti* to the side façade to Via de' Michelozzi. Five bays and two principal arched upper orders.

No. 27 is the **Casa Velluti**, with the Ridolfi family arms; at nos. 33–5 are two further **Case Velluti**, with the family arms. Owned by Baron Ferdinando Velluti in 1761, when they were altered. The houses appear different externally: no. 33 is tall and narrow, originally fourteenth century, only three bays wide, while no. 35 has six bays, with an inner courtyard, also originally fourteenth century. No. 42 is **Palazzo della Commenda**, or Corsini Suarez, formerly of the Corsini, again modernised by Gherardo Silvani in the seventeenth century. Corsini arms on the second floor. An earlier house here was sacked in the Ciompi riots of 1378, but was rebuilt in the early fifteenth century, although the stonework on the lower façade was reused. It remained in Corsini ownership until 1559, when it was sold to the Medici. In 1590 it passed to Baldassare Suarez de la Concha, who employed Silvani to alter and extend it. Silvani's modernisation included the prominent portal and ground-floor windows, and the square third-floor windows. The courtyard was enlarged, although the fine late fourteenth-century octagonal columns survive, all in *pietra serena*, as is the balcony that wraps around the *piano nobile*. Suarez donated the building to the Ordine dei Cavalieri di Santo Stefano (f. 1554), from which the title 'della Commenda' derived (*commendatore*: Knight Commander of the order).

No. 43 is the **Casa Ridolfi,** originally fourteenth century, restored in 1836 by Giovanni Pacini. It retains the severe stone façade, four bays and four orders plus mezzanine; shallow arched window heads. No. 48 is the **Casa Foggini**, once owned by the sculptor and architect Giovanni Battista Foggini, with four bays and four orders; arches to the ground floor, square lights above. No. 37 is the **Casa di Bernardo Buontalenti,** owned by the architect in the late sixteenth century, and conveniently close to Palazzo Pitti, where he worked extensively; the façade was originally decorated with *sgraffito* by Poccetti. Four bays and three orders. Nos. 50–52 is another **Palazzo Corsini**, later Rosselli del Turco. Sixteenth century, with six bays to the upper orders and a portal at each end. At the corner of Piazza San Felice is the **Casa Guidi**, two structures, originally fifteenth century, built for the Ridolfi, later joined internally. After 1847 the English poets Elizabeth Barrett Browning and Robert Browning lived here; the former died here in 1861. Contains a small museum of memorabilia and furniture.

Via Maggio enters Piazza San Felice. In the piazza: marble column erected by Cosimo I in 1572, but removed by Leopoldo II in 1838; reinstated in 1992.

San Felice in Piazza: First recorded in 1066, and dedicated to the third-century martyr, it has a fourteenth-century plan, although modernised *circa* 1457 by Michelozzo, and again in the sixteenth century. After 1557 the church was occupied by Dominican nuns. It was damaged by fire in 1926 but restored. The present simple Renaissance façade is probably by Michelozzo: a prominent portal with a rich, complex, semicircular pediment, flanked at high level by two arched windows; above is a central oculus, and on the outer pilasters are the arms of the Lippi. The whole is capped by a large triangular pediment.

An unusual interior: the first half of the long nave is divided into three, with central nave and side aisles, four bays long and divided by eight Doric columns. Above is a *barco* or nuns' choir gallery, supported by cross vaults carried by the columns. It was added for the Dominicans in 1578–9. The further part of the nave retains some fourteenth- and fifteenth-century material, with a timber beamed roof and the original flanking windows, reopened after the 1926 fire. The apses are mid-fifteenth century, and perhaps also by Michelozzo; a chancel arch, a high vault and a tall, narrow *bifora*.

First right altar: *Pietà*, fresco by Niccolò di Pietro Gerini, 1405–10; fifth altar: *Deposition* by Giovanni della Robbia, 1500–15. Chancel: a large wooden Crucifix, from the workshop of Giotto, before 1307; two panel paintings from the workshop of Botticelli. Other works by Bicci di Lorenzo, Volterrano, Neri di Bicci, Salvator Rosa and others. To the left (SW) of the façade: remaining conventual buildings, dedicated to St Peter Martyr; a central cloister. In the refectory: a large *Last Supper* by Matteo Rosselli, 1614.

From Piazza San Felice, continue SW along the Via Romana, lined with modest shops and workshops. At nos. 8–10: the **Oratorio di San Sebastiano dei Bini**, part of a hospital founded *circa* 1290 from the will of Folco Portinari and Giovanni Amidei. The oratory was built in 1496–1525. A simple interior of *pietra serena* and white plaster. Opposite, no. 17 is **Palazzo Torrigiani**, known as La Specola, since Grand Duke Pietro Leopoldo acquired it in 1771 and established an observatory here. It was transformed by Gaspare Maria Paoletti. Today it contains the Museo Zoologico, part of the Museo di Storia Naturale of the university, also founded by Pietro Leopoldo in 1775.

180 Via Maggio: general view towards the south, with Palazzo Ricasoli Firidolfi and Palazzo Michelozzi

181 Palazzo di Bianca Cappello: detail of *sgraffito* decoration of the façade, with the Medici arms, by Bernardo Buontalenti, *circa* 1570–74

182 San Felice in Piazza: main portal by Michelozzo, *circa* 1457

183 Via Romana, terminating at the Porta Romana

184 Porta Romana: detail of the original medieval gates, 1328–31

At nos. 27–31 is the ancient former **Ospizio della Buca**. On Via Santa Maria (right), at the end of a short cul-de-sac is the former **Convento di San Vincenzo d'Annalena**, founded by Annalena d'Anghiari in 1440. Adjacent is the **Teatro Goldoni**, originating in 1807, when Luigi Gargani acquired the monastic buildings, and built a ballroom in the section towards Via dei Serragli and a theatre on the side towards Via Romana. The work was completed in 1817 by Giuseppe del Rosso. It was modernised in 1875 but declined in the twentieth century, evincing major structural problems. It was closed in 1976 but restoration followed, and it reopened in 1985. A simple neo-Classical façade; inside: an oval auditorium, with four tiers of galleries. Rich stucco decoration. The adjacent Saloncino is used for dance performances.

Back in Via Romana, just beyond the junction with Via Santa Maria is a portal with the coats of arms of the Ridolfi, indicating the site of the former **Ospedale di San Pier Novello**, founded in the fourteenth century by Pietro Ridolfi.

Continuing SW, adjacent to the Giardino Scarselli is a small neo-Classical *loggetta*, built by Giuseppe Manetti for Tommaso Corsi (1801–10), in conjunction with the adjacent garden, set out in the English manner. Continuing SW, on the right (corner of Via Serumido) is **San Pier Gattolino** (or San Pietro in Gattolino), of Romanesque origin, but rebuilt in the later sixteenth century by Giuseppe Castagnoli, following serious damage during the siege of 1529–30. The façade is perhaps by Santi di Tito; rusticated quoins and a portal with split pediment. Inside: a square, box-like nave, Corinthian, with coffered, frescoed ceiling also by Castagnoli. The barrel-vaulted chancel is in the style of Gherardo Silvani, 1603. Attached is the **Oratorio del Santissimo Sacramento**, with a late eighteenth-century fresco cycle; altarpiece by Alessandro Fei, 1568.

No. 115 is the **Spedale dello Spirito Santo**, founded by the Laudesi confraternity in the early sixteenth century.

Via Romana terminates in Piazza della Calza, named after the **Convento della Calza** (no. 6), founded as a hospital in 1362, dedicated to St John the Baptist. After 1529 it was occupied by friars of the Ingesuati order. Among the works of art: early seventeenth-century high altarpiece by Jacopo da Empoli of *St John the Evangelist with the Archangel Michael*; *Crucifixion* attributed to Lorenzo Monaco.

The imposing **Porta Romana** (1328–31) is said to have been designed by Orcagna, with sections of the city wall surviving on each side. That to the NW is the longest in the city. The Porta was reduced in height in the sixteenth century, although it remains the second largest after the Porta San Frediano, and also conserves its original wooden gates. In the lunette: early fifteenth-century fresco of the *Virgin and Child with Saints*, said to be by Franciabigio. On the Via Senese, just S of the Porta, is **Sant'Ilario a Colombaia**, dedicated to St Hilary of Poitiers; founded *circa* 1000, it has a fourteenth-century portico, with contemporaneous frescoes. The campanile is from 1880.

Return to the heart of the Oltrarno and the southern bridgehead of the Ponte Vecchio.

4 VIA GUICCIARDINI, PALAZZO PITTI AND THE GIARDINO DI BOBOLI

The first tract of this busy, congested street was destroyed by the Germans in 1944. On the left (E) side is an arch carrying the Corridoio Vasariano across Via dei Bardi. Largely hidden within the fabric of the first block on this side is the **Torre degli Ubriachi**, visible from the foot of the Ponte Vecchio. Via Guicciardini opens out into the little Piazza Santa Felicità, at the back of which is

Santa Felicità: Romanesque in origin, built over the foundations of an earlier fourth-century basilica; it is therefore one of the oldest churches in the city. In 1060 it was rebuilt and consecrated by Pope Nicholas II, dedicated to the early Christian martyr. After centuries of alteration and partial reconstruction, it was completely rebuilt by Ferdinando Ruggieri in 1736–9. The Corridoio Vasariano runs across the simple façade, on a three-bay colonnade. The Medici thus had direct access to the church from the corridor, and it became the family's formal chapel. This function continued under the Lorraine dynasty. Inside the portico is a small atrium, flanked by two chapels (see below). The interior of the church itself is tall, stately and very light; a Latin-cross plan, with an aisle-less nave, but with deep chapels, three to each side. Beyond is the crossing; square transepts and chancel. All the detailing is in *pietra serena*. Paired, fluted Corinthian pilasters flank the nave; between them are semicircular arches to the flanking chapels. Above the nave: a tall clerestory with a single large arched window to each bay. At the crossing: a simple hemispherical blind cupola on pendentives. Terminating the nave is a tall chancel arch, capped by a pediment. The chancel is raised up on four steps; high altar and choir both by Cigoli, *circa* 1610.

The most notable chapel is that originally built by the Barbadori, to an early design by Brunelleschi, *circa* 1430, later passing to the Capponi. It stands to the right of the entrance vestibule, but was altered by Vasari when he built the Corridoio. It is extremely simple: a square plan, with Ionic pilasters at the corners supporting a hemispherical cupola on pendentives. The splendid paintings of the *Deposition* and the *Annunciation* (1527–8) are among the finest works by Pontormo. The *Evangelists* in the pendentives are also by Pontormo, or Bronzino. Opposite the Capponi chapel is that of the Carnigiani, with a cupola by Tommaso Gherardini and paintings by Poccetti.

Other works of art: in the sacristy: polyptych by Taddeo Gaddi, *circa* 1355; frescoes by Niccolò di Pietro Gerini; *St Felicitas* by Neri di Bicci. Also works by Volterrano, Poccetti.

Opposite the church, at Via Guiccardini nos. 10–12r, is the **Torre de' Nerli** or Galganetta, a variant of the typical model, with two bays and relatively large window openings. It was largely rebuilt after 1944.

Continuing SW, on the left (nos. 11–13) is **Palazzo Franceschi**, by Antonio Maria Ferri, and next to it, no. 15, **Palazzo Guicciardini Benizzi**. The latter was the birthplace of the historian of the republic, Francesco Guicciardini, in 1482. The earliest houses were built around a fortified tower, but were destroyed in the Ciompi riots of 1378. They were subsequently rebuilt and extended (*circa* 1390), incorporating two fortified towers. In 1515 the house was further extended towards the right by acquisition of an adjacent house of the Benizzi. The building still consists of several component elements, unified internally in 1620–25, when Gherardo Silvani formed a new main entrance, added a formal staircase within a tower once owned by the Malefici, and joined two courtyards together. Inside the entrance is an atrium, beyond which is the courtyard. The façades were partially unified by aligning the second-floor windows and building a continuous cornice. Further alterations took place in 1837. The palace was badly damaged in 1944. It is still owned by the Guicciardini. Behind, a small garden abuts that of the Boboli.

Immediately beyond, the street opens out into Piazza dei Pitti, a vast, long, open space, down the SE side of which, on a high, sloping terrace, stands the immense mass of Palazzo Pitti. The most interesting house on the W side is **Palazzo Temple Leader**, on the site of a former house of the Pitti. Rebuilt *circa* 1498; enlarged 1529. An eighteenth-century façade, but in *cinquecento* style; three orders, five large arched bays below, nine above; a prominent roof loggia. It was bought by the British nobleman and classical scholar John Temple Leader in 1857.

Palazzo Pitti: By some considerable margin the largest *palazzo* in the city, it stands on the lower slope of the Boboli hill, which rises behind it. Most unusually, the building also stands on the site of one of the *pietra forte* stone quarries, and thus directly on the quarry from which it was built.

The Exterior

The massive façade is twenty-three bays long; at each end, wings project forward to enclose the extensive forecourt. The palace was built in stages, each stage adding further to the original nucleus. This was built for the wealthy banker Luca Pitti; it was designed by Brunelleschi, who had already died by the time work began, *circa* 1458; it was probably supervised by Luca Fancelli. Pitti's intention was to build a *palazzo* to rival that of the Medici, begun in 1444 by Michelozzo, but its site and context are very different, located on a hillside on the very SE edge of the city. The façade is bolder, simpler and more ruggedly powerful than that of the Medici palace; this original element consists of the seven central bays of the main façade: three orders, each with a different degree of rustication, massive and rough-hewn to the first order, more finished on the upper two. The basic element is a single large arched opening, with radiating rusticated stone around the extrados. Seven of these elements define the two upper orders, while the lowermost has a single central one for the portal, now flanked by two others, into which an aediculed window is set, alternating with high-level squared lights. These windows were inserted later by Ammannati for Cosimo I. Each order is defined by a continuous stone balcony. Pitti's palace was not completed as intended because of his rapid financial decline.

In 1549, a century later, it was bought by Cosimo I and Eleonora di Toledo, who decided to transfer the ducal court here from the Palazzo Vecchio, and to modernise and extend the palace. The first stage came in 1558–70, when the courtyard and its enclosing wings were added to the rear, also by Ammannati, just moved to Florence from Rome. The courtyard façades are all massively rusticated in the manner of the Veronese architect Michele Sanmicheli, although the influence of the Roman Renaissance is also strong. Again three orders, this time (correctly) Doric, Ionic and Corinthian, with rustication both to the colonnade and to the wall surfaces behind and between the columns. The main courtyard façade has five bays, with a central portal leading directly from the main entrance on the piazza. The first order is simple and powerful; the second has aediculed windows with split pediments set into the arches, while the third order has windows with curved pediments. The central bays are emphasised by a large arched opening flanked by colonnettes. A similar treatment extends down the two flanks, and was continued further on the SE faces of the wings towards the Giardino di Boboli.

The next stage of expansion took place after 1619, under Giulio Parigi. It followed a competition launched by Cosimo II four years earlier. It consisted of the further extension of the original front block to the piazza by an additional three bays on each side, extending the façade to thirteen bays in all. The treatment was identical to Brunelleschi's original block, and again incorporated aediculed ground-floor windows. The southern section was begun after 1631. A further extension by Alfonso Parigi after 1640 resulted in another five bays being added to each end of this already massive façade. These new outer wings, however, have only two orders rather than three, a significant reduction of scale, focusing attention on the earlier nucleus.

The very last additions were the two outermost wings, which project forward from the main façade; the so-called *rondò* on the right was added by Giuseppe Ruggieri in 1764, that on the left by Pasquale Poccianti in 1839, again following the architectural language of all the earlier phases. Each wing has seven bays but a single order, with tall rusticated arches.

Palazzo Pitti contains a number of important collections of works of art and artefacts, the principal of which are located within the Galleria Palatina (occupying the NE half of the *piano nobile*) and the Appartamenti Reali, the equivalent apartments on the SW side.

Galleria Palatina

A brief summary of the contents. The itinerary usually begins at the top of the monumental staircase.

Sala degli Staffieri: marble statues by Baccio Bandinelli and Pietro Francavilla.

Galleria delle Statue: Roman copies of Greek statues from Villa Medici, Rome. Paintings by Luca Giordano and Tintoretto.

Sala delle Nicchie: antique statues set into niches.

Sala di Venere: rich stucco and fresco to the vaults by Pietro da Cortona. *Venus Italica* by Canova; four fine works by Titian, including

185 Palazzo Pitti: central section of the main façade, by Brunelleschi, begun *circa* 1458

186 Palazzo Pitti: main façade; ground-floor window added by Ammannati after 1558

187 Palazzo Pitti: rustication to the ground-floor colonnade, by Ammannati, 1558–70

188 Palazzo Pitti and the Giardino di Boboli: amphitheatre, begun by Niccolò Tribolo, 1550, completed by Giulio and Alfonso Parigi

portraits of *Pietro Aretino* and *Pope Julius II*; works by Rubens, Sebastiano del Piombo, Guercino and Salvator Rosa.

Sala di Apollo: fresco decoration again by Pietro da Cortona. Paintings by Rosso Fiorentino, Titian, Tintoretto, Guido Reni, Andrea del Sarto.

Sala di Marte: ceiling again by Pietro da Cortona. Paintings by Rubens, Van Dyck, Tintoretto and Veronese.

Sala di Giove: paintings by Raphael, Titian, Giorgione, Fra Bartolomeo, Bronzino, Andrea del Sarto.

Sala di Saturno: frescoes by Ciro Ferri, Pietro da Cortona's pupil. Paintings by Perugino, several by Raphael, Sebastiano del Piombo and Andrea del Sarto.

Sala dell'Iliade: early nineteenth-century decoration by Luigi Sabatelli. Paintings by Andrea del Sarto, Raphael, Velázquez, Veronese, Artemisia Gentileschi and the Carracci.

Sala dell'Educazione di Giove: *Sleeping Cupid* by Caravaggio.

Sala della Stufa: wall paintings by Pietro da Cortona.

Sala di Ulisse: paintings by Raphael, Filippino Lippi, G.B. Moroni and Andrea del Sarto.

Sala di Prometeo: paintings by Filippo Lippi, Botticelli, Signorelli, Pontormo.

Corridoio delle Colonne: Dutch and Flemish landscapes.

Sala della Giustizia: paintings by Bonifacio de' Pitati and a *Portrait of Vincenzo Mosti* by Titian.

Sala di Flora: works by Alessandro Allori and Andrea del Sarto.

Sala dei Putti: north European painters, including Rubens.

Galleria del Poccetti (reached via the Sala del Prometeo): works by Francesco Furini, Pontormo and Jusepe de Ribera.

The Sala dei Tamburi leads to the Sala del Castagnoli and thence to the former apartments of Grand Duchess Vittoria della Rovere. These include the Sala delle Allegorie, the Sala dell'Arca, the Sala delle Miniature, the Sala di Ercole and the Sala di Psiche. They contain works by Cigoli, Jacopo da Empoli, Salvator Rosa and others.

The royal apartments are richly decorated and furnished. They also contain works of art by Castagnoli, Luca Giordano, G.B. Foggini and others.

On the second *piano nobile* is located the Galleria d'Arte Moderna, covering Italian art from neo-Classicism to the twentieth century. It contains works by Pompeo Batoni, Francesco Hayez, Lorenzo Bartolini, and later works by Camille Pissarro, Giovanni Fattori and Galileo Chini. In the summer apartments of the Medici is located the Museo degli Argenti, containing not only works in silver, but also ivories, jewellery, gemstones and *pietra dura*.

Giardino di Boboli: One of most important gardens in Italy. It consists of two distinct but closely connected elements. The first is a series of formal terraces, embankments and features all aligned with the rear façade of Palazzo Pitti, and ascending the slope of the Boboli hill. At the top, on the left, this section abuts the Forte di Belvedere (see below). The second, considerably larger element, is at right angles to the first and consists of a further series of gardens, terraces and other features, which slope down SW towards the Porta Romana.

The original design is attributed to Niccolò Tribolo, and was begun following the acquisition of Palazzo Pitti by Eleonora di Toledo in 1549. It was remodelled in the seventeenth century, when it became more complex, and was further modified in the eighteenth.

Access is usually from Ammannati's rear courtyard, from which steps rise to the first terrace. On the terrace: the fine **Fontana del Carciofo**, named after the little artichoke at the top (by Giovanni Francesco Susini, 1641). Beyond this terrace extends the grandiose amphitheatre, with a central avenue on axis with the palace, and surrounded by steps and aedicules. The amphitheatre was formed out of the former stone   188
quarry. Its present appearance is largely the work of Giulio and Alfonso Parigi, after 1618, and it was intended to accommodate theatrical performances and other spectacles. The Egyptian obelisk (from Luxor) was added in 1789; the granite basin (from the Baths of Caracalla in Rome) followed in 1840.

Before ascending the terraces, turn left, down the side of the hill to the Giardino di Madama, in which is Buontalenti's **Grotto delle Capre**, the earliest grotto in the gardens, with sculptures by Baccio Bandinelli. Continuing down towards the rear of the NE wing of the palace, we reach the **Grotta Grande**; begun by Vasari in 1557, it was completed by Buontalenti in 1583–93 for Francesco I. A three-bay Doric colonnade supports a continuous entablature; flanking the loggia are two niches with statues (*Ceres* and *Apollo* by Baccio Bandinelli); the rest of the grotto is far more bizarre, with stalactites descending from the large upper arch, and a fantastical crowning of stalagmites. In the centre: the Medici arms. Interior: an outer chamber with carved figures of animals and fantastic creatures by Pietro Mati. Michelangelo's four unfinished *Prisoners* were located here by Francesco I, until they were transferred to the Accademia in 1908. Frescoes by Poccetti. In the inner chamber: a fine *Venus Emerging from her Bath* by Giambologna, *circa* 1570. Again frescoes of animal and vegetable motifs, and a marble group of *Paris and Helen* by Vincenzo de' Rossi, 1560.

Following the façade wall of the palace towards the SW, we reach the **Fontana del Bacchino**, by Valerio Cioli, 1560: a human figure mounted on a tortoise, the former modelled on Pietro Barbino, Cosimo I's court dwarf (today a copy).

Return to the amphitheatre and the main axis up the hill, and ascend the ramps towards the SE. On the first intermediate terrace: statues of *Septimus Severus* and a Roman magistrate, flanking a *Demeter*, also Roman.

Rising to the next level, we reach a broad terrace, largely occupied by the **Vivaio di Nettuno** or Fontana del Forcone, a basin of water with sirens and tritons; bronze figure of *Neptune* by Stoldo Lorenzi, 1565–8.

Taking the path to the left, we reach the **Kaffeehaus**, a pavilion by Zanobi del Rosso, 1776, built for Grand Duke Pietro Leopoldo as a summer house. Neo-Classical and restrained, but capped by a turret with a cupola. A fine view of the city from the adjacent terrace (NE).

Returning to the main axis, we rise to the uppermost terrace, and the giant statue of *Abundance*, begun by Giambologna (1608) but completed by Pietro Tacca and Sebastiano Salvini in 1637. To the left are the lower bastions of the Forte del Belvedere (see below). Turning right instead, we reach the foot of the steps that rise to the **Giardino del Cavaliere**, a small, formal, partially walled garden, on the site of one of the bastions added by Michelangelo in 1529. Delightful view from the terrace over the olive- and cypress-clad hills of the city's periphery, including San Leonardo and Bobolino.

The adjacent **Casinò del Cavaliere** (left), *circa* 1700, was built by Cosimo III for his son Gian Gastone. Since 1973 it has contained the Museo delle Porcellane.

Return down the steps, and take the left diagonal path, flanked by a long, low, ancillary building. This is the Prato dell'Uccellare, partly surrounded by cypresses; halfway along on the left is the start of the **Viottolone**, the main avenue which descends fairly steeply through the second, larger section of the Giardino, flanked by splendid cypresses. The avenue was first planted by Giulio Parigi in 1612. The Viottolone is also lined with statues, some classical, but many now copies. This

189

189   Giardino di Boboli: the Viottolone towards the north-east

190   Giardino di Boboli: the Isolotto, by Giulio and Alfonso Parigi, after 1618; central fountain by Giambologna.

191   Giardino di Boboli: the Isolotto, with fountains and dolphins, by Giulio and Alfonso Parigi

section of the garden was originally far less formal, and was used for hunting, but later interventions rendered it more ordered, with side avenues and clearings with fountains and arboreta.

The Viottolone terminates in the spacious **Piazzale dell'Isolotto**,
190 formed by Giulio and Alfonso Parigi after 1618, and enclosed by hedges of box and holly, within which are statues. In the centre is a large basin
191 of water, in the centre of which is the Isolotto, reached by bridges on the E and W sides. The island is planted with dozens of ornamental citrus trees in terracotta pots, with – in the centre – the *Fountain of the Ocean*, attributed to Giambologna or Tribolo, for Francesco I. Set in the water are figures of *Perseus* and *Andromeda*, in the manner of Giambologna, 1637. Flanking the approach bridges are columns surmounted by Capricorns, symbols of Cosimo I, flanked in turn by fountains. At the N and S ends are four cupids, while on the E and W sides are four grotesque harpies, by Giulio Parigi.

Beyond the Piazzale, still on axis with the Viottolone, is the **Prato delle Colonne**, with two pink granite columns carrying white marble vases. The Prato is surrounded by classical busts and marble figures. Beyond again, just before the gate towards the Porta Romana, is the Rondò, a terrace with *Perseus* by Vincenzo Danti.

Return towards Palazzo Pitti by taking the left-hand avenue, which follows the boundary wall. On the left is the **Limonaia** or Orangery, a substantial building by Zanobi del Rosso (late eighteenth century), which houses the orange and lemon trees from the Isolotto in winter. A short path (left) past the end of the Limonaia leads to the Grotto containing *Adam* and *Eve*, *circa* 1616, by Michelangelo Naccherino.

Continuing NE along the main path, we reach the **Palazzina della Meridiana**, the southernmost wing of Palazzo Pitti, added in 1778 by Gaspare Maria Paoletti for Pietro Leopoldo. A fine neo-Classical work, completed by Pasquale Poccianti, 1822–40. Since 1983 it has housed the Museo del Costume. The garden in front is the Prato del Pegaso, in the English manner. Return to the Palazzo.

5 THE OLTRARNO: EAST OF THE PONTE VECCHIO

From the bridgehead of the Ponte Vecchio, turn E along Via dei Bardi, passing below the Corridoio Vasariano.

The first tract of Via dei Bardi comprises buildings constructed in the 1950s to replace those lost in 1944. Nos. 46–8 is by Italo Gamberini.

Further E is Piazza Santa Maria Sopr'Arno, from which Via dei Bardi continues inland parallel to the river, while along the bank is the Lungarno Torrigiani.

No. 1 Piazza Santa Maria is **Palazzo Tempi**; see below. No. 25 on the Lungarno is **Palazzo Capponi**, with its other façade onto Via dei Bardi. The river façade was rebuilt by Giuseppe Poggi in 1866 after the construction of the Lungarno. Five bays and three orders, all with arched heads. Adjacent is the **Chiesa Evangelica Luterana**, the façade a cheerful work in Venetian neo-Romanesque-Gothic by Riccardo Mazzanti, 1901.

The Lungarno terminates in Piazza dei Mozzi, at the Ponte alle Grazie. Good views towards the N bank and the tower of the Palazzo Vecchio. On the W side is **Palazzo Torrigiani**, with principal façade to Piazza dei Mozzi (see below). There are in fact two palaces, nos. 4 and 5. The larger house (no. 5) was first built *circa* 1540 for the Nasi by Domenico di Baccio d'Agnolo; it had only five bays to the left of the portal, since the Arno was then considerably wider. It passed from the Nasi to the del Nero, and was then extended by Domenico di Baccio with a further six bays on reclaimed land towards the river. The top floor has a full-length loggia. Its NE side was again modified after construction of the Lungarno. The smaller house, no. 4, was also owned by the Nasi, then the Scarlatti; see below. Like the other house, it passed to the Torrigiani in the early nineteenth century.

The next tract of the river bank is the Lungarno Serristori, extending E to Piazza Giuseppe Poggi. After a short distance it opens out into Piazza Demidoff. In the centre: monument to Conte Nicola Demidoff (1774–1828), a Russian philanthropist. At the E end of Piazza Demidoff is **Palazzo Serristori**, 1520–22. It was built for Lorenzo Serristori, bishop of Bitetto. Adjacent was a fine garden, along the edge of the Arno. In the nineteenth century it was turned from a garden *all'italiano* to a garden *all'inglese*. Some was lost when the Lungarno was built in 1870. In conjunction with these works, the façade was altered in 1873 by Mariano Falcini, who added the two side wings. The only surviving sixteenth-century façade is that to Via dei Renai. Inside: a monumental staircase of honour leads to a large ballroom; damaged by fire in 1866 but restored.

No. 3 is the **Casa Museo Rodolfo Siviero**, noted for his role in repatriating works of art stolen by the Nazis. His private collection was opened to the public in 1992. The nineteenth-century neo-Classical house is by Poggi.

At the E end of Lungarno Serristori is Piazza Giuseppe Poggi.

192   **Porta San Niccolò**: The city gate now stands isolated in the centre of the square formed by Poggi (1865–76), one of a series of urban interventions following demolition of most of the city walls. The Porta was built in 1324, and 'matched' the Torre della Zecca on the N bank. The gate is the only one to retain its full original height; relatively tall and narrow, less massive than most of the others; three superimposed orders and prominent machicolation. It also retains its internal stairs and passageways. The piazza formed by Poggi is defined by two similar buildings, out of the four originally planned. Adjacent to the gate, a series of ramps leads up towards Piazzale Michelangelo (see below).

Between the Porta and the former *pescaia* (fishery) in the river, there stood a group of mills, the earliest from 1164, and all owned by the monastery of San Miniato. On the site today is a small garden.

From Piazza Poggi return towards the city centre inland along Via di San Niccolò and Via dei Bardi.

Much of Via di San Niccolò retains its medieval atmosphere; the first tract contains several fairly modest medieval houses. No. 2 (right) is the former **Oratorio dei Buonomini**, later deconsecrated. Further along, left, Via San Miniato leads up to the fourteenth-century **Porta San Miniato**, set into a surviving section of the medieval walls. Back in Via di San Niccolò, almost opposite the junction is

193   **San Niccolò oltr'Arno**: Recorded in 1184, and since 1374 a parish foundation, when it was modernised in the Gothic manner. In the sixteenth century it was further altered by Vasari. A very plain façade with a double-pitched roof and a large oculus; a restrained, pedimented, rather neo-Classical portal. The interior: a single nave, with a Latin-cross plan and an open timber trussed roof. The E end terminates with a central chancel and two side chapels. Badly damaged in the 1966 floods; subsequent restoration revealed fifteenth-century frescoes; one is at the first right lateral altar. On the second right altar: polychrome Crucifix attributed to Michelozzo. Third right altar: *St Urban*, another fifteenth-century fresco.

In the sacristy, also attributed to Michelozzo, set into a stone aedicule is a fresco of the *Madonna della Cintola* ('of the Girdle'), later fifteenth century.

The next section of Via di San Niccolò contains several houses of interest. On the right, no. 54 is **Palazzo del Rosso Vitelli**, sixteenth century; no. 56 is **Palazzo Demidoff**, with an eighteenth-century six-bay façade by Alfonso Parigi. An attractive internal courtyard, with

192   Porta San Niccolò (1324) from Piazzale Michelangelo

193   San Niccolò oltr'Arno and campanile from Piazzale Michelangelo

194   Palazzo Capponi 'delle Rovinate', Via dei Bardi, early fifteenth century, modernised in the sixteenth

195   The city walls in the Oltrarno from San Miniato, with the Giardino di Boboli (right)

colonnades on two sides. No. 87 (left) is the fortified medieval **Torre Quaratesi**. No. 93 (left) is **Palazzo Vegni**, originally fourteenth century (internal frescoes survive), but radically modernised after 1611; internal stair by Giulio Parigi. No. 68 (right) is **Palazzo Cambiagi**, altered in the nineteenth century. No. 99 is **Palazzo Nasi**, later Stiozzi Ridolfi, originally fourteenth century, modernised in the fifteenth, and with a sixteenth-century façade attributed to Baccio d'Agnolo. Six bays to the upper orders. The internal courtyard preserves its fourteenth-century colonnade. No. 107 is another **Palazzo Nasi**. At no. 117 is **Palazzo Pecori Giraldi**, with family coat of arms (a lion rampant).

To the right is Piazza dei Mozzi. The square occupies a site formerly partly occupied by the riverbank and the southernmost arches of the Ponte alle Grazie; it was extended further N when the Lungarno was formed and the river made considerably narrower. On the S side of the piazza (no. 2) is the stone façade of

Palazzo Mozzi: Built by the Mozzi, a prominent Guelph family of bankers. Earlier houses on this site were destroyed by the Ghibellines in 1260. Today it consists of three contiguous structures. The oldest dates from the rebuilding, *circa* 1266–73, and represents a transition between the simple fortified towers of the thirteenth century and the more mature palaces of the fourteenth, such as Palazzo Davanzati. The taller right-hand façade, with Guelph battlements, is aligned with the bridge across the river; it resembles the typical thirteenth-century tower, although the fenestration is large, regular and clearly no longer defensive. Behind the houses are extensive gardens and orchards, rising to the city walls. In the nineteenth century the houses became the property of Stefano Bardini, a notable antiquarian and collector. In 1883 the tower was roofed and the gardens remodelled in the Romantic manner. **Palazzo Corsi Bardini** (no. 1, E side of the piazza) was rebuilt in the neo-Renaissance manner and transformed into Bardini's private museum (1881), while the adjacent thirteenth-century church of San Gregorio della Pace was incorporated into the fabric. The museum was given to the city in 1922: a varied, eclectic collection including classical and later sculptures, and incorporating doorways, stairs and other elements from demolished buildings.

On the piazza: no. 3 is **Palazzo Lensi Nencioni**, fifteenth century, with a return façade onto Via dei Bardi; no. 4 is the Baroque **Palazzo Torrigiani Nasi**, with rich, complex, *sgraffito* decoration, added following its rebuilding by Alfonso Parigi, late sixteenth century. Four bays, with large rectangular lights; broken pediments to the *piano nobile*. No. 5 is the larger Palazzo Torrigiani: see above.

Continuing W along Via dei Bardi, no. 23 is **Palazzo da Uzzano**, very early fifteenth century and once the home of Niccolò da Uzzano; its design has been attributed to Lorenzo di Bicci and to Donatello, a close friend of Niccolò. The lower façade is clad with rusticated stone, probably fourteenth century; original wooden doors. The upper floors, clad with smooth ashlar, are *circa* 1427. Inside is a courtyard with octagonal stone columns. No. 24 is the little church of **Santa Lucia dei Magnoli**; founded *circa* 1078, but rebuilt several times. Above the portal is a lunette containing a glazed terracotta panel of *St Lucy between Two Angels*, attributed to Benedetto Buglioni. Inside: a nave without aisles, with altars in *pietra serena*. On the ceiling: *St Lucy in Glory* by Pietro Benvenuti, *circa* 1830. On the high altar, the present work is the *Virgin and Child Enthroned with Saints* (Florentine school, sixteenth century), replacing the celebrated *Pala de' Magnoli* by Domenico Veneziano, today in the Uffizi. First left altar: *St Lucy*, an early fourteenth-century panel painting by Pietro Lorenzetti, flanked by the two figures of the *Annunciation* by Jacopo del Sellaio, late fifteenth century. Opposite the façade: a little tabernacle recording the visit of St Francis of Assisi.

Immediately beyond the church, nos. 28–30 is the substantial **Palazzo Canigiani**, formerly Larioni Bardi, on the site of the ancient Ospedale di Santa Lucia. Originally later fourteenth century, with a long street façade; three orders, the first clad with stone, with rusticated arches to the main openings; the two upper orders very plain. Inside: a fifteenth-century courtyard, sometimes attributed to Michelozzo, perhaps completed by Benedetto da Maiano. Adjacent is the imposing **Palazzo Capponi 'delle Rovinate'**, nos. 36–8. The affix refers to the landslides for which the locality was notorious. Built by Lorenzo di Bicci (although recent hypothesis has suggested Brunelleschi) for the banker Niccolò da Uzzano in the early fifteenth century, on his death it passed to his son-in-law's family, the Capponi, in whose ownership it remains. Eight bays, with a tall rusticated ground floor, still with the original wooden doors; the rustication is perhaps the earliest on a fifteenth-century *palazzo*, and may have been the inspiration for the numerous later examples by Michelozzo and others. It is much altered, however, with some openings lost, and later aediculed windows. The upper façade is mostly original and very plain: a *piano nobile* with arched lights and two da Uzzano crests, surmounted by two lower attics. Inside, the

194

courtyard is colonnaded on all four sides, with octagonal stone columns. The Lungarno façade (see above) is by Poggi.

On the left, corner of Piazza Santa Maria Sopr'Arno, no. 1 is **Palazzo Tempi Bargagli Petrucci**; modernised by Matteo Nigetti in the seventeenth century. Five bays; the entrance to the narrow Costa San Giorgio passes below one bay. Continuing along Via dei Bardi, return towards the Ponte Vecchio.

6 THE COSTA DI SAN GIORGIO AND THE FORTE DI BELVEDERE

From the SW corner of Piazza di Santa Maria Sopr'Arno, a flight of steps, the Rampa delle Coste, rises to the little square at the start of the Costa di San Giorgio, which winds up the side of the hill. No. 2 is the **Villa Bardini**, early seventeenth century, by Gherardo Silvani. Extensive gardens are attached. It was bought by Stefano Bardini in 1913, together with Palazzo Mozzi. On the Costa are three churches at intervals. The first is **Santi Girolamo e Francesco**, since 1928 annexed to the Scuola di Sanità Militare; medieval in origin, rebuilt 1515–20; not accessible to the public, its presence is indicated solely by the campanile *alla vela* and two tall windows.

Further up, just above the junction with the Costa dei Magnoli, is

San Giorgio alla Costa (San Giorgio e lo Spirito Santo): Originally a priory, founded in the tenth century. The exterior is incomplete and very simple, but the interior was transformed by G.B. Foggini in 1705–8, into one of the most ornate Baroque church interiors in the city. Now occupied by the Romanian Orthodox Church.

A single nave with a flat timber coffered ceiling, painted and gilded, divided into large panels. A nuns' *barco* (gallery) on arches was inserted by Foggini above the entrance atrium. Three arched bays across the width of the nave supported by two marble columns; the central bay breaks forward to form a balcony, on tall volutes. All is extensively decorated with gold and white stucco.

Within the atrium: two lateral altars. To the right: altarpiece of *St Benedict* by Tommaso Redi, *circa* 1705; to the left: *Virgin and Child with St Catherine of Siena and St Dominic* by Jacopo Vignali, early seventeenth century. In the atrium ceiling: fresco of *St George in Glory* by Alessandro Gherardini, *circa* 1705.

In the nave: right altar: altarpiece of *St John Gualbert* by Passignano, early seventeenth century. Opposite: *Deposition* by Alessandro Gherardini, *circa* 1705. The high altar: stucco decoration by Foggini into which is set an oval painting of the *Descent of the Holy Spirit* by Antonio Domenico Gabbiani. To the right of the high altar: *Virgin and Child with Two Angels*, attributed variously to Giotto and Cimabue. Attached to the church is a short, simple campanile.

Nearby, at the junction with the steep Costa Scarpuccia, which descends to Via dei Bardi, is the former **Santi Agostino e Cristina**, founded in 1640 by the Grand Duchess Cristina of Lorraine, a patron of the Augustinians. Designed by Bernardino Radi and completed by Gherardo Silvani. A plain, unfinished façade; inside: nave flanked by three chapels on each side, but radically altered after deconsecration.

Further up, no. 19 is the house once owned by Galileo Galilei. Towards the top of the hill: on the left is the extensive walled garden of Villa Bardini, which descends the hillside to Palazzo Mozzi. At the top is the **Porta San Giorgio** built in 1260 on the line of the medieval walls. Very modest, but the oldest surviving city gate; on the exterior is a relief of *St George and the Dragon* (now a copy; the original is in the Palazzo Vecchio). Below the vault is a fresco of the *Virgin and Child Enthroned* by Bicci di Lorenzo, *circa* 1430.

Adjacent is the entrance to the **Forte di Belvedere**, or the Forte di San Giorgio. Founded in 1590 under Ferdinando I, it was designed by Buontalenti, with Giovanni de' Medici and Alessandro Pieroni. The plan is an irregular six-pointed star, adapted to the contours of the site, with three triangular bastions facing NW towards the city and the other three, which project beyond the city walls, facing SE. It was built principally to defend the city from external attack from the roads towards Rome, but its height and strategic location could also be used to deal with insurrections within the city. It housed a substantial munitions store.

The principal entrance is in the centre of the east side; Medici arms above the portal. The internal route around the perimeter walls gives fine views across the city. In the centre of the S part is the **Palazzina di Belvedere**, an elegant villa-like structure which pre-dates the construction of the fort. It was constructed in conjunction with the upper part of the Giardino di Boboli, and has been attributed to Ammannati, probably *circa* 1570s. The sole access to the Palazzina is by an internal staircase up from inside the adjacent basement vaults, which extend both to the N and S and form a platform on which the Palazzina stands.

It has a rectangular plan and three storeys, and, once the Forte had been completed, was occupied by its *capitano*; the Medici treasury was kept here, within the heavily fortified stone vaults. On the ground floor on the two longer façades is a colonnaded loggia; it is from these loggias that the *bel vedere* (beautiful view) originates. The Palazzina resembles the roughly contemporaneous Medici villas at La Ferdinanda and La Petraia. The clock on the N façade was added in the eighteenth century. Military use of the Forte ceased in 1859; today it is often used for temporary exhibitions.

7 PIAZZALE MICHELANGELO, SAN SALVATORE AND SAN MINIATO

The itinerary begins at Piazza Poggi, where a series of ramps, steps and paths leads up through a park planted extensively with lilies (the symbol of the city). At the top is a large parterre, Piazzale Michelangelo, created by Poggi *circa* 1875. Frequented by crowds of tourists, chiefly for the splendid panoramic views of the city from its N edge. In the square is a much-criticised monument to Michelangelo (1871), an assemblage of copies of his works: *David* and the figures from the Medici tombs in San Lorenzo, on a marble base designed by Poggi. The nearby café-restaurant, the **Villa La Loggia**, is also by Poggi, 1873, originally intended to house further copies of Michelangelo's works. Three arched bays, with a colonnade broadly based on Palladio's Basilica in Vicenza.

Behind the villa, a long flight of steps (left) off the Viale Galileo Galilei leads up to

San Salvatore al Monte: The first church on the site was built by Franciscans, *circa* 1419, and is perhaps the structure of the present *capellone* (big chapel), adjacent to the sacristy. The basic shell of the present church was probably built *circa* 1490, but its appearance is largely the work of Il Cronaca, 1499–1504.

The façade is very simple: two orders capped by a triangular pediment. A pedimented portal in the centre of the lower order, three smaller aedicules to the upper one, the central one a window, the outer two blind.

197   The interior is restrained and disciplined: a single rectangular nave, with two superimposed orders down the sides, the first time this had

196 Forte di Belvedere from Piazzale Michelangelo, with the Palazzina, *circa* 1570s, perhaps by Ammannati

197 San Salvatore al Monte: interior of the nave, by Il Cronaca, *circa* 1500

198 San Miniato al Monte: detail of the façade, with thirteenth-century mosaic of *Christ in Majesty*

199 San Miniato al Monte: nave interior, completed 1207

been seen in Florence. The order is a simple Doric throughout, all in *pietra forte* rather than the *pietra serena* used in many other early Renaissance church interiors. The lower order has bays defined by flat pilasters, between which are semicircular arches, some blind, some open, with chapels attached. A continuous entablature divides the lower order from the upper; on the latter, again flat pilasters, with a rectangular aediculed window to each bay. At the E end is a large, heavy, semicircular chancel arch, with substantial Doric pilasters to the imposts; an open timber trussed roof. The altarpieces of the side chapels are mainly seventeenth and eighteenth century.

Off the right transept is the 'double' chapel of Tanai de' Nerli, late fifteenth century; in the right section: homonymous circular tomb monument, 1405. In the left section: altarpiece of the *Virgin and Child with St John the Baptist, St John the Evangelist, St James and St Francis*, late fifteenth century. In the choir: sixteenth-century stalls in walnut. Left transept: early sixteenth-century terracotta *Deposition* by Giovanni della Robbia above the entrance to the *capellone* (normally closed).

The short distance up to San Miniato continues by following the winding Viale Galilei, also built by Poggi. Nearby are the remains of the city fortifications erected with great speed by Michelangelo in 1529 as an emergency measure to confront imperial troops; they were constructed only of brick and beaten earth and later became extensively overgrown. The defences were made more permanent by Cosimo I in 1552, under Francesco da Sangallo.

Ascend the monumental flights of steps built by Poggi by forming a break in the sixteenth-century fortifications. At the summit, at the back of the terrace is

San Miniato al Monte: Together with the baptistery, the most notable Romanesque building in the city, with a famously elegant, refined marble façade. The first church dedicated to the martyr-saint Miniato (decapitated *circa* 250 by the emperor Dacius) was built in the eighth century. In 1018 the bishop, Hildebrand, began the present church, which was constructed in stages; it was completed only in 1207. It was occupied by Benedictines until 1373, when it passed to the Olivetans.

200 The façade is prominently visible from many locations around the city. It was the last element to be completed, in the early thirteenth century. Like that of the baptistery, it is faced with white Carrara and green Prato marbles. Its profile is a direct reflection of the volumes inside, with a tall central section demarcating the nave, and two much

lower side wings terminating the aisles. The lower order has a refined five-bay colonnade of blind semicircular arches, with large rectangular doorways alternating with infill panels. The spandrels are also filled with marble cladding. Above the colonnade: a broad entablature across the full width of the façade. The central upper order has three bays, with marble cladding to the outer two, while the central one has a lower aediculed window (eleventh century) above which is a thirteenth-century mosaic of *Christ in Majesty*, giving the sign of benediction, flanked by the *Virgin Mary* and *St Miniato*. Above is a further cornice, above which is a triangular pediment, again with quite complex marble cladding, including a blind arcade of nine small arches, and an eagle, symbol of the Calimala guild, the church's patron. The two lower side wings are terminated with half-pediments, masking the aisle roofs behind; again clad with marble, with a pattern of diagonal cross-hatching. 198

The interior: very dark, but with almost all surfaces richly detailed. It is nine bays long, subdivided into three sections, each of three bays: compound piers carrying half-shafts and diaphragm arches alternate with sets of two columns. The first two sections form the nave, while the furthermost section represents the chancel, which is raised 3.3 m (approx. 11 ft) above the level of the nave, with steps rising from the aisles on either side. Below the chancel is a crypt. The transverse arches over the nave, corresponding to the three subdivisions, are all clad with marble. Most of the internal structure is eleventh century, although subject to many later restorations. The nave colonnade has capitals from a variety of dates and sources; many do not fit their columns – some are distinctly too small. Those that derive from ancient Roman sources are of white marble, Corinthian or Composite; the Romanesque capitals instead are of fired clay, painted. 199

The floor is finished with fine marble intarsia, incorporating the date (1207) just inside the portal, and with numerous symbolic figures, vegetation and zoomorphic figures; set into it are many tombs. The roof is an open timber truss, richly painted and decorated, from 1322, but heavily restored in 1861.

At the far end of the nave, free-standing in the centre, just before the chancel, is the square form of the Cappella del Crocefisso. The aedicule itself is by Michelozzo, 1448, and was intended to house the Crucifix of St John Gualbert, formerly a monk here, but who left in 1039 to found the Vallombrosan brotherhood, an austere branch of the Benedictines. He died in 1073 and was canonised in 1143. The relic was transferred in 1671 to Santa Trinità. Today the aedicule contains painted panels by Agnolo Gaddi, *circa* 1394. The extrados of the arches and the vault soffit are decorated with polychrome maiolica by Luca della Robbia, while the two gilded bronze eagles are by Maso di Bartolomeo, 1449. The chapel was patronised by Piero il Gottoso.

Nave, right aisle: on the walls a number of frescoes, thirteenth to fourteenth centuries. In sequence, they are: first: *Virgin and Child with Saints* by Paolo Schiavo, 1436; second: *Christ with St Christopher*, later thirteenth century; third: *St James*, 1387; fourth: *St Anthony Abbot*, attributed to Andrea Bonaiuti; fifth: *St Andrew, St Nicholas and St Miniato*, later fourteenth century. On the pier of the first transverse arch: *Communion of St Mary Magdalene*, later fourteenth century. Back on the walls: sixth: *St Catherine of Alexandria*, *circa* 1416; seventh: *St Miniato and St Julian*, attributed to Jacopo da Firenze, 1409; eighth: *Christ Suffering*, by Mariotto di Cristofano.

Across the end of the nave is the marble *transenna* (arcaded screen) dividing it from the much higher chancel. The screen has three bays across the width of the nave, the central one crowned by a tall semicircular arch. It is flanked by two much lower arches, from which steps give access to the crypt below.

Ascending the steps (rebuilt 1475) at the end of the right aisle, enter the chancel. Three bays, with flanking aisles, and a semicircular apse. Adjacent to the steps on the right side: *St John the Evangelist and St Lucy* by Paolo Schiavo; adjacent: *St Catherine of Alexandria* by Pietro Nelli, early eighteenth century. Across the front face of the chancel, immediately behind the large cruciform piers, is another fine enclosing *transenna*, with geometric marble decoration, *circa* 1207. Just to the right of the central opening is the pulpit, of similar date; square, supported by marble columns. A little further down this side is the doorway to the sacristy, a square vaulted hall, 1387. The walls and vaults are entirely frescoed by Spinello Aretino and his son Parri, although heavily restored in the nineteenth century. The sixteen panels around the walls illustrate the *Life of St Benedict*, and were commissioned by Benedetto Alberti. In the vaults: the *Evangelists*, also by Spinello and Parri.

Back in the chancel: to the right of the high altar: altarpiece by Jacopo del Casentino, *circa* 1320, with eight scenes from the *Life of St Miniato*. The high altar: Romanesque, 1207. The semicircular apse has a five-bay blind arcade, defined by six columns of green Prato marble; set into the panels are 'windows' of partially translucent alabaster; within the arches is further refined geometrical decoration. In the hemispherical apse vault: a fine mosaic of *Christ in Majesty with the*

Virgin Mary and St Miniato, together with *Symbols of the Four Evangelists*; the date (1297) refers to a restoration, since the work itself is some decades earlier. To the left of the central apse: altarpiece of *St John Gualbert*, 1354. On the back wall: remains of a fourteenth-century fresco (*Noli me Tangere*).

The eleventh-century crypt is the oldest part of the church, occupying the area below the raised chancel and its aisles, with simple groin vaults supported by thirty-six colonnettes. These, with their capitals (like those in the nave), have a varied provenance, some Roman, some Romanesque, with shafts of brick, *pietra serena* and different types of marble. The capitals were gilded in 1342 by Taddeo Gaddi; some gilding remains. The paintings to the chancel vaults are also by Gaddi, depicting *Saints*, *Prophets* and *Martyrs*. The altar itself is thirteenth century, and is said to contain the bones of St Miniato.

Return to the nave and complete the circuit down the left aisle walls. About halfway down is the entrance to the chapel of the Cardinale di Portogallo. It was built for Jacopo di Lusitania, cardinal archbishop of Lisbon, who died in 1459. It was completed in 1473, a fairly small square chamber with one of the richest interiors of the early Florentine Renaissance. The design is by Brunelleschi's pupil Antonio Manetti, begun in 1460, and probably completed after his death by Antonio Rossellino, *circa* 1466. It is broadly based on the Sagrestia Vecchia at San Lorenzo, but more richly finished. A rich coffered entrance arch, repeated on the other three sides of the chamber, to form niches for the monuments and altar. The fine marble floor is in *opus sectile*, marble and porphyry. Set into the pendentives of the sail vaults are four roundels of the *Cardinal Virtues* by Andrea della Robbia; in the centre is a representation of the *Holy Spirit*. In the right-side niche is the monument to the cardinal by Antonio and Bernardo Rossellino; on the back wall at high level: roundel containing the *Virgin and Child*, also by Antonio. On the opposite wall is a simple throne, again by Antonio. On the wall opposite the entrance is the altar: altarpiece of *St Eustace, St James and St Vincent*: by Antonio Pollaiolo (today a copy; the original is in the Uffizi).

Returning to the left side aisle: walking back towards the entrance, further frescoes: first *St John the Baptist* and *St Catherine of Alexandria*, late fifteenth century; then a rare late thirteenth-century Crucifix. The Crucifix is flanked by two early fifteenth-century frescoes by Mariotto di Nardo: to the right is a *Crucifixion with Seven Saints*, to the left the *Virgin and Child with Four Saints*.

Immediately adjacent to the church (right) is the **Palazzo dei Vescovi**, begun in 1295 by the bishop of Florence, Andrea de' Mozzi. It remained the property of the bishops, who used it as a retreat, until 1337, when it passed to the monastery. Most of the other surviving monastic buildings, including the chapter house, are early fifteenth century, by Bernardo Rossellino and others. The complex was radically restored after 1902, when blocked-up windows were reopened and the interiors were altered. Further careful work in 1962–87 restored several elements to their original appearance, including the cloisters. A fragment of surviving fresco in the lower order is attributed to Andrea del Castagno. In the upper order are fresco remains by Paolo Uccello, depicting *Lives of Saints*.

Also adjacent to the church (left, NE side of the piazza) is the entrance to the **Cimitero monumentale**, begun by Mariano Falcini in 1865. It occupies an extensive area enclosed by the sixteenth-century fortifications. The cemetery contains many imposing nineteenth-century monuments in a variety of styles; among the notable figures buried here is Carlo Lorenzini or Collodi (author of *Pinocchio*) and the composer Ruggero Leoncavallo.

Continue SW along the Viale Galileo Galilei. After about 2km it reaches a large square, Piazzale Galileo. Just before the Piazzale, right, a narrow lane, Via San Leonardo, leads NE, and eventually terminates at the Forte di Belvedere. About halfway along the lane is **San Leonardo in Arcetri.** Founded perhaps in the eleventh century as a rural parish church, it was comprehensively restored in 1899 and again in 1929. On the inner façade: sixteenth-century frescoes. Inside: paintings by Neri di Bicci and a triptych by Lorenzo Gerini, early fifteenth century. The fine pulpit was salvaged from San Pier Scheraggio, and is from 1193–1250; reliefs of the *Life of Christ*. The lane terminates at the Porta San Giorgio and the city walls.

The City Beyond the Walls

The City Beyond the Walls

I EAST AND NORTH-EAST

The zone to the E of the former city walls was settled significantly only after the Poggi plan of 1865, in the later nineteenth century and the early twentieth. The area between Via Aretina and the river was settled first, followed by the zone further NE towards Campo di Marte railway station.

The east zone: From the Porta alla Croce, proceed E along Via Vincenzo Gioberti. To the N, parallel to it, is Via Scipione Ammirato. It is worth a brief detour to see two Art Nouveau houses, both by Giovanni Michelazzi. No. 99, the more splendidly exuberant, is **Villino Broggi** (1911), and no. 101 is **Villino Ravazzini** (1907). Back to Via Gioberti, which, after Piazza Alberti, becomes the Via Aretina, the ancient route to Arezzo. Flanking it (left) is the suburb of Madonnone, and to the right, Bellariva. Right again, between Via Aretina and the Lungarno Aldo Moro is the RAI **television building,** by Italo Gamberini, 1962–8; a collection of different volumes and elements, articulated according to their various functions: studios, administration, etc. The finishes include brickwork and exposed reinforced concrete.

A little further is **Varlungo**; on the right: **San Pietro**, established in the twelfth century, but rebuilt in the seventeenth, and again in the later nineteenth, when the portico was lost. The interior retains some seventeenth-century elements. In the apse containing the high altar: wooden Crucifix dated 1665.

After Varlungo is **Rovezzano**, centred on two churches, **San Michele** and Sant'Andrea. The former is also twelfth century, but rebuilt in 1840; the sixteenth-century portal is attributed to Baccio d'Agnolo. Inside: on the high altar: another wooden Crucifix, *circa* 1400. Also in the chancel is a figure of *St Michael*, from the workshop of Giovanni della Robbia, *circa* 1520. Just beyond the church on the right is a fourteenth-century watermill, the **Mulino di San Michele**, one of the oldest to survive; it is linked to the Mulino delle Guazzine on the other bank by a weir.

Rovezzano was developed after 1951, following a national competition for the design of a new residential quarter. The first phase was built in 1951–7, the second in 1962–8, the third in 1984–6. The three stages were located at Via Torre degli Agli, Via Benedetto Dei and Via di Rocca Tedalda. The housing was intended to be 'minimal', cheap and rational. The architects of the first stage were Cardini, Cetica e Raspollini.

A little further along the Via Aretina is **Sant'Andrea**. Founded perhaps *circa* 1000, it retains a small Romanesque campanile; the interior, though, is neo-Classical, with a Latin-cross plan. In the right transept is a *Virgin and Child* from the workshop of Luca della Robbia, fifteenth century. To the N is the park of the **Villa Favard**, rebuilt by Baccio d'Agnolo in the early sixteenth century for Zanobi Bartolini, on the basis of a medieval structure. It was acquired by the Favard in 1855, who had the villa radically modernised by Giuseppe Poggi, 1875–7.

The north-east zone and the Campo di Marte: The large rectangular zone between the former city walls and the main railway line (Florence to Rome) was set out with a rectilinear grid of streets after the Poggi plan, and then developed. Most of the later nineteenth-century development, however, was replaced in the 1950s and 1960s with the present housing. Beyond the railway lines is another extensive zone, the result of the Piano Regolatore of 1924. This further district is isolated from the inner zones by the railway, which has few crossing points. The principal one is the Ponte al Pino, towards the NW, which leads, after a couple of turns, via Via Marconi, into the long, straight Via dei Mille and its SE continuation, Via Pasquale Paoli.

On the Via dei Mille, junction with the Via Sette Santi, is the **Chiesa dei Sette Santi Fondatori**; neo-Gothic, by Luigi Caldini, 1901–10. A rather heavy, eclectic interpretation, with a big, tall portal and the seven saints in niches across the façade directly above. Crenellation and three picturesque turrets crown the façade.

The main feature of the zone is the extensive Campo di Marte, planned by Poggi, but fully realised only in the 1960s. On the NE side is Pier Luigi Nervi's **Stadio Comunale Artemio Franchi**, a notable structure from 1931, built following a design competition and completed for the World Cup of 1934. A significant Modern Movement work, entirely in reinforced concrete, and mostly rational and functional, although it incorporates flourishes such as the tall slender tower, the Torre di Maratona (70 m / approx. 230 ft tall), which was to carry the flag; and the sculptural helical ramped stairs that link the lower and upper terraces. The stadium was altered significantly when Italy hosted the World Cup again in 1990; the level of the pitch was lowered to create additional seating (now 45,000), and new staircases were added to meet escape regulations.

On the SW side of the avenue, Viale Paoli, on a large rectangular site extending to Viale Malta (SW), is a group of sports buildings. Two main elements; the first is the **Centro Balneare** (swimming centre) by Francesco Tiezzi and others, later transformed into the Palazzetto dello Sport, with an asymmetrical plan, and a new structure built over the original swimming facilities. The other is the **Palazzo dello Sport**, again by Tiezzi. It contains a large space with a capacity of up to 7,500, and is used for a wide range of sport and entertainment activities. Begun in 1962, the complex was finally completed only in 1986.

Continue SE along Via Pasquale Paoli, the last section of which becomes Viale Enrico Cialdini. Turn right at the junction with Via Lungo l'Affrico, then, after a few hundred metres, E along Via Tito Speri, to reach Piazza di San Salvi.

San Michele a San Salvi: Said to have been founded by two French monks fleeing the Norman invasions, and taking with them the remains of St Salvi. In 1048 the church and monastic buildings were given to the founder of the Vallombrosan order, John Gualbert. In 1312 the oratory was replaced by a new church and conventual buildings. They were badly damaged in the imperial siege of the city in 1529–30. Four years later it was given to Vallombrosan monks from Faenza, who restored the church and remained until the Napoleonic suppression.

The exterior is very simple, fourteenth century, other than the rather elegant three-bay sixteenth-century arched portico. A square, rough stone campanile rises on the left. The plan is a Latin cross, with an aisle-less nave, covered by an open timber-beamed roof, and a square chancel. The interior is partly Baroque, notably the chancel frescoes, although late twentieth-century restoration returned part of the fabric to its original appearance.

In the right transept is the chapel of San Giovanni Gualberto, with a fresco cycle (early fifteenth century) showing stories from his life. A marble statue of *Blessed Humility*, a Vallombrosan foundress, is attributed to Orcagna, *circa* 1350. In the chancel: on the two side walls: early sixteenth-century reliefs of *St Salvi* and *St Michael* by Benedetto da Rovezzano, sometimes located in the adjacent cloisters. On the high altar: sixteenth-century wooden Crucifix and the *Miracle of the Child*

Revived by St Humility by Passignano. On the nave left wall: fifteenth-century fresco (detached): *Virgin and Child* by Lorenzo di Bicci.

To the right is the cloister; late fourteenth-century arcades, octagonal columns with acanthus capitals. The upper loggia is mid-fifteenth-century Renaissance, in the manner of Michelozzo. Further S again, beyond the cloister, are the monastic buildings. After the Napoleonic closures, they were used for a succession of secular functions, one of which (from 1887) was annexation by the adjacent psychiatric hospital of Vincenzo Chiarugi. The conversion was undertaken by Giacomo Roster, who retained some elements, rebuilding others in a neo-Renaissance manner. Significant damage was done in the 1966 flood, after which restoration was completed in 1981, when the **Museo del Cenacolo** di Andrea del Sarto was established (no. 16 Via di San Salvi).

The first part is a long gallery containing sixteenth-century paintings by Vasari, Pontormo and others. At the far end: reassembled elements of the funerary monument to St John Gualbert by Benedetto da Rovezzano, 1507–13, originally at the Badia di Passignano. Next is the Sala del Lavabo, and then the former kitchen, before entering the refectory. On one wall is the splendid and renowned *Last Supper* by Andrea del Sarto, 1526–7, in exceptionally good condition, with refined colouring and lively movement. The hall contains other works by Andrea: a *Pietà, circa* 1520, and an *Annunciation, circa* 1509.

2 THE NORTH-EAST FURTHER OUT: SETTIGNANO AND MAIANO

From about halfway along the Via Lungo l'Affrico, Via Gabriele d'Annunzio leads off eastwards. After 1 km it passes through the *borgo* of Coverciano. On the left: entrance to the **Villa Poggio Gherardo**, set in an extensive park. Originally a medieval fortified farmhouse, in the fourteenth century it was owned by the Baroncelli, Acciaioli and finally the Gherardo; in 1888 they sold it to the writer Henry James, who added neo-Gothic crenellations. Today it is an orphanage. Continue E to Ponte a Mensola. Beyond, the built-up suburbs end; a little further up on the left is the neo-Gothic **Castello di Mezzaratta**, a typically eclectic work by Adolfo Coppedè, 1920–21. The road approaches the attractive village of **Settignano**. In the surrounding hills are several notable villas.

On the right, Via Buonarroti terminates at the gates of the **Villa Michelangelo**, owned by the Buonarroti in the sixteenth century, and where Michelangelo lived as a young boy. Continuing, again on the right, Via della Capponcina leads to two villas, **Villa Porziuncola**, once occupied by the actress Eleanora Duse, and **Villa Capponcina**, owned by Gabriele d'Annunzio, 1898–1910; many of his most notable works were written here. **Settignano** was the place of origin of some of the city's most significant architects and sculptors, including the eponymous Desiderio da Settignano, the Rossellino family and Bartolomeo Ammannati. The central square is Piazza Niccolò Tommaseo (monument by Leopoldo Costoli, 1878), adjacent to which is **Santa Maria**, founded in the twelfth century, but rebuilt *circa* 1518. It was enlarged in 1595 when the side aisles were formed.

Inside: the pulpit (1602) is by Gherardo Silvani to a design by Buontalenti. The fifteenth-century triumphal arch was acquired from elsewhere and installed here in the seventeenth century. On the high altar: *Virgin and Child with Two Angels*, early sixteenth-century glazed terracotta by Andrea della Robbia. The frescoes in the apse depict the *Assumption*, by Piero Dandini, early eighteenth century. On the second left aisle altar is a painted terracotta *St Lucy* by Michelozzo, *circa* 1430. At the back: *Holy Trinity and Saints*, fresco by Santi di Tito, 1593.

Adjacent to the church, with façade towards the square, is the **Oratorio della Santissima Trinità**, mostly sixteenth century, with a stucco relief of the *Virgin and Child with St Giovannino* above the portal. From Piazza Tommaseo, Via di San Romano leads to the **Oratorio di San Romano**, at the junction of Via dei Cioli. Sixteenth century, with contemporaneous fresco decoration inside.

From Piazza Tommaseo, Via Simone Mosca slopes down towards Piazza Desiderio, from which there are views of the city. In the piazza: monument to *Desiderio da Settignano* by Vittorio Caradossi, 1904.

Around Settignano are several villas of note. To the SE, towards Terenzano: **Villa Gamberaia** (Via del Rossellino no. 72), with a fine garden. Originally a modest country house owned by the Rossellino family of sculptors, until 1610, when it passed to Zanobi di Andrea Lapi, who transformed it into a villa. In 1718 it passed to the Capponi, one of whom, Scipione, extended the house on a more imposing scale and set out the gardens. The villa itself has two orders and seven bays to the main façades, with a rusticated portal and large rectangular windows with *pietra serena* frames. The gardens are richly decorated with statuary, topiary and fountains, and were further embellished in 1905–15, when the parterre was added. Both house and garden were severely damaged in 1939–45 but subsequently restored.

201

Take Via dei Cioli out of Settignano, which rises to the top of the hill and the village of **Montebeni**, then continues as Via di Montebeni; then, very sharp left, into Via Vincigliata. **Vincigliata** is a small village centred on **San Lorenzo**, mostly late eighteenth century, when it was rebuilt and its orientation reversed. The façade evinces traces of the original Gothic eastern apse. Inside: a single nave with an open timber roof. The apse has modern decoration by Amalia Ciardi Duprè, 1980–86. The sacristy is now a chapel dedicated to St Lawrence. In the church: two fifteenth-century terracotta works: *Virgin and Child* attributed to Tommaso Fiamberti; and *St Lawrence*, in the manner of Antonio Rossellino.

Continuing SW, within a sweep in the road is the **Castello di Vincigliata**, first recorded in 1301, although rebuilt in the neo-Gothic style by Giuseppe Fancelli for John Temple Leader, who lived here from 1850 to 1903. Temple Leader was a wealthy businessman who turned the castle into a museum; he also contributed large sums towards the façade of Florence Cathedral.

Via Vincigliata descends through woods of pines and cypresses. At no. 26 is the well-known **Villa i Tatti**, owned for centuries by the Bardi and Alessandri, and then (1854) also bought by John Temple Leader; in 1905 it was acquired by the art historian Bernard Berenson; it was modernised for him in 1908–15 by Cecil Pinsent. The villa contains Berenson's fine library and art collection, including works by Giotto, Domenico Veneziano, Cima da Conegliano and Giovanni Bellini. It was bequeathed to Harvard University, which uses it as a centre for studies of Italian art and history.

South of the villa, taking Via San Martino, right, we reach the homonymous church of **San Martino a Mensola**. Founded in the ninth century, the present structure is mainly fifteenth century, but with an eighteenth-century portico; it was restored in 1857, and a further comprehensive restoration took place in 1969, when remains of the Romanesque church were identified below the nave. A fifteenth-century campanile.

Inside: a central nave flanked by Ionic colonnades and aisles. At the E end, a fine *pietra serena* chancel arch, with two small tabernacles. Several notable works of art: first right altar: *Virgin and Child with St Andrew and St Sebastian*, early sixteenth century. At the end of the right aisle: triptych by Taddeo Gaddi of the *Virgin and Child Flanked by Two Saints*, mid-fourteenth century, to which were added in the late fifteenth century *Four Prophets*. On the high altar: triptych of the *Virgin and Child Enthroned Flanked by the Donor and Saints*, 1391, by a follower of Orcagna, known only as the Master of San Martino. At the E end of the left aisle: *Annunciation* by Zanobi Machiavelli. On the left aisle altar: panel of the *Virgin and Child Enthroned between Four Saints* by Neri di Bicci. In the adjacent sacristy: *bancone* in wood with intarsia decoration, traditionally ascribed to Benedetto da Maiano. In an adjacent room is a wooden casket (1389) containing the relics of the apostle Andrew, patron saint of Scotland, with four panels showing episodes from his life. He is said to be buried under the church floor.

The road continues as Via di San Martino; turn right at Via di Poggio Gherardo. It then turns into Via Benedetto da Maiano.

The hamlet of **Maiano** is best known as the place of origin of Benedetto da Maiano (1442–1492) and his brother Giuliano (1432–1490), sculptors and architects. Just to the N, up Via delle Cave, on the slopes of Monte Ceceri, are the quarries from which *pietra serena* was derived until the 1960s. The Fattoria di Maiano is housed in the remains of a Benedictine monastic house, the church of which, **San Martino**, is adjacent. It was heavily restored in the nineteenth century by John Temple Leader.

From the crossroads in the village, Via del Salviatino runs back down towards the city. No. 26 is the entrance to **Villa di Maiano**, originally owned by the Pazzi, but again radically restored by John Temple Leader in an early Renaissance manner. No. 14 is the **Villa il Salviatino**, originally of the Bardi family, and rebuilt in the early sixteenth century for Alamanno Salviati. Currently owned by Stanford University. Towards the bottom of the hill, no. 6 is the **Villa Montalto**, comprehensively modernised in 1885.

3   NORTHWARDS TO FIESOLE

Fiesole is the most notable historic settlement in the vicinity of Florence. Located on a hill a little east of north, it is an important historic settlement in its own right. It is easily reached by public transport (no. 7 bus) from Piazza San Marco.

From Ponte al Pino, or nearby Le Cure, there are two or three routes to Fiesole. This one takes Via Pacinotti, and then Via della Piazzuola, which passes several villas, before joining Via San Domenico, the usual main approach route. The first villa is the present Hotel President, housed in the fifteenth-century **Collegio alla Querce**, later a monastery, before becoming a hotel. Next, after a few hundred metres, is **Villa il Garofano** (right), access from Via delle Forbici, once said to have been owned by the family of Dante Alighieri, but restored in a neo-medieval manner in 1865. No. 89 is the **Villa l'Ombrellino**, sixteenth century but modernised in the eighteenth; then **Villa Le Lune** (no. 103), at the junction with Via San Domenico, late fifteenth century, by Giuliano da Sangallo for the Salviati, but radically modernised in the Baroque era for the Guadagni, and again by Giuseppe Poggi in 1845.

An alternative route to Fiesole starts from Le Cure, near the railway, taking the main road, Viale Alessandro Volta, to reach the start of Via San Domenico in Piazza Edison. This is a busier route, also taken by the bus service, and is more direct.

202 **San Domenico**: On the homonymous piazza. Begun in 1406 at the instigation of Giovanni Dominici, a reformist Dominican; completed 1418–35, under the patronage of Barnaba degli Agli, but modernised and enlarged in the 1480s and again in the seventeenth and eighteenth centuries. Among its notable occupants were Antonino Pierozzi, arch-bishop of Florence, later canonised (1523), and Fra Angelico, who lived here until 1437, when he moved to San Marco.

In front of the façade is an elegant portico, added by Matteo Nigetti in 1635; he also rebuilt the little campanile (1611–13). The portico has rusticated quoins and three large central arched bays flanked by smaller square bays, with niches above an entablature. The plain church façade rises above and behind.

Interior: a single aisle-less nave, attributed to Giuliano da Maiano. Three chapels down each side, each approached by a decorated arch in *pietra serena*. The eighteenth-century modernisations affected the choir and chancel, rebuilt by Giovanni Battista Caccini in 1606, and raised above the nave. In the nave vault: fresco of *St Dominic in Glory* by Matteo Bonechi, 1705. Above the triumphal arch into the chancel: *St Dominic Receiving the Rosary from the Virgin* by Lorenzo del Moro and Rinaldo Botti, *circa* 1705.

First right chapel: fourteenth-century wooden Crucifix. Second right chapel: *Baptism of Christ* by Lorenzo di Credi, early sixteenth century. Third right chapel: wooden Mannerist altar. The high altar: a grandiose tabernacle in gilded wood, with figures of Dominican saints, 1617 by Andrea Balatri. The choir stalls are early seventeenth century. To the left of the chancel is the sacristy, 1606. Around the walls: benches with intarsia and intaglio decoration, late fifteenth or early sixteenth century. Adjacent is the Cappellina delle Reliquie; an *armadio*, 1606, to house reliquaries.

Back in the church, a doorway leads to the Oratorio di San Donato di Scozia. Built in 1792, it contains a gilded bust of the saint. Nave left side, third altar: *Annunciation* by Jacopo da Empoli, 1615. On the right wall: wooden Crucifix attributed to Antonio da Sangallo the elder. Second left chapel: *Adoration of the Magi* by Giovanni Antonio Sogliani, *circa* 1540. First left chapel: *Virgin and Child with Saints*, a triptych, an early work by Fra Angelico, 1425. The landscaped context is by Lorenzo di Credi, 1501.

The conventual buildings: the entrance lobby contains a refined 'spiral' staircase, 1727. The chapter house (Sala Capitolare) has a frescoed *Crucifixion* by Fra Angelico, *circa* 1430, and a second fresco, from Angelico's school, of the *Virgin and Child*. Within the chapter house (right) are remains of the earlier fourteenth-century structure, with octagonal stone columns.

Just past the church façade, Via della Badia dei Roccettini (left) descends a short distance W to the

Badia Fiesolana: Of ancient foundation, until 1028 it was the cathedral of Fiesole. It was built on the site where it is said that St Romulus was martyred, and is dedicated to him and to St Peter. Around 1028 it was rebuilt by the Camaldolesi and dedicated instead to St Bartholomew. In the fourteenth century the Benedictines occupied the house, and remained until 1439, when it passed to regular Augustinian canons. After 1456, under the patronage of Cosimo il Vecchio, the church was rebuilt on a larger scale. The present fabric is mostly later fifteenth-century Renaissance; attributed by Vasari to Brunelleschi, today it is generally said to be by collaborators of Michelozzo or Bernardo Rossellino.

The layout of the complex is of considerable interest. The site is on a hillside and the buildings are set at different levels, the church itself being the highest element. It faces NW, and stands at an angle to the adjacent conventual buildings, all built towards the S, with adjacent terraces and steps linking the elements together.

The church façade remains largely in rough stonework, but incorporates the central section of the early eleventh-century façade (*circa* 1025–8), a Romanesque survivor in the manner of the baptistery and San Miniato. All in white Carrara and green Prato marble, the lower order has three arched bays, the central narrower bay containing the portal. The outer bays are filled with rectangular decorative panels, with

203

further decoration to the spandrels of all three arches. Above is a lower blind order, again with rectangular decorative panelling and three small blind windows. The whole is capped by a small, rich frieze.

The interior: sober and restrained, mostly from 1461–4. The plan is a Latin cross, the nave flanked by four square chapels down each side. Articulation is all in *pietra serena*. The crossing is set several steps higher than the nave and the transepts have the same depth as the lateral chapels. Beyond the crossing is the deep rectangular chancel. The spaces all have simple plastered barrel vaults, with tall fluted Corinthian pilasters at the crossing; Medici arms set into the nave ceiling. The nave chapels are approached by simple arched openings, with no capitals; family arms in the vaults.

Nave: first right chapel: *Our Lady of the Rosary* by Giovanni Montini, seventeenth century. Third chapel: *Martyrdom of St Bartholomew*, in the manner of Caravaggio, 1625. Fourth chapel: Rococo decoration by Giuseppe Ruggieri, 1749. Frescoes and altarpiece by Niccolò Nannetti. At the ends of both transepts are altars by Pier Francesco Silvani, 1673–5. The high altar is of *pietre dure*, by G.B. Cennini and Pietro Tacca, 1610. Adjacent, and reached by two stone portals (1464), is a little chapel with an *Annunciation* by Raffaellino del Garbo, early sixteenth century. Back in the nave: first left chapel, of the Tornabuoni: *Deposition*, perhaps by Botticini, late fifteenth century.

The entrance to the monastery is to the right of the church. Cosimo il Vecchio de' Medici, *pater patriae*, spent considerable time here, collecting and reading rare books and manuscripts. In 1783 his library was transferred to the Biblioteca Laurenziana. In the nineteenth century the monastery was the base for a college founded by the Padri Scolopi (Piarist Fathers); after 1976 it was the seat of the Istituto Universitario Europeo.

A short way along the main corridor, on the left a staircase rises to the central cloister; seven bays by five, with elegant arched colonnades and a loggia above, by Ambrogio di Benedetto, 1460. Down the right side a doorway leads into the ante-refectory, then the refectory itself, today used as a conference hall; a richly decorated semicircular stone pulpit, by Pietro di Cecco, 1460. On the opposite (E) side of the cloister is the chapter house; lunettes with fifteenth-century frescoes. The adjacent loggia (also 1460) is again by Ambrogio di Benedetto, with refined capitals; panoramic views over the gardens.

From San Domenico, Via Giuseppe Mantellini rises towards Fiesole; the road was built in 1840 to improve access to the village, previously reached only by steep, narrow lanes. After a sharp hairpin bend, we reach the last tract, Via Fra Giovanni da Fiesole (Fra Angelico). Off a lane up on the right is the **Villa Doccia** (today a hotel), formerly owned by the Davanzati, and occupied by Franciscans, 1486–1808. The present villa is largely from 1599, by Santi di Tito, with a long pilastered portico; it incorporates remains of the monastic church, with two orders of colonnades. At the top of Via Fra Giovanni, a short, steep turn to the right brings us into

Fiesole: It is often said that Fiesole is the mother of Florence; the settlement is several centuries older than the city, and was one of the most important in pre-Roman Etruria. Its site is on a hill, below and between two higher eminences, almost 300 m above sea level, and with splendid views across the bowl of the city. It was settled in the Bronze Age, but the Etruscan settlement probably dates from the fifth century BC. The Etruscans were defeated by the Romans in 283 BC, after which it became a Roman town, Faesulae. It remained a significant settlement until the barbarian invasions, and in 854 it was subsumed within the administration of Florence. After further hostilities, in 1125 Florence gained a decisive military victory over Fiesole, during which much of the town was destroyed. In 1325 its defensive walls were strengthened by Castruccio Castracani in recognition of its continuing strategic importance. The upper part of the town was fortified further, but in 1399 became the base of a Franciscan friary, which remains there today. During the nineteenth century the village and its environs achieved great popularity among both Florentines and foreign visitors, many of whom built or acquired villas and gardens in the surrounding hills.

The long, rectangular **Piazza Mino da Fiesole** is the heart of the community, occupying the site of the Roman forum. At the W end is the imposing bulk of the **Seminario**, 1637, later extended. Four storeys plus a mezzanine, and seventeen bays long. Within the oratory (first floor) is a *Virgin and Child with Saints*, a large piece by Giovanni della Robbia, 1520. Immediately N is the **Palazzo Vescovile**, originally eleventh century but rebuilt several times; approached by impressive steps, the broad, rather low façade is from 1675; three orders and seven bays. A rusticated stone portal with the arms of the see above. To the right is a small, attractive three-sided cloister.

Opposite the Palazzo Vescovile, with its flank to the piazza, is the cathedral of **San Romolo**. Founded in 1028 by the bishop, Jacopo il Bavaro, to replace the earlier cathedral (now known as the Badia

Fiorentina; see above). It was enlarged in the thirteenth century (a date of 1260 is on the fifth right nave pier), and again in 1349–73 under Bishop Andrea Corsini. Further modernisations followed in the eighteenth century, then a radical restoration in 1878–83 by Michelangelo Maiorfi, who also rebuilt the façade. The exterior was comprehensively restored again in the early 2000s. The tall stone campanile is from 1213, although the battlements are nineteenth-century additions. The simple, broad façade has an arched central portal, surmounted by a small oculus.

The internal planning (but not the appearance) resembles San Miniato al Monte: a central nave flanked by aisles; transepts; and the chancel, terminating in a semicircular apse, raised above a crypt. The general appearance is Romanesque, simple and powerful. Stout circular stone colonnades support rich capitals from different sources; two are Roman, and some do not fit the columns; an open timber truss roof. Above the central portal: polychrome figure of *St Romulus* by Giovanni della Robbia, 1521. At the end of the nave: modern altar slab on a frontal of white and green marble, originally at the Badia Fiorentina, dated 1273. Behind the altar: three polychrome arches support the upper level of the chancel.

In the chancel, the Salutati chapel is on the right. Fifteenth-century frescoes by Cosimo Rosselli, with the *Evangelists* in the vaulted ceiling. On one wall is the monument to Bishop Leonardo Salutati, by Mino da Fiesole, also late fifteenth century. The altar dossal is also by Mino, with the *Virgin and Child with St Leonard, St Remigius and St Giovannino*. In the conch of the main apse: frescoes by Nicodemo Ferrucci of the *Life of St Romulus*, 1590. On top of the high altar: polyptych by Bicci di Lorenzo, *circa* 1450. Left of the chancel is an arch supporting the adjacent campanile; monument to the bishops Guglielmo and Roberto Folchi, sixteenth century. Enter the Cappella dei Canonici; altar dossal by Andrea Ferrucci, 1493. From this chapel we reach the eighteenth-century sacristy, containing the reliquary bust of St Romulus, 1584, gilded copper.

Below the chancel is the thirteenth-century crypt: a central nave and side aisles, with columns of stone and marble supporting capitals of various styles and dates, some again Roman. In the vaults: a series of fifteenth-century medallion frescoes; others were added in the nineteenth. To the right: granite font by Francesco del Tadda, 1569. In the centre of the crypt is the St Romulus altar, with ironwork screens (1349). The altar itself is fifteenth century. Around the curved back wall of the apse: frescoed lunettes, later fifteenth century, depicting the saint's

202 Fiesole: San Domenico, completed 1418–35, partly perhaps by Michelozzo, and Giuliano da Maiano, *circa* 1480–90

203 Fiesole: the Badia Fiesolana, the church 1456–64

204 Fiesole: façade of the Palazzo Vescovile, rebuilt 1675

205 Fiesole: Piazza Mino da Fiesole, with the Palazzo Pretorio (originally fourteenth century), left, and Santa Maria Primerana, centre

life. Below the crypt, archaeological excavations in the early 1990s found evidence of the earliest church as well as Etruscan and Roman structures.

Back in the nave: on the left side is the so-called cathedra (originally perhaps part of a choir stall) of St Andrea Corsini, 1371, by the Sienese Pietro di Lando.

Back in the piazza: at the E end are the picturesque **Palazzo Pretorio** and the little oratory of **Santa Maria Primerana**. The former is fourteenth century, but modernised in the mid-fifteenth, and on later occasions. The ground floor has a spacious trabeated four-bay colonnade of *pietra serena*; on the back wall are numerous arms of former *podestà* (governors), 1520–1808. Above is an upper loggia, also of four bays.

Immediately to the right is Santa Maria Primerana; first recorded in 966. The façade was rebuilt around the end of the sixteenth century, in a Mannerist style, with *sgraffito* decoration by Lodovico Buti, 1592–5. The portico was added in 1801. Inside: a single nave with short transepts. On the right wall: a large fifteenth-century Crucifix attributed to Bonaccorso di Cino. Transept, right arm: two reliefs by Francesco da Sangallo, 1542 and 1575. The chancel retains its Gothic appearance. In the left transept: sixteenth-century *Crucifixion with the Virgin and St Mary Magdalene*, fired terracotta from the della Robbia workshop.

The **Museo Bandini** stands behind the E end of the cathedral. It was built in 1913 by Giuseppe Castellucci to house the collection amassed by the canon Angelo Maria Bandini, and which was left on his death (1803) to the bishop and chapter. Bandini was the librarian, first of the Biblioteca Marucelliana and then the Biblioteca Laurenziana. The core of the collection consists of early painted works, thirteenth and fourteenth centuries, as well as works from later periods, including many from the della Robbia workshops.

Adjacent, on Via Giovanni Duprè, is the entrance to

The archaeological zone: The principal Etruscan settlement is from the sixth and fifth centuries BC. A substantial tract of city wall has survived along the N edge of the site, 248 m long and nearly 5 m high (approx. 814 ft and 16 ft). After 283 BC Fiesole was a Roman town, acquiring the typical characteristics such as forum, capitol and theatre. The archaeological zone covers the N part of this former Roman settlement, the rest lying below the present centre of the village.

Passing the museum up on the right, in front is the theatre, late first 206 century BC, but enlarged by the emperors Claudius (AD 41–54) and Septimius Severus (AD 193–211). It measures 34 m (approx. 112 ft) across the auditorium, and has a capacity of approximately 2,000, on nineteen tiers of stone benches. Part was excavated out of the hillside, while part is supported on manmade vaults. It is still used today. NE of the theatre are the remains of the Roman baths, perhaps from the Augustan era 207 (27 BC–AD 14), with alterations in the second and third centuries. At the W edge is a large rectangular swimming pool, then a terrace, then two smaller pools. Further E again are the remains of the calidarium, tepidarium and frigidarium. Directly N of the baths is the massive Etruscan city wall. Continuing to its W end and then walking S, we reach the remains of the Roman temple; rebuilt in the first century BC, its entrance was at the E end (the steps survive). The temple had a tetrastyle pronaos, and the stylobate is around 16 m (approx. 53 ft) long. The adjacent Etruscan temple is at a lower level; its walls survive to a height of around 2.2 m (7 ft).

Continuing SE, return to the **Archaeological Museum**. Built in 1912–14 in the form of an Ionic temple, the lower level houses finds from the excavations and other nearby sites, principally Etruscan and Roman. It was enlarged, with an upper level, in 1981 and again in 1997. These galleries display other collections, and now extend below the street with a series of display spaces, terminating below the Anti-quarium Costantini (no. 9 Via Portigiani), itself used for exhibitions and a library.

Return to Piazza Mino da Fiesole and take the lane between the Seminario and Palazzo Vescovile, which rises steeply towards San Franc-esco. At no. 7 (left) is a house containing a little fourteenth-century chapel dedicated to **San Sepolcro**, its design based on the Holy Sep-ulchre in Jerusalem. On the right: a small public garden with views over the village. To the left, a little further up: another terraced garden with two war memorials. Magnificent views of Florence from here. Further up the lane are three churches.

The first is **San Alessandro**, built on the site of a pagan temple, transformed in the sixth century into a church. In the ninth century the dedication was changed from San Pietro to San Alessandro, after a beatified bishop of Fiesole. Modernised in 1570, and again in 1782; finally by Giuseppe del Rosso in 1815–19, who added the present neo-Classical façade. After 1956 it was restored yet again, reinstating more of its earlier appearance. A basilica plan, with nave and side aisles, with two colonnades of *cipollino* marble, with bases and Ionic capitals probably taken from the nearby Roman ruins.

A little further on the left is the chapel of **Santa Cecilia**, late fifteenth century.

San Francesco: Finally, at the top of the hill, at an altitude of 346 m (approx. 1,135 ft), is the site of the Etruscan acropolis, then that of the Romans, then in succession, the early medieval castle, and finally in the fourteenth century, the present Franciscan friary. The medieval castle was destroyed by the Florentines in 1125, but the oratory then built here was adopted by Franciscans in 1399. Altered over the following centuries, it was radically restored in 1905–7 by Giuseppe Castellucci. The façade is still of early fifteenth-century appearance, although the rose window was remade by Castellucci. The portal has a boldly projecting canopy, faced with a cusped Gothic arch.

Interior: a single nave, very dark, three bays long, with a pointed barrel vault articulated by simple transverse arches; at the sides are two pairs of rather elaborate nineteenth-century neo-Gothic ogee aedicules, decorated with figures of saints. Right side, first altar: *Marriage of St Catherine*, attributed to Cenni di Francesco, late fourteenth or early fifteenth century. Second altar: *Immaculate Conception* by Piero di Cosimo, dated, apparently falsely, to 1480. On the left side: second altar: *Annunciation* by Raffaellino del Garbo, early sixteenth century; first altar: *Adoration of the Magi*, school of Cosimo Rosselli, late fifteenth century.

In the chancel: Renaissance chancel arch, Corinthian, in *pietra serena*; attributed to Benedetto da Maiano. The stalls are early sixteenth century, with intarsia decoration. Leading off the chancel is the sacristy, and then the chapel of San Antonio, with a *Nativity Crib* by the della Robbia workshop.

Just outside the sacristy a little fifteenth-century cloister gives access to the Museo Etnografico Missionario, containing a miscellany of objects and artefacts brought back by Franciscan missionaries from China, Egypt and elsewhere.

To the right of the church are two more cloisters, one fourteenth century, the other fifteenth. The delightful small first cloister may be visited; steep steps just inside the lobby lead to an upper wing containing two rows of small friars' cells. This was the home for several years of (St) Bernardino of Siena, superior of the convent after 1417. The

208

206 Fiesole: the Roman theatre

207 Fiesole: remains of the Roman baths with the campanile of the cathedral of San Romolo

208 Fiesole: San Francesco; detail of the portal, after 1330

final, larger rectangular cloister is eighteenth century, and not normally accessible, since it is still in use by the friars.

The return route to Florence may be varied to include the nearby Medici villa. Return to Piazza Mino da Fiesole, and then take the Via Vecchia Fiesolana, towards the SW rather than Via Fra Giovanni, the road by which we arrived. A short distance down on the right is the **Villa Medici**, also known as the Palagio di Fiesole. Built on land acquired by Cosimo il Vecchio from the Bardi; it was built in 1458–62 for Giovanni di Cosimo by Michelozzo, with considerable terracing to deal with the difficult site. It was used extensively by Lorenzo il Magnifico for literary and philosophical gatherings; his Accademia Platonica was transferred here in 1479, and which Pico della Mirandola, Marsilio Ficino and Angelo Poliziano attended. It was sold by the Medici in 1671 to Vincenzo del Sera, succeeded by a series of owners. Extended in the eighteenth century by Lady Orford, the original form of the villa was a pure cube. It was radically modernised in 1780 by Gaspare Maria Paoletti. In 1857 it was acquired by the British artist William Spence, and became a centre for the Pre-Raphaelite movement, including such figures as Holman Hunt and Millais.

4 THE NORTHERN DISTRICTS: MONTUGHI AND LA PIETRA

This rather ill-defined zone is bounded to the E by the Mugnone stream, and to the NW extends towards the eminence of Careggi. It contains suburbs principally built after 1900, but further out are several notable historic villas. A circular route beginning and ending at Piazza della Libertà visits most of them.

Take Via del Ponte Rosso the short distance to the crossroads at Ponte Rosso, then turn NW onto the long Via Vittorio Emanuele. About halfway along, right, set back from the road, is **Villa Fabbricotti**, an impressive pile by Vincenzo Micheli, 1860s. A little further on the right is Via Federico Stibbert, leading to the noted homonymous villa.

Villa Stibbert: The museum is based on the collections amassed by Frederick Stibbert (1838–1906), an Englishman born in Florence of a Florentine mother. Stibbert's father and grandfather were bankers and financiers, and he was bequeathed a substantial fortune, from which he acquired a rich collection of arms and costumes, paintings and a library. On his death, his collections were left to the British nation, but the government ceded them to the city of Florence. In 1908 a foundation was established to administer them.

The present villa consists of two originally separate farmhouses, united and extended by Stibbert, mainly in 1880–88, ultimately to contain more than sixty rooms; they form a long, linked collection of structures along the Via Montughi. His architect was Gaetano Fortini. The styles are widely divergent, from neo-medieval to neo-Classical. In the grounds are further eclectic structures, including a Hellenistic rotunda and an Egyptian temple. Among the paintings are works by Allori, G.B. Tiepolo and Luca Giordano, although the emphasis of the collection centres on arms and armour, and costume. The Japanese and Asiatic armoury may be the finest in Europe.

To the w of the villa's entrance gates is **L'Immacolata e San Martino a Montughi**, rebuilt in the early twentieth century, but containing a polychrome lunette, *Deposition with Angels* by the della Robbia, sixteenth century. The adjacent canons' house (1539) is by Baccio d'Agnolo.

Return to Via Vitttorio Emanuele and continue NW; then, just after Piazza Giorgini, take Via dei Cappuccini, right. Immediately on the left is **San Francesco e Santa Chiara**, also known as Le Cappuccine di Montughi. It was assigned to Capuchin Franciscans by Cosimo I, after its reconstruction following the siege of 1530. The church was recon-secrated in 1623, but was rebuilt in 1793 by Giuseppe Manetti. Inside: a single nave, with three lateral chapels down each side. At the end of the nave: a triumphal arch in *pietra serena*, beyond which is the chancel. Most of the fittings are in wood decorated with intaglio, much exe-cuted by the friars themselves. First right chapel: *St Anthony of Padua* by Lorenzo Lippi, 1659. On the high altar: a wooden Crucifix, late fifteenth century. Second left chapel: *St Francis Receiving the Stigmata*, a fine work by Jacopo da Empoli, late sixteenth century.

Continue N along Via dei Cappuccini. After passing the Facultà di Ingegneria (engineering) of the university, the road becomes Via Santa Marta; a few hundred metres further, left, is the **Convento di Santa Marta**, founded in 1336 by the wealthy Florentine Lottieri Davanzati, and originally occupied by the Umiliati. It was also badly damaged in 1530, but was rebuilt by the Davanzati. Today occupied by an enclosed order of Benedictine nuns.

The gateway on the road leads to an atrium with two stone portals (1599); one gives access to the conventual buildings, the other to the *foresteria*, lodgings for visitors. A third, original fourteenth-century doorway, with the Davanzati coat of arms, leads into the church: a single aisle-less nave, with early seventeenth-century altars in *pietra serena*. On the high altar: a fragmentary frescoed *Crucifixion*, attributed to Orcagna, *circa* 1350.

At the Villa della Cisterna, Via Santa Marta turns right and then left, continuing NE as Via del Poggiolino to its junction with the Via Bolognese (SS 65). Continue NE for a short distance on SS 65. Just before its junction with Via Salviati (right), a narrow lane, Vicolo del Cionfo, leads S to the **Villa la Loggia**; first built as early as the 1200s, it was then owned by Brunetto Latini, the teacher of Dante; later acquired by the Pazzi. Today it has material of various dates, including the fine homonymous early fifteenth-century loggia. In 1724 it was bought by Jacopo Panciatichi, who established a notable botanical garden. Today owned by the Giunti publishing house.

Returning to Via Bolognese, after a very short distance, turn right into Via Salviati. After 100 m or so, on the right is the **Villa Salviati**. The oldest nucleus is fourteenth century, with cantilevered crenellations; modernised in the early Renaissance in a restrained Michelozzian style for Alamanno Salviati, who acquired the estate in 1445. It was enlarged in the seventeenth century. To the rear (S) are seventeenth-century gardens.

Return to the Via Bolognese. A further excursion N takes us to the notable park at Pratolino. Continue N along the SS 65, passing through the hamlet of La Lastra. A little further N is Monte Rinaldi, where the road (Via Bolognese Nuova) turns sharply around the hill. On the hillside: a complex of villas designed by Leonardo Ricci, terraced into the hill, 1952–62; the first was built for himself, the second for the Petrelli. The forms derive from Frank Lloyd Wright, and are sensitively and ingeniously integrated into the landscape. Passing through Trespiano and Montorsoli, we reach the extensive estate of the **Villa Demidoff**, just before Pratolino. The site was acquired by Francesco I de' Medici in 1568, who appointed Buontalenti to design a notable villa. Under Ferdinando II and Cosimo III it became a famous centre of cultural gatherings, with a theatre and concerts directed by Handel and Domenico Scarlatti. It declined in the Lorraine era, and in 1822–4 the villa was demolished. The park was redesigned to become the most important Romantic garden in Tuscany. In 1872 the Savoy dynasty sold it to Paolo Demidoff, who turned the former servants' wing into a family house and remodelled the gardens. They remained thus until the early twentieth century, when the estate declined once more; in 1969 it was acquired by the provincial government and restored. In addition to the extensive parkland, the main interest is the surviving sculptures by Giambologna. The most notable are the giant figure of *Apennino* (1579–89), the *Fontana del Mugnone* (1577), the *Grotto of Cupid* (1577) and the *Fontana delle Maschere*. The villa's chapel and stables, both by Buontalenti, also survive.

Return down Via Bolognese towards the city. About 1 km after the side road to Villa Salviati, on the left is **Villa Finaly**, of medieval origin, but rebuilt by Poggi in the mid-nineteenth century. Today a study centre for Paris University. A little further down, in the village of La Pietra, again left, and at the end of a long avenue of cypresses, is the **Villa La Pietra**. It was originally built in the 1460s for the Sassetti, one of whom, Francesco, was general manager of the Medici bank. It was sold to the Capponi in 1545. Its present appearance is the work of Carlo Fontana and Ferdinando Ruggieri, who rebuilt the villa for the Capponi, *circa* 1700. A substantial square plan, with a central axial progression of rooms, leading to the gardens; again, formal terraces on axis. To the NE is another extensive formal garden. In 1907 the villa was bought by Hortense Mitchell, the American wife of Arthur Acton, and parents of Harold, the art historian and collector, who had been born here in 1904 and died in 1994. Harold left the villa to New York University, and today it is used as a study centre. It retains his collection of paintings. The gardens were laid out in the early 1900s by Arthur Acton, and after decades of neglect were restored by the British landscape architect Kim Wilkie, 2002–4.

To complete the tour of these northern districts, return to Villa Salviati, and continue E along Via Salviati, turning right after a couple of hundred metres, into Via Faentina. After about 300 m on the right is the Benedictine convent of **San Giovanni Battista a Lapo**, with the church dedicated to Santa Maria del Fiore. The façade is by Benci di Cione, retaining part of its earlier fourteenth-century appearance.

Continue down Via Faentina back towards the city; after a couple of hundred metres, turn left into Via Francesco Caracciolo, which runs along the bank of the Mugnone stream. Cross the bridge onto Via Giovanni Boccaccio, and then return N again along Via Boccaccio, this time along the east bank. On the right is the **Villa Palmieri**. Built in the fifteenth century by Matteo Palmieri, it was extensively modernised in

1697. In 1873 it was bought by the Englishman Alexander Lindsay, earl of Crawford, who extended the villa's Italian garden with a new garden in the Romantic manner. Return to the Via Faentina and continue SW back towards the city. On the right is **San Marco Vecchio**, first documented in 1058; the present structure is from 1894, with a further enlargement in the early 1930s. Continue down Via Faenza to Piazza delle Cure, and cross the railway bridge to return to Piazza della Libertà.

5 THE NORTH-WEST: CAREGGI

This zone was urbanised rapidly immediately after 1945, both with large-scale industrial development (including a FIAT plant) and with accompanying residential districts. The district is divided into two by the railway lines out of Santa Maria Novella, which run via Rifredi towards Prato. The E section includes Rifredi, Le Panche and Careggi, about 2 km N of the Fortezza da Basso. Take Viale Filippo Strozzi along the E side of the Fortezza; at the crossroads, take Viale Giovanni Milton on the E side. One block along Viale Milton is the **Chiesa Ortodossa Russa**, a splendid confection by Michail Presbashenskij, 1899–1903, a full-blooded transposition of the Russian church vernacular, richly carved and decorated, and with a cluster of onion domes on the skyline. Although designed in Russia, it was built by local craftsmen. Return to the main junction and continue NW along Via dello Statuto, Via Cesare Guasti (crossing the railway) and Via Francesco Gianni to Piazza Pietro Leopoldo, then straight on along Via Angelo Tavanti, and its continuation, Via Vittorio Emanuele, as far as Piazza Dalmazia. Continue N along Via Reginaldo Giuliani. To the W is Rifredi station; this zone, particularly that to the W of the railway lines, is in the process of radical transformation in conjunction with the new TAV (Treni di Alta Velocità) railway line. A new TAV station has been planned, designed by Norman Foster, who won an international competition in 2002. Continue on Via Giuliani, and then after a short distance turn right on Via dello Steccuto into Via delle Panche. Directly opposite is **Santo Stefano in Pane**, founded perhaps in the ninth century; the present church is twelfth or thirteenth century, although modernised in the seventeenth. Basically Romanesque; in front of the façade is a seventeenth-century portico. On the façade: arms of the Tornabuoni by the della Robbia workshop. Return S a short way down Via delle Panche, then turn left into Via di Santo Stefano in Pane and its continuation,

209 Villa Salviati from Fiesole in morning mist, after 1445

210 Ospedale Pediatrico Meyer at Careggi, 2000–07 by CSPE: detail of ward wings

Via Dino del Garbo. At Via Taddeo Alderotti, turn left. On the right, after half a kilometre, is the extensive Centro Traumatologico Ortopedico (CTO), one of the principal tertiary orthopaedic centres in Italy; by Pier Luigi Spadolini, 1955–62. A little further N is the large general hospital of Careggi (see below).

The villas of Careggi and Castello

Villa Medici di Careggi: The zone of Careggi has been popular since the early medieval era. The land undulates slightly, with modest hills and valleys, originally interspersed with rich farmland and vineyards.

To reach the first of the Medici villas, start from the Largo Palagi to the N of the CTO, and take Viale Gaetano Pieraccini. About 1 km to the N, the **Villa Medici** (nos. 15, 17 and 21) is on the left, set in a small wooded park. In the fourteenth century the property was owned by Tommaso Lippi, but was bought by Giovanni di Bicci de' Medici in 1417. It was then modernised and enlarged, perhaps by Michelozzo, a process that continued until 1459. It was probably the most important villa to the Medici, who spent a considerable time here; Lorenzo il Magnifico's Accademia Platonica also assembled here, and it became the hub of the humanist movement in the city, whose members included Marsilio Ficino and Pico della Mirandola. Cosimo il Vecchio and Lorenzo de' Medici both died at the villa. It was badly damaged when the Medici were expelled from the city in 1494 but was restored by Cosimo I, who commissioned a famous cycle of frescoes by Pontormo and Bronzino (now lost). The gardens were reordered *circa* 1617, perhaps by Giulio Parigi. In 1779 it was sold to Conte Vincenzo Orsi; in the early nineteenth century it was owned by Lord Holland, and after 1848 by Francis Sloane, who restored the villa and replanned the gardens, much as they remain. Today it is used as administrative offices for the adjacent hospital.

The external appearance remains transitional, part way between a medieval fortified manor house and a semi-rural noble villa. The prominent crenellations have survived on the principal façades, although the lower parts were modernised in the fifteenth century. The plan, too, evinces the emergent villa typology, with two extended wings forming an overall U shape, enclosing a courtyard. The interior centres on an irregularly shaped internal courtyard, perhaps by Michelozzo, while the wings towards the garden each have three bays, with large glazed openings. Above one wing is an Ionic loggia, again perhaps by Michelozzo or Giuliano da Sangallo.

Ospedale Universitaria di Careggi: Founded in 1934, the hospital occupies an extensive site SW of the villa, and is bisected by a road, Viale San Luca. To the E it is bounded by Viale Pieraccini. It is the principal acute and teaching hospital of the city. Many of the older buildings have little architectural merit, although the hospital is in the course of an extensive modernisation programme, among which are the trauma and emergency services building (a substantial block, mostly red brick) and the new 'gateway' or entrance block (the Portone), at the S end of Viale San Luca, 2010; extensively glazed, simple, refined, but impressive. Both are by CSPE (Centro Studi Progetti Edilizia).

Ospedale Pediatrico Meyer: E side of Viale Pieraccini, opposite the Medici villa. The new children's hospital is based around the pre-existing nineteenth-century neo-Classical Villa Ognissanti, with an extensive English garden. Again designed by CSPE, 2000–07. The new building is towards the rear of the site, behind sturdy three-storey early twentieth-century neo-Classical blocks (restored, now used for post-graduate studies and a parents' hotel); two curved, glazed, colonnaded cloisters link the front blocks to the new hospital, which is partly set into the hillside; it is extremely energy efficient, with 'green roofs' and a greenhouse-gallery with photovoltaic cells. It contains around 200 beds, and is built on three levels of terraced accommodation, mostly clad with copper roof panels.

210

Continuing N up Viale Pieraccini, after a few hundred metres we reach the Piazza Careggi, on which stands the imposing, crenellated, medieval **Torre di Careggi**, since 1936 part of the adjacent Convento delle Suore Oblate. The adjacent buildings are wrapped around a courtyard, all fourteenth century in origin, but altered towards the end of the sixteenth century. For much of its history the tower was also owned by the Medici, who used it as a *foresteria* (accommodation for guests) and a farmhouse for the adjacent estates. Many works of art were transferred here by the sisters from their earlier base at the Arcis-pedale di Santa Maria Nuova. They include works by Matteo Rosselli, Bernardo Daddi and Giuliano da Sangallo.

Return a short distance down Viale Pieraccini, right along Via delle Oblate, down towards the Terzolle stream. Then turn left on Via delle Gore and right onto Via della Quiete.

On the right is the **Villa Bellini**, modernised in recent times but still identifiable as a substantial traditional villa-farmhouse. To the NW, also on Via della Quiete, is the

Villa La Quiete: Built by the Orlandini in the medieval period; in 1438 it became the property of the *condottiere* Niccolò da Tolentino, and then in 1452 of the Medici. In 1627 it was acquired by Cristina di Lorena, after which it became the seat of notable social events and festivities. In 1650 it was acquired by Eleonora Ramirez de Montalvo, who established a conservatory for noble girls. After her death, the conservatory was taken over by Vittoria della Rovere, who built the adjacent chapel in 1686. After 1724 the last of the Medici, Anna Maria Luisa, lived here. Since 1937 it has been the base for the Suore Montalve, who continue the tradition of education.

The adjacent church is by Pier Francesco Silvani; two choirs, one above and one below, the upper one with a frescoed vault by Giuseppe Masini and Giuseppe Tonelli, very late seventeenth century. Also in the upper choir: tomb monument to *Eleonora Ramirez de Montalvo* by Antonio Corbellini, 1689. Within the adjacent conventual buildings, works by Botticelli, Giovanni dellla Robbia, Domenico Ghirlandaio, Neri di Bicci and others.

Villa Corsini a Castello: From Villa La Quiete, take Via delle Montalve down to Via delle Panche and its continuation, Via Giuliani; then turn right onto Via della Querciola and right at Via di Castello. This terminates in front of the villa. Its impressive late Baroque façade conceals its fifteenth-century origins. Originally owned by the Strozzi, it was sold in 1460 to the Rinieri, and then, after many changes of ownership, in 1697 it passed to Lucrezia Rinuccini, wife of Marchese Filippo Corsini, who employed Antonio Maria Ferri in 1698–9 to modernise the façade. The central bay is particularly rich, flanked by broad pilasters; two orders surmounted by a large complex attic, flanked by volutes and capped by a powerful pediment. In the centre is a large clock, surrounded by sculpted decoration. Above the Mannerist portal is a balcony, at the top of which is a large, ostentatious Corsini coat of arms.

Inside, the plan centres on a courtyard, with colonnades on three sides. The principal hall is a double-height *salone*, with white stucco decoration and frescoes of rural scenes. The attractive garden is in the Italian style, with sculpture by Tribolo and a large exedra known as the Giardino delle Quattro Stagioni.

Villa Medici della Petraia: From Villa Corsini, Via della Petraia rises NE a few hundred metres towards the Medici villa. Originally owned by the Brunelleschi, then the Strozzi; the nucleus of this first structure survives in the form of the big, square, crenellated tower, rising above the villa. It became Medici property in 1530, and in 1576 Ferdinando I began its modernisation under Buontalenti, *circa* 1589–94. Further modernisations followed in 1636–48, when Lorenzo, Ferdinando's son, commissioned Volterrano to fresco the internal courtyard, illustrating the splendours of the Medici dynasty. In the same period (*circa* 1620) Parigi set out the piazza at the front and the surrounding gardens. In the period of Lorraine ownership, the grounds were separated from those of the adjacent Villa di Castello by ironwork fences, 1785. The gardens were first opened to the public in 1805. During Florence's brief period as capital of Italy, it was used as a hunting lodge by Vittorio Emanuele II. It became state property in 1919.

The plan is a rectangle, with two long main façades towards the road and the garden. The main façade is symmetrical, with a low basement and two *piani nobili*. Three bays on each side of the central entrance bay, which is denoted by a large arched portal with the Medici coat of arms above. Simple rectangular fenestration, and plastered walls, with *pietra forte* for all the detailing. The villa is planned around a large central *salone*, while the massive medieval tower rises at the back towards the gardens.

From the entrance, we reach the courtyard, with loggias on two sides, but now roofed over with a glass and iron roof, to become a ballroom. On the two other walls are frescoes by Cosimo Daddi, 1591–4, made in the period of Ferdinando I's reign. Also on the ground floor is the Sala da Pranzo, nineteenth-century furnishings; the Sala di Musica, with Louis XV furniture; and the Studio di Vittorio Emanuele.

On the *piano nobile* are the king's private apartments. The *studiolo* has *trompe l'oeil* frescoes (late sixteenth century); opposite is the old chapel, also with late sixteenth-century frescoes, attributed to Cosimo Daddi.

The gardens are on three levels, following the hillside; laid out in the late sixteenth century, they were altered significantly in the nineteenth. On the uppermost level, that of the villa itself, are formal terraces; the intermediate level has a large fishpond, traversed by a bridge-staircase that rises to the level of the villa. The lowermost level is much larger and is laid out in the Italian manner, formal and geometrical, with a central marble fountain on axis with the house, flanked by two groups of trees.

Return to Villa Corsini, and take Via di Castello NW to the piazza in front of the

Villa Medici di Castello: The first fortified farmhouse was built in the twelfth or thirteenth centuries. It was modernised in the fourteenth, and again after 1477 by Lorenzo and Giovanni, sons of Pierfrancesco de' Medici, nephew of Cosimo il Vecchio. It became a favourite of Cosimo I, and was further modernised for him by Tribolo, who enlarged the house, 'regularised' the long façades and set out the garden. In the same period, the interior was decorated by Bronzino and Pontormo. Later again, there were further additions by Buontalenti (late sixteenth century), who added the rusticated portal and balcony to the long main façade. Following the end of the Medici dynasty, Pietro Leopoldo of Lorraine modernised both the interior and the gardens after 1766. The villa became the property of the state in 1924, and after 1974 was the base of the Accademia della Crusca, founded in 1583 as a learned society, whose principal role is the study, conservation and dissemination of the Italian language.

The main façade has two orders plus a mezzanine and a low attic, and five bays on each side of the central one. Each bay has a rectangular window to each principal order, with small square lights to the mezzanines and attic.

The garden was set out by Tribolo immediately after 1537. It was divided into sections, with the formal central part planned around a basin of water, in which was later added (1583) Ammannati's sculpture of *Appenino*; it now stands on the upper terrace surrounded by holly woods. On the terrace around the basin are classical statues, and *putti* surround the central basin itself. It was originally crowned by Ammannati's bronze *Hercules and Antaeus*, now kept in storage at the villa. The gardens were completed *circa* 1590. They have been much altered (part were replanned in the nineteenth century in the Romantic manner), but Tribolo's complex Grotta degli Animali survives, with stalactites and animal figures; it was completed *circa* 1550 by Vasari. The important collections of citrus trees and herbs also survive.

Just E of the villa façade, a lane winding through the parkland, Via di San Michele, takes us to the homonymous church. **San Michele** is of medieval origin but was rebuilt by Ferdinando III in 1817.

Sesto is so named because it stood on the 6-mile mark on the Roman road out of Florence. It is a substantial industrial town (pop. approx. 50,000), the origins of which lay in the establishment of the famous porcelain works at Doccia in 1737 by Carlo di Leonardo Ginori. The town expanded notably after 1945, to encompass several outlying villages. It centres on the main axis of Via Reginaldo Giuliani /Via Antonio Gramsci, the main road between Florence and Prato. The urban hub is Piazza Ginori, from which the other streets radiate. Two parallel streets, Via Dante Alighieri and Via Verdi, meet at Piazza Vittorio Veneto. The parish church of **San Martino** is recorded in the first millennium, but has been modernised and altered many times. In front of the façade is a colonnaded Tuscan portico, added in 1602. Inside: nave and side aisles, with an open timber roof; much twelfth-century Romanesque material has survived. The flanking altars in *pietra serena* are from 1633; the chancel was rebuilt in the early 1950s by Lando Bartali.

The major public buildings stand on Via Gramsci, SE of Piazza Vittorio Veneto. The **Palazzo Pretorio** (no. 332) has the arms of the *podestà* on the façade. Further down, at no. 456, is the **Villa Guicciardini**, formerly Corsi-Salviati, recorded in 1502, but modernised in 1632 and 1738. The interior is used for exhibitions and other events.

A couple of kilometres beyond Sesto is the complex road junction where the A1 (Autostrada del Sole) crosses the Autostrada Firenze-Mare. Adjacent to this 'spaghetti junction' (NE corner) is one of the most remarkable twentieth-century buildings in the vicinity of Florence, Giovanni Michelucci's church of **San Giovanni Battista** or '**Chiesa dell'Autostrada**'. Built in 1960–64, as a pilgrimage church dedicated to those who died in the construction of the great engineering feat of the Autostrada del Sole. The plan is cruciform, and the superstructure rises from a base of rusticated stonework. It is a complex three-dimensional form, reinforced concrete, intended as a reinterpretation of a tent, with raking concrete columns resembling tree trunks and branches, and a folded concrete roof structure. The external 'sails' are clad with copper. The interior is a dramatic, dynamic space, with equally dramatic contrasts of light and dark.

Novoli to Le Cascine: Return to Piazza Dalmazia in Rifredi; then continue SW on Via Giovan Filippo Mariti, passing below the railway.

At the end of Via Mariti, a left turn along Viale Francesco Redi takes us to the former **Macelli**, slaughterhouses, by Felice Francolini, 1878. Following their closure, the complex was used for a school and other functions; restored and converted in the 1980s, it now houses the Museo di Storia Naturale. Returning down Viale Redi, continue NW over Ponte San Donato, then along the Via di Novoli. On the right is the site of the former extensive FIAT complex; this, and adjacent sites, were subject to a master plan for redevelopment in the late 1980s (involving Richard Rogers, Leonardo Ricci, Lawrence Halprin and Bruno Zevi), but it was highly controversial and then abandoned. A new plan was drawn up by Leon Krier in the early 1990s. The zone has now been partially redeveloped, one section becoming the Parco San Donato; the NE part, adjacent to Viale Alessandro Guidoni, houses administrative buildings of the Regione Toscana and the **Palazzo di Giustizia**, a cluster of partly glass-walled towers by Ricci and others. Further recent developments include housing (by Gabetti e Isola, 2005) and university buildings, *circa* 2004.

On the SW side of Via di Novoli is **San Donato**, after which the locality is named. Documented as early as 1187, it is identifiable mainly by the campanile; the church itself was rebuilt in 1963. At the NW end of Via di Novoli (approx. 1 km), Via Alessandro Allori, left, contains the little church of **San Cristofano**. Romanesque in origin, it was largely rebuilt in 1873, but the façade is fifteenth century, with traces of fresco. Inside are further fourteenth- and fifteenth-century frescoes. Marsilio Ficino was the rector here in 1473.

Le Cascine: The itinerary may be completed by returning to Ponte San Donato, and then taking Viale Francesco Redi SW. After a short distance, it opens out into Piazza Puccini. On the W corner is the **Teatro Puccini**, a good example of late 1930s Fascist modern architecture (1939, by the Ufficio Tecnico del Monopolio dello Stato). Originally built as a recreation and social centre for tobacco factory workers. The main block is low and reticent, but on the corner is a tall obelisk-like glazed tower containing a 'spiral', actually helical, stair, and below which is a large double portal with relief sculpture between the two doorways. The building had a variety of uses after 1945, including a ballroom and a cinema. Since 1991 it has been used as a theatre. Continue SW down Via delle Cascine to reach the long, narrow riverside park, **Le Cascine**. It extends for 3 km along the N bank of the Arno and covers around 118 ha. In the sixteenth century the zone was an island between the Arno and the Mugnone stream, and was owned by the Medici. Once used for hunting, it was then used for raising cattle (*cascine*: dairy farms); later it was partly planted with trees, and in the seventeenth century a botanic garden was established here. At the beginning of the nineteenth century it was opened to the public, and since then has been one of the most popular and heavily frequented open spaces in the city.

Enter the park about halfway down its length, at Piazzale delle Cascine. The **Palazzina Reale** was built for Grand Duke Pietro Leopoldo in 1787 by Giuseppe Manetti. Today part of the university; an elegant, restrained, neo-Classical structure, with two orders and seven bays. The lower order is colonnaded, the arches alternating with small rectangular openings. The upper order has rectangular aediculed windows, with alternating triangular and segmental pediments.

Towards the NW the park is bordered by the Via dell'Aeronautica, flanking the extensive Prato del Quercione. Viale del Pegaso traverses the Cascine halfway along this section; on the right, the **Istituto Militare Aeronautica** by Raffaele Fagnoni, 1937. The furthermost part of the Cascine is the Prato delle Mulina, in the centre of which is an amphitheatre. At the end is the Piazzaletto dell'Indiano; adjacent is the bridge across the Arno, the **Ponte all'Indiano**, by Fabrizio de Miranda, Adriano Montemagni and Paolo Sica, 1969–76. A suspension bridge with an elegant single span of 220 m (approx. 722 ft), supported by two inclined steel piers (48 m / approx. 157 ft high), from which suspension cables radiate. The bridge has two decks: that for vehicles above, and a pedestrian route hung underneath it. The name derives from the maharaja of Kolhapur who died in Florence in 1870, and was cremated here where the Mugnone meets the Arno; monument in the park nearby.

Return to the central Piazzale, and to the city centre along the SE part of the Cascine. The principal route is the long, straight Viale degli Olmi, along the NE side of which are various sports facilities including a horse-racing circuit and a velodrome. Alternatively, one can take the Viale Abramo Lincoln, which flanks the Arno.

7 WESTWARDS FURTHER OUT: THE MEDICI VILLAS AT ARTIMINO AND POGGIO A CAIANO

This itinerary covers the outer NW sector, beyond the route of the Autostrada del Sole (A1), which wraps around the outer western suburbs. Starting at the Porta al Prato, take Via del Ponte alle Mosse, which continues as Via Francesco Baracca and then, after the major intersection near the Ponte all'Indiano, as Via Pratese. Passing through Peretola, after about 2.5 km we arrive at **Campi Bisenzio**. A substantial town, mostly of modern appearance. After crossing the Ponte del Bisenzio, we reach the **Rocca degli Strozzi**, owned by the Strozzi since the early fifteenth century, but radically modernised in the seventeenth. Turning S, after less than 1 km we reach the junction with SS 66, the road to Pistoia. Turn right (W), and continue for a further 4 km. As the road rises slightly, we reach the village of Poggio a Caiano.

Villa Medici di Poggio a Caiano: The most famous of all the Medici villas. The entrance is directly off the SS 66, on the N side; the village lies mainly to the SW. Originally a fortified castle-farmhouse, in 1480 it was bought by Lorenzo il Magnifico de' Medici, who had the house rebuilt by Giuliano da Sangallo, *circa* 1485–94. A major landmark in the history of the development of the rural villa, with no residual defensive functions; its design was extremely influential, and was the forebear of dozens of other country villas for urban nobility, not only in Tuscany but also in the Venetian Terraferma and many other locations. The villa remained the principal summer residence of the Medici for generations. It was further elaborated under Lorenzo's successor Giovanni (later Pope Leo X), and further alterations took place under both the Medici grand dukes and the Lorraine dynasty. It was the setting for major events in the Medici's history, including the marriages of Alessandro and Margherita of Austria (1536), Cosimo I and Eleanora di Toledo (1539) and that of Francesco I and Bianca Cappello (1579); the last lived here until her death in 1587. After 1919 it was the property of the state, but today is managed by the comune.

The villa stands on a modest eminence, sufficiently high to have views over the Arno plain. It is approached by a gate in a wall, at the outer corners of which are short, square towers, the only nominally defensive element. Through the gate is a garden, with the main entrance to the villa on axis. The present curved stairs are by Pasquale Poccianti, 1807, and replace the original rectilinear stairs with straight flights.

211 Villa Medici at Poggio a Caiano: detail of entrance portico, by Giuliano da Sangallo, begun 1485

212 Villa Medici at Poggio a Caiano: façade towards the formal garden

213 Villa Medici at Poggio a Caiano: detail of barrel vault in the entrance portico

The villa has a square plan, and stands on a plinth, which surrounds it on all four sides. The plinth contains many practical functions such as stores and cellars, and other necessities associated with the management of the surrounding estate. It also contains a billiard room and a small theatre. It is treated differently from the more *signorile* villa itself, its robust, rustic arches forming an open colonnade on all four sides.

The villa has two storeys, clad with white render and capped by a boldly oversailing Tuscan roof. The entrance is marked by a five-bay Ionic portico, which appears to project from the façade, but is actually recessed behind the plane of the front wall; it is capped by a bold triangular pediment, the first time in the Renaissance that this classical device was used on a secular building. Above, in the centre is a small turret with a clock, added in the eighteenth century.

The plan is an H, and is divided into three elements, the whole contained within a perfect square. Across the front and rear façades are larger rectangular wings, while in the centre is a narrower section, containing the main central *salone*, with a small courtyard at each end. All the subordinate elements are contained within a pattern of squares of two different sizes, the larger square having sides twice the length of the smaller.

The interior: on the ground floor (the 'plinth') are the apartments of Bianca Cappello, mostly with considerably later decoration; the attractive little theatre and billiard room are also accessible, the former complete with proscenium arch and miniature galleries. On the principal storey: the entrance loggia has a rich barrel-vaulted ceiling with the Medici arms, *circa* 1490. The original *frontone* (the relief decoration in the pediment) of the entrance portico is a terracotta frieze, attributed to Andrea Sansovino, with mythological themes (now a copy). Directly inside is the reception hall, with monochrome frescoes by Luigi Catani (*circa* 1811). To the left is a small suite of rooms, including the neo-Classical bedchamber of King Vittorio Emanuele II. Directly beyond the entrance hall, but with its long axis at right angles, is the splendid central *salone* (Salone di Leone X) with a fine, rich, barrel-vaulted ceiling (1513), with gilded, coffered decoration. Around the walls: painted Corinthian pilasters, between which are frescoes by Andrea del Sarto, Pontormo and Franciabigio, 1519–21, and a second phase by Alessandro Allori, 1579–82. They all glorify the house of Medici, principally using classical history and mythology. Beyond the *salone*, still on axis, is the dining room, with frescoed ceiling by Antonio Domenico Gabbiani, 1698; views over the gardens. Adjacent to the left and right are two more small suites of rooms, again once occupied by Vittorio

Emanuele II and his queen, 'la bella Rosina'; notable is the neo-Classical bathroom by Giuseppe Cacialli, 1811.

Within the grounds and gardens are a *tempietto* and an ice-house. Along the Via Pratese are the stables, begun by Baccio Bigio in 1516 and completed by Tribolo in 1545–8.

Villa Medici di Artimino: Around 3 km SW of Poggio is another Medici villa, at Artimino. The village itself is Etruscan in origin, and retains its medieval fortifications. The Medici villa, also known as La Ferdinanda, stands on a wooded hill. It was designed by Buontalenti for Ferdinando I, and built in 1594–8. The principal function was as a hunting lodge. It was originally decorated internally by a noted series of lunettes painted by Giusto Utens in 1599, each depicting a different Medici villa with its gardens and estates; today the series is in the Museo di Firenze.

La Ferdinanda is broadly modelled on Sangallo's villa at Poggio, with a long, relatively low façade, terminating in projecting corner towers with rusticated quoins. In the centre is a recessed entrance loggia, of five bays, with a flat architrave and a split pediment to the central bay. The wall surface is plain white plaster, with a basement storey, a single *piano nobile* and two subsidiary attic storeys. The fenestration is simple, with relatively small windows. Above the oversailing eaves is a rich variety of decorative chimneys, contrasting with the rather reticent façade below and giving the villa its nickname, 'dei cento camini' (of 100 chimneys). The prominent main external stair is modern (1930), but based on Buontalenti's design, with two curved lower flights meeting at a central landing and a long straight flight up to the portico. The plan is a compact rectangle. The villa is privately owned, although the local Museo Archeologico Comunale was ('temporarily') installed in the basement storey in the 1980s. Much of the rich internal decoration is by Passignano. The villa is used for conferences, cultural events and exhibitions.

8 THE SOUTH-EAST STRIP: SORGANE AND GAVINANA

The route begins at Piazza Ferrucci in front of Ponte San Niccolò. Lungarno Francesco Ferrucci flanks the river, while the parallel Via Coluccio Salutati takes a similar route 100 m or so inland. Via Salutati ends at Piazza Gavinana. These districts, Ricorboli and Gavinana, were laid out in 1924, with a regularly planned network of rectangular city blocks, mostly of two-storey terrace housing.

From Piazza Gavinana, take Viale Donato Giannotti SE, then its continuation, Viale Europa. At the junction with Via di Badia di Ripoli, turn right. On the Piazza di Badia is the **Badia a Ripoli**. The oldest monastic house within the city limits, it was founded as a nunnery in the seventh or eighth century; the formal dedication is to San Bartolomeo. It later passed to the Vallombrosans, who remained until the Napoleonic closures in 1808; today it has parish functions. It was modernised in 1598, restored in 1892 and again in 1931. In front of the church is a sixteenth-century portico. Inside: a single nave with side altars. Paintings by Jacopo Vignali, Francesco Curradi, and two frescoes by Poccetti, 1585 and 1601.

Continue along the Via di Badia N, crossing Viale Europa. After a few minutes we reach (right) the **Castello di Bisarno**, a Mannerist villa with eighteenth-century crenellations, and the adjacent **San Piero in Palco**, founded *circa* 1000, in a period when the Arno had two branches here and the church stood on an island between them; reconsecrated in 1360, and modernised again in the sixteenth and eighteenth centuries. Restoration in 1990 uncovered fourteenth-century frescoes. Return to the piazza and continue E along Via di Ripoli. To the right is the modern suburb of **Sorgane**. It was developed by three groups of architects under the leadership of Leonardo Ricci, Leonardo Savioli and others, in 1962–70. It followed a much more ambitious initial master plan by Michelucci in 1957, which envisaged a 'new town' of 12,000. The scaled-down result is more modest, with around 4,000 residents. The layout is based on a principal N–S axis, with branches to E and W containing the residential blocks.

9 THE SOUTH: POGGIO IMPERIALE AND THE CERTOSA DEL GALLUZZO

Poggio Imperiale: The imposing villa of Poggio Imperiale is easily reached from the Porta Romana. The long, straight Viale del Poggio Imperiale, lined with cypresses, rises to terminate directly in front of the villa's façade. The land on which it stands was confiscated in 1565 by Cosimo I from the Salviati. It was given to his daughter Isabella, and in 1622 was acquired by Grand Duchess Maria Maddalena, wife of Cosimo II and sister of the Habsburg emperor Ferdinand II. A pre-existing house was then demolished, and rebuilt on a much larger scale by Giulio Parigi, 1622–4. It was further enlarged, with a new S wing, in 1681–3 by Ferdinando Tacca. After the end of Medici rule, it became an important centre for the Lorraine dynasty. Under Pietro Leopoldo, in 1767–82 it was modernised by Gaspare Maria Paoletti. Its impressive external appearance is neo-Classical, largely by Pasquale Poccianti, who, with Giuseppe Cacialli, designed the main façade, 1807–23. After 1865 it became a women's college dedicated to the Santissima Annunziata.

The long façade has two orders. The central section, all rusticated, has a lower order of five tall arches, with radiating rustication. Directly above, the second order has five equally large windows separated by Ionic colonnettes. The whole is capped by a large triangular pediment. The outer wings are treated differently; rectangular lights to both orders. At the two outer ends, single-storey wings project forward to enclose the entrance courtyard.

Part of the ground floor can be visited. Four rooms are frescoed by Matteo Rosselli and others, 1623; on the *piano nobile*, the main hall is by Paoletti, with stucco decoration by Giocondo and Grato Albertolli, 1779–82.

Arcetri and Pian dei Giullari: At the NE corner of the Piazzale in front of the villa is Largo Enrico Fermi, from which a lane, Via Guglielmo Righini, leads first to the Istituto di Fisica, and then the Istituto di Astronomia of the university, and the nearby observatory, founded 1872. Continue NE on Via Righini to its junction with Via del Pian dei Giullari. At the junction is the **Villa Capponi**, with a Renaissance garden, planted in 1572; continuing right (SE) towards the hamlet of Pian. On the left is the prominent **Torre del Gallo**, a neo-medieval work built by the antiquarian Stefano Bardini, 1904–6. Along the Via del Pian are a number of villas, including **Villa Alinari** (no. 27), originally thirteenth century but now of seventeenth-century appearance; **Villa il Gioiello** (no. 42), where Galileo was forced to live from 1633 to his death (1642); and **Villa Ravà** (no. 71), where Francesco Guicciardini lived from 1533 to his death in 1540.

Continuing SE and then NE, past Villa Roster, we reach **Santa Margherita a Montici**, left, fourteenth century, with a crenellated campanile. In the right transept: *Virgin and Child* by the Master of St Cecilia, *circa* 1300. The road continues NE as Via Santa Margherita and then Via Benedetto Fortini, as far as Ricorboli, from which we can return to the city centre.

Certosa del Galluzzo (Certosa Fiorentina): The Certosa is also easily reached from the Porta Romana. This time, take the Via Senese directly S to the village of Galluzzo and the Certosa (Charterhouse). Halfway along the first section of the Via Senese is the village of San Gaggio; the **Villa Bayon** is a striking modern villa (1966) by Leonardo Savioli and Danilo Santi; rectilinear forms set below a dramatically cantilevered canopy-roof.

Just after the junction of the Via Senese and Via del Gelsomino is the small village of **Le Due Strade**, so called because two roads lead SW towards Galluzzo; to the W is the lower 'new road', nineteenth century, while to the SE is the more attractive, higher 'old road', the Via del Podestà. At no. 79 is the **Villa Corboli** (sixteenth to eighteenth century), and at no. 86 the **Convento del Portico**, an Augustinian house founded in 1340, today occupied by the Suore Stimmatine. The church contains a wooden Crucifix (*circa* 1340), and a high altarpiece by Piero Dandini.

After about 2.5 km both roads take us into Galluzzo at Piazza Niccolò Acciaioli; after 1415 Galluzzo was the seat of a *podestà*, whose palace is on the left of the main road; the present building is fifteenth century, based on an earlier house of the Canigiani. On the façade: a series of coats of arms in stone and terracotta from the della Robbia workshops. The Via Senese continues S through the village. After a short distance we reach the imposing, severe pile of the **Certosa**, looming over the road to the right (W); it resembles a fortress rather than a monastic house. The site was fortified before its acquisition by Niccolò Acciaioli in 1342, who then founded the charterhouse; it received many donations from wealthy Florentines as well as the Visconti of Milan. The Carthusians remained in occupation until 1958, when they were replaced by Cistercians, who remain there today.

214   The original core is the **Palazzo Acciaioli**, all in stone, and built by the Dominican friar Jacopo Passavanti and Jacopo Talenti after 1342; it was intended to be the residence of Niccolò Acciaioli. Not complete when he died, the first floor was added in the mid-fifteenth century. The entrance leads to a small and irregularly planned courtyard, and then a long flight of steps up to the first floor of the Palazzo Acciaioli or degli Studi, founded as a place where young Florentine noblemen could meet and study. Two storeys, with two prominent external façades towards the surrounding landscape. The lower order has narrow windows, the upper much larger pointed-arch windows, and the whole is capped by crenellation. The large upper hall is presently an art gallery, contain-

ing five frescoes by Pontormo from the *Passion of Christ*, 1522–5, formerly in the large cloister (recently restored). Also a Crucifix (*circa* 1350) and five paintings by Jacopo da Empoli, copies of Pontormo lunettes.

Directly beyond the great hall is a broad rectangular courtyard, with its long axis from left to right, and with the church façade directly opposite. **San Lorenzo** is also fourteenth century, but the present façade is by Giovanni Fancelli, sixteenth-century Renaissance; tall and rather fussy, with two principal orders and three bays, the whole capped by a substantial pedimented attic, flanked by volutes. The two lower orders are different; the first has applied Corinthian semi-columns on tall plinths, with a central portal capped by a segmental pediment; niches with statues to the outer bays. The second order has flat pilasters; in the centre a *bifora* below a semicircular arch. In the outer bays: niches again but no statues.

Inside: an entrance lobby, the Coro dei Conversi, added in 1556–8. Altars to left and right, the latter with a figure of *St Philip Neri* by Felice Ficherelli, 1657–9. To the left: *St Benedict* by Tommaso Garelli, 1601. The church interior retains its fourteenth-century appearance, a single nave, three bays long, with rib vaults on Gothic pilasters. In the vaults of the third bay, and on the walls: frescoes by Bernardino Poccetti, 1591–3. Carved walnut choir stalls, with intarsia decoration, 1570–90, by various masters. At the end of the nave (right) is the Cappella delle Reliquie, originally built by Acciaoli but rebuilt in the seventeenth century. Opposite is the sacristy, with refined late eighteenth-century decoration.

A doorway, left, leads to the Colloquio, where the Carthusians received visitors; sixteenth-century grisaille glass. Beyond is a small cloister, rebuilt in 1558–61, perhaps by Fancelli. Lunette of *St Lawrence between Two Angels* by Benedetto da Maiano, 1496. Above the chapter-house doorway: two lunette paintings by Bronzino, *circa* 1520. The chapter house was rebuilt after 1496, with a pavement of polychrome marble, installed under the prior Leonardo Buonafede, 1539. His tomb is by Francesco da Sangallo, 1545. A doorway leads out into the great cloister, a very large square space behind the apse of the church. Early sixteenth century, in the style of Brunelleschi, and surrounded by Composite colonnades supporting elegant semicircular arches. In the spandrels between the arches are sixty-six roundels containing terracotta busts of *Old Testament Figures*, *Saints*, *Evangelists* and *Apostles*, from Andrea and Giovanni della Robbia's workshop. The cloister walks are roofed by simple groin vaults on corbels.

The monks' cells are ranged around three sides of the great cloister. Each cell is in fact a small apartment, with an antechamber, dining room and day room, and upstairs, a bedroom and loggia. Attached to each cell is an *orticello* (allotment). The refectory is reached by a doorway and an anteroom, off the access way to the cloisters; rebuilt at the end of the fifteenth century. At the end of the walkway is the Chiostrino dei Conversi, 1475–85, with two orders of colonnades.

10 THE SOUTH-WEST: BELLOSGUARDO AND MONTE ULIVETO

These districts lie just SW of the city walls of the Oltrarno. They can be easily reached from Piazza Torquato Tasso, which lies in a gap in the surviving city wall. Take Via Villani, which runs directly SW out of the piazza. Just to the left is Via Giano della Bella, in which are two 'Liberty' (Art Nouveau) villas by Giovanni Michelazzi, 1905–7, both known as **Villa Lampredi** (nos. 9 and 13). No. 13 is the more eclectic and expressive, with a central balcony supported by large stone dragons, and curvilinear ironwork. At the far end, Via Villani opens into Piazza San Francesco di Paola; no. 7 is **Villa Pagani**, a neo-medieval work by Adolfo Coppedè, 1906. Also on the piazza is **San Francesco di Paola**, originally by Gherardo Silvani, mid-seventeenth century, but much modified in the eighteenth. Inside: a series of six oval paintings, late seventeenth century, showing the *Life of St Francesco di Paola*. On the right wall is a detached fresco by Taddeo Gaddi, the *Madonna del Parto*, *circa* 1355. On the high altar: early fifteenth-century wooden Crucifix.

Past the right flank of the church, Via di Bellosguardo rises up the hill of Monte Rimorchi, which passes the **Villa dello Strozzino**, owned by the Strozzi from the sixteenth century to the nineteenth. It has been attributed to Il Cronaca, particularly for the loggia on the first floor at the corner.

Adjacent on the right is the Via Monte Uliveto; a short distance along is the church of **Santi Vito e Modesto**, originally eleventh century, but now mostly nineteenth. At the end is the monastic complex of **San Bartolomeo**, most recently part of an adjacent military hospital. It was built from the funds of Bartolomeo Capponi, 1377. In 1454–72 it was rebuilt, perhaps by Michelozzo, but was modernised in the early seventeenth century and again in 1725. Inside: a single nave

214 The Certosa at Galluzzo: the Palazzo Acciaioli, founded by Niccolò Acciaioli in 1342

215 Bellosguardo from the city, with the fourteenth-century Torre di Bellosguardo

with groin vaults on corbels. Works by Bernardino Poccetti, Passignano, Sodoma and Santi di Tito.

Return to the Prato dello Strozzino in front of the homonymous villa, and this time take the Via di Bellosguardo S. On the right, just before the piazza, is the **Villa Brichieri Colombi**, where Henry James lived in 1887, writing *The Aspern Papers*. A little further, the road reaches the Piazza di Bellosguardo, the centre of this little settlement. Adjacent are several villas. To the right (NW) is **Villa Mercede**, or Villa al Saraceno (nos. 6–7), built by Pier Francesco Borgherini to a design by Baccio d'Agnolo, *circa* 1520. Said to have been the setting for Henry James's *Portrait of a Lady*.

To the left of the piazza are the grounds of the **Villa dell'Ombrellino**, no. 12, today a hotel, but noted as the home of Galileo, 1617–31. Like several other villas here, it was much frequented by the Anglo-Florentine literary circle in the nineteenth and twentieth centuries, including Virginia Woolf and Vita Sackville-West. To the south of the villa, near the edge of the estate, is the **Torre di Bellosguardo**; originally a fourteenth-century castle owned by the Cavalcanti. Rebuilt as a villa after 1583 and restored in the early twentieth century, again as a hotel, with neo-medieval features. Taking Via San Carlo (left), down the hill past Villa Mercede, we reach the **Castello di Montauto**, with fourteenth-century crenellations; it was transformed into a villa in the seventeenth century.

Return to the piazza, and this time take Via Piana S. After about 0.5 km, we reach the junction with Via di Marignolle. Turn right (W). After about 1 km, on the right is the **Villa Medici di Marignolle**, nos. 30–32. Originally owned by the Sacchetti, it was rebuilt by Buontalenti for Francesco I, *circa* 1585, and was modernised in the eighteenth century. A relatively modest house, two storeys, with a rectangular plan. A symmetrical façade with a central pedimented portal, flanked by pairs of single lights, also pedimented. In 1621 it was sold by the Medici to the grandson of Gino Capponi; it remains in private hands. A little further, also on the right, is the **Castello di Marignolle**, once owned by the Canigiani. Its present neo-Gothic appearance is the result of a 'modernisation' by the antiquarian Stefano Bardini at the beginning of the twentieth century. A hundred metres further again, we reach **Santa Maria a Marignolle**, rebuilt in 1903.

The itinerary may be completed by returning a short way N along Via di Marignolle, then taking Via di San Quirichino, right, which after 1 km or so joins the Via Senese N of Galluzzo, the main road back into the city from the SW.

This itinerary covers the SW part of the city beyond the lines of the medieval walls; it is bounded to the N by the Arno.

The route begins at Piazza Taddeo Gaddi, at the foot of **Ponte della Vittoria**. The bridge was first built in 1835 for Grand Duke Leopold II, and was designed by the engineers Seguin as a suspension bridge. It was rebuilt in 1925, but destroyed in 1944; it was rebuilt in 1946, with three arched spans, and is an important element in the city's inner orbital road network. The suburb of Pignone lies between the river and Monte Uliveto.

The zone along the river was settled on a significant scale only after the Piano Generale of 1924, when the district of Isolotto was designated for important residential expansion. It is reached by taking the Lungarno del Pignone, and then Via Baccio Bandinelli and Lungarno dei Pioppi, turning left along Via delle Magnolie.

L'Isolotto was the first substantial development by the housing agency known as Ina Casa; it was planned in 1951, and completed by 1958. Conceived as a collection of six sub-districts, each with its own public and social facilities, among those who designed elements were Italo Gamberini and Giovanni Michelucci. They centre on the rectangular Piazza dell'Isolotto, and the zone is divided in two by the green strip of the Viale dei Bambini. To the east, on Via del Palazzo dei Diavoli, is the pre-existing oratory church of the **Madonna della Querce**, early fifteenth-century Renaissance, with a centralised plan and showing the influence of Brunelleschi. At the front is a contemporary portico, filled in during the seventeenth century. Most of the housing, totalling 1,600 units, has between two and four floors, and represents a fusion of elements of the traditional vernacular, elements of the suburban and parts of the legacy of the English garden city movement.

To the SW of the Isolotto is the public housing of Torri a Cintoia, 1964–76, adjacent to which is the little church of **San Bartolo**, 1304, with a contemporaneous fresco of the *Virgin and Child with Saints*.

Scandicci: From Piazza Taddeo Gaddi, take the short Via del Ponte Sospeso to Piazza Pier Vettori, and then turn right onto the Via Pisana; continue for less than 1 km and then turn left onto Via Scandicci. After about 2 km on the left is the **Nuovo Ospedale di San Giovanni di Dio** by Pier Luigi Spadolini, 1968–82. Continue for a further 1 km past the suburb of Le Bagnese and cross the Greve river. Scandicci is a substantial town (pop. 54,000), but with little architectural merit; its main axis is Via Dante Alighieri and its continuation, Via Roma. Just to the SE, reached by Via Sant'Antonio, is Scandicci Alto, the rather fragmented original medieval settlement. Adjacent is the **Villa Passerini**, built in 1622 by the Altoviti on the remains of the castle, but refaced in the nineteenth century. Returning to Via Roma, turn left and then right to reach Piazza Don Giulio Cioppi, at the end of which is the parish church of **Santa Maria**; founded in 1070, but rebuilt in the thirteenth century, and modernised several times thereafter. Most of the present structure is from 1926. Inside, on the left wall: an early sixteenth-century terracotta *Virgin and Child* from the workshop of Giovanni della Robbia.

Appendix 1
Glossary of Terms

altana
Roof terrace, usually built of timber, and reached by a dormer

androne
Entrance hall of a *palazzo*

archetti
Small arches, usually in rows, and supporting a cornice or entablature

arte
Trade guild

bifora
Two-light window

borgo
A suburb of the city, originally outside the walls, but now within them, after successive enlargements, notably that of 1284–1333

bugnato
Rustication, as of stonework

camino
Chimney

canto(n)
Corner at the intersection of two streets; often named after an adjacent *palazzo*

cantoria
Choir loft or organ loft

casinò
Summer house or small villa, used for retreat from the city, especially in summer

cason(e)
Shed or outbuilding

cava
Stone quarry

chiasso
Narrow lane or alley, often linking two streets together

chiostro
Cloister

costa
A roadway or lane up the side of a hill

cupola
Cupola, often erroneously in English called a dome

duomo
Cathedral

finestra
A window; *finestron(e)* = a large or multi-light window

formella
Panel of stone carved in relief, and affixed to a structure

fresco
Correctly *affresco*; the technique of painting, using water-based paint, onto fresh plaster, so that the pigment is absorbed by the plaster and 'fuses' with it

giardino
Garden; diminutive *giardinetto*

insula
An urban 'island' surrounded by streets; in the medieval era *insulae* were frequently owned by the same family or a group of similarly aligned families, for purposes of defence

largo
A broad spacious street or promenade

liagò
Covered terrace on the top floor of a *palazzo*, with the roof above supported on a colonnade

loggia
Roofed, colonnaded structure; sometimes constructed by noble families for their own use; others were used by the *arti* or as covered markets.

Lungarno
Quay or embankment that borders the Arno river

macigno
A type of calcareous sandstone used in construction

merlatura
Crenellation, as applied to fortified buildings such as the Bargello and
the Palazzo Vecchio

monofora
Single-light window

occhio
Circular window or oculus, so called since it resembles an eye

Oltrarno (or Oltr'Arno)
The district of Florence on the south or 'other' side of the Arno river

piano nobile
Principal floor of a noble residence; usually the first floor but
occasionally the second

Piazza, *piazzale*
Piazza is the general term for a public square; *piazzale* is a particularly
large, spacious piazza. In the old city, *piazze* are often little more than
courtyards, but are still always called by this name.

pietra (forte, viva, serena)
Stone; *pietra forte* is the most widely used building stone of Florence and
is usually yellowish-brown in colour; *pietra serena* is bluish-grey. *Pietra
viva* is simply 'real' stone. *Pietra cotta* is brickwork (literally 'cooked
stone')

pluteo
Decorative stone panel, often carved in rich relief, and often placed in
series to form a low screen across the front of the chancel of a church

poggio
Small hill

prato
Meadow; also the name of an important textile manufacturing city
north-west of Florence.

quartiere, sestiere
Administrative subdivisions of the city; literally quarters and sixths

ricetto
Lobby or reception hall

sala madornale
Principal day living room of a *palazzo*; effectively synonymous with *salone*

scarsella
Small chancel or chapel containing the high altar

Serliana

Type of window used in the Renaissance, and named after the architect, writer and theorist Sebastiano Serlio. It consists of a large central light, usually arched, and flanked by smaller, narrower side lights; the more complex ones have two additional small square lights above the lower outer ones

sgraffito

The technique of etching ('scratching') decorative patterns or images using two thin layers of differently coloured plaster; the outer layer is removed, following a pattern, to reveal the contrasting colour of the base layer. Popular in Florence from the late sixteenth century

sporto

Jetty supporting the cantileved upper floor(s) of a building. Frequently used in the older parts of the city to gain extra space on the upper floors. Usually built of stone, sometimes of timber

stemma

Coat of arms, either of a noble family or of one of the *arti*

tabernacolo

Street-side shrine, usually in the form of an aedicule, and usually containing a venerated image, generally of the *Virgin and Child* ('Madonna')

tondo

Circular stone relief carving, also a circular painted panel

torre

Tower; dozens of tall, narrow stone towers were built in the city in the eleventh and twelfth centuries for families' individual defence. Diminutive *torreselle*, or turret

torrente

Stream, usually fast-flowing

vela, alla

Applied to a campanile that has a broad, flat-fronted façade, with an opening in which the bells are hung

via, viale, viuzzo

Via is the general name for a road, *viale* is an avenue; *viuzzo* is a particularly narrow street

vicolo

Lane or alley, much the same as *chiasso*

Appendix 2
The Guilds (*le arti*)
with their Arms and Patron Saints

ARTI MAGGIORI

Calimala / Mercatanzia (cloth merchants)
A gold eagle holding a bolt of cloth on a red field; patron: St John the
Baptist

Cambio (bankers and money-changers)
Gold coins on a red field; patron: St Matthew

Giudici e Notai (judges and notaries)
A gold star on a blue field; patron: St Luke

Lana (wool workers), popularly known as the **Ciompi**
The *Agnus Dei* on a blue field; patron: St Stephen

Medici e Speziali (physicians and pharmacists)
The *Virgin and Child Enthroned*; patron: Madonna della Rosa (Our Lady
of the Rose)

Por Santa Maria / Setaiuoli e Orafi (silk and gold workers)
A portal with a red door; patron: St John the Evangelist

Vaiai e Pelliciai (tanners and furriers)
Rows of small white shields on a black ground with the *Agnus Dei* in
the corner; patron: the apostle St James the Greater

ARTI MINORI

Beccai (butchers)
A black goat on a gold field; patron: St Peter

Calzolai (shoemakers)
Alternating black and white horizontal stripes; patron: St Philip

Fabbri / Maniscalchi (blacksmiths / farriers)
A pair of black pliers on a white ground; patron: St Eligio

Linaiuoli, Rigattieri e Sarti (workers in linen, dealers and tailors)
A shield halved vertically, red and white; patron: St Mark

Maestri di Pietra e Legname (stonemasons and carpenters)
An axe on a red ground; patrons: the Quattro Santi Coronati
('Four Crowned Saints', early Christian martyrs: Castorius, Simpronian,
Nicostratus and Simplicius)

The following minor guilds were later absorbed into the above:

Albergatori (innkeepers)
A red star on a white ground

Chiavaioli (locksmiths)
Two gold keys on a red ground

Corrazai e Spadai/Armaiuoli (armourers and sword-makers)
A sword with a red ribbon and a piece of chest armour

Corregiai (harness-makers)
A shield halved horizontally, white above, red and grey stripes below

Cuoiai e Galigai/Conciapelli (leather workers and tanners)
A shield halved vertically, black and white

Fornai (bakers)
A white star on a red ground

Legnaioli (furniture-makers)
A tree and a *cassone*

Oliandoli e Pizzicandoli (oil and cheesemongers)
A red lion rampant holding an olive branch

Vinattieri (vintners)
A red chalice on a white ground

Appendix 3
Rulers of Florence

Giovanni di Bicci (Averardo) de' Medici (1360–1429)

Cosimo il Vecchio, son of Giovanni di Bicci (b. 1389; r. 1434–64);
later known as 'father of the nation', *pater patriae*

Piero il Gottoso (the gouty), son of Cosimo il Vecchio (b. 1416;
r. 1464–9)

Lorenzo il Magnifico, son of Piero (b. 1449; r. 1469–92)

Piero II, son of Lorenzo (b. 1472; r. 1492–4)

In 1494 the Medici were forced to flee, and a republican government
was established (1494–1512).

Giovanni di Lorenzo de' Medici (later Pope Leo X) (b. 1475;
r. 1512–13)

Giuliano di Lorenzo de' Medici, duke of Nemours (b. 1479; r. 1513)

Lorenzo II di Piero de' Medici, duke of Urbino, son of Piero II
(b. 1492; r. 1513–19)

Giulio di Giuliano de' Medici (later Pope Clement VII) (b. 1478;
r. 1519–23)

Ippolito de' Medici (natural son of Giuliano) (b. 1511; r. 1523–7, jointly
with Alessandro)

Alessandro de' Medici (natural son of Lorenzo II) (b. 1511; r. 1523–7,
jointly with Ippolito)

From 1527 to 1530 there was a further republican interlude.

Alessandro de' Medici again (r. 1531–7)

Cosimo I de' Medici (b. 1519; r. 1537–74), son of Ludovico, who was the
great-great-grandson of Giovanni di Bicci; duke of Florence from 1537;
grand duke from 1569

Francesco I de' Medici, first son of Cosimo I (b. 1541; r. 1574–87),
grand duke

Ferdinando I de' Medici, second son of Cosimo I (b.1549;
r. 1587–1609), grand duke

Cosimo II de' Medici, son of Ferdinando I (b. 1590; r. 1609–21),
grand duke

Ferdinando II de' Medici, son of Cosimo II (b. 1610; r. 1621–70),
grand duke

Cosimo III de' Medici, son of Ferdinando II (b. 1642; r. 1670–1723), grand duke

Gian Gastone de' Medici, son of Cosimo III (b. 1671; r. 1723–37), grand duke

On the death of Gian Gastone, the Medici line became extinct.

House of Lorraine:

Francesco Stefano di Lorena [Lorraine] (r. 1737–65), grand duke

Pietro Leopoldo, second son of Francesco Stefano (r. 1766–90), grand duke; in 1790 he ceded the title of grand duke to his second son, Ferdinando III (r. 1791–9)

Napoleonic conquest and interregnum, 1799–1814:

    Lodovico di Borbone [Bourbon], hereditary prince of Parma, grand duke 1801–3

    Carlo Lodovico di Borbone, son of Lodovico, grand duke 1803–8

    Tuscany subject to the French Empire, 1808–9

    Elisa Baciocchi, sister of Napoleon, grand duchess, 1809–14

Ferdinando III returns (r. 1814–24)

Leopoldo II, son of Ferdinando III (r. 1824–59), grand duke, although there was a democratic government in 1848–9. He abandoned the grand duchy in 1859.

Plebiscite for the Unification of Tuscany into kingdom of Sardinia and then of Italy, 1860–61

Florence was capital of unified Italy from 1865 until 1870, when it was finally transferred to Rome.

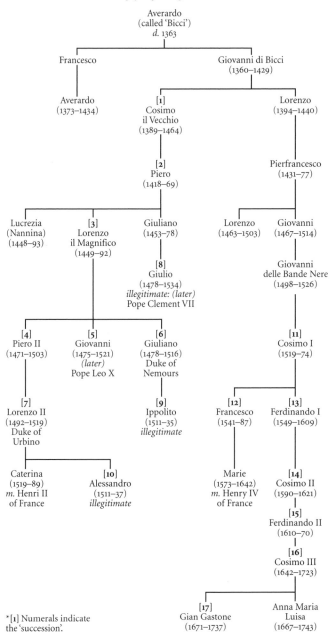

THE MEDICI

Simplified genealogical table*

Averardo
(called 'Bicci')
d. 1363

Francesco

Averardo
(1373–1434)

Giovanni di Bicci
(1360–1429)

[1]
Cosimo
il Vecchio
(1389–1464)

Lorenzo
(1394–1440)

[2]
Piero
(1418–69)

Pierfrancesco
(1431–77)

Lucrezia
(Nannina)
(1448–93)

[3]
Lorenzo
il Magnifico
(1449–92)

Giuliano
(1453–78)

Lorenzo
(1463–1503)

Giovanni
(1467–1514)

[8]
Giulio
(1478–1534)
illegitimate: (later)
Pope Clement VII

Giovanni
delle Bande Nere
(1498–1526)

[4]
Piero II
(1471–1503)

[5]
Giovanni
(1475–1521)
(later)
Pope Leo X

[6]
Giuliano
(1478–1516)
Duke of
Nemours

[11]
Cosimo I
(1519–74)

[7]
Lorenzo II
(1492–1519)
Duke of
Urbino

[9]
Ippolito
(1511–35)
illegitimate

[12]
Francesco
(1541–87)

[13]
Ferdinando I
(1549–1609)

Caterina
(1519–89)
m. Henri II
of France

[10]
Alessandro
(1511–37)
illegitimate

Marie
(1573–1642)
m. Henry IV
of France

[14]
Cosimo II
(1590–1621)

[15]
Ferdinando II
(1610–70)

[16]
Cosimo III
(1642–1723)

[17]
Gian Gastone
(1671–1737)

Anna Maria
Luisa
(1667–1743)

*[1] Numerals indicate
the 'succession'.

Appendix 4:
Principal Architects and Sculptors
Active in Florence

Alberti, Leon Battista

b. Genoa, 14 February 1404; d. Rome, April 1472. Architect, sculptor, painter and writer. A seminal figure of the early Renaissance and one of the most important architectural writers and theorists of all. His *De re aedificatoria*, written after 1455, first published in 1485 (published in English in 1726 as *The Ten Books of Architecture*), was the first architectural treatise since the classical texts of Vitruvius, and was enormously influential. His work in Florence was patronised by the humanist and banker Giovanni di Paolo Rucellai: façade of Santa Maria Novella, begun *circa* 1458; Rucellai chapel at San Pancrazio, *circa* 1465–7; Palazzo Rucellai, begun *circa* 1455; Loggia Rucellai, 1463–6. His principal works elsewhere are: San Francesco, Rimini, begun 1450; San Sebastiano, Mantua, begun 1460; Sant'Andrea, Mantua, begun 1472.

Ammannati, Bartolomeo

b. Settignano, 18 June 1511; d. Florence, 13 April 1592. Architect and sculptor. One of the central figures of the later sixteenth century; influenced by Michelangelo and Jacopo Sansovino, and developed a rather idiosyncratic early Baroque manner. Work and attributions in Florence: *Fontana di Nettuno*, Piazza della Signoria, 1563–75; extensions to Palazzo Pitti, 1558–70; Palazzo Grifoni Budini Gattai in Piazza della Santissima Annunziata, 1563–74; Palazzo Giugni, Via degli Alfani, *circa* 1577; Palazzo Ramirez de Montalvo, 1568; Ponte Santa Trinità, 1567–70. Attributions include: Palazzo Pucci, *circa* 1565–70; Palazzo Mondragone, 1567–72; Palazzo Peruzzi, *circa* 1570s?.

Arnoldi, Alberto

Recorded from 1351; d. *circa* 1377. Sculptor and architect. The Loggia del Bigallo is generally attributed to him, as are some of the relief panels of the campanile of the cathedral.

Arnolfo di Cambio

b. Colle di Val d'Elsa, 1245; d. Florence, before 1310. Sculptor, stonemason and architect. The central figure of Florence's great period of urban renewal in the late thirteenth and early fourteenth centuries. Works: the cathedral of Santa Maria del Fiore, begun 1296; Palazzo Vecchio, begun 1299; Santa Croce, begun 1295. Among his sculptures: various figures for the façade of the cathedral, including the *Virgin and Child*, *St Reparata*, *Pope Boniface VIII*, *Madonna della Natività* (all now in the Museo dell'Opera).

Baccio d'Agnolo [Bartolomeo d'Agnolo di Donato Baglioni]
b. Florence, 19 May 1462; d. Florence, 6 May 1543. Architect. A central architect of the middle Renaissance, with a long, prolific career; also a notable woodcarver. Among his works and attributions is a series of palaces for the Florentine nobility: Palazzo Cocchi Donati Serristori, *circa* 1470; Palazzo Rosselli del Turco, *circa* 1517; Palazzo Taddei, *circa* 1503–4; Palazzo Ginori, 1510–16; Palazzo Sertini, 1515–20; Palazzo Lanfredini, 1515. Other works include the Loggiato dei Servi (with Antonio da Sangallo the elder). Later palaces include Palazzo Bartolini Salimbeni, 1520–23, probably his masterpiece.

Benci di Cione
b. Como?; active in Florence, *circa* 1337–86. Architect and mason. Works: completed the Loggia dei Lanzi, with Simone Talenti, 1376–82; San Carlo dei Lombardi, with Neri di Fioravante, begun 1349; he began Orsanmichele, with Neri and Francesco Talenti, 1337.

Brunelleschi, Filippo
b. Florence, 1377; d. Florence, 16 April 1446. Architect, engineer and sculptor. The most important architect of the early Renaissance, whose work was enormously influential throughout Italy and Europe. The cupola of the cathedral remains one of the world's great feats of engineering. Works and attributions: cathedral cupola, 1418–36; exedra, 1439, and lantern, 1443–68; Ospedale degli Innocenti, 1419–39; Barbadori chapel at Santa Felicità, 1419–23; San Lorenzo: Sagrestia Vecchia, 1421–6; church after 1434; Pazzi chapel at Santa Croce, designed 1420s, built 1442–*circa* 1465; Palazzo dei Capitani della Parte Guelfa, 1420s and after 1442; Santa Maria degli Angioli, begun 1434–7; Santo Spirito, 1436–82.

Buonarroti, Michelangelo [Michelangiolo]
b. Caprese, ?6 March 1475; d. Rome, 18 February 1564. Sculptor, painter and architect. One of the most remarkably gifted and multi-talented masters in the history of art; the central figure of the high Renaissance in both Florence and Rome. His work in all media is characterised by a powerfully expressive style, which in his later architectural work is decidedly Mannerist. Works in Florence: architecture: San Lorenzo, Sagrestia Nuova, 1519–33; Biblioteca Laurenziana, 1524–62; project for the façade of San Lorenzo (unrealised), 1516. Sculpture: *St Matthew*, 1505–6; four *Slaves* or *Prisoners*, *circa* 1520s; *David*, 1502–4 (all Accademia); *Battle of the Centaurs* and

Madonna della Scala, both before 1492 (Casa Buonarroti); funeral monuments in the Sagrestia Nuova of San Lorenzo, 1519–33; *Pietà*, late 1540s–1555 (Museo dell'Opera).

Buontalenti, Bernardo (delle Girandole)

b. Florence, *circa* 1531; d. Florence, 6 June 1608. Architect, painter and military engineer. A notable and prolific high Renaissance polymath. Much of his work was for the courts of Cosimo I and then Ferdinando I, with whom he shared interests in alchemy; several of his works are bizarrely Mannerist. Works and attributions: Palazzo di Bianca Cappello, 1570–74; the villa and gardens at Pratolino, after 1469 (mostly lost); Casinò Mediceo, 1574; grotto in the Giardino di Boboli, after 1583; Uffizi galleries, after 1574; Palazzo Vecchio interiors, after 1588; Palazzo Nonfinito, 1593–1600; Medici villas at Marignolle, 1587, Castello, 1591, Artimino, 1597, and Petraia, completed *circa* 1594; façade of Santa Trinità, 1593; Forte di Belvedere, 1590–95. Many fortifications elsewhere in Tuscany, including Pisa, Prato, Livorno and Siena.

Caccini, Giovanni Battista

b. Rome, 24 October 1556; d. Florence, *circa* 15 March 1613. Sculptor and architect, pupil of Giovanni Antonio Dosio. Moved to Florence from Rome in 1575, and remained. Works and attributions: architecture: high altar at Santo Spirito, 1599–1613; portico of Santissima Annunziata, 1599–1601; choir and high altar at San Domenico, Fiesole, 1606; Palazzo Nonfinito, 1600–10. Sculptures in: Bargello, Santissima Annunziata, Palazzo Vecchio, Giardino di Boboli, Santa Trinità and on Ponte Santa Trinità.

Cellini, Benvenuto

b. Florence, 3 November 1500; d. Florence, 13 February 1571. Goldsmith, sculptor and writer. One of the most notable Mannerist artists of the era; lived in Rome 1519–27, working for successive popes; in France 1540–45. Principal works in Florence: *Apollo and Hyacinth*, 1548–57; *Ganymede*, 1548–50; *Narcissus*, *circa* 1548–57 (all in the Bargello); *Perseus and the Head of Medusa*, 1545–53 (Loggia dei Lanzi). His autobiography, the *Vita di Benvenuto Cellini*, written 1558–67, first printed in Naples in 1728, is an important milestone in art history.

Cronaca, Il [Simone di Tommaso del Pollaiolo]

b. Florence, 30 October 1457; d. Florence, 27 September 1508. Architect and sculptor. In Rome until 1485, then moved back to Florence. Works: Palazzo Strozzi, 1490–1504; Palazzo Vecchio, Sala dei Cinquecento, 1495–7; San Salvatore al Monte, *circa* 1490–1504. Attributions: Palazzo Corsi Alberti (Museo Horne), *circa* 1480–90; Palazzo Dei Guadagni, Oltrarno, 1503–6.

Donatello [Donato di Niccolò Bardi]

b. Florence, 1386 or 1387; d. Florence, 13 December 1466. Sculptor.
The most important sculptor of the early Renaissance, extremely
creative, skilful and versatile. Works: Two *Prophets*, 1406, and *St John the
Evangelist*, 1415, for the cathedral; marble *David*, 1408 (Bargello);
St Mark, 1411–13, and *St George*, *circa* 1414, both for Orsanmichele;
St Louis of Toulouse, Santa Croce, 1422; *Jeremiah* and *Habbakuk* for the
campanile of the cathedral (Museo dell'Opera), 1415 onwards; *cantoria*
for the cathedral, 1433–9 (Museo dell'Opera); tabernacle of the
Annunciation, Santa Croce, *circa* 1435; reliefs in the Sagrestia Vecchia,
San Lorenzo, after 1433; bronze *David*, *circa* 1439 (Bargello); *St Mary
Magdalene*, *circa* 1455 (Museo dell'Opera).

Ferri, Antonio Maria

b. Florence, 1651; d. Florence, 1716. Architect. His work ranges from
neo-Classical to Baroque. Works in Florence: Palazzo Corsini al
Parione (later stages), after 1686; Palazzo Gondi 'di Francia' (Orlandini
del Beccuto), 1679; Villa Corsini at Castello, 1698–9.

Foggini, Giovanni Battista

b. Florence, 1652; d. Florence, 1725. Architect and sculptor. Works and
attributions: Palazzo Medici Riccardi extension, 1670–85; Palazzo
Viviani della Robbia, 1693–6; San Giorgio alla Costa interior, 1705.

Gamberini, Italo

b. 21 September 1907; d. 14 November 1990. Modernist architect. One
of the founders and (with Michelucci) the most notable member of
the Gruppo Toscano. A long, varied career. Works: Stazione centrale di
Santa Maria Novella (with other members of the Gruppo), 1932–4;
Ponte della Vittoria (with others), 1945–6; reconstruction around the
Ponte Vecchio after war damage, from 1950; Assicurazione Generali,
Via dei Bardi, 1950; Cinema Italia, Via Nazionale, 1955; RAI television
buildings, 1962–8; Archivio di Stato, 1972–88; Hotel Brunelleschi,
1974–88; Stadio Comunale Artemio Franchi (with Pier Luigi Nervi
and others), 1984–90.

Ghiberti, Lorenzo

b. Florence, 1378; d. Florence, 1 December 1455. Sculptor, goldsmith,
architect and writer. A multi-faceted master, he was the chief bronze
sculptor of the first half of the fifteenth century. Principal works:
north doors to the baptistery, 1403–24; *St John the Baptist*, 1413–14,
St Matthew, 1419–22, and *St Stephen*, 1425–9, all for Orsanmichele;
Porta del Paradiso of the baptistery, *circa* 1426–52.

Giambologna [Giovanni Bologna, Jean de Boulogne]

b. Douai, 1529; d. Florence, 1608. Sculptor and bronze founder. The most important sculptor of the second half of the sixteenth century. He was in Florence from 1552, where he became the court sculptor to the Medici. Worked in both marble and bronze, and was both very prolific and extraordinarily technically skilful. Works and attributions: the Isolotto in the Giardino di Boboli; many small bronze pieces in the Bargello; *Rape of the Sabines*, 1582, and *Hercules and the Centaur*, 1599 (both Loggia dei Lanzi); *Apennino* for the Villa Demidoff at Pratolino, 1570–80; equestrian figure of *Cosimo I de' Medici*, Piazza della Signoria, 1587–93; equestrian figure of *Ferdinando I de' Medici*, Piazza della Santissima Annunziata, 1601–8.

Giotto di Bondone

b. Vespignano, Florence, *circa* 1267–75; d. Florence, 8 January 1337. Painter and designer. A prolific and highly creative master, the central figure of the 'pre-Renaissance'. Many works in fresco at Assisi (San Francesco), although many attributions are uncertain or controversial, and Padua (Arena chapel), as well as Florence. His only known major work of architecture was an initial design for the campanile of the cathedral, later adapted by Talenti. Principal paintings include: the painted Crucifix in Santa Maria Novella, *circa* 1300; the fresco cycles in the Bardi and Peruzzi chapels at Santa Croce, *circa* 1320.

Maiano, da

An important family of woodcarvers, stonemasons, sculptors and architects, from Maiano, just east of Florence; among the most significant of the early to mid-Renaissance. The principal members were the brothers:

Giuliano (b. Maiano, 1432; d. Naples, 17 October 1490)

Works and attributions: Palazzo dello Strozzino, *circa* 1462; Palazzo Pazzi Quaratesi, *circa* 1462–1470s; San Domenico, Fiesole, 1480–90; Palazzo Antinori, 1461–6.

Benedetto (b. Maiano, 1442; d. Florence, 24 May 1497)

Works and attributions: pulpit in Santa Croce; doorways in the Palazzo Vecchio (with Giuliano), 1476–81; tomb of Filippo Strozzi in Santa Maria Novella, 1491–7.

Michelozzo di Bartolomeo

b. Florence, 1396; d. Florence, 7 October 1472. Notable sculptor and prolific architect, one of the most outstanding of the early Renaissance generation of Alberti and Brunelleschi. He became the 'house architect' to Cosimo il Vecchio de' Medici. Works and attributions: monastic buildings and library at San Marco, begun 1436; Medici chapel at Santa Croce, 1440s; Palazzo Medici Riccardi, begun 1444; Medici villa at Careggi, 1457–82; Medici villa at Fiesole, *circa* 1460; tribune and two cloisters at the Santissima Annunziata, from 1444; San Felice in Piazza, *circa* 1457; Palazzo Lenzi, *circa* 1430; Palazzo dello Strozzino, *circa* 1451–62.

Michelucci, Giovanni

b. Pistoia, 2 January 1891; d. Florence, 31 December 1990. Notable Modern Movement architect; prolific and long-lived. A founder member of the Gruppo Toscano, but completed many other works in the post-war era. Works in Florence: Stazione centrale di Santa Maria Novella (with Italo Gamberini and others), 1932–4; Ponte alle Grazie, 1946–53; Cassa di Risparmio, 1953–7; Sede Provinciale delle Poste e Telegrafi, 1959–67; San Giovanni Battista ('Chiesa dell'Autostrada'), 1960–64.

Neri di Fioravante

Recorded 1340–84. Architect and sculptor. A crucial figure of the late Gothic era. Works and attributions: San Carlo dei Lombardi, 1349–1404; Ponte Vecchio, 1345; Orsanmichele, after 1337; Santa Trinità, 1365–1405; Bargello upper hall, 1340–45.

Nigetti, Matteo

circa 1560–*circa* 1649. Baroque architect, one of the leading figures of the early seventeenth century. Works and attributions: San Gaetano, 1604–30; Ognissanti, 1627–37; Cappella dei Principi, 1604–44, and cupola, 1640; San Francesco dei Vanchetoni, 1602–20; Santa Maria degli Angioli, Chiostro Grande; San Pier Maggiore, portico, from 1638; San Domenico, Fiesole, portico, 1635.

Parigi

Family of architects. Principal members:

Giulio (1571–1635). Works and attributions: Arcispedale di Santa Maria Nuova, from 1606; Palazzo Pitti expansion, 1619–35; Palazzo dell'Antella, 1619; Giardino di Boboli, after 1618.

Alfonso the younger (?1606–1656). Works: San Giovannino degli Scolopi; Giardino di Boboli, after *circa* 1625; Palazzo Pitti expansion, after 1640.

Poggi, Giuseppe

b. 3 April 1811; d. 5 March 1901. Architect, engineer and town planner, responsible for a major series of urban interventions following the designation of Florence as capital of united Italy in 1865. These included the demolition of most of the medieval city walls and the laying out of the avenues between the gates. Principal works: Villa

Favard, 1857; Palazzo Calcagnini Arese, 1857–77; Piazza Beccaria, 1865–74; Piazza della Libertà, 1865–73; Piazza della Mulina (today Piazza Giuseppe Poggi), 1865–76; Piazzale Michelangelo, *circa* 1875, and the Viale dei Colli (Viale Michelangelo and Viale Galilei), 1871–6.

Raphael [Raffaello Sanzio]
b. Urbino, ?28 March 1483; d. Rome, 6 April 1520. Painter and architect. One of the most important artists of the high Renaissance, together with Michelangelo, Titian and Leonardo. He developed an extraordinarily refined painting technique, with rich tone and coloration. Many works are in Rome, although some important paintings are in the Uffizi. In Florence his only known work of architecture is Palazzo Pandolfini, supervised on site by the Sangallo, after 1516.

Rossellino, Bernardo
b. Settignano, *circa* 1409; d. Florence, 1464. Sculptor and architect. A noted master of the mid-fifteenth century. His most famous work is the remodelling of the village of Corsignano for Pope Pius II, to become the miniature Renaissance city of Pienza. Works and attributions in Florence: tomb of Leonardo Bruni, Santa Croce, *circa* 1446–8; the second cloister at Santa Croce, *circa* 1453; Palazzo Rucellai façade (to a design by Alberti), *circa* 1450–64.

Sangallo
Important family of masons, sculptors and architects. Principal members:
   Giuliano (b. Florence, *circa* 1445; d. Florence, 20 October 1516)
A highly skilled Renaissance master, the 'house architect' of Lorenzo il Magnifico de' Medici. Works and attributions: Villa Medici at Poggio a Caiano, 1486–94, 1515–16; Santa Maria Maddalena de' Pazzi, 1490s; sacristy, 1489–96, and vestibule, 1492, at Santo Spirito; model for Palazzo Strozzi, 1489; Palazzo Gondi, from 1490. He also designed the remarkable Santa Maria delle Carceri at Prato, 1485–99.
   Antonio the elder, brother of Giuliano (b. Florence, *circa* 1460; d. Florence, 27 December 1534). Works: Palazzo Vecchio, Sala dei Cinquecento; Loggiato dei Serviti, with Baccio d'Agnolo, 1510–11.
   Aristotele, nephew of Giuliano and Antonio (b. Florence, 1481; d. Florence, 31 May 1551). Works: Palazzo Pandolfini (for Raphael), 1530–32; Fortezza da Basso (with Antonio the younger, his cousin).

Silvani, Gherardo
b. Florence, 1579; d. Florence, 1675. Architect. Significant Baroque figure of the early to mid-seventeenth century. Works and attributions: Madonna de' Ricci façade, 1604; San Gaetano, after 1630; Santi Simone e Giuda, 1628–30; Palazzo Covoni, 1623; Palazzo Marucelli Fenzi,

1634; Palazzo di San Clemente, *circa* 1640. His son Pier Francesco (Florence, 1620–1685) collaborated with him and succeeded him on several projects.

Vasari, Giorgio

b. Arezzo, 30 July 1511; d. Florence, 27 June 1574. Artist, architect and writer. A pivotal figure in sixteenth-century Florence. He was prolific in all three fields, with extensive programmes of painting in the Palazzo Vecchio, *circa* 1555–72; the architecture of the Uffizi, 1560s–1580s; the Corridoio Vasariano, 1565; internal remodelling at Santa Maria Novella and Santa Croce, both 1560s. Equally noted for his *Vite . . . degli pittori* (1550), the first work of art biography and history ever published, and the source of extensive information on the lives of his contemporaries and predecessors. It was published in English as *Lives of the Artists*, in many different editions.

Verrocchio, Andrea del

b. Florence, 1435; d. Venice, ?30 June 1488. Principal sculptor in Florence in the later fifteenth century; he was Leonardo's teacher. Versatile, with works in bronze, marble and some paintings. Works and attributions: two sculpted groups of *St Thomas* for Orsanmichele; tomb of Cosimo il Vecchio, San Lorenzo, 1465; tombs of Piero il Gottoso and of Giovanni de' Medici, 1472, both in the Sagrestia Vecchia, San Lorenzo. Also a *David*, *circa* 1475 (Bargello).

Select Bibliography

GENERAL HISTORIES AND GUIDES

G. Boffito and A. Mori, eds, *Firenze nelle vedute e piante*, Rome, 1926

M.-F. Bonetti, ed., *G. Zocchi: vedute di Firenze nel '700*, Rome, n.d.

M. Brion, *The Medici*, London, 1980

F. Cesati, *Le strade di Firenze*, 2 vols, Rome, 2003

C. Cresti et al., *Guida di Firenze architettura*, Turin, 2nd edn 1998

E. Detti, *Firenze scomparsa*, Florence, 1970

M. Dezzi Bardeschi, ed., *Florence: Architecture, City, Landscape*, Rome, 2006

G. Fanelli, *Firenze* (Le Città nella Storia d'Italia), Rome, 1981

— et al., *Firenze e provincia* (TCI Guide), Milan, 1993

R. J. Goy, *Florence: The City and its Architecture*, London and New York, 2002

J. R. Hale, *Florence and the Medici: The Pattern of Control*, London and New York, 1977

C. Hibbert, *Florence: The Biography of a City*, London, 1993

—, *The Rise and Fall of the House of Medici*, London, 1974; new edn 1998

M. Levey, *Florence: A Portrait*, London, 1996

A. Macadam, *Florence* (Blue Guides), London and New York, 2005

J. M. Najemy, *A History of Florence, 1200–1575*, Chichester, 2008

T. Parks, *Medici Money: Banking, Metaphysics and Art in Fifteenth-century Florence*, London, 2006

G. Poggi, *Sui lavori per l'ingrandimento di Firenze, 1864–77*, Florence, 1882

N. Rubinstein, *The Government of Florence under the Medici, 1434–94*, Oxford, 1966

P. Strathern, *The Medici: Godfathers of the Renaissance*, London, 2005

G. Zucconi, *Firenze: guida all'architettura*, Venice, 1995

MONOGRAPHS ON INDIVIDUAL ARCHITECTS AND SCULPTORS

J. S. Ackerman, *The Architecture of Michelangelo*, London, 1961

C. Avery, *Donatello: An Introduction*, New York, 1994

—, *Giambologna: The Complete Sculpture*, Oxford, 1987

E. Battisti, *Filippo Brunelleschi*, Milan, 1976

F. Borsi, *Leon Battista Alberti: l'opera completa*, Milan, 1975

S. Borsi, *Giuliano da Sangallo*, Rome, 1985

G. Brunetti, *Ghiberti*, Florence, 1966

C. Conforti, *Giorgio Vasari architetto*, Milan, 1993

G. Fanelli, *Brunelleschi*, Florence, 1980

A. Fara, *Bernardo Buontalenti*, Milan, 1995

M. Ferrara and F. Quinterio, *Michelozzo di Bartolomeo*, Florence, 1984

J. Gadol, *Leon Battista Alberti: Universal Man of the Early Renaissance*,
Chicago, 1969

L. Gori Montanelli, *Brunelleschi e Michelozzo*, Florence, 1957

A. Grafton, *Leon Battista Alberti*, London, 2000

H. Hibbard, *Michelangelo*, new edn, London, 2002

H. W. Janson, *The Sculpture of Donatello*, Princeton, 1957

M. Kiene, *Bartolomeo Ammannati architetto*, Milan, 1995

H. Klotz, *Brunelleschi: The Early Works and the Medieval Tradition*,
New York, 1990

G. Marchini, *Giuliano da Sangallo*, Florence, 1942

—, *Ghiberti architetto*, Florence, 1978

V. Mariani, *Arnolfo di Cambio*, Rome, 1943

G. Milanesi, ed., *Le opere di Giorgio Vasari*, 4 vols, Florence, 1878–85

O. Morisani, *Michelozzo architetto*, Turin, 1951

N. Ponente, *Raphael*, Geneva, 1990

J. Pope-Hennessey, *Luca della Robbia*, Oxford, 1980

P. Portoghesi and B. Zevi, eds, *Michelangelo architetto*, Turin, 1964

R. Tavernor, *On Alberti and the Art of Building*, London and New Haven,
1998

MONOGRAPHS ON INDIVIDUAL BUILDINGS AND TYPOLOGIES

L. Artusi and S. Gabrielli, *Orsanmichele in Firenze*, 2nd edn, Florence, 2006

U. Baldini, ed., *Santa Maria Novella: la basilica, il convento, i chiostri
monumentali*, Florence, 1981

S. Bardazzi and E. Castellani, *La villa medicea di Poggio a Caiano*, 2 vols,
Prato, 1981

E. Bargilli, *La cattedrale di Fiesole*, Florence, 1883

L. Bartoli, *Il disegno della cupola di Brunelleschi*, Florence, 1984

C. Berti, *Palazzo Davanzati*, Florence, 1958

M. Bucci, *La basilica di Santa Croce*, Florence, 1965

— and R. Bencini, *Palazzi di Firenze*, 4 vols, Florence, 1973

A. Busignani and R. Bencini, *Chiese di Firenze*, 4 vols, Florence, 1972–82

M. Carniani, *Santa Maria del Carmine*, Florence, n.d.

C. J. Cavallucci, *Santa Maria del Fiore: storia documentata*, Florence, 1881

F. Cesati, *Le chiese di Firenze*, Rome, 2005

G. Cherubini and G. Fanelli, *Il Palazzo Medici Riccardi di Firenze*,
Florence, 1990

P. Fabbri, *Palaces of Florence*, Venice, 2000

F. Grimaldi, *Le 'case-torri' di Firenze*, Florence, 2005

O. Guaita, *Le ville di Firenze*, Rome, 1996

A. Lensi, *Palazzo Vecchio*, Milan and Rome, 1929

A. Lillie, *Florentine Villas in the Fifteenth Century*, Cambridge, 2005

G. Marchini, *Il battistero e il duomo di Firenze*, Florence, 1972

D. Mignani, *Le ville medicee di Giusto Utens*, Florence, 1980

G. Morozzi, *Santa Reparata: l'antica cattedrale di Firenze*, Florence, 1987

M. Preti, *Museo dell'Opera del Duomo di Firenze*, Milan, 1989

G. Rocchi, ed., *Santa Maria del Fiore: piazza, battistero, campanile*, Florence, 1996

B. Santi, *San Lorenzo and the Medici Chapels*, Florence, n.d.

G. C. Sciolla, *Ville medicee*, Novara, 1982

F. Tarani, *La basilica di San Miniato al Monte*, Florence, 1910

A. Tarquini, *Santa Maria Novella*, Florence, 2000

THE RENAISSANCE: GENERAL

J. S. Ackerman, *Distance Points: Essays in Theory and Renaissance Art and Architecture*, Cambridge, MA, and London, 1991

L. B. Alberti, *The Ten Books of Architecture* [Leoni edn, London, 1755], New York, 1986

B. Berenson, *Italian Painters of the Renaissance*, Oxford, 1930

G. Brucker, *Renaissance Florence*, Florence, 1994

J. Burckhardt, *The Civilization of the Renaissance in Italy*, 2nd edn, New York, 1981

B. Cole, *The Renaissance Artist at Work*, New York, 1983

V. Cronin, *The Florentine Renaissance*, London, 1967; new edn 2001

R. J. Crum and J.T. Paoletti, eds, *Renaissance Florence: A Social History*, Cambridge, 2008

M. Furnari, *Formal Design in Renaissance Architecture*, New York, 1995

R. Goldthwaite, *The Building of Renaissance Florence*, Baltimore, 1980

—, *The Economy of Renaissance Florence*, Baltimore, 2009

J. R. Hale, *The Civilization of Europe in the Renaissance*, London and New York, 1993

G. Holmes, *The Florentine Enlightenment, 1400–1450*, Oxford, 1969

P. Lee Rubin and A. Wright, eds, *Renaissance Florence: The Art of the 1470s*, London and New Haven, 1999

R. Mackenney, *Renaissances: The Cultures of Italy, c.1300 to c.1600*, Basingstoke and New York, 2005

F. Schevill, *Medieval and Renaissance Florence*, London, 1961

S. Serlio, *The Five Books of Architecture* [London, 1611], New York, 1982

M. Tafuri, *Interpreting the Renaissance: Princes, Cities, Architects*, London and New Haven (with Harvard University), 2006

J. S. Turner, ed., *Encyclopedia of Italian Renaissance and Mannerist Art*, 2 vols, London and New York, 2000

R. Turner, *Renaissance Florence: The Invention of a New Art*, London and New York, 1997

G. Vasari, *Lives of the Painters*, 5 vols, London, 1878 [complete edn]

A FEW USEFUL WEBSITES

it.wikipedia.org/wiki/Firenze (English version: en.wikipedia.org/wiki/Florence)
with numerous links to other sites

www.treccani.it
online encyclopedia, good for bibliographies

www.michelucci.it
twentieth-century architecture

www.palazzospinelli.org (English version available)
archives of maps and plans

www.sba.unifi.it/.../sviluppo strade
history of the city's streets and squares

www.ordinearchitetti.fi.it
future architecture in the city

www.fondazionearchitettifirenze.it
history of architecture and construction methods and techniques

www.palazzostrozzi.org (English version available)
history of Palazzo Strozzi, with details of temporary exhibitions, etc.

www.firenze.guidatoscana.it (English version available)
general architectural guide

www.travelitalia.com/it/guide/firenze
general architectural guide

www.comune.firenze.it (English version available)

Index of Places

Index of People